Postwar Higher Education in America

Postwar Higher Education in America

Just Yesterday

Richard B. Schwartz

Hamilton Books
Lanham • Boulder • New York • London

Copyright © 2018 by The Rowman & Littlefield Publishing Group, Inc.
An imprint of The Rowman & Littlefield Publishing Group, Inc.
4501 Forbes Boulevard, Suite 200, Lanham, Maryland 20706
Hamilton Books Acquisitions Department (301) 459-3366

Unit A, Whitacre Mews, 26-34 Stannary Street, London SE11 4AB

All rights reserved
Printed in the United States of America
British Library Cataloguing in Publication Information Available

Library of Congress Control Number: 2018948749
ISBN: 978-0-7618-7054-8 (pbk : alk. paper)—ISBN: 978-0-7618-7055-5 (electronic)

For my family—Judith, Jonathan, Kirsten, Katharine, and Caroline

Table of Contents

Preface		ix
1	The Monastery and the Corporation	1
2	The Faculty Vanishes	25
3	Vacuums and Mazes	49
4	For a Living or a Life?	71
5	The New School of Mortuary Science	93
6	Fever Dreams	115
7	I Came to Cornell to Become an Engineer	147
8	Every Man His Own Carver	173
9	Physics for Poets	197
10	Out of the Dark	221
Bibliography		247
Index		261
About the Author		271
Also by Richard B. Schwartz		273

Preface

Studies of American Higher Education tend to be part-memoir, part-history, part-analysis and part-policy prescription. While some are written by journalists and some by independent scholars, those written by insiders are often focused upon the university or college with which the author is principally associated. Bok writes about Harvard, Bowen about Princeton, Duderstadt about Michigan, Ehrenberg about Cornell, and so on. This is extremely helpful, since these authors have access to information concerning their institutions that would not usually be revealed to the reading public.

Faculty also write such books and they can be of particular value because they are written at eye-level, with passion and insight. The faculty, however, are not privy to the activities in the trustees' chambers, as the president is, and they have not, in general, made seven-figure development asks, been beaten about the head and shoulders by a legislative caucus or been on the receiving end of the faculty senate's ire.

Presidents and "senior administrators," on the other hand, are distant from the classroom (if, indeed, they have ever stood at the front of one), do not receive course evaluations from failing students and are not writing books or scholarly/scientific articles that will be subjected to rigorous peer review.

Deans are somewhere in between. They hear the voice of the faculty every day; many continue to teach and to write while they serve in an administrative capacity and they also find themselves amid the travails and triumphs of the provost and president. The graduate dean is the only academic officer beyond the president (and sometimes the provost) who has some responsibility for the institution as a whole.

I thought that my twenty-nine years of decanal experience, first in graduate education and then as a dean of arts and science, might enable me to offer some observations that could be instructive and, hopefully, useful. My experience is relatively unique in that I attended a private university (Notre Dame) for college, an AAU public flagship (Illinois) for graduate school, taught at West Point for two years to satisfy my active-duty obligation, then spent twelve years at Wisconsin (associate dean for the Humanities in the graduate school, four years), seventeen years at Georgetown (graduate dean and twice interim provost) and have been at Missouri (dean of arts and science, eight years) since 1998. Those who do administration in private schools generally stay in the private sector; those who do administration in state institutions generally stay in the public.

I began my college studies in 1959 and completed my graduate studies in 1967. Thus, I experienced a direct connection with individuals from both the GI Bill generation and with those from a bygone, pre-war era. My Old English teacher at Illinois was a student of the legendary George Lyman Kittredge (1860–1941) at Harvard and was in England in 1939 when the Sutton Hoo burial cenotaph was excavated. As a graduate student I attended lectures by such individuals as the great philologist Kemp Malone, who began his teaching career at Johns Hopkins in 1924.

As a young professor my role models and friends were individuals now thought of as ancient presences, people such as Jim Clifford, Jean Hagstrum and Donald Greene. I am aware of the "old ways" through direct experience as well as the reading and writing of books.

While I missed the Dow riots at Wisconsin I was there for the Teaching Assistants Association strike and the 1970 bombing of Sterling Hall by the so-called New Year's Gang. I experienced directly the ethos of the "60's," heard the curriculum debates first hand, and taught in classrooms permeated by tear gas. I served for ten years on the research committee which allocated WARF funds to faculty investigators, served multiple terms in the faculty senate and represented the graduate school in various capacities at the state capitol in Madison and before the national educational establishment in Washington. I arrived at Georgetown at a time when their application pools had dramatically raised their national profile. They had been invited to join the COFHE schools, were in the midst of an accreditation study designed to enhance their graduate programming and were beginning their first significant development campaign. I served Missouri in a number of capacities, seeing the College of Arts and Science through a mission enhancement exercise, chairing a committee for the Chancellor whose purpose was to reduce costs across the 1,400-acre campus, serving on the committee to design, build and staff the University's life science center, chairing the search committee which identified the leadership for our successful billion-dollar advancement campaign and sitting on the research board which allocated funds to support research across the four-campus system.

I was fortunate to serve under some truly gifted administrators for the majority of my career and learned from a few others through negative example. Drawing on this experience and my reading within the educational literature my conclusions can be briefly stated. I believe, with Jonathan Cole, that the American research university is an incomparable national resource, one whose achievements should be celebrated and whose mission should be protected and enhanced. At the same time, I believe that culturally and organizationally our higher education institutions have been disserved in a multiplicity of ways. They are now, in their broad totality, structured to survive rather than to achieve excellence. No single entity is responsible for their problems. On the contrary, a series of unfortunate isolated events and decisions have combined to create an enterprise that is now often grotesquely overpriced and potentially vacuous at its core, *potentially* because we have abandoned what a manufacturer would term quality control. Diplomas have been reduced to simple certificates of attendance; we have abandoned *signatures* for *brands*, treated students as consumers or, worse, customers rather than apprentices, awarded grades that are inflated and degrees that carry no guarantees that an appropriate, identifiable body of knowledge has been obtained.

The abandonment of the structures and expectations of the past has aligned higher education with K-12 culture. Adulthood is postponed and results plummet as quasi-romantic "educational" principles are invoked and peripheral activities grow and multiply.

This has all occurred in less than the space of a single lifetime. I remember my own college experience as if it had happened yesterday and while it was far from perfect its ways and means enjoyed considerably more success than the methods of proceeding that characterize what is now the higher education "industry." I would not advocate that we return, in toto, to the ways of the recent past, but if we do not begin to reverse our current practices we will see our present circumstances amplified: higher prices, greater indebtedness, further failure, additional credential creep and greater intellectual vacuity. We cannot continue to fob off our educational failures on the next level of instruction. Grammar schools and high schools are unable to produce students who perform at grade level; rather than confront that reality we require all students to attend college. We gut college so that at least half can graduate. They still cannot secure appropriate employment and so we send them to graduate school. One graduate degree is inadequate and so we expect two, three or more. This is cruel, wasteful, unsustainable and nearly mad.

Having said that, one must quickly add that none of this is a problem for a select number of students. They can afford private education; they have social capital; they can resist infantilization and construct their own educational paths around the current labyrinths and dead ends. They will prosper; we need not worry about them. On the other hand, for many other individuals, inequalities within our society will widen and those who begin with the greatest number of disadvantages will be at even greater risk of being lost. Among the harshest realities of our current condition is the fact that those most in need of authentic education remain the principal sufferers within a system putatively structured for their specific needs.

Andrew Delbanco (2012, p. 150) has identified four genres of books on higher education: jeremiads, elegies, calls to arms and funeral dirges. My book includes elements of each, with an emphasis on the third. I do believe that if we are to reverse any or all of the declines surrounding us, the hour is late, as the individuals who remember different, often more effective ways of proceeding, diminish in number. Fortunately, the issues themselves are generally clear—how complicated is it to acknowledge that awarding A's for C work engenders delusion and false hope? The problems and challenges' etiologies and connectedness, however, are often quite complex. To elucidate them I have given them discrete chapters, but I have overlapped my arguments from chapter to chapter to reinforce core points.

While I glance occasionally at grammar school and high school education, these are not my areas of expertise. I am not, however, innocent of the concerns of those who *are* expert in them. My wife served for many years as a K-12 teacher with special expertise as a reading specialist. She is my lifelong love, best friend and principal sounding board. Her doctoral field is developmental psychology. She and her former fellow teachers are my ongoing resource for understanding the public education system which attempts to prepare our students for college.

To her I owe my greatest debts in preparing this book. I would also like to thank Ivan R. Dee, who published the ebook which preceded this volume and offered many helpful suggestions to its author; Jim Cogswell, who provided information and advice; Luke Menand, who made a number of cogent suggestions; my friends, colleagues and former chairs, among them Melvin Platt, Mike Podgursky, John Petrocik, David Read, Ted Tarkow, Mike O'Brien, Jerry Atwood, Mike Collins, Tim Materer, Tom Quirk and Elias Saab, who taught me many things in many ways and whose ongoing support is deeply appreciated.

Higher education in America is a mercurial subject. In commenting on it, one is usually treating large, statistical patterns, not the individual experience of a particular student or the individual practices of a particular institution. The reality of the situation forces us to hedge: "The overall situation is distressing, but not at *our* institution, at least not in *this* particular aspect, although President X's recent arrival gives us pause. . . ." It is a general fact that athletics are subsidized, often to a significant degree, at nearly every American college and university. A handful of schools are exceptions, but not exceptions in *every* year. Stating this does not represent toe-digging; it represents the reality of the situation. I have tried to be as straightforward as possible in my observations and analysis, but the subject can be very slippery when one gets down to individual cases.

There is also the issue of educational statistics. While some are collected annually or at least regularly, many are the result of discrete studies conducted under specific assumptions within limited time parameters. I have cited a lot of statistics, but I have not attempted to replicate and update all of the studies to which I have made reference. That would be impossible anyway, since many of the studies required large numbers of staff and hundreds of thousands or millions of dollars in grant support. The result is more broad-brush historiography than the kind of rigorous focus on a single issue or single set of issues examined within small time constraints.

The rigor that I might desire is, at any rate, impossible, since this branch of intellectual, social and cultural history proceeds in a broad-brush manner anyway. The impact of the French Nietzscheans on the Humanities, e.g., was, for a time, important, but how does one date it? Derrida came to the U.S. in 1966. Some paid no attention whatsoever. Others fell at his feet and worshiped at his altar. Some paid a respectful degree of attention but saw his work within wider, longer contexts. Now we hear of trends in terms of decades, with a lot of wiggle room around the edges. That is not inappropriate. Sadly, the long term trends have been rather consistent: the reduction of state support for public higher education, the erosion of required core curricula, the admission of an ever-larger number of students requiring remediation, the consistent lowering of expectations, the growth of vocational instruction at the expense of the liberal arts and, most palpably, the stratospheric rise in costs.

The popular press is often concerned with the politicization of our institutions of higher education. While there is such a thing as political correctness and while it does have significant implications for our practices, there are gradations within political correctness. The more important issues concern larger practices rather than simple nomenclature (though the latter can metastasize into the former). It is one thing to forbid the use of the word "girls" or "ladies" in describing young women, quite another to forbid the discussion of important subjects or to mandate and enforce a monolithic approach to them. I see our most deleterious situations resulting from the use of ideological constructs to accelerate the abandonment of rigorous standards and high expectations—*standards and expectations which once materially benefited students*. To ask that an instructor relieve a student of the responsibility of reading a classic book because it might contain elements that offend the student's sensibility is, implicitly, to *reduce the requirements of the course* and to deny the student an experience possessed by classically-educated individuals, thus expanding the disparities between the "sensitive" student's intellectual resources and those with whom he or she will interact in the larger world.

The rubrics and practices which I regret most are relatively recent phenomena. Regardless of its political inclinations (generally on the left, particularly in the Humanities and social sciences), the postwar professoriate was far more "traditional" in its espousal of academic principles. That was the ethos in which I was educated in college and trained in graduate school and I see its replacement by one of "student-centeredness," "nonjudgmentalism" and "validation" as a central concern. Very "liberal" and "left-leaning" faculty once staunchly defended principles and standards which have now been eroded or abandoned, while many elements and offices within the contemporary university are once again espousing the notions of "progressive education" and its offshoots, notions which had been subjected to withering (and, one might have thought, definitive) criticism generations ago, by such formidable voices as Arthur Bestor's and Richard Hofstadter's. I write as a traditionalist, frequently utilizing the arguments and voices of those to my political left, sometimes to my far left, in order to reinforce the point that while the postwar professoriate (regardless of its political impulses) was generally contemptuous of the colleges of education's quasi-romantic ideology, that ideology has resurfaced, merged with corporatism, identity politics and victimology and systematically reduced the stature of our enterprise.

My intended audience encompasses the full range of those invested in our efforts. My fervent hope is that together we can face the reality of our condition and begin to ameliorate it. I am haunted by the gulf between the programs and experiences offered to my generation and the far more expensive though far less substantive opportunities that we now provide for the children we love, the grandchildren we love and the children and grandchildren of our fellow citizens who have previously been marginalized and who now, at a time when they most require an authentic education, are being offered pablum at the cost of foie gras.

Chapter One

The Monastery and the Corporation

Consider the experience of an aged alumnus, walking across the campus of his alma mater in 2018. Tousled faculty carrying books and lecture notes have been replaced by corporatist men and women in suits with clipboards and file folders, hurrying from meeting to meeting. Cranes and dumpsters surround construction sites for facilities that will house unfamiliar organizations with unfamiliar functions. Along each walkway there is a security box with buttons and speakers. Students walk and text, deleting a stream of emails from administrators and middle managers. In the academic buildings the faculty doors are largely closed, but the offices of advisors, counselors and tutors are pulsing with activity. Part-time faculty hurry from the parking ramps to their classrooms, pulling pieces of wheeled, carry-on luggage containing the materials they will use to produce a PowerPoint presentation or launch a succession of film clips or illustrative images. Students sit in stairwells, balancing their tablets and laptops, taking mandatory instruction on diversity, sexual harassment and Title IX rules. Small buildings house advocacy centers for minority groups and women. Demonstrators sweep through cafeterias, libraries and student-commons space, shouting rhymed demands.

Where am I, the alumnus wonders? The straightforward, vaguely-monastic campus of his youth has been altered. It is noisy and frenetic, heavily-politicized and divided. The students are older; they have part-time jobs which take them to and from campus; they are tense and harried, pursuing training in fields that seem vocational in the extreme. Athletics have been all but completely professionalized, the student/athletes' facilities, training tables and tutors set apart from those of their classmates; they inhabit a special space, their commonalities with other undergraduates fewer and fewer in number.

As he walks, the alumnus hears one omnipresent and overriding concern: cost. Whatever this new entity is—this largely-corporate enterprise—it is very, very expensive, and yet the students appear to be well-to-do products of privilege. They pay Starbucks prices without a blink of an eye, carry multiple electronic devices in their purses and backpacks and drive better cars than many members of the faculty. Academics are but one part of their lives, sometimes a relatively unimportant part. They go to the library for coffee as much as for books or study space. When he inquires, the aged alum is told that all libraries now have coffee bars because their budgets are driven in part by patron visits and this is the best way to increase their number. As he walks behind them he sees that the students are not reading course materials on their electronic devices; they are watching films and television episodes featuring vampires and zombies. One student is actually reading a book. It is called *Fifty Shades Darker.* The alum falls back against the tile wall. Where are the shelves of books and the stacks of journals, the maps and other historical artifacts? The sounds of pens and pencils on notebook sheets, of pages being turned and volumes stacked, have been replaced with electronic clicks and social chatter. The library feels like a giant break room in an insurance company. Who is in charge of this larger operation and how have we reached this point? And why, why is it so incredibly expensive?

When my parents drove me to college in 1959 my father was a recently-promoted partner in a small Cincinnati law firm. One-ninth of his annual salary of $18,000 was sufficient to cover my tuition and room and board at the University of Notre Dame. If we were driving there today (2017–2018) my father would require a salary of $620,955 in order to devote one-ninth to the university's tuition of $51,105 and room/board fee of $14,890 (+$3,000 in other expenses). In 1959 and in my succeeding undergraduate years tuition and room/board cost more or less the same: around $1,000 each. Correcting for inflation, using the CPI from 1960–2018, the $2,000 charge should now be $16,820, not $65,995 (plus those fees for books, et al.).

All parents and students now face costs this daunting, but their choices and opportunities are far more complex. It is imprecise to say starkly that families once sent their children to those schools which they could afford, but it is certainly the case that financial aid policies and subsidization from third party payers (federal and state governments, university endowments) have radically changed this portion of our cultural landscape. The lessons now are that you can attend any school you choose (assuming that you meet admissions criteria), so long as you realize that you may have to borrow money to do so (and, if you fail, you will not be able to remove the debt through bankruptcy proceedings). Options have multiplied, but so have the risks.

This is a sobering thought in light of the fact that nearly half of the nation's four-year college students fail to complete the requirements for baccalaureate degrees in *six* years (57 percent at publics, 66 percent at nonprofit privates, 32 percent at private for-profits). In some institutions the completion rate is far lower. In 6 years, Idaho State graduates 20 percent, the University of Texas-El Paso 29 percent, Medgar Evers-CUNY 10 percent (Toby, 2010, p. 93). At the for-profit University of Phoenix, which, in 2010, enrolled 470,800 students, the graduation rate was less than 27 percent (Alva, p. 2).

It has never been easier to gain admission to college, since the number of institutions and places has been expanded, well beyond (some argue) the actual need. Only 8 percent of American institutions accept less than 50 percent of their applicants. Fifty percent admit 50–80 percent of their applicants and 42 percent admit more than 80 percent of their applicants (Maeroff in Hersh and Merrow, 2005, p. 14). Most college doors are bolted in the *OPEN* position.

At the same time the pressures on admission to the most selective schools have never been higher, since their slots have not expanded to meet their exploding applicant pools. In 1900 22.77 students per thousand, aged 18–24, attended college. By 1960 that number had risen to 225.68 per thousand; in 2000 the number was 544.92 per thousand (Toby 2010, p. 12). Put another way: in 1870 52,000 students were enrolled in college; after World War II, 2,000,000, in 1994 15,000,000 (Hunt, in Kernan 1997, p. 18), and in 2017—20,400,000 $\pm$. James B. Conant, who took his Ph.D. in Chemistry at Harvard in 1916 and became its president in 1933, thought that an appropriate number for college attendance in America was one-half of 1 percent of the population (Lewis 2006, p. 51). We have, clearly, proceeded in a different direction.

The most competitive schools, which offered relatively easy access in the 1950's, now admit fewer than 10 percent of their applicants. Harvard takes 6 percent. In one recent class Stanford received 32,022 applications and accepted 7 percent, Brown 30,135 applications, accepting 9 percent. The depth of the applicant pool, however, is only part of the story. Tulane received more applications than Stanford—44,000; it then admitted 10,000 of those applicants but only 16 percent of those admitted actually matriculated (Hoover 2010, pp. 1, 8). Some schools are "stretches," others "fallbacks." Institutions that admit to schools rather than to the university—as Georgetown does—may be far more competitive than the omnibus admissions number suggests. The School of Nursing, for example, might admit a far higher percentage of applicants than the College of Arts and Science. At Georgetown it was common for students to apply to the easiest port of entry and then, once admitted, attempt to transfer to another college or school. Under such circumstances the initial port of entry might frontload required courses in order to create disincentives for transfer.

Entering a college campus now is like entering the cabin of a commercial aircraft: everyone is going from point A to point B together, but each is paying a different fare. Some are paying the highest published fare; some are paying nothing at all. Most are paying some number in between. Each applicant's family will wrestle with the same financial aid forms (a bout requiring sufficient social capital that the application process itself will dissuade some from participating, though some institutions provide help with the process), but each school to which the student makes application might evaluate the data provided (and, thus, assess individual need) differently. (For example, can the institution reasonably expect a contribution from a divorced parent who has remarried? What sort of contribution?)

Once having determined need, each school will package support in a different way, with different percentages of the "support" devoted to loans and to grants. An institution with $20,000 tuition that offers $1,000 in grants and $19,000 in loans can still claim to have met full need. The shapes of these packages will vary within the same school's applicant pool, with more favored students receiving a higher percentage of grants than loans. (A *tiny* percentage of schools provide grants, exclusively.) One student is offered full tuition through grants; another receives a combination of grants and loans, combined with the expectation that the student will perform work/study duties. Both students' needs are said to be met, but the first student's package is far more attractive because that student, for one reason or another, is considered to be more desirable.

Many students and parents refuse to accept the first offer and attempt to negotiate more attractive packages. Some schools, e.g., will change their loan/grant mix when they are informed of other institutions' offers. This is called "dialing for dollars" (Ehrenberg 2002, p. 78).

There may well be more favorable terms offered to those who fill a need—an applicant proposing to pursue an undersubscribed major, a viola player filling a vacancy in a string quartet, a minority student who meets a diversity need or, very often, an athlete. Some schools "buy" National Merit Scholars; others, by policy, do not. The first type of institution highlights the number of such scholars there as a brag point, trading off the attractive statistic for the fact that they may have overpaid to obtain them. The COFHE schools (the Consortium on Financing Higher Education, the nation's [with a few exceptions] top privates) have a policy of making all aid need-based. They resent the fact that some distinguished privates "buy" students with merit-based aid. The top public institutions, on the other hand, often have a great number of merit-based scholarships, some of them formal entitlements within their states.

If the student applies for early admission he or she may enhance the chances for a positive response. At the same time, that applicant who elects to apply in this way and then commits upon acceptance will deny him or herself the opportunity to see the offers that might have been tendered by other institutions. Early admission favors the institution because it boosts their yield rate (a significant brag point) and reduces the need to offer an aggressive financial aid package.

And then there are the unforeseen breaks. Institutions now worry that the number of women in attendance may be reaching a tipping point. There is much talk of an unspoken 60–40 rule: a school with 60 percent women has become a "women's school" and hence, to some (particularly the women), less desirable. For over three decades now, some institutions have been favoring men in the admission process in order to achieve gender parity and not permit the women—who often have stronger credentials—to squeeze out the men in the applicant pool. Hence the opportunity now for special consideration for less-qualified male students. In 2007 Brown admitted 13 percent of its women applicants, but 16 percent of the men (Hacker and Dreifus 2010, p. 183).

At the same time that elite institutions are concerned about the nuances involved in *shaping* a class, there are desperate institutions that are doing everything in their power to simply *fill* one. With half a tuition better than none, their last-minute offers might well entail far more generous packages for far less-qualified students, *need*, at this point being a secondary or tertiary consideration.

In the face of this complexity and uncertainty—with parents and students trying to balance their desire for admission to their school or schools of choice with the far more (or far less) favorable financial aid terms offered by the other institutions to which they have made application—cost (for all but the very wealthy) becomes a crucial decision point.

Whether the differences between institutions are actually all that great (an issue we will address later) it is important to ask why the costs of college and university attendance have risen so dramatically and why their ethos has become so commercial. (The wishes of small-town newspaper editors and dimbulb legislators that universities and colleges "should be run more like a business" are radically uninformed; they have been run like businesses for generations.)

The answers with regard to expanded costs are actually quite simple. State support for public institutions has been shrinking for over forty years. At the same time, flagship public institutions continue to compete with elite private institutions for the best faculty and the best graduate students. Hence they must attempt to provide attractive levels of support in order to draw the people needed to sustain programs of high quality. They have struggled to do this, with the gaps in compensation between privates and publics widening every year, though cost-of-living differentials between the South, the Midwest, the Mountain States, the Southwest, the Northern Plains and the Coasts often help to reduce that gap. Top faculty seek top students and top students are attracted to top faculty. When those students are graduate students they play an important role in their universities' research endeavors and teaching programs. Attracting top graduate students thus has a direct effect on the quality of undergraduate instruction, both in the freestanding classroom and in the laboratory. You are either in that competition or you are not and if you are, the costs are high.

Both instrumentation costs and construction costs continue to rise and those costs must be borne by public institutions with reduced state subsidies and private institutions with volatile endowments. At the top schools there is sufficient elasticity with regard to tuition to turn, early and often, to that source for a solution to budgetary challenges.

When the Board of Directors at Georgetown asked President Tim Healy about "running the university more like a business" he promptly told them that they wouldn't really care for that. "Our applicant pools are deep enough that we could charge $100,000 a year in tuition. We don't want to do that and I don't think you'd want us to do that, but that's precisely what a business would do." They sat quietly, shaking their heads "No, we wouldn't want you to do that." Before long, however, we will see $100,000 tuition/fee levels at some schools. At 4 percent rates of growth many institutions would reach $100,000 levels before 2030.

People speak of the "arms race" for top faculty. This is actually only an issue at the top schools (200 or fewer of approximately 4,500 institutions). The salary differentials between the top schools and the average ones are not insignificant but they are nothing like the differences between the salary of a country lawyer and the salary of a partner at Williams and Connelly or Covington and Burling. (The *average* 2010/2011 salary of an assistant professor at Yale was $87,500; these numbers skew skyward because they *include* the far higher compensation paid to engineering and law faculty. The starting salary for a new associate at Covington and Burling was $160,000, a salary just below the average for the most senior faculty at Yale, individuals who are thirty years older and enjoy international reputations for lifetimes of significant achievement. An equivalent full professor at the University of Wisconsin, Madison makes some 36 percent less than a colleague at Yale.)

The salaries are not munificent, once one considers the schooling required for them, the years of potential income that are foregone and the credentials that are expected. The vast majority of college professors are paid relatively modest salaries and those salaries have become radically compressed as a result of budget cuts. If you seek to hire the best faculty—the indispensable element in university stature and university success—you are compelled to pay the market rate for entry-level positions, but then, unfortunately, the compression sets in. At Wisconsin in the late 1970s the salary differential between entering computer science teachers (a then fast-growing field) and their senior colleagues was little more than $100 (per year). When I entered graduate school in 1963 it was expected that a senior full professor would make 2.5x the salary of an entry-level assistant professor. This was a "best practices" number. The top faculty salaries in the Illinois English department in the mid 1960's were in the low $20 thousands, the starting salary approximately $8,000. Fifty years later, in four-year colleges and universities across the country the average salary for an assistant professor in English was $55,716, the average salary for a full professor $85,404.

The teaching loads and leave opportunities at the top institutions are more attractive than those at average institutions, but those loads and leaves assume a significant research stream and their costs (in simple dollars) are not automatically passed on to students, for budgets can be balanced and curricula covered by hiring contingent faculty at lower rates. Even the most elite departments have non-tenure-track faculty filling out the curriculum. In addition to the graduate students who lead discussion sections at Harvard, for example, that institution's departments will also include non-tenure-track holders of terminal degrees (approximately 20 percent of the English faculty, e.g., though one assumes that many if not all of those individuals are, at Harvard, paid through endowments). The personnel ladder within colleges and universities continues to resemble that of a medieval guild (cf. the *master's* degree), in which apprentices and journeymen remain very much in evidence.

With science faculty the startup costs for an initial hire can be huge, though one expects them to be offset quickly by the receipt of grants (which will generate university overhead in addition to the new faculty member's direct research costs). I was taken aback in the late 1970s when my boss at Wisconsin allocated $500,000 in startup funds to a young chemist. Those sorts of numbers would occasion no surprise today.

New additions to the faculty are often housed in temporarily-unused (or otherwise-used) space that is renovated to meet their needs. (The faculty positions are often *banked* for several years, the saved salary money then expended on a one-time basis to meet or at least reduce the renovation and startup costs.) Recent additions to our Biological Sciences Division, for example, required $250,000 in renovation costs per laboratory and additional, often significant funding for instrumentation. Biologists do not enjoy the levels of compensation that economists, Law faculty or Finance professors see, but they need decent laboratories in order to begin the work which will then attract federal, state, corporate and foundation funding. The astronomical salaries of university surgeons are, of course, offset by clinical income and the salaries of prominent coaches could/*should* be offset by ticket revenue and licensing income.

I have seen startup packages for the most senior faculty reach levels in the tens of millions of dollars, though it should be noted that such individuals bring major grant support with them; many then interact with faculty and students in multiple departments and can literally alter a university (economically, intellectually, culturally) by their presence and labors. When Professor

Har Gobind Khorana left Wisconsin in 1970 to go to MIT the local legislators expressed surprise at the fact that a building was being provided for his research. The university was surprised by their surprise, since Professor Khorana had a building at Wisconsin. Some members of the legislature had earlier expressed surprise at his level of compensation. Questions such as, "Who is this person?" were heard. The answer was that he was the recipient of the Nobel Prize for Medicine in 1968, the first to demonstrate the role of nucleotides in nucleic acids, which carry the cell's genetic code and control its synthesis of proteins. He was also to receive the National Medal of Science in 1987.

Professional salaries rise faster than the cost of, e.g., durable goods, so university faculties have "become more expensive" *vis à vis* the cost of refrigerators or microwaves (see, e.g., Archibald and Feldman 2011, p. 21). Their numbers, however, have not risen significantly above the increase in the number of students, while the portion of the universities' budgets dedicated to instruction has generally not risen appreciably. In many cases it has diminished significantly as universities have struggled to develop other activities to create revenue streams to offset the reduction in state subsidies. One observer estimates the portion of university budgets dedicated to instruction at, on average, twenty-one cents on the dollar (Brandon 2010, p. 30). Another estimates the cost of instruction—at four-year public institutions—at twenty-six cents on the dollar (Ferguson 2011, p. 177). In 2008-9 the University of California System reported its instructional budget at 11 percent of the whole, with another 11 percent for "academic support" (libraries, museums, etc.). As interim provost at Georgetown my utopian fantasy number for the instructional budget was 40 percent of the Main Campus budget; we never got there.

The rankings of a college or university may be of greater interest to a prospective undergraduate than the specific quality of its faculty or the dimensions of its instructional budget. Since the ranking system can be gamed it can drive behavior as well as the budget. One southern institution, for example, urged *US News* to alter its assessment of the resources invested in faculty by keying them to the local cost of living, a change which was of great benefit to the institution in question.

Emory (with many others rumored to follow their example) does not accept their *best* applicants (who are unlikely to come) because it would hurt their yield rate and thus negatively affect their rankings (Kirp 2003, p. 26). One institution, which shall remain nameless, went so far as to hire a relative of an official at *US News* in order to enhance access and, potentially, increase the chances for influencing him.

Sometimes you can persuade the ranker to change; sometimes you must change (or consider changing) in order to leverage the rankings. Missouri, for example, suffered in the rankings because it had putatively small applicant pools and accepted a high percentage of those who applied. The reason was that we were very explicit with regard to our expectations and did not want students to waste time and resources in applying when they were unlikely to be admitted. This was a kind thing to do. Unfortunately, it was not very shrewd or calculating; the way to work the system is to encourage students to apply—covering them in warm fuzzies—so that you can then reject the vast majority of them and hype your "selectivity." The cost of the warm fuzzies is then passed on to the enrollees in the form of higher tuition charges. In the mid 1980s, for example, when Brown was working hard to raise their profile, they (as many do) purchased SAT results and approached students within certain numerical parameters. Our son received seven mailings from them, even though he had not expressed interest in applying there.

A far greater driver of current costs is enhanced and expanded information technology. Alan Turing may have used the colossus computer at Bletchley Park to help break the German codes, but I did not see word processors in university offices until the late 1970s. As an associate dean in the Wisconsin graduate school at that time I was very happy to have my own IBM Selectric typewriter. The university's computer resources were metered out to graduate students there and then with an upper limit of $500 of "time" per doctoral student (for their dissertation research) and it was expected that students would use the computers during slow periods (i.e. 2:00 a.m.$\pm$) in order to maximize the availability of the resource. The academic computing committee—the ACC, but termed the "ACK-ACK" committee because of the struggles for resources which it governed, was one of the most difficult and contentious committees on which one might be asked to serve.

Laser printers were among the major desiderata of distinguished researchers. In the mid-80s HP's were $3,000-$4,000 and the only college office which was sure to have one was the office of admissions. All of these costs have come down, but the use of information technology has risen astronomically. Bottom line rule: information technology increases productivity but it does *not* reduce costs.

At that time it was common for academic research libraries to *hope* for a budget consisting of approximately 4 percent of the university operating budget (a "best practices" number). They were often lucky to receive 2 percent. Costs for information technology today are not commonly shared (or easily ascertained) but one hears numbers in the neighborhood of 8 percent of the university's budget. Thus, IT is probably costing at least twice what libraries once *hoped* to receive, though we now operate *both*. The undergraduate students, of course, are most interested in bandwidth for the downloading of music and streaming of video. When schools attempt to meter this out and add surcharges for excessive use (as Cornell, e.g., has recently done) the natives respond with a great deal of restlessness (See Zou 2011).

In 1997 Cornell spent $80,000,000 for information technology on the Ithaca campus—8 percent of campus expenditures. Its library budget was $28,400,000 or 2.8 percent of the budget (Ehrenberg 2002, pp. 191, 194). In 1996-7 the Harvard library budget was $70,900,000, $9,000,000+ less than Cornell's IT budget (Ehrenberg 2002, p. 194). Keep in mind, of course, that the Harvard library collections are the envy of the academic world.

When I was a student at Notre Dame we enjoyed access to the Rockne Memorial—a gym with a pool. Adjoining it was an eighteen-hole golf course, an exceptional resource at the time. The golf course now has only nine holes as the university has built additional dormitories on that site. The Rockne Memorial now includes a climbing wall and other emoluments. Exercise facilities at American universities are among the institutions' most important draws. At Missouri we are reputed to have the nation's finest. This is either a significant comparative advantage or a dubious cost, depending on one's perspective.

Students love and expect such facilities (though they may not use them regularly). Their costs are generally added to tuition. In the outside world, those who want to use such facilities pay for them on a fee-for-service basis. The exercise facility nearest to me charges approximately $100 per month for the use of its facilities, the nearby country club far more. This has led pundits to say that the university which was once monastic in its facilities (and, to a degree, in its costs) has now become a country club. Country club facilities are expensive, but students enjoy them and, more important, expect them.

The University of Houston offers a $53M "wellness center" that includes hot tubs, waterfalls and a five-story climbing wall, though Houston's hot tubs are doubtless surpassed by Washington State University's Jacuzzi that holds fifty-three people. (*The Bachelor/Bachelorette/BachelorPad/Bachelor-in-Paradise* meet the groves of academe.) Indiana University of Pennsylvania offers room-sized golf simulators and the University of Wisconsin-Oshkosh provides massages, manicures and pedicures (Toby 2010, p. 98). In addition to batting cages, the Ohio State exercise complex (at $140M/657,000 square feet) offers a kayak and canoe course (Brandon p. 24).

With regard to amenities my personal favorite is High Point University in North Carolina, which offers both valet parking and concierge services in selected residence facilities, automated wake-up calls and lobster and steak on its lunch menu (Brandon 2010, p. 24).

I would like to taste that High Point lobster and steak. It might also be enjoyable to sample life in the Princeton dorm complex which cost $272,000 per student to build when the average cost of a single family *home* in 2010 was $183,400 (Rosen 2011, pp. 47-48). In my time, the dorm rooms at Notre Dame were of vastly different vintage and they varied markedly in size and quality, but students chose them in the order of their grade point averages. The food, however, was consistently appalling. Usually there were two choices, which sometimes rhymed, viz. "lamb or ham." During my graduation week at Notre Dame the university (very deviously) prepared special foods for our parents. Their response: "I don't see why you've been complaining so much about the food. . . ." After their initial, special, offerings, however, the cafeteria staff reverted to form and served the parents still remaining on campus the sort of food that we had been receiving. My fiancée's father asked the question, "What is this thing we're eating?" I responded that it was called a "chuck wagon steak." His follow-up question: "Why is it that I can't chew it with my teeth or cut it with my knife?" That dining hall now offers a plethora of choices with a multiplicity of preparation stations, with commensurately-higher costs. In 2002, Cornell offered five entrées for dinner, including a vegetarian main dish (Ehrenberg 2002, p. 249).

Recently, our students at Missouri requested enlarged and enhanced union facilities. We actually have two: the traditional, quiet union with gothic tower and meeting room space and—a few hundred yards to the south—the student commons union space with fast food, retail outlets and recreational facilities. To expand the latter the students were asked if they were willing to fund the construction through increased fees. They said yes, overwhelmingly and immediately. Now we have the facilities and they are very impressive, though fees have been increased in perpetuity.

Athletics, another budget item of importance to multiple segments of the university community, are nearly always subsidized, sometimes heavily subsidized. It recently came to light, e.g., that Rutgers was subsidizing athletics to the tune of $27,000,000 annually. This was better, at least, than UNLV's $34,073,391 (*USA Today*, 6/23/11). To mount its golf team USC invests $33,961 per player; Bowdoin, with only 1,771 students, supports thirty-seven athletic squads, all of them losing money (Hacker August 17, 2010, p. 1). A very small number of institutions, no more than fourteen in 2009, including Florida, Alabama, Ohio State, Missouri, Texas and Tennessee, did not have to subsidize athletics. We were very pleased to be included in that number.

Some institutions which appear, culturally, to downplay the importance of athletics (the Ivies, for example) often subsidize athletics more heavily than the schools with large athletic programs because the latter have significant income to offset costs, while the Ivies do not. At Georgetown in the 1980s a few hundred people paid $5 to sit in high school bleachers to watch a football game. Our stadium at Missouri holds 70,000+ (small by Michigan standards); the sky boxes, holding 16 seats, were initially $60,000 each *per season* (cheap by true "football factory" school standards).

The wisdom of these investments can be questioned, but just as an isolated seven-figure screenplay sale awakens the hopes of writers, the *perceived* importance of athletics is something with which the president or chancellor must conjure. When Northwestern appeared in the Rose Bowl in 1996 it experienced a 30 percent increase in applications, a nearly twenty point rise in its average freshman SAT scores, an increase in alumni giving and a rise in licensing revenue from $60,000 to $600,000 (Ehrenberg 2002, p. 234).

Athletic costs have been affected by Title IX, which attempted to bring gender equity to collegiate athletics. This has been a visible, widely-discussed issue. Parents and students are far less likely to be aware of other regulatory requirements and the costs that they entail.

The poshest facilities on any campus are likely to be those in which experimental animals are housed. With regard to cleanliness and habitability the animal facilities markedly exceed that of classroom space. Federal inspectors expect them to be at least as fresh and well-supervised as a hospital nursery.

Federal regulations entail both capital costs and administrative costs. There were few offices of research two generations ago, certainly very few at the order of magnitude that we find today. Research administration was something done by the graduate school with its managerial left hand. Now, these offices are very large (ours consists of 100 individuals) and one must have them if one is to comply with federal regulations, manage a large number of grants and seek to obtain more. And one *must* have a large number of grants (with the tech transfer personnel, patent administrators and incubator facilities to exploit their research results) if one is to compensate for the continuing reduction of support from state governments. Many flagship public institutions now receive less than 10 percent of their operating budgets from their states. The commonly-repeated witticism, originally made by James Duderstadt, past president of the University of Michigan, is that public institutions were once state-*funded*. Then they were state-*supported*. Now they are state-*located*. (They, of course, continue to be state-*regulated*.)

If a public university does not have the wherewithal to redesign itself, to, in effect, construct a new "economy" capable of, in some ways, "privatizing" the campus by developing new revenue streams, it is largely doomed, particularly if its state legislature (as nearly every one does) controls its ability to raise its tuition. That is why public flagships now conduct $1B development campaigns. That is why athletic conference realignment and the resulting distribution of television revenue result in banner headlines. That is why, in part, modern universities increasingly look like and feel like large corporate entities.

Cities and states generally applaud all of these self-help efforts. They expect universities to contribute directly to economic development and legislators are delighted to see the progeny of happy constituents admitted to the "U" at minimum cost to the state. The economy of the state—upon which the universities once depended—is increasingly dependent on the universities. One additional home football game in our city has literally saved a significant number of local businesses from bankruptcy and the economic development wing of our university system administration generally draws more attention and concern than its academic offices.

This puts the flagship publics in a difficult bind. While governors and legislatures continue to press for "access" and "efficiency," i.e., the inexpensive production of vast numbers of bachelor's degree recipients, they simultaneously press for greater research capacity that will contribute materially to economic development. At the same time, we hear the research-versus-teaching meme invoked, the rhetorical point being that research is a questionable, often trivial activity that takes the faculty out of the classroom. "If only the faculty teaching loads were increased, we would see major steps forward for public education."

In effect, the politicians want their flagships to function like very large, glorified high schools containing internationally-recognized science laboratories. The research university should *not* attempt to function in that manner. However, it often does, schizophrenically, turning out those baccalaureate-degree graduates using large classes, graduate student and adjunct instructors, soft majors and soft schools, while continuing to do what it can to develop new knowledge. The governors and legislatures are then satisfied and the magnitude of the next budget cut may be slightly reduced. This is, in part, why the number of tenure-ladder faculty has been reduced at many universities and the number of contingent faculty has increased so dramatically—in response to a demand for "efficiency" at the same time that budgets are being reduced and research expectations publicly vilified but privately applauded.

There are other costs, some of them enormous, which have grown in recent decades. The first is omnipresent litigiousness, far less common in the 1950s when authority seemed to command more respect and a sense of shame would keep many from making preposterous claims. As a graduate dean at Georgetown I had a department which required doctoral students to present themselves for an interim program review which would assess progress, monitor the past meeting of requirements, and chart the course to the completion of the degree. One student refused to appear for her review. She disregarded requests, she disregarded calls and she disregarded registered letters. When she was dropped from the program, she appealed. The grounds were that she could not be dropped from the program because that program required a review which had not occurred. Hence the department had violated its own rules *vis à vis* the requirements for the completion of a degree (though, obviously, they could *not* "honor" those rules, because *she* had refused to appear before them).

On another occasion one of my departments had a doctoral student who refused to take any direction in the writing of her dissertation. She would submit thesis chapters to her mentor and the mentor would make comments ("condense here, add here, reorganize this chapter," etc.). The student thanked the mentor and then resubmitted the chapters with no changes whatsoever. Eventually the mentor resigned from the task of directing the dissertation. The student then worked her way through the other faculty in the department and when she refused to take direction from any of them and they resigned we obtained a director from another university who, eventually, also resigned. The student was dropped and promptly sued the graduate school. Such examples could be multiplied. Litigiousness drains time and requires additional administrative staff, including both in-house and (very expensive) external legal staff.

The corporatizing and bureaucratizing of the university has brought its own costs, both intellectual and financial, particularly when administrators' business priorities supersede academic ones. One problem (among many) with "running the university like a business" is that businesses are not monolithic enterprises. It is very different to manage a mortuary, a musical instruments store, or an investment firm. The ethos of a software development enterprise is very different from that of a foundry.

Many of the "business" aspects of the university have long been addressed by administrators with business expertise, but they have served under academic leadership. When academic interests are supplanted by purely commercial interests the "academic business" suffers, for individuals without academic experience often fail to understand the university's ethos, processes and "product" (the development of new knowledge and the dissemination to students of both new and existing knowledge). This is why some universities broker the selling of cable TV services in dormitories in order to develop an additional revenue stream, without considering the fact that this might increase student debt and further reduce the time that students now devote to their studies.

The university *is*, in certain senses, a business—a nonprofit business with for-profit competitors. To manage such a business, however, requires familiarity with the nature of *that* business. Generic business people are sometimes nonplussed by universities because they do not understand the details of their operations. To give one example: they often seek to standardize computer policies in order to achieve efficiency and greater ease of management. They institute one-size-fits-all requirements, not realizing that Economics and Mathematics departments might require different operating systems than Humanities departments and will surely require hardware with more enhanced capacities than departments which largely do simple word processing. Fine arts and graphic design faculty, for example, generally use Macs rather than PCs because of the Macs' special capabilities. One-size-fits-all IT approaches can significantly disrupt the activities of key university disciplines.

The expansion of bureaucracy adds to costs in two ways. The university is first required to pay the salary, fringe benefits and overhead for the bureaucrats (and the salaries, benefits and overhead for their support staff). It then must pay for the entropy which the bureaucrats introduce into the system.

One example: several years ago our campus was pressed to create a faculty-accomplishments data base that would demonstrate our productivity and enable "oversight groups" to *generate reports*. The faculty resisted its one-size-fits-all templates because each discipline records accomplishments with different protocols in different formats. The crucial element in these documents is the material "between the lines." Standardization blurs discipline-specific practices and privileges the quantitative over the qualitative.

Such data bases exemplify the bureaucratic passion for fixity, but that putative fixity distorts the realities of academic life. In this particular case one mandated data template conflated the multiple, highly-varied entries that could fall under the category, "books". Simple, edited books (at Wisconsin we called them "nonbooks") were lumped together with efforts requiring decades of work. At the moment I am reading David Wootton's *The Invention of Science: A New History of the Scientific Revolution*. This monumental opus of some 783 pp. would have been included in the list of faculty "books" with the same fanfare as a government report, a freestanding pamphlet or a short compilation actually prepared by a professor's graduate assistant.

While some "snapshot" studies might be generated from these templates, the faculty effort required to construct the data base (and the salaries of supervisory administrators, the software costs and the software firm's consultancy costs) was out of all proportion to its actual usefulness. Ultimately, the result was a mammoth compilation that no individual or group of individuals could possibly study. A thirty pp. c.v. multiplied by 1500 faculty, for example, generates a document of 45,000 pages or 225 volumes (@200pp./volume) and the content of those 225 volumes would change every moment of every day. The "reports that might be generated" would be fatuous brag pieces that spoke simply to quantity and not to quality or significance.

One monstrous source of increased costs has been the use of computer systems (for finance, administration, admissions, human resources and student life) that were designed for businesses, not universities. One of these systems, PeopleSoft, has entailed investments that have been gargantuan—approaching $100,000,000 for large institutions and tens of millions of dollars for medium-sized institutions (See Olsen, 1999, who reports costs of $84,000,000 for Ohio State). These systems have required elaborate installation costs, but also adaptation costs, so that the generic product could be tailored (again and again, institution by institution) to meet individual needs. The systems then need to be sustained over time and on-campus offices are created for that purpose. The university pays for the software and pays for its installation, adaptation and ongoing sustenance. It also pays for the training that the software requires individuals to undergo so that they can actually utilize it. In nearly every case the administrative staff report that the new system is far more complex and cumbersome than the system it replaced. Of course, staff members are unavailable for other functions when they are attending their training sessions.

This particular system was so complex and convoluted that the software company producing it regularly took out ads in *The Chronicle of Higher Education*, actually announcing its product's successful installation at individual institutions. Imagine Toyota proudly advertising that Professor X had purchased one of its products and that the product had successfully started and actually conveyed the professor to her chosen destination, where the brakes functioned and the vehicle was able to stop without incident.

Some investments are forced upon universities by external threats. When I was at Madison I calculated that my travel vouchers were being monitored at least seven times and that, in some cases, the monitoring was costing more than the actual travel. When I brought this to the attention of one of the auditors he said, "You don't understand, young man" (I *was* much younger then). "Our purpose is not to save money; it's to keep the university's name off of the front page of the *Capital Times*." That newspaper's reporters were, e.g., acquiring institutional phone records and calling every number on the lists, hoping to find an inappropriate use of university telephones that would publicly embarrass the campus. Hence the (expensive) preemptive attempts by our auditors to protect us with regard to travel expenses.

There are many other reasons for the rise in costs, many of them hidden to parents and students, some of them arcane like the costs incurred to meet the requirements for historic preservation or the demands of so-called "sunshine" laws. When states require universities to interview potential senior administrators publicly the result is that a significant number of attractive candidates refuse to be considered. The odds are against their being hired and they do not want to jeopardize their positions at their current universities. They also do not want anyone to know that they failed to secure the job. Under such circumstances you are more likely to attract desperate candidates than attractive ones. These laws can sometimes be evaded if you interview out of state, which universities do, trading off the travel costs for their search committees for the likelihood of securing far better leadership. Even schools in states without sunshine laws take extraordinary steps to avoid the efforts of investigative reporters who stake out airport hotel lobbies and other likely interview sites. The hiring of a new football or basketball coach, of course, attracts even more attention from local newspapers.

Some universities pay "PILOTs"—*payments in lieu of taxation*—to their surrounding communities. Yale has long done this, for example. Georgetown was pressured to do so, but generally resisted by compiling lists of the millions of dollars of services which the university provided *gratis* to the District of Columbia.

Part of the cost of attending an elite private college or university includes the aforementioned charges for marketing efforts which the institution has incurred in order to deepen their applicant pools. This has been estimated at $5,000 for each student enrolled (Kidd in Hersh and Merrow 2005, p. 202), an amount larger than an entire year's tuition at many public institutions.

A particularly significant addition to costs has been the explosion in growth of nonteaching academic staff. Over the last several decades, the number of students has risen significantly. The number of faculty has risen as well, commensurate with the growth in the number of students. The number of senior, line administrators has grown, but not to the degree that many have thought or claimed. The number of blue collar workers and secretarial staff has generally diminished. What has grown, dramatically, enormously, is the number of "academic professional" staff who are not members of the ordinary or (except by special arrangement) adjunct faculty.

Between 1975 and 2005 the faculty (tracking the students) have risen by 51 percent; the executive/managerial line administrators have grown by 85 percent. The latter number is a cause for concern, but the cause for alarm is the growth in the number of nonteaching academic professionals: 240 percent (Ginsberg 2011, p. 25).

Some of these appointments are to be expected: information technology specialists, development specialists (who bring in money, ideally [and commonly] for less than 16 cents on the dollar, sometimes for as little as 8 cents on the dollar). As we will see in succeeding chapters, these numbers include academic advisers (often the result of excessively complex curricular requirements that are installed one at a time over decades but that no one can now understand, except for those who deal with this issue and nothing else).

Their numbers include tutors and supervisors of tutors whose business is remediation—a growth industry with the increase in the number of unprepared and underprepared students in America's colleges. The growing ranks of the academic staff also include administrators within the so-called "diversity industry" and the managers of centers for various minority or even majority (the "women's center") student groups. They include "student life" staff, counselors for students suffering from anxiety and for those with more severe psychological challenges. All of these groups and offices seek to expand. The newest addition to the bureaucracy is the "sustainability industry," which might actually serve to reduce costs, though most universities have long taken steps to reduce energy use and recycle materials by utilizing the wisdom of preexisting individuals in the offices of Buildings and Grounds.

It would be interesting to ask the consumers of student services whether or not they would forego these services in exchange for lower tuition. (My own students have said that the services are probably of use to some first-year students.) Many corporations keep benefit costs under control by offering "cafeteria plans" in which the individual employee selects a specific *set* of benefits. With students, on the other hand, *all generally pay for everything whether they need or use a service or not.*

Presidents and Chancellors were once thought of as academic leaders. One thinks of an Eliot, a Conant or a Hutchins, for example. They were later considered managers of what Clark Kerr called the "multiversity," a large, complex, in some ways alienating, institution whose ethos may have led directly to some student pushback and strident or even violent student activism. Now (our imagined aged alumnus would discover) college presidents are more like mayors of small cities. Those cities operate large entertainment complexes and farm team facilities for professional athletic teams; they provide security and energy, operate restaurants and retail sales outlets, supervise residential housing complexes, hire state and federal lobbyists, offer medical care and psychological services, house chapels and churches, conduct military training, hire planners for traffic control (both vehicular and pedestrian) and planners for architectural efficiency and integrity. Some operate secondary schools and nearly all operate daycare centers. Some even have ambassadors. Georgetown, for example, had a liaison with the city government, a liaison with the federal government and a liaison with the three neighborhood associations surrounding the campus. The university "cities" offer services that often duplicate those in the surrounding community, but services that are paid for by all. The number of these services is growing rather than shrinking. Their offices within the bureaucracy are seldom eliminated, even though the curtailing of some of these operations and/or the privatization of others could result in significant cost savings that could be used to reduce tuition and/or enhance instruction.

Reducing tuition would, after all, be preferable to increasing "scholarships" (particularly among the elite privates), for as tuition rises, financial aid budgets expand, particularly for those institutions committed to meeting full financial need. The more that you charge, the more that you need to sequester to offset the tuition hikes.

So what are cash-strapped parents and students to do? Irreducibly, America's colleges and universities, particularly the elite ones, are the preserves of the wealthy. The wealthy have the means to afford private grammar schools and private secondary education; they can afford good nutrition, travel, books and cultural experiences. They have social capital. They know how to complete forms and how to work systems. They can afford (and actually do pay for) admissions services that cost thousands of dollars. It has been estimated that one in four private college students use one of these services; Katherine Cohen's platinum package of admissions advice costs $40,000 (Ferguson 2011, p. 11). "Merlyn's Pen" will help you with your "personal" admissions-application essay for a mere $595 (Hacker/Dreifus 2010, p. 185).

Our son was on the tennis team at his Madison high school. When he got to Langley High School in McLean, Virginia he discovered that many of the students on the tennis team had their own tennis courts and, in many cases, their own private coaches. These are the students who apply for places at the most competitive institutions. President *emeritus* Duderstadt (2007, p. 312) reports that the average family income for University of Michigan undergraduates in 2006-7 was $120,000. At the top 146 colleges and universities 75 percent of the students come from the top income quartile; 3 percent come from the bottom income quartile (Washburn 2005, p. 208).

Every public voice in higher education cries out for greater access for the needy and the poor. Much has been done to help them, but, again, irreducibly, the bulk of the slots in our institutions of higher education are occupied by the well-to-do and the upper middle class. The wealthy or wealthier classmates of the cash-strapped expect and demand what they already experience in their daily lives: a far higher standard of living than was experienced or expected in the 1950's—better food, better accommodations, extensive support services, a wide choice of entertainment and recreational facilities, in short, comforts and luxuries. Some were surprised to see St. Louis University build luxury dorms, but SLU's experience was that luxury dorms filled quickly. Students and parents perceive a palpable difference between the monk's cell and the room with a view (and balcony) and are prepared to pay for those differences.

When my classmates and I exercised at the Rockne Memorial we were somehow able to do so without personal trainers. There was no university travel service. We formed dues-free regional clubs and chartered DC-3's from Purdue Airlines at approximately 80 percent of standard commercial rates. We incurred no parking fees because cars were not permitted for undergraduates. We incurred no phone bills because there was a (single) pay phone on each dormitory floor. We were not tempted to play video games because they did not yet exist and contemporary counterparts such as pinball machines were not available on campus because the university administration would have considered them lowbrow and a distraction from academic pursuits (despite the fact that they might have generated revenue). A life like this is unthinkable to modern students but their parents continue to complain about costs (and the students about the debt that they have incurred). That simpler life actually occurred, however, and it was survivable. We take our current condition as "reality" and fail to see the alternatives with which others regularly deal, internationally, and the alternatives which *we* might choose to reduce costs and actually enhance access for those with lower incomes.

No prominent university has yet stepped forward and announced the availability of first-rate education with more austere facilities and support systems, *at a dramatically-reduced price*. If anything, many institutions would look first to the nature of their quality-of-life facilities and services and secondarily to the academic, since their ultimate desire is to bring tuition payers through the front gates. The university-as-country-club-cum-nanny-state is a corporatist institution, not an academic one. In 1984 at the Johnson meeting at Pembroke College we were given the opportunity to stay in college rooms. There was no visible centralized heating or air conditioning and no private bathrooms. The public restroom deserved the term "bog." The food was good, particularly for those who enjoy jugged hare, but when we inquired of the Oxford faculty what their *students* ate we heard words such as *swill* and *slop*. The student commons room furniture looked as if it had been handed down through multiple generations of graduate students and exposed to the elements on repeated occasions. Tapping a piece of upholstered furniture resulted in a palpable cloud of dust motes. Oxford's reputation has managed to survive such realities, however, and their sticker-price tuition for British citizens would quickly catch the attention of American students contemplating the costs of the Ivy league and its imitators (ca. £9,000 x1.40 [3/20/18] =$12,600).

Politically, American universities are sympathetic to the needy, but the "needy" are not necessarily those in simple financial need. They are those who require "support" and "validation." I can imagine an institution lowering its costs and offering less of its brand of "support" but far more favorable tuition levels. I can imagine it, but I do not expect it to happen anytime soon. The closing of "support" services, even if the closings were accompanied by tuition reductions—which would be a great help for the financially needy—would evoke political responses that our risk-averse presidents and chancellors would find intolerable. Brandon (2010, p. 164) argues that a "no-frills college" could reduce tuition by 75 percent; he reports that Pennsylvania, at least, is looking into this possibility.

The for-profits offer a curious set of alternatives. They are free of the costs of a host of traditional functions, including the costs of intercollegiate athletics; they provide limited support services and they maintain no bona fide research libraries, laboratories, core instrumentation facilities, or museums, but they still charge Oxbridge-level tuition. Nevertheless, in these days of increased vocationalism they do not want for customers.

They also have access to federal financial aid (an issue last addressed aggressively by Secretary Bennett, who knew that some proprietary schools [of various kinds] were taking the tuition money of students and offering little to them in return besides the resulting indebtedness). In some respects the for-profits are freeriders, for their students pay them tuition but use public or university libraries in their regions. We had a comparable situation at Georgetown. I discovered that one institution in our local library consortium had decided to invest in computers rather than in books. Their students would surf the electronic catalogues of member universities' libraries, learn what books they possessed and then access them through interlibrary loan. We acquired, catalogued, shelved, circulated and controlled the climate for the books; our students and donors paid for them; their students used them. While cooperation and collaboration remain important ideals, corporatized universities are prepared to base their own success on the exploitation of their competitors'/colleagues' resources.

Absent a change in the system as a whole, middle- and low-income American families have little choice but to work very hard to seek a quality education at a modest price. Lynn O'Shaughnessy's guide (2012) provides excellent help in this regard. There is no question that a college education offers *some* value. Statistically, college graduates have greater lifetime earnings than high school graduates, the current estimates differing, but all clearly favoring the recipient of a baccalaureate degree. Jacobs and Hyman (2010, p. 6) report a lifetime salary differential of $279,893; Donoghue (2008, p. 85) argues for a $900,000 differential (we frequently hear the figure of $1M); Hoxby (Donoghue 2008, p. 113) claims a differential of $1.2M between the graduates of elite colleges and the graduates of non-competitive colleges. With regard to Hoxby's point, other studies have shown no differences (see, e.g., Farrell 2010), if, e.g., you evaluate based on SAT scores (the quality of the student) rather than by college acceptance rates (the putative quality of the college); by their behavior, however, the consumers appear to believe Hoxby, for they continue to flood the elite institutions with applications.

Of course, this differential cannot be expected in all cases, though it may be true in large statistical terms. An electrician or plumber who goes on to establish his own business may make many times more than a college graduate who spends his or her life in middle management. The "millionaire next door," it has been argued, is often the proprietor of a successful beauty salon or the owner of an auto repair shop. Similarly, it is not necessarily the case that the college graduate will secure the job because he or she has learned more in college. Toby (2010, pp. 132-7) argues, for example, that the successful applicant may have learned more in high school. He or she may be more disciplined and more motivated. He or she may possess soft skills: showing up on time, cooperating, managing time well (all of which could be learned in the military as well as in college). Irreducibly, the college graduate is four to six years older than the high school graduate and has more life experience, experience that is likely to include greater experience with computers and other information technology.

The "value," however, has changed public perception. If college graduates make more money than high school graduates and if we *know* that they will attend college because of that incentive, why should the state contribute significantly to their education? They will come anyway. The result of that attitude (or discovery) is that education is increasingly perceived as a private good rather than a public good and it is funded accordingly. State contributions have diminished and this—as day follows night—has resulted in higher tuition. I could repeat the facts that my chancellor once placed on our university website. A college degree adds to lifetime income and that increases the state income- and sales taxes paid by those graduates. The state will receive far more in taxes than it will cost to subsidize the education of the individual student/taxpayer. Supporting higher education is thus among the best investments that a state can make, a classic no-brainer. It is all true but it makes little difference to the legislature; they know that students will come anyway.

The number of individuals now attending college has exacerbated the *need* to do so, for so many now hold college degrees that we have experienced significant "credential creep." One has to have a baccalaureate degree now in order to secure a job previously held by a high school graduate and a graduate degree in order to secure a position that was earlier made possible by a bachelor's degree. Some now speak of K-16 education, arguing that "college is the new high school." Though college students are biological adults they are treated like grammar school students, "validation" trumping "testing" (in multiple senses of the term).

My father-in-law was unable to complete high school. He went on to be a parcel post driver and eventually director of delivery for Cincinnati and finally a senior postal executive in the Ohio/Kentucky/Indiana region. He served as postmaster of Louisville and postmaster of Cleveland. He was offered the position of director of delivery for the United States in the Kennedy administration. This would never happen today. One of the most effective associate deans in the Wisconsin graduate school managed the graduate school admission system and worked with the divisional deans on all special cases, probationary admissions, terminations, appeals, and so on. She was a high school graduate (but with high school training from the 1940s). Again, this would never happen today. A director of graduate admissions at a major institution would now be expected to hold at least a master's degree.

Forty years ago 3 percent of mailmen had bachelor's degrees; now 13 percent do (Ferguson 2011, pp. 176–7). One 2006 estimate claimed that 7,000,000 college graduates were in jobs that did not require a degree (Brandon 2010, p. 145). Stossel (2011, following Vedder) notes that 80,000 bartenders in America have bachelor's degrees, along with 17 percent of baggage porters and bellmen and 15 percent of taxi and limousine drivers.

Regrettably, the credential creep has resulted in part from a reduction in standards. Colleges are filled with unmotivated students who attend because they feel that they have to, not because they want to. The tuition collectors have been happy to have their business, along with that of the unprepared and underprepared. When you ask faculty how many students actually belong in college they might offer pieties about equal opportunity and "community," but when pressed, when asked what percentage is actually prepared for college, actually will enjoy college, benefit from college, have their lives changed by college, seek an education for personal growth and not just vocational opportunity, the number that one is most likely to hear is 10 percent.

I have heard that guesstimate number since the 1950s, when a far smaller percentage of students attended college. In 1959 at Notre Dame, as at other universities, there was an array of sections of freshman English, dozens and dozens of them. When we arrived, however, we discovered that the dean's office (or some invisible hand) had created three sections designed for students expected to participate in what was termed the "committee on academic progress." This was a kind of honors program with its own faculty adviser. Prior to registration, certain sections of required courses would be set aside for these students and in some cases they would be permitted to take graduate classes while still undergraduates.

Ninety students were so chosen, perhaps 6 percent of the total class. These were the "serious" students, those who would most commonly be seen on the dean's list, those most likely to receive Woodrow Wilson or Danforth fellowships, those most likely to become college professors, physicians and prominent attorneys.

A National Survey of Student Engagement (Brandon 2010, pp. 5, 64) estimates the number of "truly engaged" students at 10 percent of the total. Charles Murray is more generous (2008, p. 67), arguing that 10-20 percent of potential students can cope with genuine college-level material. The mean IQ of college graduates in the 1950s was 115 (the top 16 percent). Today, 28 percent have college diplomas. The College Board conducted a study of 41 schools (both public and private) and selected out those students with a 65 percent probability of achieving a freshman GPA of 2.7 or higher (B-). Those students averaged scores of 590 on the SAT-verbal, 610 on the SAT-math and combined scores of 1180 or higher. The number of takers of the SAT that met those benchmarks: 9–12 percent (Murray, 2008, pp. 69-70).

CNNMoney recently reported that students *graduating* in 2013 averaged $35,200 in college-related debt, i.e., including credit card debt and funds owed to family members (Ellis, 2013). In a ten-year follow-up study of 1992–1993 graduates, the National Center for Education Statistics reported that 20 percent of those who owed $15,000 or more were in default. African-American graduates defaulted at 5x the rate of white/non-Hispanics and at 9x the rate of Asian-Americans. The repayment of college loans is burdensome to all, but crippling to those unable to find suitable employment and destructive to those who fail to graduate but still carry a debt burden.

I believe it is fair to say that the system has been overbuilt to accommodate potential demand. There is no problem finding an institution willing to accept a student's, *any* student's, tuition. The tuition-dependent institutions, a significant number of the schools within the larger system, are hungry for paying customers. Seen as corporate entities now, they wish to survive at any cost. Hence, one sees struggling "liberal arts colleges" with elaborate extension programs, cash-cow master's programs operating in the evenings and on the weekends, programs on the internet and in foreign climes. Retention is a survival mechanism and hence their summum bonum, sometimes retention at nearly any cost. Look closely at many of these institutions and you will see core faculties of little more than a handful—forty or fifty individuals in an institution with a thousand students (and $20,000-$30,000 tuition, plus room and board). Structurally, they are very, very expensive high schools. Look even more closely and you will see administrative pressure exerted on the faculty to contribute to the process of retention by reducing expectations. While the top institutions may have relaxed standards for ideological reasons (increasing access, reducing "competition," combating "elitism," teaching "the whole person," and so on), the more desperate institutions have done so in order to survive.

There is a growing body of literature concerning the tuition *bubble* that is about to burst (Barone 2010; Chavez 2012; Frezza 2011; Gilley 2012; Reynolds 2011, 2012; Wood 2010). If the past is indeed prologue, that is unlikely to occur. A few schools will close (as they do now, each year) and new schools will arise (as they do now, each year). The schools most in jeopardy will ramp up their public relations activities, purchase television advertising, alter their missions, open up branches in strip malls, offer unaccredited professional programs, quietly reduce their full-time faculty, hire more part-time replacements, give credit for life experiences and proceed blithely on their way.

Failing on those fronts there is always the "global economy." Institutions can hire third parties to deliver foreign graduate students. The Missouri State MBA program, for example, hired the International Management Education Center recruiters to find students at $10,000-$12,000 per matriculant. The question is: will firms such as this help find students of quality or will they collude with students as desperate as the U.S. schools seeking them? One estimate claims that 90 percent of Chinese applicants for programs such as Missouri State's were submitting phony recommendations, 70 percent were using essays written by others and 50 percent were falsifying their transcripts (Associated Press 2011, p. 3). Times may be tough, but as that celebrated moralist J. R. Ewing once opined, "Once you give up integrity the rest is easy."

Chapter Two

The Faculty Vanishes

In 2011 Naomi Schaefer Riley published a book entitled *The Faculty Lounges: And Other Reasons Why You Won't Get the College Education You Pay For*. One of the principal thematic thrusts of the book is that American higher education could be improved if we stopped awarding tenure to faculty. As she defends that point, however, she is clearly aware of all of the arguments that run counter to it.

Tenure is a form of compensation; without it, salaries would rise. Sooner or later someone would realize that long-term or rolling term contracts would be attractive to faculty and represent an opportunity to save money. Hence, tenure would return. At present, no institutions that have declined to award tenure have achieved the distinction of the institutions that *do* award it.

Many of the perceived "problems" of higher education are with the Humanities and it is in the Humanities that tenure has most seriously eroded. The rise in cost at universities is not due to faculty tenure but to expanded student services, exploding bureaucracies, enhanced quality-of-life facilities, litigation, regulatory costs, reduced state contributions, subsidization of athletics, the growth in information technology and other matters discussed in the previous chapter.

The absence of tenured faculty would exacerbate the problems besetting the curriculum because the tenured and tenure/track faculty within departments carry the responsibility for structuring programs and coursework. In the absence of such individuals the fashioning of the curriculum would be ceded to administrators, many of whom, today, would be more interested in tuition revenue and the bottom line than in the process of cultivating intellect.

Most important of all, we are already well on our way to radically restricting the number of tenured faculty because we have continued to solve budget problems by replacing tenure/track faculty with contingent faculty. In most cases these individuals teach far higher loads (or a course or two at a time) for far less money. Many do so without offices, support staff or fringe benefits. While some long-term adjuncts are committed to their institutions, others teach at multiple institutions (driving the freeways between classes, in the common image) and a large number are spending a significant portion of their time looking for full-time, tenure/track employment. Because of their vulnerability they may be inclined to coddle and inflate grades because their livelihood turns on the anonymous evaluations they receive from their students.

The growth of contingent faculty, Marc Bousquet and others would argue, is the source of a far larger number of problems in contemporary higher education than the existence of tenure, which, we sometimes forget, is still necessary to protect academic freedom. In a world where envy, spite and significant disagreements concerning the value and appropriateness of research are not unfamiliar, the protections of tenure really do help to permit the conducting of controversial studies. More to the point, in *today's* ethos, tenure protects whole disciplines from the potential ravages of corporatist administrators, inclined to eliminate entire fields of study because their enrollments are less attractive than those in some ephemeral field which might, momentarily, throw more money to the bottom line.

In 1970, 77.9 percent of the nation's faculty were full-time; in 2005 only 52.4 percent were (Archibald and Feldman 2011, p. 115). The hiring of contingent faculty (in far greater numbers at regional publics and struggling privates) enables the desperate to achieve so-called "efficiency," but this "efficiency" (the same or a greater number of students being admitted at less cost) is only real if the quality of *learning* is unaffected.

The situation is often characterized as a purely financial issue and, indeed, it *is* a financial issue. Tenure/track faculty in the Humanities at research institutions generally teach four courses per year at beginning salaries of approximately $55,000–$65,000. Full-time adjuncts might teach six to eight courses for salaries in the mid $30s. Course-at-a-time contingent faculty might be paid as little as $1,500–$2,000 per course.

Faced with horrific budget cuts, deans and departments will turn to this device in order to keep threatened programs afloat, even if quality is jeopardized or palpably reduced. And, yes, many of the contingent faculty are superb teachers, but there is a limit to which you can dilute an enterprise and still sustain its quality.

There is another pattern at work here, however. The budget may be cut by state legislatures and governors or by the volatility of the market and other investments that undergird endowments, but there is another threat to the *core* of the academic enterprise, *the university's instructional budget:* the reallocation of instructional resources to other offices and agencies within the university.

Angry commentators (often faculty commentators) see the instructional budget drained in the interest of, e.g., administrative "edifice complexes." Cranes and bulldozers appear and buildings arise from the earth while those individuals at the center of the instructional and research enterprise dwindle in number and experience frozen salaries and reduced fringe benefits. While this does occur, buildings are usually funded from separate pools, pools that are generally not fungible. A state government, for example, might be far more willing to provide capital costs which will stimulate the local economy than invest in faculty and instruction. A donor might be far happier to see a building bearing his or her name appear rather than contributing to the protection of what he or she perceives to be the routine cost of doing business. (The reallocations from general purpose funds [including the instructional budget] to building projects would usually come in the form of *maintenance costs*, which are seldom covered by bonds or gift/endowment funds and can be substantial.)

What does unquestionably occur, however, is the growth of bureaucracy at the expense of the instructional budget and this bureaucracy can be of several sorts. As noted in the previous chapter, the number of "higher" administrators has grown at a greater rate than the number of faculty, but the number of nonteaching professional staff has grown at a rate approximately 300 percent greater than that of the new vice presidents, associate vice presidents, vice-provosts, deanlets and deanlings.

Faculty see this trend fatalistically. This is the new normal; there is little that can be done about it. We must simply suck it up and soldier on. They seldom see it for what it actually represents—an ongoing struggle for control of the university. Nor do they see their complicity in it. Once upon a time the faculty exerted far more control over the university's processes than they do now, from student life to institutional planning. The claim of those who would happily displace the faculty is that they perform work which the faculty is *unable or unwilling to do*, while the now supine faculty cannot even imagine stepping forward to challenge them. (Indeed, some of the things that the bureaucrats are prepared to do *are* a waste of time and energy, but the faculty need to say that and stop serving as their silent enablers.) There are far better ways of proceeding than the current models, but the faculty must press for them and refuse to be co-opted by a system which lines pockets but does not enhance learning.

The common acceptance of the status quo can be traced to several causes. One is the general decline of intellectual leadership within the academy; the faculty increasingly see "leadership" roles as corporatist career paths. They see administrators as beings who are simply different in kind and they see them, sometimes with good reason, as doing decidedly unpleasant things whose benefits do not outweigh their costs.

Another cause is the sameness that pervades higher education, the pursuit of "brand" rather than "signature." The bottom line: it's this way everywhere, so there's nothing that can be done . . . where once upon a time the president of Harvard and the president of Princeton participated in vocal debates on how universities should educate, when Columbia maintained elements of its core curriculum in the face of Harvard's abandonment of their's, when Chicago had a unique approach to both curriculum and university structure, when Michigan highlighted the quantitative in the social sciences and Harvard the institutional. As everything becomes, increasingly, the "same," the belief that institutions can be altered for the better wanes.

Part of the perception is the belief that one must choose between administration and serious intellectual activity, that one simply cannot do both. In American universities prior to the civil war, the university president was the institution's most serious academic presence, often entrusted with teaching the capstone course which completed the students' education. To modern faculty this seems so remote that it might as well have occurred in the twelfth century.

There are, however, notable exceptions. When David Baltimore was brought to Caltech as its president in 1997, our son (who staffed the search, working with Kip Thorne and the faculty committee and Gordon Moore and the trustees' committee) was told that the expectation was that any presidential candidate would have to be at least as intelligent as 80 percent of the Caltech faculty in order to be credible and effective (expecting more than 80 percent was seen to be unreasonable). In 2013 *The Chronicle of Higher Education's* Ian Wilhelm reported that Caltech was again voted the top university in the world.

At the University of Wisconsin in the 1970s and beyond, virtually every significant academic/administrative position in the institution was part-time with a small handful of exceptions: the chancellorship, the dean of the college of letters and science. All of the divisional associate deans in the graduate school were part-time. (Ian Loram simultaneously served as department chair in German.) The dean, a distinguished biochemist named Robert Bock, effectively made himself part-time by spending two afternoons a week in his laboratory, mentoring students (including undergraduates) and doing work that some said was of Nobel quality.

This was not a minor administrative role. The graduate school was responsible for the distribution of the Wisconsin Alumni Research Foundation (WARF) funds that directly supported faculty research. The WARF portfolio, anchored by a number of significant faculty patents, generated an annual payout, through the graduate school, of millions of dollars. The graduate school used them for a multiplicity of purposes; it also supervised major centers and institutes, the University of Wisconsin Press and the full admissions/academic progress/degree certification functions common to graduate schools. The dean (carrying full responsibility for this operation) characteristically dressed for work in laboratory clothes and wore a coat and tie only when he was pressed to serve, for brief periods, as executive vice-chancellor.

My social science counterpart, Larry Cummings, was president of the Academy of Management, a later chair holder at the Kellogg School at Northwestern and at the University of Minnesota. He was one of the most prominent business school faculty members in America. My later social science counterpart, Peter Smith, went on to chair the Humanities department at MIT and hold a chair in political science at the University of California, San Diego. He is one of the most important quantitative historians and Latin American specialists in the country. My biological sciences counterpart, June Osborn, went on to become dean of the school of public health at Michigan. She was named a member of the American Academy of Arts and Sciences in 1994 and has been, in multiple capacities, a leader in the field of public health in America. My physical sciences counterpart, Marv Ebel, is one of the country's major physicists. He served at Los Alamos, studied with Niels Bohr and, like all of the graduate school scientists, operated a laboratory while he simultaneously discharged his administrative responsibilities.

Administrative tasks are somewhat more complex now because universities are more complex now, but they are also more "challenging" because of self-imposed conditions. Bureaucratic thinking breeds bureaucratic behavior and that behavior wastes time to a nearly unimaginable degree. When you install people for whom bureaucracy itself is the highest good you create career paths which serious academics will shun. When you install faculty-administrators for whom teaching and research represent the highest goods you discover that they can nearly always find a way to perform administrative duties efficiently and simultaneously bring an academic perspective to the work, thus safeguarding the core mission of the institution without making excessive demands on its budget.

One of the best studies of our current condition is Benjamin Ginsberg's recent book, *The Fall of the Faculty*. He writes that "the bulwark of administrative power within the university" creates an autonomous administration, the result of which is explicit marginalization of the faculty (2011, p. 25). Why have we done this? He offers three explanations: a) the growth in demand for administrative services (IT, lobbying, advancement); b) regulations and data demands from federal and state governments and licensure and accreditation bodies (laboratory animal protection, campus crime reporting requirements); and c) a faculty that does not want to perform these tasks while it presses administrators to create jobs for its spouses and partners (2011, pp. 27-32).

He finds the root cause in something more basic: administrative self-aggrandizement, their need to invent new functions and, failing that, to take over the functions of others. Suddenly we awake to discover the existence of a "Dual Credit Coordinator" and a "Coordinator of College Liaisons" (2011, p. 35). Nonfaculty administrators have to featherbed; they have nothing else. Faculty administrators are far less tempted to featherbed, because they do not see administration as an end in itself; they plan to complete their term of service and return to the faculty. This is not an option for nonfaculty administrators because they generally lack the qualifications to secure faculty positions (2011, pp. 36-37).

They are not measured by their academic credentials. They are measured by their "responsibilities" and by the number of their "direct reports." (I was once headhunted for a college presidency and the first question asked by the search firm was, "How many direct reports do you have?" Thinking through the number of office staff who reported to me, I suddenly realized that I could count my department chairs as direct reports. My numbers instantaneously went from the high single digits to somewhere around forty or fifty and the headhunters' eyes lit up.)

Unlike faculty, bureaucratic administrators seek ways to fill their time. Our system administration continually redoes its website. Others (system administrators included) pursue association work, meetings, conferences, retreats, and the construction of strategic plans (that often obviate the need for real action). Ginsberg mentions retreats on "Reflective Resensitizing" and "Waking Up the Inner World" (2011, p. 44). My own favorite retreats are the "imagining" retreats, the ones in which you evade your current challenges and responsibilities by asking, "where do you want to be in five years?" Honest answer: "in a quiet corner of the Bodleian or on a sun-drenched porch in Montecito."

So-called strategic planning (2011, p. 47ff.) can be one of the most egregious of activities. It is often used to co-opt the faculty, making them feel as if they are actually participating in something important (as they sit behind their specially-printed name cards, among the administrative presences, feeding on sweet rolls in the morning and hard candy in the afternoon).

The strategic plan is sometimes a complete fiction. Administrators routinely use a thirty- or forty-paged, beautifully-printed table of pieties to co-opt and palliate campus constituencies while some (in darker mode) use it as a cover for inactivity and self-promotion. Departments are held at bay and told that financial decisions and long-term commitments cannot be made until the strategic plan is in place. Then, when the plan is finally approaching completion, the administrator goes on the job market, touting the fact that among his many other accomplishments in his current role there is the crown jewel: the construction of a broad-based, faculty-supported strategic plan. He then promises prospective employers that it will be his first act in his new role to lead a strategic planning process *for them*. I have seen this done so crassly as to boggle the imagination. One provost, for example, told the faculty that the planning process on which he wished them to embark would lead to the freeing up of resources in the millions of dollars. In other words, if they would just cease frustrating his efforts and instead cooperate with him and participate in his planning process, there would be a pot of gold at the end of the academic rainbow and they would be able to participate in the decisions concerning its joyful distribution. This was a complete fabrication. They swallowed every word and he promptly left for his next position without accomplishing anything of lasting or even ephemeral value.

The "long-form" strategic plan (as opposed to a plan to meet a small handful of truly important goals) has a subsidiary "benefit" in that it extends and proliferates bureaucracy. Individuals are assigned responsibility for each of the individual items in the plan. Then, year-by-year, each is required to submit a report on progress-to-date. While the full meeting of the goals seldom occurs (if the problems were solved, the process would become unnecessary), reports are submitted; trees are slain; toner cartridges are depleted; emails fill in-boxes and protracted meetings are held. Otherwise minor players in the university are given the chance to speak before the institution's "leaders" and bonhomie reigns. The documents are presented to the Board of Directors and the assembled worthies there smile approvingly, believing that the university's chief executive has things "well in hand."

The faculty is most easily co-opted when administrators appeal to their sensibilities using hot-button issues. Ginsberg comments: "Disarmed by its own progressive commitments, the faculty has been largely silent as administrators have used the language of diversity and civility to trample on faculty prerogatives and to advance administrative agendas. Administrative abuse of multicultural programs, diversity planning, civility rules, and the like should be a punishable offense" (2011, p 128).

He gives the example of administrators expanding diversity bureaucracies and then forcing the faculty to accept representatives or consultants from those bureaucracies to guide search processes. The faculty seek diversity, of course, but many of the diversity bureaucrats know far less about issues of race, ethnicity and gender than the faculty do (and have little or no interest in intellectual or political diversity). They are forced on the faculty, willy-nilly, even if there are virtually no minority faculty available in the field of the job search. A friend of mine at one major university was in a department that studied a branch of forestry. The university had a rule that no one could be appointed to a faculty position without a minority candidate on each short list and bureaucrats were in place to enforce this rule. I asked him how many minority faculty there were in his entire field in the entire country, at all ranks. He said, "Four." Fortunately, one of them allowed his name to be placed on all short lists so that the department could hire faculty. The real subtext here is that the administration should control job searches, not the faculty, and elements within its bureaucracy should grow and prosper, even if the processes which it manages are sometimes shams.

When bureaucracies oversee hot-button issues any potential opposition can be labeled racist, sexist, or homophobic. On less heated issues (2011, pp. 157–58), the administration must tread more carefully. For example, in program development whose goal is to generate vocational or other programs that might receive faculty pushback, charges are made, very gently, that hidebound tenured faculty have difficulty adapting to "new ideas and methods." Deanlets and deanlings then shape programs desired by the administration for financial or other reasons (the palliation of specific legislators, trustees or donors, e.g.). The subtext is that new ideas and programs cannot be developed by the faculty, who are incapable of performing such tasks.

Ginsberg suggests some strategies for reducing these problems and reasserting the role and function of the university faculty: Boards should press university presidents to reduce non-faculty administrators and staff. More faculty should be appointed as part-time administrators. Boards should be given statistics on the percentage of administrators per 100 students and be encouraged to see high percentages as detrimental to the institution's core mission. We should, in short, stigmatize administrative bloat. Publications which "evaluate" and "rank" institutions should count administrative bloat against offending schools (2011, pp. 203–9).

I would add that the size of the university's instructional budget should be a *key indicator* for all oversight boards, including accrediting agencies. Administrative evaluation and compensation should be tied to its annual growth, both in absolute numbers and as a percentage of the total budget.

The admission of unprepared and underprepared students throws money to the bottom line but shifts resources from collegiate instruction to remediation. The development of a complex, labyrinthine curriculum initially co-opts the faculty planners but ultimately increases the number of professional advisers, expanding the bureaucracy and further marginalizing the faculty. Both practices are all too common. Beneath the smiley faces of the "student-centered" bureaucracy lies a struggle for control. The outcome of that struggle (day by day, issue by issue) is central to the nature of the university and its success.

When I attended Notre Dame (1959–1963), there was little or no evidence of non-academic bureaucrats hoping to dislodge or diminish the faculty. If I had a significant issue with one of my classes I went directly to either the department chair, John T. Frederick, or to the dean of the college, Fr. Charles Sheedy. In the two cases that I can remember in particular I met to drop courses that were either incompetently taught or markedly different from how they had been advertised. This is what was done in the days before anonymous student evaluations. You presented yourself to the relevant administrator and he could then evaluate your request and your case in the context of your argument and your personal academic history.

There was little or no academic bureaucracy because the curriculum was explicitly prescribed and rigidly enforced, with a few exceptions offered for those who had exhibited high performance. Students on the dean's list were permitted unlimited cuts, a privilege that disappeared whenever one fell off the list. For all others, the maximum number of cuts was the number of credits in the course. Faculty now will tell you that during the period prior to and just after break periods, attendance falls off dramatically. At Notre Dame any cut of a class prior to or just after a break period was multiplied by the number of credits in the class. In other words, if you cut then you could not cut at any other time during the semester or you would fail the class, unless you were on the dean's list, in which case you could extend your vacation by a day or two or three in either or both direction(s). Students participating in the honors program-like "Committee on Academic Progress" generally took the same courses as their classmates, but in special, accelerated, sections. On some occasions they could take graduate courses. For some, this pattern of rules and behaviors will seem to have been a totalitarian hell or part of some grand elitist plot. For us, the lesson inculcated was that those who studied hard received rewards for doing so. At the least it was a form of quality control and the insuring (in the case of the cut system) that a number of classes each semester would not simply be wasted or abandoned. Proper academic and personal behavior trumped the receipt of tuition revenue and the administration never balked at expelling students when their behavior warranted it.

(Parenthetically, I probably earned the most respect from the senior officers at West Point when I "quilled" [wrote up and required to walk punishment tours] a cadet who said "F-ck" in a stage whisper when he received a paper that I had graded. No one instructed me to be tolerant of student feelings.)

While Notre Dame in the early 1960s had pretensions to research acclaim (though not of the order that it now enjoys), the faculty teaching load was higher, by one course per term. I was never taught by a teaching assistant (except my quiz section leader in math). The faculty served as sponsors for academic clubs, occasionally invited us into their homes and played a role (usually a relatively small one) in our lives outside the classroom; "student services" types did not, to my knowledge, even exist. Any personal issues that you were undergoing could be taken up with the hall rector or floor prefect, individuals who had full-time academic jobs.

The resulting ethos was very different from today's. When I think of experiences beyond the classroom then they were either social (films and bars in South Bend, bull sessions in the dorms), intellectual entertainment (films and plays on campus or concerts in South Bend), or explicitly academic/co-curricular. For example, the faculty held public debates (Castro: friend or foe?). Each year the university sponsored a classic film series. This provided the student body an opportunity (in the days before modern technology) of seeing canonical films by Griffith, Eisenstein, Renoir, et al. This was seen as part of the development of one's cultural literacy.

The same thing occurred at West Point, though the purpose was as much entertainment as education. As a faculty member I had the responsibility for organizing and presenting the "Great Films Festival." There were specific guidelines and constraints (a $1200 budget for rentals, the requirement to show at least one documentary and one classic film). I showed several controversial films—Peter Ustinov's *Billy Budd*, Kubrick's *Paths of Glory*—and what turned out to be a very bad choice during February "gloom period," *The Seventh Seal*. Attendance was very strong, though it was not required. Attendance for our superb external lecturers (Howard Nemerov, Gilbert Highet, Alfred Kazin, et al.) was always strong because it was always required in lieu of a class meeting.

The ethos of today's universities is very different and it is related, in part, to the configuration of the university. The nonteaching professional staff whose numbers have multiplied so dramatically control many aspects of daily life in our colleges and universities and they see their role as explicitly *non-intellectual* (though they are unlikely to characterize it in that way). Like their former teachers (in many cases) in the colleges of education they believe that the university's role is to educate the entire individual. Their concern is the shaping of "life" and personhood writ large and not simply the cultivation of intellect. This provides their entry point within the bureaucracy. Education should be "holistic." The faculty is only interested in the *intellectual*. Ergo, the university requires brigades of service providers to complete the educational process.

"Holistic education" as opposed to the development of intellect is not a new issue. It is an issue which has had an extremely important impact on K-12 and higher education since the early twentieth century. Many believe that that impact has, nearly always, proven to be deleterious.

It is related to several aspects of so-called progressive education and it bears on such phenomena as the "life adjustment" and "open classroom" movements. It is "student-centered" and sees the teacher (often contemptuously referred to as the "sage on a stage") as one who constrains curiosity and enforces discipline for discipline's sake, focusing on "intellectual" material which is often irrelevant for "real life." It sees life "holistically" and assumes that professional "educators" (as opposed to scholar-teachers) are best positioned to take responsibility for the training of the entire person. This has sometimes led to a diminution of the academic in favor of the more pragmatic and it has sometimes suggested—through its theories and presuppositions—that very few students are capable of serious study, that it is not particularly useful anyway, and that the educational establishment should devote the bulk of its energies to helping the nonacademic majority. It is likely to substitute check-writing for mathematics, domestic economy for formal economics, practical plumbing for hydrodynamics, and so on. This will seem to some to be an unfair caricature, but it is not mine. It is Richard Hofstadter's and this strain within the thought of prominent educationists is one of his central examples of the anti-intellectualism that pervades American life.

On this, more later, but I should say now that I stand with such administrators as Robert Maynard Hutchins and such commentators as Hofstadter and Diane Ravitch (more timid than Hofstadter generally), rather than with the followers of Dewey (to the extent that Dewey's actual positions can be determined) in diverting the processes of education from their core role—the development of intellect. I will also argue that "life" as defined by those who want to shape and improve it within the university is a far narrower construct than the "life" which many imagine when the notion is invoked.

The resulting ethos—an academic world that has in part been fashioned by nonteaching professional staff—is not necessarily an evil one, but neither is it a particularly interesting one. It offers diversion, entertainment, an opportunity for "belonging" and for free pizza and tee shirts. It feels very much like the "real" world, assuming that your real world principally consists of new ageism, narcissism, self-indulgence, physical self-help and political correctness. It is, in many respects, the world of David Brooks's Bobos—the bohemian bourgeoisie. To provide a sense of its texture I would like to offer a pertinent example.

Every two weeks at my university we receive a mass emailing from "MU Info." Ranging in length from two to ten pages, single-spaced, a year's worth of such announcements is approximately the length of a large novel. The mailing includes information concerning a host of university events and services. For some elements within the bureaucracy it represents "free" advertising, though the documents must be written, compiled, edited and circulated. "MU Info" does not, of course, replace mailings from System Administration or the Chancellor's, Provost's, Deans', Departments' and Institutes' offices. It is only one portion of a withering volume of information, much of which, I am assured by my colleagues, is never read at all. "I automatically delete anything that comes from X," one friend of mine commented.

How many actually sift through this range of material is difficult to say, but when Don DeLillo set his novel *White Noise* in a contemporary (fictional) college he knew what he was doing. It is fair to say that the bureaucratization of information dispersal has materially increased college costs, particularly given the fact that bureaucracies seek to perpetuate themselves by increasing their visibility and multiplying (or appearing to multiply) their output. No one within the current system is incented to reduce the white noise. Instead, of course, as new elements within the bureaucracy arise, they add to it.

"MU Info" principally announces the dates and details of events, activities and services and there is nothing in these efflorescences of the university's many, many offices that could be considered evil--silly perhaps, trivial perhaps, but nothing that would not find at least a handful of defenders. However, there is almost nothing among its lists of events and services that could be legitimately considered *free*. Each carries costs because each requires resources for its implementation. That is not to say that all such events and services are inappropriate. A great many are useful and even central to the university's mission. Flu shots for students, faculty and staff with university insurance contribute to community health. Lectures by learned visitors can contribute significantly to the education of those who attend them. Notices inviting participation in human-subject research can make important contributions to knowledge.

What strikes me in the list is the number of events and services that did not exist in the university of the 1950s and early 1960s. None of the meetings or activities in my four years as an undergraduate carried the promise of "free" pizza, "free" tee shirts or "free" entertainment.

The organizations in which my classmates participated were nearly all academic or at least co-curricular. There were political organizations (few in number and relatively traditional in conception), but most student activities involved hobbies, intramural athletics or, principally, academics. Other than the provision of classroom space, at night, there was no ongoing budget or one-off financial contribution from the university to support these activities. Refreshments were not served unless we brought them. Some groups simply met in dorm lounges.

The following appeared in one year's installment of "MU Info":

HEALTHY FOR LIFE OFFERS STRESS REDUCTION PROGRAM

The Mindfulness-Based Stress Reduction Program is an 8 week class that teaches skills for responding to stress with greater skill and creativity using formal mindfulness skills (meditation, yoga, body scan) and information about stress, communication and wellness. Participants will be expected to engage in daily practice exercises outside of class . . . .

FREE SUMMER REJUVENATION SEMINAR ON JULY 21

Join X. X., MD, board-certified in facial plastic surgery, for a free seminar on *Wednesday, July 21 at 6 p.m.* Dr. X will discuss surgical and non-surgical options for your eyes, ears, nose, face and skin. Plan to attend and bring a friend while enjoying light refreshments and an open discussion. . . . This summer, Columbia Facial Plastic Surgery will offer 25 percent off PCA skin care products for facial maintenance and restoration. In addition, everyone who attends the free seminar on July 21 will receive *$25 off a Botox or Restylane treatment*. . . .

SUSTAINABLE COTTON SUMMIT ON SEPT. 21 AND 22

Are you interested in learning more about sustainability and the clothes you wear? The . . . *Mizzou TAM Sustainable Cotton Summit* . . . will focus on cotton and sustainability in textiles and apparel. Industry representatives including cotton farmers, seed companies, manufacturers, and retailers will be featured. . . . *Student participants will be eligible to win t-shirts, meals with the speakers, and scholarships.* . . .

9TH ANNUAL PAGAN PRIDE DAY—SUNDAY, SEP 19, 12-6 PM, PEACE PARK

. . . Come join the fun . . . from noon to six in Peace Park! Be carried away by the melodies of Raven Wolf and enchanted by the Deva Dancers as they weave their magic. Enjoy the eye candy of renowned artist Mickle Mueller, who's [sic] most recent work includes the Voice of Trees Tarot deck! . . . . Mid-Missouri Pagan Pride will also be collecting food donations for Loaves and Fishes food pantry to help with the drastic need for food this winter . . . .

SPA NIGHT-FRIDAY OCT. 8

It's back! Spa Night is a favorite at Mizzou and returns to offer much needed relaxation through numerous activities. We will offer free haircuts, massages, aromatherapy and much more! Create your own spa crafts and enjoy free food. All services and supplies are on a first-come basis. Free to MU students with a valid student ID. . . .

LOVE YOUR BODY DAY AND KEYNOTE

Thursday, October 7. . . . Body-positive buttons, freshly screen-printed posters, advice from fitness and nutrition experts, 'zines, t-shirts and more!. . . .

Learn strategies for increasing self-esteem with the body and person you have and are right now with a focus on health, sexuality, and identity for bodies of all sizes and shapes, and the importance of positivity and self-love. . . .

FREE PIZZA AND T-SHIRT AT THE SAFE SPRING BREAK RESOURCE FAIR NEXT WEDNESDAY

Countdown to spring break! Join the Wellness Resource Center as we celebrate spring break being right around the corner. There are many things to consider in order to stay safe and healthy while enjoying your break. We will provide this information as well as FREE PIZZA, TSHIRTS, and other goodies on Wednesday, March 23. . . .

This is a miniscule selection of the entries in the "MU Info" mailings. Every event and service requires staff, facilities, utilities and, depending on the size and nature of the event, security. Are these services and activities worth the costs that accompany them? At our colleges and universities, all students are charged student fees for events and activities in which many (usually the vast majority) choose not to participate. Given the choice, would they choose to see these events and activities be held on a fee-for-services basis, with the positive tradeoff of reduced tuition and mandatory fees?

No one is coming forward to offer them that choice, of course, because the bureaucracies are entrenched and each has a constituency which can be rallied politically should the question ever be raised. Plus, our rival, the University of X and the universities within our peer group, Y, Y, Y, et al., offer comparable events and activities. This is, quite simply, the way things are.

These activities and services, at my university, exist at a time when tuition has risen precipitously, the faculty and staff have experienced years without pay raises, enrollments are up (until very recently), facilities pinched and cuts have been made to academic programs. At many regional publics in our state, key programs in the sciences and foreign languages have been closed. Indeed, foreign language programs have been closed at institutions with the stature of the State University of New York, Albany.

In times of vast riches one could imagine a wealth of services and activities with constant giveaways, but these are not those times. "MU Info" announces a plethora of programs for stress reduction. How many would prefer to see their stress reduced by increased pay and increased job security or reduced tuition and enhanced instruction rather than the proliferation of hand holders and meditation leaders?

Who are these service providers? What are their goals and what is the etiology of the situation which they have helped to create? One evening at the Washington Navy Yard I heard Tom Clancy talk about the origin of *The Hunt for Red October*. In the course of the talk he referred to the "political officer" who served on Soviet naval vessels, describing him as "a kind of chaplain for atheists." University service providers are not chaplains for atheists but in a sense they are chaplains for secularists. I say that because their view of human development principally involves secular concerns. (In some ways that is quite appropriate; we do not want student service personnel serving as theology instructors.)

I suggest the description "chaplains for secularists" because of the things that are left out of their developmental vision. In part, this is a bureaucratic issue, since the issues with which they do *not* deal *are,* sometimes, dealt with elsewhere. The issue is one of *emphasis*: what is most important in their putative bailiwick--the non-academic development of students? Ans.: The student service providers often tend to focus on the politically-correct triumvirate of race, class and gender (with sexual orientation included in the broad grouping).

Race, class and gender are, of course, important issues in our development, but there are other areas in which students live and move and have their being: in their churches, in ROTC, in athletics, in dramatics, in Greek life, in co-curricular and extra-curricular clubs. Our two granddaughters were very active in band in high school; it consumed a significant part of their time and was an important aspect of their lives. In college, one of our granddaughters became interested in crew and she eventually devoted a significant portion of her free time to coxing for crews consisting of breast cancer survivors. Our other granddaughter was an Emergency Medical Technician, working with the fire department in her college town. In neither case did these activities bear directly on their majors (Molecular Genetics, Computer Science/Math/Psychology). These are simply the things that they did outside of class which contributed materially to their personal development.

My suspicion is that most of our students (my granddaughters studied at a representative institution—our largest feeder school—Parkway West High School in St. Louis) would have already encountered issues of race/class/gender long before they went off to college. Despite the protestations of student service personnel, our young people today are far more comfortable with diverse sexual orientations than their grandparents' generation was. They are also far more comfortable with racial diversity, for it has been simple reality to them throughout their lives.

Even more to the point, the foundational demographics of contemporary higher education suggest a certain quaintness in the (in my opinion, often fabricated) urgency of student service responses to questions of race/class/gender. The narrative that is presented is that many backwoods students come to college innocent of human diversity. It is thus the mission of service providers to acculturate them, purge them of racism, sexism and homophobism and oversee their proper "development" as contemporary citizens.

The bottom line, however, is that in contemporary higher education a mere 16 percent attend the kind of full-time, residential colleges which putatively require the constant attendance of service providers (Donoghue 2008, pp. 89-90). The average age of a "college student" in America today is twenty-nine. Two-thirds of the students at four-year institutions work and one-third work sixteen hours per week or more (Toby 2010, p. 94). At many institutions (this was particularly true at Georgetown) the students have internships, paying jobs and volunteer work over and above their co-curricular and purely academic activities. The vast majority of my students (sophomores, juniors, seniors and graduate students) live off campus, in apartments, with cars and with jobs. In other words, they live as fully-functioning adults.

There are other obvious factors deserving of consideration in this regard: earlier puberty, career/health information now readily available on the internet and, of course, the maturation of our society, in which women are increasingly so dominant that colleges have installed affirmative action for men. The nation has twice elected an African-American president. For good (societal maturation) or ill (student study time), it is no longer 1955. One might add the comment of Julie Johnson Kidd: "An environment with the nonstop provision of services does not equip [today's students] for life after college" (Hersh and Merrow 2005, p. 202).

And yet, the support staff are still with us. The percentage of campus employees who do not teach is 85 percent at Vanderbilt, 80 percent at Princeton, 75 percent at Harvard, 68 percent at Emory (Chace 2006, p. 304*n*). As the leaders go, so go the nation's aspirants and imitators. This is the sport of kings, of course, for this level of support is extremely expensive. The elites simply charge more; when other institutions follow their lead in hiring support staff they are frequently forced to hire fewer full-time faculty. They reduce quality in the hope of increasing tuition revenue. Globally, of course, we are the outlier. As Derek Bok reminds us, "No [other] country offers undergraduates such a wealth of student services and extracurricular activities" (2003, p. 23).

The well-to-do do not want to give up their personal trainers, hot tubs and climbing walls and the potentially-aggrieved will not want to give up their identity-politics centers, advocates and counselors. The corporatist administrators thus give them what they want, figuring, probably correctly, that the reduced quality of education is far less likely to result in student pushback than the reduction of services. Meanwhile, our global competitors focus on education *per se*.

The faculty must realize that these practices consciously and systematically weaken and marginalize them. They are being deprofessionalized, reduced from their previous standing as permanent officers of the university (Yale's sometime designation for its faculty) and treated as, essentially, high school teachers in a K-16 system who must obey those in authority, even if those in authority lack the experience and qualifications for an entry-level faculty position. Under this dispensation the faculty are now urged to give mid-semester grades (to provide warnings to the unprepared, underprepared, at-risk, tuition-paying students the administrators have chosen to admit and are now desperate to retain). In this system faculty are forced to complete mandatory training/indoctrination to reinforce administrative programs and edicts. They become the grist for the corporatist administrative mills which seek to expand and prosper by palliating internal and external forces by demonstrating their faculties' subservience to administrative power. In the contemporary university elements of the bureaucracy advance themselves and their organizations by insinuating themselves into the curriculum and the personal authority of the faculty by inserting "norms" into student evaluations and tenure-and-promotion templates. Has the instructor made use of information technology (whether appropriate or not)? Has the instructor explicitly contributed to diversity and inclusivity (regardless of the subject matter of the course or teaching format)?

Over twenty-five years ago Camille Paglia "fired a prophetic warning shot about the takeover of American universities by an expanding class of intrusive administrators, leading to today's disastrous loss of faculty power" (2017, p. xxi). She singled out, in particular, "Student Life deans and the freshmen orientation staff" for leading the process of politically-correct social indoctrination (2017, p. 82).

Paglia is a traditional academic, one who places her trust in scholarship and hard-won authority. One alternative to the promotion of "human development" by support staff would be for students to actually read the literature on human development. Who would you trust more—Erik Erikson, Jean Piaget, Eleanor Maccoby, Lawrence Kohlberg, Arnold Gesell, Urie Bronfenbrenner, Albert Bandura or the nice young man down the hall with the master's degree from the college of education in counseling psychology? The student services establishment's answer: the nice young man down the hall. Their goal is not to engender curiosity, but rather to create sensitivity and allay victimhood. "Know thyself" has been replaced by "know thy gender, sexuality, class and residual racism, sexism and homophobism" (with the help of your student affairs staff).

It might be considered unfair for me to characterize them when they can speak for themselves. Let me provide some quotations from two of their bibles, *Foundations of Student Affairs Practice* (Hamrick et al., 2002) and *Student Services: A Handbook for the Profession* (Delworth et al., 1989).

Their desired outcomes (Hamrick et al., 2002, p. xiii): "(1) a self-aware and interpersonally sensitive individual, (2) a democratic citizen, (3) an educated person, (4), a skilled worker, and (5) a life skills manager." (We should, presumably, be grateful that education comes in third rather than fifth; note the "life adjustment" overtones of the fifth goal.)

Helms and Cook (in Hamrick et al., 2002, pp. 47-48) on what is of prime importance: "As global consciousness increases and as the diversity of our country and college student population grows, racial and ethnic identity becomes salient . . . determining how one wishes to present oneself and relate to others often takes precedence over other developmental issues."

And no, we haven't forgotten sexual issues (2002, p. 50): "If all students, including those who are gay, lesbian, and bisexual, are to be given equal opportunity for growth and development, services must be available to assist them in negotiating the challenges they face. The college must address the developmental needs of gay, lesbian, and bisexual students through counseling, support groups, and social outlets as well as educate heterosexual students about this population."

Parenthetically, it is fair to ask how many college students still believe in "traditional" gender roles in a monolithic way? Simone de Beauvoir's *The Second Sex* appeared in 1949. The major books by writers such as Germaine Greer, Betty Friedan and Mary Ellmann appeared, respectively, in 1970, 1963 and 1968, Mary Wollstonecraft's in 1792. It may be that our students need a greater awareness of intellectual and social history rather than the ministrations of *bien pensant* support staff.

Aside: budgets are not infinitely expandable. We need to see support services as more than budgetary additions. When forced to choose between such services and traditional skills, corporatists choose the services. We must remember that we have simultaneously lost *writing skills, geography skills, public speaking skills, foreign language skills* and other advantages that are crucial if we are to compete within a global economy.

Citing M. L. Upcraft (Hamrick et al., 2002, p. 123), "student development theory" is proposed as the "primary justification underlying student affairs work." This follows the demise of the practice of *in loco parentis*. Why student affairs personnel rather than the faculty? "The justification for this student affairs role is simple: faculty members have neither the time nor the know-how to develop a total range of experiences to advance student learning, and since out-of-class experiences have been clearly demonstrated to work, duplication of effort is unnecessary" (=hire less faculty; hire more student affairs staff).

While student services advocates wish to increase their numbers and power, they acknowledge the realities (Fenske, in Delworth et al. 1989, p. 6): "[These staff are] taking over necessary and sometimes unpopular tasks abandoned by trustees, administrators, and faculty. The field of student services has grown into a ubiquitous but almost invisible empire in virtually every institution of higher education." [They are seen, interestingly, as both indispensable and somehow peripheral. The question, of course, is how *necessary* the tasks were which the faculty, et al. putatively abandoned. The unspoken assumptions here would appear to include the following: university students are not adults; students' beliefs and personalities will not have been shaped by their parents, churches or high schools; bureaucrats are more appropriate mentors than parents, pastors, rabbis, faculty and civil authorities. We are presiding over something somewhere between a nursery school and a high school summer camp, rather than an institution of *bona fide* higher education.]

Note that there have indeed been significant changes in American higher education that have altered the faculty's sense of its role, principally the acceptance of German ideals with regard to research that were exemplified by the founding of Johns Hopkins University in 1876, an event whose eventual results brought a bifurcated approach to higher education, with the English residential college model for undergraduates yoked to the German research model for graduate students. The former is student-centered, the latter faculty-centered. So, at least, goes the narrative. I will address this in greater detail in chapter 8.

Fenske (cited above), is an informed and thoughtful commentator. He notes (Delworth et al. 1989, p. 26) that the Great Depression brought financial stress to universities and that, in response, student services budgets were cut drastically. Their numbers have increased dramatically since then, but their role, Fenske argues, remains unclear (1989, p. 27): "The fact is that almost throughout the field's historical existence it has never had a single functional focus, has never been stable in its role over significant periods of time, and has never had a consensual integrative philosophy. [As a profession, it is not a] mighty oak [like the medical profession] . . . but a disorderly thicket of stunted saplings, each fighting the others for its place in the sun and the crowded, tangled roots all seeking sustenance from the same inadequate source."

The leading post-Depression assertor of the "overriding value of intellect rather than character or personality development, in higher education" (1989, p. 33) was Robert Maynard Hutchins, who stressed intellectual virtues and knowledge. Dewey and his followers (1989, p. 34) retaliated, inveighing against "monastic seclusion" but the debate was mooted by the financial constraints of the Depression.

Parenthetically, I would add that a financial crisis sometimes compared with the Great Depression has recently returned, a fact of which we might take note. I would also argue that our *business* is intellectual. That is what we do best; that is what we are best equipped to do. That is why students come to us; that is why they incur debt—to receive higher *education*. I am personally dismayed at the notion of entrusting our students' human, moral and character development to student services personnel. At my university, for example, we have an exceptionally strong clinical psychology practice within our distinguished department of Psychological Sciences. If a student asked me to recommend professionals to help him or her I would refer the student immediately to those individuals, and never to student services personnel.

In addressing these issues we should be aware of the messianic orientation of the student services leadership. In her inaugural speech to the American College Personnel Association (1984), Margaret Barr said that "student services professionals serve as *the conscience of the campus*" (cited by Canon in Delworth et al. 1989, p. 58, my emphases). He himself comments: "These professionals, more than any other constituent group in higher education, attend to the human needs of students and respond to concerns about individual differences. In doing so, they sustain an awareness of inequities imposed on students by the system, by the fact of individual differences and needs."

These individuals, it is argued, are different in kind (Canon 1989, p. 70): "Student service professionals, by disposition and choice, are more inclined to acknowledge needing the support and stimulation of their colleagues than are their faculty counterparts." (I take this to mean that they are more "touchy-feely" than the faculty. They are *sensitive* and, one must say, somewhat single-minded in their orientation.) He refers (1989, p. 71) to "their almost unique awareness of the range of injustices visited upon students by other students, faculty, administrators, and the system itself." Their concerns and commitments address what he terms *care* issues (1989, p. 71): "Peace issues and caring relationships: the international arms race; programs for international students; programs fostering multicultural awareness and sensitivity; spouse abuse; conflict resolution."

We have clearly moved beyond the notion of holistic learning and into the area of "character development" and "personality shaping" of a particular kind. I would be the first to argue that the "system" of higher education does not always serve us well and that, in some cases, it does things that are negative or hurtful. Hence, it is the responsibility of the university to identify those problems and do all in its power to *solve* them, not create sensitivity sessions. The latter would enable the negative behavior by suggesting that handholding is an appropriate response to a horrid situation rather than identifying the abuses or evils and removing them root and branch.

I believe that Fenske's characterizations are quite accurate. In the student services establishment we have a largely invisible (because most do not utilize it or even know of its existence) but costly empire whose mission lacks focus but whose politically-correct ethos is immediately recognizable. Lacking a core mission, its primary mission becomes survival and proliferation.

There is no question that many of our students require professional help of various sorts. The help should be precisely that: *professional*. Trained medical personnel, trained health providers, trained psychologists, trained clergymen and other professionals should be the first line of defense for troubled students, not well-meaning amateurs.

While our current situation is traceable in part to the corporatization of the university and the redefinition of the faculty's role, there are other elements within our social history that have led to our current condition.

David Mamet (2011, pp. 30–31) has impishly suggested that the shortage of positions for individuals in the Humanities has encouraged them to create previously-nonexistent jobs which have a professional feel. He offers the examples of "feng-shui experts" and "past-lives counselors." It is true that radical graduate students in the late 1960s would say that "college teaching is one of the things that I am *willing* to do," the point being that their alienation from capitalism and the prosecution of the war in Vietnam drastically limited the kinds of positions that they were willing to take. It may be true that many feng-shui experts and past-lives counselors are long-lost English majors, but I consider it more likely that the student services staff's academic genealogy leads to the college of education rather than the college of arts and science.

Mamet also (again, impishly) cites Veblen's argument that the rich have difficulty in exhibiting all of their wealth. They can exhibit their leisure, but there are only twenty-four hours in the day. Hence, they exhibit their capacity for hiring "staff" as a way of demonstrating their means. One thinks of the entourages that accompany prominent athletes, actors and vocal artists.

While these suggestions may carry hints of the larger truth, there are two proximate explanations for the multiplication of "support staff" in our universities. One is the simple growth in "support staff" in our lives. We now require "personal trainers" to manage our exercise regimens; we have financial advisors to help us handle our money, tax preparers to guide us through the thickets of ever-changing federal and state legislation, genetic counselors to guide us in our decisions with regard to procreation, wedding planners, travel planners, funeral planners, and, let us not forget, college admission advisors. We are now guided by "experts" more often than by leaders and that carries over into our lives as students.

The second obvious reason for the proliferation of support staff is the routine admission of unprepared and underprepared students. Universities wish to continue to collect tuition and they wish to be able to report high retention rates. Hence they hire armies of tutors and, as we will discuss in the next chapter, professional advisors. They also hire individuals to aid students in the reduction of the stress and depression that predictably result from conditions which are found to be excessively challenging, though it is clear that the academic challenges have been significantly *reduced* in the decades since the war. One reflection of these realities is the fact that graduation statistics are now judged within a framework of six years, not four. For a number of reasons, many students require the extra two years to complete their programs. This is a boon to the corporatists who can now collect tuition for an additional four semesters.

For an overview of the culture in which these phenomena are embedded, the classic text remains Christopher Lasch's *The Culture of Narcissism* (1979), the origin of which was anticipated in Lasch's book *Haven in a Heartless World* (1977), in which he details the manner in which "professionals" took over roles and duties that had previously been performed directly by the family. They have now taken over activities that were either handled directly by students themselves or were facilitated by college and university faculties.

As in the case of the texts of student service professionals, I would like to permit Lasch to speak in his own compelling voice. The degree to which his insights still hold true (or are even more compelling) 39 years after their original articulation is striking.

"The narcissist . . . sees the world as a mirror of himself and has no interest in external events except as they throw back a reflection of his own image" (1979, p. 47). Some causes: bureaucracy, "in which work assumes an abstract quality almost wholly divorced from performance" (1979, p. 47) and "the society of the spectacle" in which life is "a succession of images or electronic signals . . . thoroughly mediated by electronic images" (1979, p. 47).

"The bureaucratization of the business career . . . made the acquisition of educational credentials essential to a business or professional career and thus created in large numbers a new kind of student, utterly indifferent to higher learning but forced to undergo it for purely economic reasons" (1979, p. 119).

Lasch traces our historical condition, in part, to the manner in which the modern educational system developed (1979, pp. 127–40). He argues that mass education *did not democratize the higher culture of the privileged classes*; it stupefied the privileged themselves.

(Now following Bettelheim): "Formerly religion, myth, and fairy tale retained enough childlike elements to offer a convincing view of the world to a child. Science cannot take their place. Hence the widespread regression among young people to magical thinking of the most primitive kind. . . ." (1979, p. 151). [See *Thrones, Game of* and the continuing interest in zombies, vampires, werewolves and other "paranormal" phenomena which now enjoy a separate section—targeted at teenagers—at Barnes and Noble.]

"Because the narcissist has so few inner resources, he looks to others to validate his sense of self" (1979, p. 210). [Hence the endless series of awards bestowed by the contemporary university?]

And the crucial point: "The real value of the accumulated wisdom of a lifetime is that it can be handed on to future generations. Our society, however, has lost this conception of wisdom and knowledge. It holds an instrumental view of knowledge, according to which technological change constantly renders knowledge obsolete and therefore nontransferable" (1979, p. 213). [We will return to this point with the consideration of Hofstadter's insights with regard to anti-intellectualism in America. It explains why the two professional schools which have displaced liberal arts education in the modern university—the college of business and the college of education—continually develop new methods and approaches, new buzz words and new acronyms that often merely restate commonsensical principles. In the case of colleges of education there is often an ideological opposition to "content" and academic substance and an argument for "technique" and "method," the promised shortcuts that often prove disastrous when put into practice.]

Finally, I would stress a pivotal concern of Lasch's. The challenges of contemporary higher education can ultimately be traced to specific attitudes that have been debated since the eighteenth century. The principal sources of our challenges are persistent elements of Romanticism which continue to call to us like the Homeric Sirens.

Narcissism, Lasch argues, (1979, p. 241), is, ultimately, the longing to be free from longing. Humans are born too soon; they are born utterly dependent and they are faced with the overwhelming reality that they must endure the pain of *separation*. This, Lasch argues, is the original source of the human malaise. The feeling of loss and separation is also, in many ways, the central lesson of Romanticism 101.

The antidote, Lasch argues, is the recognition that we must accept our limits and deal with them. My humbler formulation would be that in a university that offers the temporary nostrums of "help" and "support" (ephemeral if well-meaning gestures that will remain behind when we set out on our real lives) *we* must take responsibility for our educations as well as for our lives and take heart in the fact that there are still living examples of the millions who *did just that* with profound success. They are not otherworldly beings who populate the sword-and-sorcery fantasies of our popular entertainments. They are our relatives, friends and neighbors who embraced the opportunity offered by the GI Bill and, in the process, radically altered American higher education and brought it to its apogee.

Chapter Three

Vacuums and Mazes

Like most universities mine has a "student success center"—a building filled with advisors, counselors and computer stations, whose purpose is to increase retention, persistence and graduation rates. A high graduation rate (high meaning 60–70 percent in public education) serves as a significant brag point and the muting of a potential vulnerability when the next year's state budget is being built and the next-year's evaluative magazines are going to press.

Such facilities may also include tutors, since remediation is a growth industry in American higher education. Within the California State System, in 1998, 50 percent of the students took one or more remedial classes (Toby 2010, p. 39). In 2002–2003, 29 percent of entering freshmen (across the American system) required a remedial reading, writing or mathematics class.

The professional advisors are, now, largely necessary. George Harper, the late Blakean and Yeatsian, told me that he had once accomplished something that most would find daunting. He sat down and set himself the task of actually understanding, in all of its details, his college's academic rules and regulations. He retained that information for approximately one year. Had he tried to learn the rules of the arts and letters college at Notre Dame in the early 1960s the task would have been far easier, since the rules were few in number. They were, accordingly, far less expensive to administer. College rules now are like English common law or the U.S. tax code. They have grown over a period of time, by accretion, and few are able to understand them but full-time professionals.

Where once most institutions had basic core requirements—Comp I, Math I, American History I, etc.—they have now often moved to recondite systems of specific course requirements and more generalized distribution requirements, including requirements that apply to all students, requirements that apply to individual colleges only and requirements that apply to specific tracks and majors. All may require math, e.g., but a different math course, program by program (the B.S. in Biology vs. the B.A. in Biology, e.g.) or major by major. When a student transfers colleges or majors within the university he or she may lose some credits, be required to take a different version of Calculus than the one already taken, and so on. This is not just endlessly complicated for the students; it is also extremely challenging for the faculty. Given the stakes—additional registrations/additional tuition—the faculty are reticent to offer advice without administrative guidance.

This fits the professional advisors' career templates perfectly. They are happy to see the growth in the layers of complexity because they are putatively taking over work that "the faculty refuse to do." As a result, they seek status and longevity comparable to the faculty's and consume resources which could be invested in the instructional, research or financial aid budgets.

The fact that requirements may now be convoluted or recondite does not guarantee that they will be challenging. Nor does it mean that they will necessarily be coherent, integrated or sensible. What they represent, most often, is the work of a sequence of committees over a period of decades. The results are seldom models of clarity; they are instead the products of special pleading and compromise, the works of individuals who have crafted systems which they themselves will never have to administer. They may be mazes or they may be vacuums; sometimes they are both.

The decline of traditional curricular requirements is not a phenomenon that can be blamed exclusively on the 1960s activists who protested all forms of authority and demanded endless, free-flowing student choice. To the extent that they influenced current policies they were operating within a long-standing tradition.

Charles W. Eliot is sometimes termed Harvard's greatest president. A mathematician and chemist, Eliot became Harvard's 21st president in 1869 and served in that capacity for 40 years. While many of his personal views would now be considered reactionary, he did several good things. He required baccalaureate degrees for admission to professional schools, whose standards then were extremely lax (Menand 2010, pp. 45–46). He also wanted liberal *education* (understood as the pursuit of knowledge for its own sake) to be separated from professional *training* (Menand 2010, p. 49).

At the same time, he was opposed to core requirements at the undergraduate level. After his "reforms" the Harvard undergraduate curriculum carried only two requirements: English composition and one foreign language. In his judgment, the prewar curriculum had been more "moral" than intellectual. Classroom rigor was designed to shape character and instill discipline, while Eliot believed that the curriculum should satisfy curiosity and expand the imagination.

Eliot's way sounds wonderful if one is a curious and self-motivated individual, well-prepared for college and seeking to pursue *intellectual* interests in the company of a highly-gifted faculty (Eliot's model). He correctly felt that requiring a core curriculum would play to the needs of the weaker students at the expense of the stronger, but this, of course, is the nub of the issue—what percentage of current university matriculants will meet Eliot's expectations, conscientiously embrace his system and flourish within it? In our time, when a vast number of students attend college (Eliot expected a miniscule percentage to attend) the vast majority consists of the intellectually-needy who would benefit from, indeed who would require, a strong core curriculum.

In point of fact, Eliot's plan was something of a misfire in his own day. Many students, then as now, were not academically inclined. They exploited the opportunity that he offered them and took easy courses, which they termed "bow-wows." As students do now, they took a large number of introductory courses. While they might have achieved some depth of knowledge in a particular field, the rest of their courses could be both scattered and thin.

Clifford Adelman's research confirms that that is largely our situation today. Studying thousands of American transcripts, he discovered that students' non-major courses were largely taught at an introductory level. In many cases, students would be learning little more than introductory taxonomy ("the primary fields of psychology are . . . developmental . . . social . . . clinical . . ."), often taught utilizing PowerPoint slides, requiring memorization of bullet points for the exams and leading to the quick forgetting of nearly all that had been "learned" shortly thereafter.

By the 1970s, the Harvard core consisted of an introduction to disciplines, essentially a system of distribution requirements that invited the student to become familiar with the theories and methods of discrete divisions of learning. While such a system may seem appropriate for Harvard's students (with top prep school educations, off-the-charts SAT scores, a lifetime of travel and exposure to books and information technology) that sort of system can be gamed.

The faculty offer coursework within their specialties (which are then judged, by some coordinating committee, to be appropriate for one or more of the distribution categories), viz. Professor X's course on health delivery systems in Senegal fits the rubric for "history"; Professor Y's course on protest movements in the 1960s fits the rubric for "social thought". The system is gamed by students taking the easiest courses and/or those whose material is confined to the twentieth or twenty-first centuries. A student might take a course that meets the "history" requirement but have no idea which came first—the Renaissance or the Enlightenment. A student might satisfy the "social thought" requirement but remain innocent of classical political theory or statistical reasoning.

The most frequent explanation for our current situation is that faculty are not interested in teaching general education courses and students are not interested in taking them. Faculty are not interested because the university reward system is focused upon research rather than teaching (and certainly not introductory-level teaching). They are also *not equipped to do so*, in many cases. Teaching classes that encompass large swaths of material in cogent and interesting ways is very difficult to do. As a result, students may be less interested in general education courses because they are seldom taught well; they also perceive that the responsibility for such courses is shunted off on graduate students and adjunct faculty. If the institution doesn't take the courses seriously, why should they?

Indeed, general education courses are largely seen as a bother—by students, faculty, and by politicians, who continually urge universities to liberalize their policies with regard to transfer of credit. The simple fact is that a great number of students today attend multiple institutions before settling on the institution from which they will take their baccalaureate degree. Two, three or four prior institutions are commonplace. Many of these students lack the specific general education courses required by the baccalaureate institution.

When colleges hold the line (viz. "we will not graduate students who lack college algebra, an intermediate knowledge of at least one foreign language and a laboratory science course") they are pressured by governors and legislatures to be more "efficient" and move the students along, so that they can complete the *important* part of a college "education"—the vocational training in a professional school which will lead to satisfactory employment. This pressure is exerted through system administrations and state coordinating councils, in addition to direct phone calls, pleading the case of the politician's disappointed constituents.

The resulting problems are obvious. Fully half of a student's undergraduate education is often being treated, institutionally, as trivial or of marginal importance. While the practice may masquerade as either "efficient" or "student-centered" it puts the student at a significant disadvantage both in the eventual job market and in the choice of majors. The student who lacks core, general education knowledge will have difficulty competing in a global economy. At the same time, such a student will foreclose educational options within his or her bachelor's degree program. Absent mathematical skills, for example, there will be no opportunity to study within a host of fields and, *a fortiori*, hold a host of positions in later life.

The simple but sometimes forgotten fact is that the acquisition of a strong "general education" is also essential for research. This point was made repeatedly by Jary Pelikan, sometime graduate dean and Sterling Professor of History at Yale, as well as the President of the American Academy of Arts and Sciences. His point was straightforward; following Kuhn, most researchers burrow in tunnels, doing "normal science." They emerge from those tunnels and take whole disciplines in new directions by drawing on some aspect of their "general education" which had been overlooked by those too immersed in their narrow specialties.

We see this every day when we read masterpieces of scholarship. Significant thinkers startle us by their knowledge of related and even distant academic fields. That is one of the reasons why their work endures when more "specialized" research is often ephemeral. I served on a dissertation exam once with the prominent medieval historian, David Herlihy, whose library now graces Georgetown's villa in Fiesole. The dissertation was on Romantic literature and the proceeding became very awkward when David (very modestly) demonstrated that he knew as much about Romanticism as one of my English department colleagues who specialized in that period.

The politicians who urge the finessing of general education requirements and the corporatist administrators who permit it do not really concern themselves with such research or with the opportunities and prospects of the individual student. Their primary goals are not personal enrichment and authentic *education*, but rather reelection, the acquisition of tuition and administrative advancement. Their actions suggest that they do not believe, ultimately, that individual students struggling with requirements and offering up multiple transcripts can ever do anything beyond receiving a credential that will facilitate receipt of a job. Indeed, they are comfortable with removing any "obstacles" that are obstructing that process. The purpose of college, after all, is to receive a diploma, not an education that will enrich the totality of a student's life.

Our nomenclature must be reexamined. Politicians and corporatists may refer to something called a "college education," but if that process is so denuded of content and challenge that we can no longer consider it an authentic college education we must see it rather as a "college" education, a certificate of attendance at something we now call *college* but which might be any number of things, certifying any number of levels of achievement.

Those who suffer the most within this ethos are those who are most at risk—the students Eliot sought to overlook, those most in need of a core curriculum and a command of basic skills, those most likely to drop out, those most likely to incur debt and then default on it, those whose financial lives (in the eventual face of poor employment or unemployment) will be most damaged by such debt. What do we offer them? Admission, loans, remediation and—beyond the entrance gate and the treasurer's office—an array of smiling tutors.

English programs at British universities were established in the nineteenth century; they grew out of technical institutes, the bottom-line belief being that while the rich drank wine and the poor drank beer the elites would study the Greek and Roman classics and the working class would study something appropriate to their lower station and more modest abilities: English literature.

Now, with many "nontraditional" learners in the academy, we had two clear courses that we might have followed. The first was to sustain traditional standards and traditional curricula and provide new matriculants the same opportunities and education once enjoyed by the select few. Social capital would then have been built through personal achievement and the knowledge once held by elites would now be held by all willing to attain it. Raymond Chandler once said that he wanted a classic education in order to protect himself from those who already had one. The new students would have been so protected and along with their learning and their new, transferable skills they would have enjoyed hard-earned confidence, personal pride and a multiplicity of employment opportunities.

The second course was, regrettably, the one that we continue to follow: a systematic reduction in expectations. The result has been a national tragedy. Grades have been inflated; core curricula have been dismantled; language requirements have been removed, special identity-based courses and programs have been installed. Students in need of significant remediation have been admitted. Students keep journals rather than write papers. PowerPoint notes are distributed electronically so that students need not attend class. Study time and reading/writing assignments have been radically reduced.

The further tragedy is that none of this has *worked* (except in the sense that institutions have survived on increased tuition). Completion rates remain low, indebtedness high, marketability reduced, anxiety increased; all of this has occurred in the face of the fact that we now participate in an unforgiving world economy in which jobs move freely across the globe.

In 1941 the mean SAT-verbal was 501; in 1990 it was 425. In 1941 the mean SAT-math was 502, in 1990, 475. In 1983 the National Commission on Excellence in Education had issued the controversial study, "A Nation at Risk: The Imperative for Education Reform." What was done? The Educational Testing Service "recentered" the SAT scores, turning a 425 into a 501. The average entering student in 1970 had a GPA of 2.95; by 2001 that number had risen to 3.37 (Vedder 2004, p. 112). Performance plummeted; grades rose.

The American Council of Trustees and Alumni recently issued a study (see Parker 2010) that examined a number of institutions based on their retention of a required core of general education courses in Composition, Literature, Foreign Languages, U.S. Government or History, Economics, Mathematics and Science. They then graded the institutions. A's went to Baylor, Brooklyn College-CUNY, Texas A&M, Arkansas, the United States Military Academy, et al. B's went to Missouri, Chicago, Columbia, Notre Dame, et al. Princeton and William and Mary (the latter often thought to have an intact, traditional curriculum) received C's; Harvard, Illinois, Wisconsin and Georgetown were awarded D's and F's were given to Brown, Vassar, Yale, UC-Berkeley, Kenyon and Washington University in St. Louis. That does not mean that elite institutions do not offer coursework in these areas; what it means is that if you wish to receive a liberal arts education with general education courses in specific, important areas you have to seek them out for yourself.

In fairness, some of these institutions still maintain "distribution requirements" which target specific areas of the traditional curriculum, but these often consist of a partitioned menu of electives that do not guarantee the inclusion of core knowledge. The frequent assumption is that students will have learned particular content in high school and now will want to choose their own coursework in college. And that may be correct, depending on the high school that the students attended. The students most at risk, however, are not those who attended expensive preparatory schools; they are the students from the second, third and fourth tiers.

Opponents of core curricula sometimes call up memories of lockstep, grill-and-drill instruction designed to instill discipline and develop character but largely consisting of sadistic bullying. Others point to the evils perpetrated by western civilization and question the perpetuation of such a "civilization's" culture. Such arguments involve the creation of great straw men which are then unceremoniously toppled.

The unspoken assumption is that happy mediums can never be realistically sought. One can, surely, inculcate discipline and develop character without brutalizing students, just as one can (and must) understand both the accomplishments *and* the shortcomings of the past, for we have nothing else but the past. The unavoidable question is: can one say that a student possesses an *education* at the bachelor's degree level if that student is ignorant of the most basic material?

An Oxbridge "first" or "upper second" degree once meant something. There were expectations with regard to what one would read and know and a further expectation that the quality of the degree determined upon examination by the faculty could be trusted, a certain level of quality consequently being expected for certain types of employment, particularly in the civil service. When Alvin Kernan studied at Oxford (1949–1951) his *undergraduate* degree required four and a half days of exams—three hours in the morning, three in the afternoon (Kernan 1999, p. 56). An American degree, unless it carries the distinction of Latin honors, insures very little now and even the Latin honors will be driven by grades (without regard to the level of difficulty of the courses taken) at a time of considerable grade inflation.

We reduced standards for several reasons: first, because many quietly (though wrongly) believed that the new students were incapable of facing traditional challenges; second, because some of the students *demanded* relaxed and/or altered standards (contrary to their own best interests), and finally because the politicians wanted to be reelected and the corporatists wanted to collect the tuition revenue.

Courses that have been failed can be retaken; sometimes that fact is noted on the transcript, sometimes it is masked. Transcripts are often sanitized, personal behavior incidents being effaced. At one point the Board of Directors at Georgetown refused to permit us to expel a student who had started a fire in a dormitory. I give credit to those who wished to expel that student, but those who handle student disciplinary cases now do so in a world in which some prominent universities consciously suppress information concerning such actions. It is very much like the arguments concerning grade inflation: if your institution "holds the line" you are putting your students at a disadvantage in the marketplace. You are also, of course, participating in a system "designed for student success" whose honesty and integrity have been compromised.

Despite these issues, there is still quality and opportunity in American higher education; in many cases, the student must conscientiously and tenaciously seek it out. He or she is aided in that process by information technology, but that technology can tempt as well as facilitate. Electronic devices both inform and distract; their use turns on the nature of their users' curiosity.

The French encyclopedia, an Enlightenment landmark, the great project of Diderot and d'Alembert, was designed to be a revolutionary device. Basic content (how to construct a well or how to operate a printing press) would be disseminated to all. Knowledge would indeed be power. The world would be changed. The lines of traditional authority would be redrawn. The poor could become rich, the hungry fed, the ignorant taught. Their thirst for knowledge was driven by their often desperate circumstances. Now we can hold the knowledge that they labored to accumulate and disseminate in the palms of our hands. Will students seek such knowledge or will they play video games and consult social media websites?

One July day in 1763 Johnson and Boswell were travelling down the Thames to Greenwich. They hired a sculler at the stairs by the Temple and set out. The young waterman rowing them listened to their talk as he transported them. (This was a very dangerous job, particularly when the journey took the vessel below London Bridge, with swift currents running between narrow stone pillars and the cries of the drowning frequently being heard by those above.) They discussed learning, Boswell saying that many go through life, quite successfully, without it. Johnson acknowledged that there was some knowledge that was not of "direct use," but he argued for the overall advantages which it offered. "It is wonderful," he said, "what a difference learning makes upon people even in the common intercourse of life, which does not appear to be much connected with it." He noted that the waterman could row just as well without the knowledge, for example, of the song of Orpheus sung to the Argonauts, but life, as Johnson well knew, is about more than simply rowing. He then asked the boy, "What would you give, my lad, to know about the Argonauts?" "Sir," the boy responded, "I would give what I have." They gave him a double fare, Johnson saying that "a desire of knowledge is the natural feeling of mankind; and every human being, whose mind is not debauched, will be willing to give all that he has to get [it]."

I am not sure that Johnson is correct in the latter statement, for I regularly encounter people who appear to care little for the acquisition of knowledge. A related view of Johnson's, a restatement of the above principle, is closer, I believe, to common experience, namely the notion that the greatest indication of a strong and healthy mind is an active curiosity.

We test for intelligence and we test for aptitude. We ask for writing samples and we seek lists of extracurricular activities. Sometimes we even test for content. We do not test for curiosity. Jary Pelikan once said that there is only one issue of importance in the hiring of faculty: "Will the individual's curiosity run out before his contract does?"

Curiosity is the key; it is the central attribute of the 10 percent (or, hopefully, many, many more) who should attend college. It is not dependent on intelligence and it has little to do with wealth, though wealth can help to satisfy it. It is said to be an emotion and not an instinct. The Latin *curiosus* is related to *cura*, care, and it includes the concept of diligence. We share it with our cats and our dogs and while they are sometimes more successful than us in following it we exceed them in our ability to be curious about curiosity itself, taking that interest to ever higher levels of abstraction.

It is the *sine qua non* for a student and those who possess it and seek to satisfy it will be embraced enthusiastically by every college or university's faculty, for the faculty are just as dismayed by the corporatized university and just as demoralized as students hoping to find a way through the gray corridors of consumerism, branding, sham strategic plans, nanny statism and institutional cowardice.

Moreover, the resources are all there. American universities, particularly American graduate schools, are still the world's model and canny undergraduates benefit directly from the campus presence of graduate programming. Our libraries, laboratories, instrumentation and information technology are unsurpassed, even in a time of constrained budgets. Diffuse curricula require students to choose wisely and well, but those students will not lack help, particularly as they seek to specialize. Their challenge will be to reconstruct the liberal arts core which most institutions have largely abandoned and to familiarize themselves with the texts and traditions which have shaped civilization (and, yes, sometimes retarded it).

The existence of a curriculum, even one sought personally by the individual student, does not, however, guarantee challenge. In addition to opportunities, there must be expectations. In 2011 Richard Arum and Josipa Roksa startled the academy with a book entitled *Academically Adrift: Limited*

Learning on College Campuses. They noted that a survey of student time use from the 1920s until today had shown that through the 1960s students devoted approximately forty hours per week to academic pursuits. That time has now shrunk to twenty-seven hours. In 1961 students studied approximately twenty-five hours per week; now (2003) they study, on average, thirteen. That was just the beginning.

In 1963 26 percent of students admitted to cheating on tests and examinations, in 1993, 52 percent (2011, p. 14). On average, students now work five hours more per week than students in the 1960s (p. 16). While fewer than one in six full-time students work more than twenty hours per week, a workload of fifteen hours is huge, particularly when one includes travel time; it essentially consumes every weekday afternoon.

Hence, Arum and Roksa's pivotal question: what are students learning? And the answer, in many cases: precious little. The authors joined with the Council for Aid to Education and twenty-four colleges and universities whose students were scheduled to take the CLA exam—the Collegiate Learning Assessment—in their first semester (fall 2005) and at the conclusion of their sophomore year (spring 2007). In addition to surveys and transcript data, the authors had access to longitudinal data on 2,322 students on diverse campuses (2011, p. 19ff.).

The CLA does not assess the acquisition of specific content, but tests overall intellectual competencies. It provides you with background documents on a particular issue and then asks you to study and respond to them. The documents—previously unfamiliar to the test taker—pose "real world" problems and require the individual to think critically, reason analytically, solve problems and communicate clearly (2011, pp. 21–22). The skills necessary to excel in the exercise are precisely those skills which are generally touted on college websites.

Aside: keep in mind that despite these website promises with regard to reasoning and communication skills, few or no institutions now require the study of Logic and few require systematic courses in public speaking. The mathematics sequence at West Point, for example—one of the Academy's signatures—was designed to instill confidence and build communication skills. It was rooted in nineteenth-century practice. Students solved problems at the board and then defended their proofs to their classmates. This required them to think on their feet and explain themselves in a crisp, clear manner. If possible, they "recited" every class period.

Forty-five percent of the students who took the CLA in the Arum/Roksa study showed no change at all in their basic abilities after three semesters of college. This prompted the authors to ask whether or not education promotes social mobility or simply sustains existing inequalities (2011, p. 37). Their conclusion: "Since schools expect but do not teach these cultural competencies, children from less advantaged families are left to fend for themselves, and in the process they typically reproduce their class location" (2011, p. 37).

White students scored one standard deviation above African-American students and other non-white racial/ethnic groups made progress similar to that of white students. Women demonstrated the same level of critical thinking, complex reasoning and writing skills as men (2011, pp. 38-39). This is attributable in part to the fact that the majority of African-American students (66 percent) were enrolled in less selective institutions, while only 12 percent of whites were enrolled there. The bottom line, however, is that all of these institutions are charging tuition; their students are incurring debt and the results of the CLA suggest that they are not all experiencing real academic growth (2011, p. 55).

There is, however, more to the story. A number of students appear to be prospering. The top 10 percent of the CLA sample improved by 1.5 standard deviations (43 percentile points) and those numbers included students from *all* family backgrounds and *all* racial/ethnic groups, as well as students who came to college with very different levels of academic preparation (2011, p. 56).

Why? What college experiences and practices actually facilitate student learning? In the first place, the strongest influences on students are their peers and their teachers. Thus, one obvious question for those interested in enhancing student achievement would be, "How can one reduce the out-of-class time spent on socializing and leisure activities and make peer culture more academic?"

On the faculty-influence side, Arum and Roksa report that the greater the selectivity of the individual college the greater the degree of student-faculty interaction outside of class (2011, pp. 66–67). They discovered other things as well. On average, students studied twelve hours per week; 37 percent studied less than five hours a week. Fifty percent had not taken a course in the prior semester that required twenty pages or more of writing over the course of the semester. One-third had not taken a course in the prior semester that required forty pages of reading per week. Highly selective colleges tended to require more of students than the less selective ones (2011, pp. 69–72).

Aside: when I taught freshman composition at the University of Illinois in 1964–1966 the first-semester students wrote fifteen papers, one a week. In the second semester they wrote twelve papers and then a term paper. At Harvard at the turn of the twentieth century students wrote every day in their composition classes. As the expectations steadily erode, the students who suffer most are the students who are the least prepared to do college work. Inequalities are perpetuated.

Some would argue that higher expectations are difficult to sustain when students must work more and more hours to meet today's costs. I agree. This is why we must reduce those costs; they not only impose a financial burden, they significantly diminish the college (intellectual) experience.

The best performance on the CLA by major: the Humanities, social sciences, the physical and life sciences and Mathematics. The worst: business, education and social work (2011, pp. 104–6). Health majors perform significantly higher on the CLA than do business majors, even though both are applied fields (2011, p. 108).

Another interesting finding: studying by oneself appears to be more beneficial than studying in groups (2011, p. 100). This is not counterintuitive. Despite the pieties concerning "study groups" and "collaborative learning," "the reality of implementation is much more challenging" (2011, pp. 100–1). The reason is simple: when studying in groups it is very difficult to keep on task and it is very hard to eliminate freeriding.

I am sure that business schools will promptly respond that working in groups is how business is actually done and problems are actually solved, but the real world is different from the artificial world of the business school, *American Idol* or *The Apprentice*. In the real world, when one leads a group the leader has at his or her disposal real carrots and real sticks.

Arum and Roksa studied the student allocation of time and found the following: classroom/laboratory time 9 percent; studying 7 percent; working/volunteering 9 percent; sleeping 24 percent; socializing and leisure, a stunning 51 percent (2011, p. 97). If that "socializing" is non-academic, a significant portion of what could be "peer learning" is lost. Some estimate the percentage of peer learning that constitutes higher education as high as 40 percent of the total.

To summarize Arum and Roksa's conclusions, students are most likely to succeed if they:

> Have educated parents;
> Secure grants rather than loans;
> Do not work long hours in jobs;
> Study alone;
> Take demanding courses (= those that require twenty pp. of writing each semester/forty pp. of reading, weekly);
> Spend no time on sorority or fraternity activities;
> Study a great deal;
> Attend more-selective rather than less-selective institutions;
> Study with demanding faculty;
> Interact out-of-class with those faculty;
> Major in the liberal arts and sciences rather than in business, education or social work.

Today's jobs, the authors conclude, require knowledge, learning, information and skilled-intelligence, cognitive abilities that can be learned and developed in college (2011, p. 123). It is difficult, however, to hone those abilities in a world in which one-third of recent college graduates took at least one remedial course (2011, p. 126), a world in which dormitories are too often seen as revenue centers and revenue generators rather than instruments for enhancing academic development (2011, p. 128), a world in which "undergraduate learning is peripheral to the concerns of the vast majority of those involved with the higher-education system" (p. 143), a world in which only 24 percent of adults, aged 18-24, read a newspaper and 34 percent receive no news from any source on a daily basis (2011, p. 243).

Employers still seek to hire entry-level employees. Surveys conducted with such employers reveal that a *small* proportion of college graduates now exhibit the skills which they require: in the case of the ability to excel in written communication—16–26 percent; in the ability to excel in critical thinking or problem solving—22–28 percent. What do the employers do? They hire foreign workers who do have those skills or they hire American students with advanced degrees (2011, p. 143), thus extending the credential creep and the warehousing.

Assuming that a general education curriculum, of some sort, is preferable to a random listing of unrelated coursework, how should that curriculum be conceived? We can look at five common responses, the first one being no core curriculum at all, a common pattern among elite institutions. Faculty at such institutions will generally hasten to observe that their students make their choices within a system of conscientious advising. This is not an idle walk through a cafeteria, but a structured plan tailored to specific needs with input from both the student and one or more faculty mentors. If so, fine, particularly in the context of a student cohort trained in the nation's finest secondary schools and possessing an awareness of the nature of the decisions being made. A top student might decide between a political theory course which focuses upon the thought of classical antiquity or that of the Enlightenment. An underprepared or marginal student, on the other hand, may not even be aware of the differences between the choices or even of the concept of "political theory" per se.

A second approach is also seen with some frequency—the (easily-gamed) general education menu that offers insights into the theories and methods of specific disciplines. As noted above, the individual courses often simply represent the research interests of the faculty and are not designed to be elements within a formal core curriculum, one where the courses are "freestanding"—designed specifically to be part of an identifiable, extra-departmental core.

It is likely that a good student will already have some sense of the processes and procedures of a multiplicity of disciplines. He or she will not have studied linguistics or other collegiate subjects at the secondary level, but such students will have studied mathematics, language, literature, physical and/or life science and social science there. Either way, a lower-level course at a university is unlikely to inculcate a sense of what real historians or real physicists actually do. Such courses will seldom require archival work with primary sources or the utilization of an ancient, medieval or modern foreign language and students will not do laboratory experiments beyond the standardized activities that one commonly sees. Nor are they likely to work with advanced instrumentation. A chemist friend of mine once said that there are two processes in science—knowing the notes and hearing the music. Most introductory courses will focus on the former and many of those notes will already have been learned in high school.

Beyond those possibilities—the non-curriculum and the introduction-to-disciplines curriculum—there are three noteworthy core curricular patterns. The first focuses upon *transferable skills*, with content being subsidiary; the second focuses upon *cultural literacy*, with common content taking precedence, while the third focuses upon *great thinkers/artists and great thoughts/works*. There is, of course, the preferable but rare choice—a core which builds cultural literacy, exposes the student to works of uncommon quality and importance and, simultaneously, helps develop transferable skills.

At Portland State, for example, a system of interdisciplinary seminars has been designed for the first two years of the college experience. The seminars are designed to enhance and extend students' core skills. In the words of Dan Berrett, a senior reporter for the *Chronicle of Higher Education*, "the approach taken by Portland State is dominant and growing. It sees the explicit cultivation of core skills, such as critical thinking, writing and quantitative literacy, as the goal of undergraduate education" (2011, p. 1).

Core skills rather than *specific knowledge* are the institutional goal. Thus, Portland State's first-year students can satisfy general education requirements taking such courses as "Human/Nature," "Sustainability," and "Design and Society." Not surprisingly, the American Council of Trustees and Alumni give Portland State's curriculum an F, their preference being for content-driven courses within specific academic areas.

Of course, as Mr. Berrett goes on to say, "Core skills and core content are linked with one another . . . because neither can realistically be taught in isolation" (2011, p. 3). Josipa Roksa has argued that the desire to draw a sharp distinction between content knowledge and critical thinking represents a "false dichotomy that we don't need and is actually very counterproductive" (Berrett 2011, p. 3). My advice for an institution considering installing a curriculum that focuses on skills would be that they should not settle for a partial loaf when they can inculcate and develop those skills while also providing important content.

The content/skills dichotomy is at the heart of E. D. Hirsch, Jr.'s (as we now say) *intervention*. A Yale-trained English teacher, Hirsch began his career studying Romanticism and hermeneutics. Moving from Yale to Virginia, he became responsible for the U-VA composition program and worked to discover the most effective ways of teaching writing.

In that process, he experienced some epiphanies which will now strike readers as rather obvious. One, for example, concerned the work of a researcher at the University of Illinois who was studying the relationship between content knowledge and communication skills. He looked specifically at students' writings on weddings. He found that Indian students could write more effectively on Indian weddings than American students and that American students could write more effectively on American weddings than Indian students. Why? Because each had greater, prior knowledge of the cultural specificities of their own country's practices.

While this would appear to be obvious, it flew in the face of skill-based writing theory and argued that rather than simply possessing *skills* we also need *knowledge* if we are to become effective writers. It positioned Hirsch against the shibboleths of the colleges of education and against the Deweyesque principles associated with so-called progressive education and other early twentieth-century tendencies.

The result was Hirsch's book, *Cultural Literacy: What Every American Needs to Know*. The book fortuitously appeared in 1987 and was paired with Allan Bloom's 1987 bestseller, *The Closing of the American Mind: How Higher Education Has Failed Democracy and Impoverished the Souls of Today's Students*. Bloom was a Straussite, writing about cultural decay and the ravages of cultural relativism. Hirsch was a traditional liberal talking about a specific pedagogical issue (with wide-ranging implications). The two, as Johnson said of the heterogeneous ideas of the metaphysical poets, "were yoked by violence together." Both books were phenomenal and unanticipated bestsellers, obviously tapping into a deep set of preexisting anxieties. Hirsch's financial success led to the establishment of a foundation, one that has issued a series of volumes that are designed to facilitate the acquisition of cultural literacy. His program and materials have been adopted by individual school districts, with claims of significant success.

Bloom, a prominent member of the University of Chicago faculty, was arguing for more of a "great books" approach while Hirsch was arguing for a more systematic, integrated, content-based approach. While he and Bloom might have shared certain ideas and principles in common, the thrust of their core arguments and their overarching purposes were very different. Nevertheless, Hirsch was vilified and even demonized for suggesting that we should develop core curricula which would help insure that all students could achieve a certain degree of cultural literacy. Critics claimed that this curriculum would be too white, too monolithic, too "undemocratic" for a country as richly diverse as our own.

Hirsch would answer that the absence of consistent, common curricula at the K-12 level would most hurt the poor. For one thing, they move more frequently—as often as every nine months in the inner city. Children move from school to school and never catch on or catch up because of the absence of consistent curricula across the grades. He would also answer that the absence of coherent core curricula accounts for many of the problems with K-12 education in general and the fact that for all of our investments at that level, our students lag behind the achievements of students in other countries, which do have core curricula. In response to the criticism that our country is more diverse and that this accounts for our lagging performance, he would respond that other countries are equally diverse and that they are better served by strong core curricula.

In some ways the issue is a prudential one. No one likes the idea of a panel of bureaucrats (troglodyte, fundamentalist yokels in the fantasies of the left, fire-breathing, America-hating radicals in the fantasies of the right) determining and requiring what our children will learn. On a theoretical level, the issue appears to raise significant problems. On the practical level, however, the issues are much clearer. Do we want students to proceed through our school system without a knowledge of key issues? The Deweyesque planners wanted students to learn basic skills—how to balance a checkbook, how to change a tire. Hirsch wanted students to know the essential facts with regard to such things as our system of government.

He was also concerned and continues to be concerned with regard to the issue of social integrity. Can we, in fact, function as a society if significant numbers of our countrymen do not know basic things? How can we communicate with one another without cultural literacy? In a sense, he would argue that the acquisition of cultural literacy is of supreme *pragmatic* value, for it makes communication possible.

One way to think about this is to say that "cultural literacy" is that which is left out of a discussion (Willingham 2009, p. 47). A thriller writer says, for example, that "Smith flew to Washington, taxied directly to the Hoover Building and met with his counterpart there." The writer does not tell us that Washington, D.C. is the nation's capital or that the Hoover Building houses the Federal Bureau of Investigation, an arm of the Department of Justice, named for a former director who not only markedly advanced the profile of the Bureau but later embarrassed it when it was revealed that he had a penchant for dressing up in cocktail frocks. An individual ignorant of this basic cultural information will be unable to understand a simple passage in a piece of genre fiction or sense its possible nuances and overtones, much less be able—as a citizen and voter—to assess the proper role of the FBI in our contemporary society.

There are other, obvious devices that Hirsch uses to demolish a skills-based approach to, e.g., reading. He will give the reader a paragraph concerning a cricket match. Every *word* is known by an American reader but even if the reader possesses advanced "reading *skills*" the entire paragraph may be completely unintelligible to him or her because the comprehension of the paragraph requires a knowledge of the detailed rules and procedures of cricket. He will give the reader a paragraph from Kant's *Critique of Pure Reason* and suggest that the passage is unintelligible without the prior knowledge of a single element—e.g., Kant's particular use of the word *manifold*. Without prior knowledge there is limited or no comprehension. Decoding, in and of itself, is insufficient.

As obvious as this might seem, there are still theoretical battles raging beneath the surface. Deweyesque critics, for example, would say that much of the foundational knowledge associated with "traditional" education is useless because it does not lead to practical application but rather simply to the acquisition of more knowledge. Why learn Italian? It will not enable you to balance a checkbook or change a tire; it will simply enable you to read texts in that language. We will later look at Richard Hofstadter's arguments that pragmatic approaches to education—characteristic of much of twentieth-century educational orthodoxy—are decidedly anti-intellectual.

Hirsch would say just the opposite of the Deweyesque critics. He would say that the absence of cultural literacy obstructs your ability to learn, period, and that it is absurd and cruel to ask our students to compete in a global economy when many of their number cannot even identify the nation's vice president or describe in a sentence or two the purposes of the office.

In the early twentieth century students completing grammar school in rural, one-room, Kansas schoolhouses were required to define such terms as *zenith* and *panegyric*, spell words like *elucidation* and *animosity*, exhibit a significant familiarity with geography and history and do such arithmetic problems as finding the amount earned on a $900 note, at 8 percent interest, after two years, two months and six days (Sowell 1993, pp. 7–8). The expectation of such a level of cultural literacy might render many of today's college students apoplectic. The students in the elite Georgetown School of Foreign Service chafed under the requirement that they take the course "Map of the Modern World." They scornfully called it "Coloring for Credit," but it was a necessary course, particularly when one of their master's degree students (with 10+ applicants for each of the highly-coveted places in the program) commented on the contiguous land border between England and Germany (perhaps thinking of the good old days back in Laurasia and Gondwanaland?)

David Gelernter's recent book, *America-Lite: How Imperial Academia Dismantled Our Culture (and Ushered in the Obamacrats)* raises an interesting possibility. He argues that the many afflictions with which we now must deal turn on a specific change within our elite colleges. They have moved from being "society colleges" to being "intellectuals' colleges." On the face of it, that would seem to be a very positive development. Rather than educating the upper classes within a clubby ethos, one that perpetuated inequalities and fostered such institutions as dining clubs and secret societies, universities have now focused on the development and dissemination of knowledge.

The point is a bit more subtle than that, however. The "society college" was not exclusively driven by a desire to perpetuate wealth and class. It was driven, in part, by a specific pedagogy, one that concerned general education and the core curriculum.

When James Bryant Conant was president of Harvard (1933–1953) he held general education in much higher regard than Charles W. Eliot had. His General Education Committee released a book entitled *General Education in a Free Society*, a text that is most often called the "Harvard red book." Its purpose was to set the direction for both secondary and college curricula for ensuing generations.

Eliot, for all of his love of the elective system, was no philistine. He is associated with the "five-foot shelf" containing the fifty volumes constituting the Harvard Classics, the introduction to which he wrote in 1910. He did not conceive of the collection as being comparable to something like Mortimer Adler's "Great Books" series, but rather as a sort of portable university that might encapsulate the materials undergirding six great courses which would serve to demonstrate the upward progress of the human mind.

The red book's purposes were related, but also significantly different. As Louis Menand writes, its norm was to utilize specific books to create a cultural lingua franca, a common fund of human knowledge that would bind us as a people and reduce the divisions that separate us (in particular the economic and political ones). The Harvard system of general education would thus represent what Menand calls a form of "social glue" (2010, pp. 39–42).

These "social" purposes are part of Gelernter's argument. They are similar in kind to the desires behind Hirsch's urgings for enhanced "cultural literacy." They are also different from the University of Chicago model, which sees great books as articulating, as Menand says, timeless truths (2010, p. 41). This was a key element in Strauss's thought and one that is seen in other elements of Chicago thought. While Strauss idolized Plato, e.g., R. S. Crane and his literary colleagues idolized Aristotle. As one reads the book that represented their "school," *Critics and Criticism: Ancient and Modern* (1952) one sees the mindset at work. While Hirsch's program would insure that students are familiar with Plato's "myth of the cave" and the differences between the more idealist Plato and more empiricist Aristotle, Crane and his colleagues would focus on Aristotle's *Poetics* as a crucial element in the understanding of literature. For Hirsch, it is important that we be familiar with key notions and concepts; for the Chicago critics and Strauss-site social scientists it is important that we study specific works and specific authors in great depth, their work not just being "important to know about" but absolutely foundational for human learning.

President Eliot, a chemist, was interested in the progress of human thought, but the Humanities represent non-cumulative knowledge rather than the cumulative knowledge of the natural sciences, where coursework is necessarily presented sequentially. The Humanities do not necessarily "progress." All philosophy is a footnote to Plato, Whitehead thought, and nearly every successful narrative from *Middlemarch* to an episode of *Frasier* contains the pattern of plot arcs that Aristotle found in Greek drama.

For Hirsch we need cultural literacy to learn (further) and to communicate with one another; for Crane we turn to the *Poetics* not simply to be able to discuss it or build upon it, but in order to understand, fundamentally, crucial elements of human expression.

Johnson once said that classical quotation was the *parole* of literary men all over the world. Individuals from different countries and different educational systems could communicate with one another because of the shared cultural commonality of the thought of antiquity. Our *parole* may be different in kind but it is no less important.

I remember seeing a clip of Sinatra performing a new song in the studio and commenting that "it was longer than the first act of Hamlet." Last evening my wife and I were watching a television show that included the often-repeated line that the scenario in question "was like Hamlet without the prince." When one of my college professors' father died another commented that "he took it like Hamlet." This is normal English speech and Hirsch is at pains to insure that all members of our society will share enough of a common culture to be able to understand it and, hence, one another.

At West Point we required a course in World Literature for yearlings/sophomores. They would read sections of the Bible, *Oedipus the King*, segments of Dante's *Inferno*, the first act and parts of the second act of Goethe's *Faust*, and chunks of Chaucer, Shakespeare, Milton, Swift, Yeats and others. One explicit purpose of the course was to attempt to insure that our graduates would be able to move among educated individuals across the globe, understand references to classic works of literature and make their own contributions to serious conversations.

Kenneth Burke's celebrated essay, "Literature as Equipment for Living," imagines literature as a language whose noteworthy incidents, emblems, scenes and characters serve as both aids to understanding and communication shorthand. The expression, "the fidelity of Cordelia" serves as a way of understanding, comprehending and describing a specific segment of human experience. When P. D. James names her protagonist Cordelia Gray in *An*

Unsuitable Job for a Woman the name is designed to carry overtones and associations that bear directly on the character and, ultimately, the plot.

To lack such cultural literacy is to be ignorant in some contexts and to be utterly silenced in others. It isolates the individual from intellectual company (and, in some cases, the most elementary forms of understanding) and reinforces and widens prior inequalities. Such information and experience is most important for those students that Eliot thought would drag down his elective-driven curriculum, in which the elites would thrive. The non-elites who would have distorted his curriculum by constraining it and formalizing it would have been part of a tiny echelon at the top. Now, with some 60 percent of the country's population attending college, cultural literacy is at what must surely be an all-time low, though at a time when it should be in greatest demand.

The "great books" represent a related issue. They play less of a role at Chicago than they once did. At Notre Dame in the early 1960s there was considerable interplay between the two universities. The Chicago emphasis on the "great books" manifested itself at Notre Dame in a required seminar for juniors. The notion was that all members of the faculty would be tapped to teach the course, so that students and faculty could learn together, in fruitful dialogue.

Such at least was the piety. My instructor was a kindly mathematician who knew very little about the great books and who, interestingly, believed that Freud was possessed by the devil. The discussions were not of the sort that they might have been, had they been conducted by political theorists or members of the Classics department, but at least all Notre Dame juniors in the college were exposed to a succession of serious and important texts. They all were familiar with Plato's "myth of the cave" because they read *The Republic* in toto.

The remaining fully-institutionalized remnants of the concept are the great books-driven curricula at the campuses of St. John's College in Annapolis and Santa Fe. I have colleagues who studied at St. John's and their seriousness and learning are very impressive.

Unfortunately, St. John's remains a tiny beacon in a sea of institutions offering degree programs in Parks and Recreation and Leisure and Fitness Studies. As Derek Bok points out (2008, pp. 264–65), the great books approach requires small classes and (far more difficult to secure) faculty members competent to teach within that system. Students are not fond of heavily-prescribed curricula and in a day when students are "consumers" and "customers" rather than apprentices, they are given what they want.

In 2013 St. John's-Annapolis had 342 applicants and accepted 81 percent of them; in 2015 it accepted 87.1 percent. Schools with no general education requirements at all can attract 20 or 30 times the number of St. John's applicants and simultaneously pride themselves on the high rejection rates that they are then able to report to *US News*. Since deep applicant pools engender strong bond ratings and afford the opportunity to borrow at favorable rates, the die is effectively cast. I once mentioned St. John's and its curriculum to our director of admissions at Georgetown. He responded in a nanosecond with a detailed recital of St. John's admission statistics.

For all of the commercial issues, however, we now risk graduating students who are largely ignorant of the basic elements of our cultural life. Gelernter (2012, p. 109) cites Sandra Day O'Connor's comment that only a third of Americans can name the three branches of American government, but 75 percent of the nation's youth can name the *American Idol* judges. "With no past," he comments, "you are no one. And a nation without a past is likewise stripped of identity. Failing to teach America's history makes America faceless, a mere generic Western nation" (2012, p. 149).

It was not always so. When Johns Hopkins was established, modeled upon the German universities that towered above American ones in research, it created a revolution in American higher education whose various results continue today. The philological underpinnings of its language and literature areas drove a historical approach to research which continues today on a much-reduced scale. The historical approach, which goes hand in glove with many approaches to "core curricula" has much to recommend it, not the least of which is its attractiveness to the human brain.

As the cognitive scientist Daniel Willingham points out, factual knowledge must precede skills; skills require it (2009, p. 25). [Full disclosure: Willingham is a colleague of Hirsch's at Virginia.] The so-called 4th grade slump is attributable to the fact that reading levels diverge then. All may be able to decode well, initially, but by the fourth grade students with greater content knowledge are able to read more complex materials more effectively, with disadvantaged students falling farther behind (2009, p. 37).

"Logical thinking," Willingham states, is actually memory retrieval (2009, p. 37). Memory is the cognitive process of first resort and factual knowledge improves memory (2009, p. 42). When Einstein said that imagination was more important than knowledge he was, unfortunately, wrong. Knowledge is necessary for imagination (2009, p. 45). Willingham cites the Spanish truism: "The Devil is not wise because he is the Devil. The Devil is wise because he is *old*" (2009, p. 47).

The brain "chunks," combining related bits of information in order to relieve pressure on short-term memory. Memory, ultimately, is "the residue of thought," that which remains after the consideration of a multiplicity of material (2009, pp. 34–36, 40, 54). Although emotion is not necessary for learning, we seem to remember things that evoke an emotional reaction. Since most schoolwork does not involve emotional reactions, schoolwork is less interesting to young learners (2009, p. 57).

Repetition aids memory, since you tend to remember whatever you tend to think about. Meaning is particularly memorable. So too is the factual. The brain is "lazy" and it does not care for abstractions; it prefers the concrete (2009, pp. 58, 61, 87). We understand new things in the context of things we already know and most of what we already know *is* concrete (2009, p. 88). Understanding is, thus, remembering in disguise (2009, p.88).

It is next to impossible to become proficient at a mental task without extended practice (2009, p. 107). Children do differ in intelligence, but intelligence can be changed through sustained hard work (2009, p. 170). Hence, the bottom line: students love facts and they love the concrete. They also love stories, because the "lazy" brain does not want to be burdened with abstractions. At the same time, it does not want to be bored with dull drivel. With stories the brain is stimulated and kept active because of stories' utilization of the "four C's": causality, conflict, complications and character (2009, pp. 65–68). They are not too easy and not too hard and thus they offer the kinds of tasks which the brain embraces.

The much-maligned Mr. Gradgrind turns out to have been right after all, but with a series of important provisos. He needed to enliven the facts—the concrete realities—by embedding them in stories and concrete images. Hence the conclusion (for the curriculum planner): students require content knowledge that is often historical, factual and concrete and their learning is enhanced when they acquire content knowledge through the reading of memorable texts. The "cultural literacy," great books and transferable skills approaches can and should be combined in a way that is most effective because it is commensurate with the processes of the human brain.

Chapter Four

For a Living or a Life?

If Aristotle were writing a book about colleges and universities his first question might concern their *purpose* and *end*. That more contemporary intellectual, Dr. Hannibal Lecter, would urge us to read Marcus Aurelius: "The Emperor counsels simplicity. First principles. Of each particular thing, ask: What is it in itself, in its own constitution?" What, after all, *is* the purpose of higher education? What is this institution designed to accomplish? Why does it exist? Why do we suspend our lives to experience it and why do we incur its vast costs?

There are generally two answers given. The first answer may appear to be crass; hence we tend to dress it up. "College prepares you for your future" sounds so much nicer than "College enables you to get a job." If that still sounds too utilitarian we can gussy it up a bit more: "College prepares you for the global economy in the twenty-first century."

Does it prepare you to *make a living* or does it prepare you to *live a life*? The two are not mutually exclusive, of course, but our hopes concerning personal growth are often overwhelmed by our desire for employment and that desire may become so intense as to eclipse education per se, in which case college becomes a mundane form of training. It is one of the curiosities of American life that we eschew vocational training in our high schools because it would constrain our children, narrow their vision and condemn them to working with their hands. The college track should be for all, we proclaim, but then we turn around and accede to the notion that college should be little more than vocational training.

There is a history to these phenomena and I will discuss it, but let us begin with a more nuanced view of the purposes of higher education—Louis Menand's *New Yorker* piece (2011), "Live and Learn: Why we Have College."

Menand identifies four purposes of higher education. The first is to *sort* for the country. Our society requires intellectual and social capital and it has made a large investment in higher education to provide it. Higher education takes these federal resources (NIH grants, Pell grants, NEH fellowships . . .) and offers the government results—an MIT-trained linguist, a Caltech physicist, a Columbia historian, an Eastman cellist, a Wharton MBA, and so on. This sorting process parallels the British recruitment of a strong civil service, which looks to the quality of university degrees for aid in its efforts.

The American sorting process, as Menand notes (2011, p. 5), is made more difficult by the number of individuals now attending college. In Britain, on the other hand, the initial sort is more stringent, though acceptance rates at Britain's very top institutions are higher—21 percent at Cambridge and 18 percent at Oxford versus 6 percent at Harvard and less than 8 percent at Columbia, Yale and Stanford (2011, p. 5).

The second possible purpose of higher education is to promote individual *growth*, a growth that is independent of career interests. As Bart Giamatti put it, liberal education is dedicated to "the proposition that growth in thought, and in the power to think, increases the pleasure, breadth, and value of life" (1990, p. 121).

The third possible purpose, Menand writes, is a purely *vocational* one. Higher education enables graduates to secure jobs; institutions of higher education are principally credentialing services. The fourth possible purpose is to place undergraduates on specific tracks. Elite liberal arts colleges, for example, prepare the students who will, eventually, matriculate in the nation's elite professional schools.

One does not have to look too closely to see that Menand's first and fourth possible purposes relate directly to the third. There are ultimately only two purposes for higher education—higher education for a life or higher education for a living.

Andrew Delbanco's formulation (2012) is similar to Menand's. Delbanco identifies three discrete purposes that are commonly suggested for college and university attendance (2012, pp. 25–32). The first is *economic*. College attendance helps the nation's and states' economies as it increases the earnings of the individual graduates, whose taxes more than repay the state and federal government for their educational subsidies.

As Delbanco notes, the economic argument is resonant with the wealthy. They know the 'value' of education and have long sought it. For a student from a family making $90,000 or more, the odds of getting a baccalaureate degree by the age of 24 is 1 in 2. If the family has income of $60,000-$90,000 the odds are 1 in 4. If the family income is less than $35,000 the odds are 1 in 17. With comparable grades and test scores, the affluent are 4x more likely to attend a selective college (2012, p. 26).

The second possible purpose in Delbanco's formulation is *political*. Education prepares us for citizenship. As many of the founding fathers argued, an educated populace is necessary for a functioning democracy (2012, p. 28). Voters must be discerning; hence, as Delbanco puts it, "we might say that the most important thing one can acquire in college is a well-functioning bullshit meter" (2012, p. 29).

This point is related to the qualities of mind that Delbanco believes should be developed in college (2012, p. 3): a skeptical discontent with the present, informed by a sense of the past; the ability to make connections among seemingly disparate phenomena; an appreciation of the natural world, enhanced by knowledge of both science and the arts; a willingness to imagine experience from other perspectives than one's own; and a sense of ethical responsibility. I would add, parenthetically, that these are largely Enlightenment principles and that the ultimate debate with regard to forms of education in the twentieth and twenty-first centuries comes down to a clash between Enlightenment ideals and Romantic ones.

The third possible function of a college or university education is to teach us how to enjoy *life* (2012, p. 32). This education, liberal education, serves as a hedge against purely utilitarian values and it protects us from the blandishments of unexamined dogma. The *artes liberales* were designed by the Greeks and Romans for those (in their time, free men) who were possessed of the leisure necessary for study. Such an education, Delbanco reminds us, was the possession of ruling elites down to and through the Enlightenment (2012, p. 33).

The nineteenth century, as Bliss Carnochan points out, and as Delbanco is aware, added some other principles. While Oxford focused on the classics and Cambridge focused on mathematics (1993, p. 21), Newman and Arnold addressed the relationship between religion and secular learning (1993, p. 40). For Newman, knowledge is different from virtue. Liberal education does not make you a Christian; it makes you a gentleman, i.e., an eighteenth-century benevolist "who never inflicts pain" (1993, p. 43). For Newman, the study of literature provides an education for a fallen world, an education steeped in the awareness of sin. It thus prepares the student "to swim in troubled waters" (1993, p. 44).

While Newman's followers regret the corruption of the world, they see literature as being palliative, whereas Arnoldians think that the great tradition—the best that has been thought and said—will actually help set things right (1993, p. 46). With Newman we have "Catholic humanism," with Arnold "cultural religion" (1993, p. 50).

The Newman/Arnold debate ultimately concerns the notion of higher education as a preparation for life, not for a job. How is one to obtain it? Is there an overarching method that extends, in some way, to all of the liberal arts? My own preferred method is indicated by Carnochan's convenient citation of the thoughts of Iowa State Senator Preston M. Sutton in 1884 (the year of the founding of the American Historical Association): "There is not a respectable college in the country but makes History one of its leading and most essential studies. . . . History is not only absolutely essential to learning but *history may be said to be learning itself*. Learning without history is Hamlet with Hamlet left out" (1993, p. 60, my italics).

As Delbanco argues, postwar American higher education neither requires the education formerly possessed by western elites for current elites, nor for the "new" students who had previously been marginalized, but has instead succumbed to the short-term attractions of the vocational. He writes, "In today's America, at every kind of institution—from underfunded community colleges to the wealthiest Ivies—this kind of education [liberal arts education] is at risk" (2012, p. 34).

Every college, Delbanco argues, should defend the opportunity for *reflection and contemplation*. And they should do so for the rich, the middle class and the poor, "who have the capacity to embrace the precious chance to think and reflect before life engulfs them" (2012, p. 35).

The residential college which helps promote this activity (a far more monastic than corporate one) is, Delbanco comments, virtually unknown outside the Anglo-American world, one of its great benefits being what he terms "lateral learning"—students learning from their classmates (2012, pp. 54–55). As Emerson put it, "I pay the schoolmaster, but 'tis the schoolboys that educate my son." (And, we should add, they do so for good or ill.)

The American "system" may be an odd one—grafting the German research university atop the English undergraduate college—but it has significant benefits when the two are seen as complementary rather than in conflict. Unfortunately, Delbanco argues, much of the disintegration and decay of American higher education results from the fact that universities (unlike freestanding residential colleges) simply do not care about the undergraduate "division" and they do not, ultimately, care about undergraduate students. They collect their tuition happily, but then invest the resulting resources in research and graduate education (2012, p. 85).

The isolation and separation are exacerbated by the dominance of professional/vocational training. For professional schools the ideal is not integration but independence. A business school faculty member at Georgetown once commented to me that her hero was a business school dean in Australia who had negotiated a relationship with his university that provided the business school utter autonomy while continuing to permit it to utilize the university's name. This is precisely what has occurred at the University of Virginia, with the physical separation of the Darden School, which returns a portion of its tuition to the university as a form of tribute.

In 2011 Alexander Astin (the dean of American statistical researchers in the field of higher education) and his colleagues published a book entitled

Cultivating the Spirit: How College Can Enhance Students' Inner Lives. It looks at the practices of "reflection," "thinking" and "meditation" in a more secular way—with the university conceived more as something like an Esalen Institute than a secularized monastery.

Astin's point is that the student's "spiritual quest," the development of self-awareness that used to be encapsulated in the phrase "know thyself'" receives very little attention in our colleges and universities (2011, p. 2). Where others speak of education for a living or for a life Astin talks about the "inner" and "outer" aspects of students' lives and argues that they are now seriously out of balance in our institutions of higher learning.

He and his colleagues assume that the student's personal quest should involve the addressing of such "spiritual questions" as the following: Who am I? What are my most deeply felt values? Do I have a mission or purpose in my life? Why am I in college? What kind of person do I want to become? What sort of world do I want to help create?

He is troubled by the fact that the responses to questions concerning values and purposes in inventories of freshman attitudes have altered significantly. The desire to "be very well off financially" has increased dramatically, while the desire to "develop a meaningful philosophy of life"—the highest ranked concern in the 1970s—has fallen sharply.

The purpose of his study is, then, to determine how students change spiritually in the course of college and identify the ways in which college can contribute positively to this developmental process. He concludes that students become slightly less religiously engaged as a result of college, but that they mature spiritually to a considerable degree (2011, p. 10 and *passim*).

An Astin study in 2005 surveyed faculty and revealed that while 64 percent are "religious," 81 percent are "spiritual" (2011, p. 6). Spiritual growth is very important, Astin argues, because it enhances other outcomes: academic performance, psychological well-being, the ability to lead and the degree to which one is satisfied with the college experience (2011, p. 10).

While student spiritual growth is impeded by television watching and the playing of video games, it is stimulated by such college experiences as study abroad and service learning. It is also stimulated by meditation and self-reflection (2011, p. 10). This is not meditation in the general sense—reflection and contemplation—but meditation in the Hindu or Buddhist sense. (For some, prayer is a form of meditation, but Astin lists them separately.) He notes that one college student in six meditates at least several times a week (2011, p. 54).

Some of his other findings are interesting. He notes that 80 percent of freshmen students attended some form of religious service in the year before college; 44 percent did so frequently. Seventy-seven percent believe in God, while 16 percent are "not sure." Sixty-nine percent pray. While students' religious commitments change very little during college, their attendance at formal religious services shows a steep decline (2011, pp. 83–89).

Astin also found sharp declines in religious and social conservatism, for example, with regard to abortion, casual sex and atheism (2011, p. 99). Religious struggles appear to be heightened when students major in English, but not when they major in business (2011, p. 106).

Astin's most interesting conclusion is his belief that the prototypical defining quality of a spiritual person is *equanimity* (2011, p. 142). Described as a student's feeling *at peace and centered*, its promotion leads to improved GPA's (2011, p. 119). Equanimity correlates with both high grades and psychological well-being. It is facilitated by meditation, prayer and self-reflection (2011, p. 54).

In defining an engaged and passionate student, both Johnson and Churchill would differ, opting for *curiosity* and *appetite* over equanimity. They would think of him or her *devouring* books (in Bacon's famous metaphor) rather than sitting in a corner, meditating. Nevertheless, Astin's formulation is interesting and contrasts dramatically with the ethos of vocational training.

Other prominent voices have turned to parallel issues. Vartan Gregorian has identified six major challenges to the American university (Hersh and Merrow, 2005, pp. 77–78): the information glut and the parallel fragmentation of knowledge; the curricular crisis, particularly within the liberal arts; the commercialization of research; the two-tiered faculty, one part-time, the other (diminishing in numbers) full-time; issues of quality, particularly within colleges of education; and the alteration of higher education that has resulted from the emergence of distance learning and e-learning.

It is striking that this distinguished historian does not mention vocationalism, the displacement of liberal arts education by professional training, but a closer look reveals that that rupture is at work in each of the problems he has identified. The expansion of knowledge, e.g., has not produced an expansive vision. At a time when we need larger, integrated perspectives we get more narrow, personalized ones. Rather than embracing a multiplicity of new material, we often filter "our" specific portion of material through a single theoretical lens. Professional schools deal in still simpler forms of knowledge (Hofstadter calls them "frozen ideas"): learn X (settled, accepted dogma) and you will qualify for a job in Y.

The "curriculum crisis within the liberal arts" has, in subtle ways, turned the liberal into the vocational. As the undergraduate takes fewer (and narrower) survey courses and instead follows the instructor into his or her microspecialty, the student experiences a simulacrum of "basic research." The student might, e.g., be made aware of his or her teacher's preoccupation—the complexities in interpreting *King Lear* because of the variations within its quarto and folio texts—but not be exposed to Shakespeare's sonnets, history plays, comedies, problem comedies, or other tragedies. The undergraduate jumps to the research issues without first establishing the foundations for that research. What was once undergraduate *education* now becomes more like graduate *training*.

The commercialization of research brings special temptations. Consider the simple example of drug trials within a medical center. The dollar amounts involved and the manner in which results can be reported (or suppressed) put our concupiscence to a very severe test.

Such choices between financial need (or greed) and the objective results of research carry the risk of diminishing the university's integrity, underscoring its now-corporate rather than academic nature and privileging utilitarian values over traditional ideals. In effect, they risk turning the university into a purely financial enterprise rather than an intellectual one, highlighting *its* need to make a living, whatever the accompanying, negative results might entail.

The two-tiered faculty represents a many-sided problem. The principal issues are the question of instructional quality and the diminution of coordinated planning that results when short-term, part-time faculty replace full-time ones. As noted above, when there is a dearth of full-time faculty the door is opened to corporatist administrators and their minions to capture the planning process and, very often, replace traditional programs with faddish, often vocational ones.

The bottom line is that the diminishing number of full-time faculty in American universities is usually either an honest response to a desperate financial situation or an expression of a corporatist wish to control, sometimes both. If one is anxious to install a group of cash-cow vocational programs this is the easiest way to do it.

Issues of quality, particularly in our colleges of education, is the subject of a later discussion. The simple fact is that the local college of education is likely to be the university's second largest vocational draw, after the school of business, and the progenitor of a great number of ideas which are, often, utilitarian in the worst senses of the term.

Finally, the changes in contemporary education that result from the development of information technology represent another many-sided issue. As noted above, information technology brings the intellectual wealth of the ages to our hands, literally. The availability of course materials, online, from top universities such as MIT and Stanford, is a positive development that can contribute to "democratic" purposes in profound ways. Everyone, literally, can gain access to the information and knowledge previously possessed by elites.

At the same time, electronic materials can displace serious study. Students can text and email from the back of the lecture hall rather than attend to what is being said by the sage on the stage. They can desperately try to get to stage three of the Angry Birds game rather than download the best that has been thought, written and said.

In the case of for-profit learning, students might return to a mechanical form of instruction which is very useful for utilitarian purposes but not particularly conducive to the kind of discussion which would help the student learn how to lead a life rather than, simply, attain a job.

The Army, for example, has long excelled at certain aspects of self-guided instruction. In addition to field manuals that spell out, in endless detail, the manner in which one addresses important, practical issues, they will take you through the planning steps that precede an operation and as Willingham would say, help the brain to "chunk" by providing acronyms and mnemonics, such as the four P's: PriorPlanningProperPerformance. As in for-profit education, the learner can study at his or her own pace, in his or her own location, at his or her own favorite or most convenient time.

This is a fine way to learn certain kinds of material, important material, but not intellectual material per se. It works for the rudiments of "platoon in the attack" but it does not work so well when one is attempting to determine the validity of Tom Carhart's recent speculation on Lee's "real" plan for the third day's battle at Gettysburg, or the relative importance of the theories of Clausewitz and their pertinence for our own time. Distance learning and self-guided instruction command a niche, but their forte is in the area of the vocational and the utilitarian rather than the intellectual.

Derek Bok, noting the statistics concerning student desires to become wealthy rather than acquire "a meaningful philosophy of life," says (realistically, perhaps, but sadly) that it is only natural that colleges play to these attitudes (2008, p. 26). The President *emeritus* of Harvard is aware of the fact that the most popular major in his college is not Philosophy, but Economics. He is also aware of the fact that other institutions (Harvey Mudd, e.g.) have a larger portion of their graduating classes going on to take Ph.D.'s than Harvard does.

He is aware of the subsidies provided to athletics, particularly at institutions such as the Ivies, where ticket revenue, licensing fees and bowl and conference income are tiny compared to those in the SEC, Big 12 and Big 10. He knows that athletics can displace academics and that many invest in athletics for utilitarian motives. He knows, as well, that college athletics in America began in a very humble and crassly economic setting. The first intercollegiate athletic contest occurred in 1852. A crew race between Harvard and Yale on Lake Winnipesaukee, it was sponsored by a railroad owner cum real estate developer who wanted to stir interest in the many charms of southern New Hampshire (Bok 2003, p. 35).

In a small college, student athletes can represent as much as 20 percent of an entering class. This is unlikely to do serious damage to the SAT averages in the case of women athletes, but when a college or university enters the world of major league football and basketball the SAT differences are stark. In the class of '93, selective public institutions such as Michigan and Penn State saw student athlete SAT's that were 237 points lower than those of their classmates. In selective privates such as Duke and Stanford, football players had SAT's that were 292 points lower than those of their classmates, while basketball players had SAT's that were 307 points lower (Bok 2003, p. 41).

For many of these athletes college is vocational, no matter what their major might be, for they aspire to play professionally. The reality, of course, is that only 2 percent of college football players will become professionals and only 0.5 percent of basketball players (Bok 2003, p. 45).

Still, we allow athletics to distort our values, in part because we believe that the payoff can be huge (as in the case of the Northwestern statistics previously cited). The University of Oregon nearly always finds itself at or near the bottom of the faculty salary scale of AAU public universities. Nevertheless, in 2001 it spent a quarter of a million dollars to install a hundred-foot high billboard near Madison Square Garden to promote the chances of their quarterback, Joey Harrington, in the Heisman trophy race. Eric Crouch of Nebraska won (Bok 2003, p. 55).

Athletics, of course, are not the only temptation that strolls before the desk of a college president in search of cash or recognition. We often think of the University of Chicago as a bastion of academic strength, cherishing tradition and going its own way with regard to curriculum and academic administrative structure. It was, however, President William Rainey Harper (a name that lives in august memory) who created a correspondence school at Chicago (1892) and refused to provide refunds to students who dropped out. He also pioneered extension programs during the evenings and on the weekends (Bok 2003, pp. 81–82).

Bok is fond of citing these facts, but he is honest enough to acknowledge that there is no institution which exceeds Mother Harvard's ingenuity in crafting cash-cow programming. With approximately 18,000 in regular degree programs, there are some 60,000 who come to Harvard for a few days, weeks or a year (Bok 2003, p. 83). If you throw a Wham-O super ball into a Washington watering hole near 17th and K streets or into a crowded metro station, you are certain to hit a significant number of people who proudly display a Harvard credential on their *curriculum vitae*. It is not a degree, but it may look like one. The one thing that can be guaranteed is that it was not cheap.

One of our recent system presidents touted the fact that he was selected to participate in Harvard Business School's Advanced Management Program. The "Advanced Management Program" ("Transforming Proven Leaders into Global Executives") is not an advanced management program in the sense of an executive MBA program. It is a short course of less than two months. In

2018, the times are 2 April–17 May and 9 September–25 October. The cost: a cool $80,000.

Johns Hopkins, the once-termed Göttingen of Baltimore, is also adept at developing subsidiary programming, though their quality is high; they were our principal "continuing ed" competitor when I was at Georgetown. The University of Maryland has long commanded a leadership position in international programming for the military.

There is nothing wrong with such programs, if there is a market and if there is bona fide value for dollar offered. I mention them to indicate that while students must choose between an education that helps provide a life or an education that provides a living, the institutions themselves must make such choices. To the extent that they choose the latter they are, more often than not, diminishing themselves.

That may seem harsh, but the objective search for what we might quaintly call the truth is a noble endeavor and it is respected as such. Bart Giamatti once said that part of the appeal of the university is that people can look to it, as a physical presence, and be comforted by the fact that somehow or other, to some degree or other, our questions can be answered there. To the degree that we are a simple provider of educational services, we are something of a lesser order.

Giamatti wrote of such university ideals in 1990 in a book entitled *A Free and Ordered Space: The Real World of the University*. Actually a collection of various pieces written for different occasions, it is a remarkable book, particularly for its time. It is exactly the kind of book that one might expect from a distinguished scholar and teacher, immersed in traditional ideals, who suddenly enters the world of "higher" administration and confronts the realities of the modern university.

He saw three trends that were particularly disturbing: *codification* (legalisms and the enactment of codes and rules); *corporatization* (which he opposed to "ecclesiastical" approaches); and the *splitting of the faculty from the administration* (1990, p. 39ff.). Since the nineteenth century the Yale statutes had described the senior members of the faculty as the "permanent officers" of the university (the president, of course, being an impermanent officer), a notion which he underscores strongly (1990, p. 43).

He is extremely vocal with regard to what he terms the "moral minority." He speaks of:

> the voices that for every cause—social, political, academic, sexual, religious, or ethnic—demand satisfaction, NOW. These voices are scornful of complexity, indifferent to ambiguity, contemptuous of competitive views or values. They are the enemies of give-and-take, of the open conversation that is the process of education. Hungering for Decree, for Absolutes, these voices are encouraged because they

are said to be 'idealistic'. What they are is precisely not idealistic,
but in their simplifying, reductionistic . . . they invariably and
inevitably create a counterreaction they cannot handle or resist. By
then, conversation, the conversation that is free and open, has ceased
(1990, pp. 44–45).

If the conversation is lost, he writes, "the place degenerates into a center of crisis management and competing special interests" (1990, p. 45). This is why universities do all that they can to mollify and distract; they are prepared to do anything to avoid such turbulence.

Actually writing in 1986, he assails those "who lust for the simple answers of doctrine or decree. They are on the Left and the Right. They are not confined to a single part of the society. They are terrorists of the mind" (1990, p. 90).

Part two of the book—"The Earthly Use of a Liberal Education" is particularly germane to our purposes. He says that liberal education at Yale follows Newman; it is disinterested and non-utilitarian; it pursues learning for learning's sake, the direct opposite of the "professional" (1990, p. 120). It is dedicated to "the proposition that growth in thought, and in the power to think, increases the pleasure, breadth, and value of life" (1990, p. 121).

Giamatti was, of course, a specialist in the Renaissance, though he acknowledged that the concepts of the "renaissance" and the "humanism" associated with it are nineteenth-century ones. "Humanist" was part of student slang in the fifteenth-sixteenth century Italian universities. *Umanista* indicated the professors and students of the Greek and Latin classics; the *studia humanitatis* (grammar, rhetoric, history, poetry and moral philosophy) came from the Romans. The method of the humanities was *philological*—the study, he states, of what was really *said*, not what we think was said (1990, pp. 132–33).

Then the kicker: "The humanities, in short, were elite culture but not the private property of the elite" (1990, p. 134). Higher education, in short, introduces all who are interested to the subjects of thought and the methods of thought of those who have enjoyed privilege in the past and who, to some degree, have held the rest of us in thrall. The opportunity to take their learning as our own, as the Enlightenment would have added, is the door to freedom.

He spells out the task of the Yale entering class in a clear and memorable fashion, urging them "to place at the center of your college education three efforts: to deepen a sense of history, so you will know who you are as human beings and as Americans; to develop your capacity to think analytically and creatively; and to hone the ability to express your thinking in speech and writing with logic, clarity, and grace" (1990, p. 136).

He sees the Humanities at the center of the university and words and texts as central to the Humanities. Language is "the bearer of tradition"; words "give first principles and last things"; etymology and eschatology clarify human life, the life of an individual and the life of a people (1990, pp. 138–39).

Writing in the late 70's he argues that "in the last decade incoherence has often been institutionalized," curricula permitted to decay, requirements being replaced by "guidelines." He confronts the Humanities faculty directly and says that they themselves did not believe in the Humanities; *they* participated in the gutting of the curricula, undermined the writing and foreign language requirements and helped contribute to grade inflation. They displaced themselves. They willed themselves to the periphery (1990, pp. 139–41).

At a conference I hosted in the late 1980s a speaker commented, disapprovingly, on the notion that the Humanities might be able to serve the function of integrating the rest of the curriculum. My friend and colleague, J. Paul Hunter spoke up immediately, saying that, in fact, the Humanities *do* integrate the rest of the curriculum, a point with which Giamatti would agree. He argued that literature departments should be like area studies programs, studying literature but also art, history, the history of science, philosophy and religion. Medieval Studies have often done just that and so too have Eighteenth-Century Studies.

Giamatti called for a reassertion of the values and the value of a liberal arts education in a time of rampant vocationalism and he asserted that the core of a liberal education is a *required curriculum* (1990, p. 216). He also said, echoing the eighteenth-century notion of the so-called concrete universal (seeking the general within the specific example) that we now, unfortunately, "rush to define issues only in terms of constituencies rather than in terms of commonalities" (1990, p. 218). "There is in America," he writes, "a retreat from structures of mutuality to strategies for special accommodation. . . . Any institution that responds only to localized, political pressure and not to broader claims of civic principle splits its polity and fragments itself" (1990, p. 218).

Again striking the democratic note, he cites Jefferson's hope for a "natural aristocracy of talent" rather than an "artificial aristocracy of birth" (1990, p. 240). This recalls the University of Michigan goal, articulated by its President James Angell (1871-1909)—"an uncommon education for the common man" (Duderstadt 2007, p. 15). I think of Buster Kilrain in Michael Shaara's *The Killer Angels*, saying that anyone who judges by the group is a peawit. "I'm Kilrain," he says, "and I God damn all gentlemen. I don't know who me father was and I don't give a damn. There's only one aristocracy, and that's right here__" (tapping his skull with a thick finger).

Giamatti then goes on (1990, pp. 272–73) to approvingly quote Edmund Burke. One might think, from my summary, that Bart Giamatti was that rarest of academics, an explicit, forthright, out-of-the-closet political conservative. He was not. He was a model *traditionalist*. In the course of *A Free and Ordered Space* he hammers Secretary William Bennett and he bludgeons E. D. Hirsch (and Bloom, of course) in a manner that can only be described as reflexive and, certainly in the case of Hirsch, a way that is ultimately quite misguided. It is as if Giamatti's political impulses have stirred him and he is forced to strike out at what appears to be a possible threat.

He surely did not share Bill Bennett's political orientation, but he would have been comfortable with Hirsch's and he should have been comfortable with Hirsch's desire to bring content-based structure to a disintegrated curriculum in order to prepare students for the world of intellect and citizens for the responsibilities of civic participation.

Academic traditionalism was once the rule and not the exception. I had a colleague at Wisconsin who was one of the towering scholars in American literature studies, an individual who was a great philologist in Giamatti's sense of the term. In one election cycle he was disappointed in the democrat candidates on offer and said, "Well, I suppose I'll just have to vote Socialist again."

The bottom line is that it was once quite possible to vote in any number of ways but still require and defend a traditional approach to education and to scholarship. The popular press and the partisan press are fond of writing stories about the predominantly liberal professoriate. They have identified the departments which are most "liberal" or "leftist" and those that are (barely, usually) moderate. This is seen to be a huge problem. In twenty-nine years of deaning I only encountered one specific case of a faculty member overtly politicizing a class. He was inveighing, in no uncertain terms, against the current president (of the country, not the university). This was not a faculty member in a Sociology or English department; he was in a department in the natural sciences. I did not have to counsel him (i.e. have what the British term an "interview without coffee"); his chairman did that immediately.

The principal problem in the modern university is not overt politicization. It is the institutionalization of an attitude that shuns traditionalism and sees the adherence to its standards, principles and values as somehow harsh and "judgmental."

The faculty senate at the University of Wisconsin in the 1970s was a contentious body in which arguments were made and answered and principles were debated with passion and point. Giamatti would have approved. Now, somehow, faculty accede; they cower. They seem to believe that to disagree in an important cause is somehow to wound and that the reduction of any possibility of hurt feelings trumps the need to adhere to and defend principle. In the process they "will themselves to the periphery," in Giamatti's powerful phrase, and they reduce the degree of public respect which they once commanded.

A half-century ago Richard Hofstadter confronted some of these issues and his arguments remain as compelling today as they were then. *Anti-Intellectualism in American Life* received the Pulitzer Prize in 1964 and it remains one of the foundational texts in American social science.

Hofstadter begins with a useful distinction. Intellect is not the same as intelligence. Intellect "is the critical, creative, and contemplative side of mind" (1963, p. 25), while intelligence is something quite different, something more mundane. "Intelligence" is the possession and utilization of "frozen ideas," i.e. more or less settled professional information. Professionals are essentially technicians. In our society, very often, they are "specialists," individuals with expertise that is exploitable for profit. When we educate for life we are cultivating intellect; when we train someone to earn a particular type of living we are cultivating intelligence.

Intellectuals are those whose interests are more tentative and more speculative. They exhibit a taste for the disinterested but passionate pursuit of knowledge; they seek the power to generalize from individual examples; they foster free speculation, fresh observation, creative novelty, and, sometimes, radical criticism (1963, p. 27).

The life of thought, Hofstadter writes, is "the highest form of human activity" (1963, p. 28), but he warns that those who live for ideas must be careful not to live for a single idea, lest they become "obsessive or grotesque." Zealotry, he says, is a possible defect of the breed but it is not of the essence of the breed (1963, p. 29).

He introduces Schiller's notion that "man is perfectly human only when he plays" and then uses "playfulness" as a counterpoise to the seriousness and earnestness that can become morbid. "Intellect may be taken as the healthy animal spirits of the mind, which comes into exercise when the surplus of mental energies is released from the tasks required for utility and mere survival" (1963, p. 30).

This brings to mind a book that we read as undergraduates, Josef Pieper's *Leisure: the Basis for Culture*. Hofstadter is "locating" the work (and play) of the intellectual in that time which is beyond the merely utilitarian and the need for self-preservation. It is reminiscent of Johnson's teasing Boswell over the relative absence of trees in Scotland, Johnson arguing that it takes a civilized intellect to plant something that he himself will never enjoy. It is a mark of both personal and cultural maturity to be able to see beyond the needs of the moment.

Americans, however, are not quite as comfortable as Johnson with such attitudes. They have been utilitarian from the outset. They are people who came here in order to consciously flee the past. They live in a country, Hofstadter says, without ruins and without monuments (1963, p. 238). Our contempt for the past combines with a tradition of self-help in personal advancement in which, he says, even religious faith can be seen primarily as an agency of practicality (1963, p. 238). This is exacerbated by such concepts as Jacksonian democracy which privileges the man of action over the man of intellect and celebrates native intuition and the power to act over an ethos of intellect regularly described by its detractors as *sterile* (1963, p. 160). The negative nuances of the metaphor are stark and shrill.

Since business is often stigmatized by intellectuals as the natural enemy of intellect, the two inevitably clash and intellect is regularly seen as potentially threatening to any and every fixed center of power (1963, p. 233). Coolidge famously stated that the business of America *is* business, so the implications are vast.

One of the obvious ways in which this attitude manifests itself is in our reward system: medical researchers make less money than orthopedic surgeons, though the latter may largely be skilled technicians. There are additional reasons for this, of course. When our life or mobility are on the line, we want the scalpel holder to be the most skilled at his trade and we pay the tradesman, in our hour of compelling need, more than the theoretician (the creator or discoverer of the now so-called "frozen ideas") who might have originally developed the procedure which the tradesman now performs.

This does not mean that Americans are unable to offer support and even acclaim to the efforts of intellect. In some cases it may be grudging, but at other times it is passionate. Hofstadter reports the story of Andrew Carnegie walking through the streets of New York and seeing the far richer Cornelius Vanderbilt on the opposite side of 5th Avenue. Carnegie turned to his companion and said, "I would not exchange his millions for my knowledge of Shakespeare" (1963, p. 259).

Vanderbilt, it is said, only read a single book in his life—*Pilgrim's Progress*—but it is reported that he once said to his minister, "I'd give a million dollars today, Doctor, if I had your education" (1963, p. 258).

Part of the culture of anti-intellectualism is traceable directly to educational theory. Hofstadter discusses "progressive education," e.g., and notes that while its core had principles that were both sound and important, its advocates included extremists whose views proved ultimately to be very detrimental. Reducing authoritarianism in the classroom is a good thing (to the extent that it is an important reality there) and so too is enlivening the child's interests, but one cannot dissolve the entire curriculum in the process and believe that what might work in a single, very special, experimental situation can be totally generalized to the rest of American education (1963, p. 360).

Dewey is leaned on heavily within these movements, but Dewey is an elusive writer whose ultimate goals were never quite spelled out. His view of the child is romantic and even primitivist. He surrounds the figure of the child with "the penumbra of sanctity" (1963, p. 363). Dewey refers respectfully to Rousseau and characteristically opposes the "natural child" to the "artificial society." Hofstadter cites Wordsworth's notion of the child "trailing clouds of glory," an idea to which I will return later.

One must, of course, pause and think very carefully before one introduces the ideas of Rousseau into a real-world system of education. Rousseau said, after all, that *reading* is the curse of childhood (1963, p. 369*n*). While progressive education was clear on its techniques it was vague with regard to its goals. Thus, leveraging some of these ideas with regard to curricular systems proved devastating. Dewey's ideas were utopian but he never quite tells us of what that utopia should consist. He saw the past as only interesting, Hofstadter says, in its direct bearing on the present and he saw culture as "an ornament and solace; a refuge and an asylum." It thus, Hofstadter writes, "loses its capacity to be a transforming agent, one that can improve the present and create the future" (1963, p. 388).

Dewey believed that the child should be the center of the school and today we frequently hear the phrase "a student-centered institution." It sounds attractive. Obviously, we don't want institutions in which students will always reside on the periphery, but Dewey believed that the students' interests and impulses should diminish both the authority of the teacher and the weight of the traditional curriculum. He saw this resulting in social reform (1963, p. 363), but one must be very careful in displacing authority lest there be nothing remaining in its place.

The notion of a passionately curious student who wishes to move beyond classroom drills is an attractive one. Throwing off constraints and following ideas wherever they might lead is part and parcel of *intellect*ual behavior, as Hofstadter describes it and this may occasionally work, for example for the better students among the miniscule percentage of American citizens choosing electives in Eliot's Harvard, but what if the student displaces the faculty and the curriculum in order to begin a four-year pursuit of the ultimate keg party? (They did so, of course, in earlier times and also introduced snakes, fireworks and other substances into faculty offices. Binge drinking is not a new phenomenon; nor is casual sex.)

While Hofstadter has significant problems with progressive education, the "life adjustment" movement of the 30's and 40's is his most important quarry. Its theorists looked across the landscape of American education and came to a disquieting conclusion. Twenty percent of high school students would go to college, while another 20 percent would enter skilled trades. The remaining 60 percent should be given education for "life adjustment." This represented, in effect, the writing off of 60 percent of American students as, in some important way, uneducable. Instead of receiving "knowledge" they would be taught "how to live," in very basic senses of that phrase (1963, p. 344).

Given their numbers—this was the majority of students—the potential results for the overall curriculum could be cataclysmic. The life adjustment theorists dodged this issue by arguing that there were, in fact, *no such things as transferable skills*. Hence there was no reason to learn mathematics or Latin because they did not actually refine and/or extend mental capacity. They enabled you to learn more mathematics or more Latin, but what their study finally represented was little more than the acquisition of isolated, useless facts.

Thus the life adjustment theorists saw the traditional curriculum as an impediment to the training of the masses. By the 1940s and 1950s, Hofstadter writes, "the demands of the life-adjustment educators for the destruction of the academic curriculum had become practically insatiable" (1963, p. 341).

The university faculties essentially did nothing to prevent it because they held educational theorists to be beneath contempt and would not waste their time challenging them. I remember my freshman English teacher (trained at Chicago in the mid 1940s) being asked a question about high school educators and dismissing the question as well as the high school teachers, referring to them as "those drabs."

I recall a similar experience with a distinguished friend and colleague of mine whose field is sociolinguistics. I asked her about some notions that enjoyed great currency in some of the faddish Humanities programs in the late 1980s and 1990s, notions that I found questionable. She said that the ideas in question were ridiculous. I responded that it would be very nice if she would say so publicly because if I did I would be assaulted as a reactionary. She said that she and her serious colleagues would not do so because the ideas were so silly that attacking them would represent a waste of their time.

Hofstadter, at Columbia, was in the very belly of the beast, with Columbia Teachers College just a few steps away. He repeats the quip that 120th Street was the widest street in the world, since the separation between the Teachers College and the rest of the university "became symbolic of a larger cleavage in the structure of American education. Professional educators were left to develop their ideas without being subjected to the intellectual discipline that might have come out of a dialogue with university scholars" (1963, p. 338).

At West Point we used Irwin Edman's *Arts and the Man* in our advanced composition class. Edman, a philosopher and prominent member of the Columbia faculty, once said that education is the process of casting false pearls before real swine. A rather odd thing to say, I was told that this was Edman's response to a plan by Teachers College to recreate the Columbia College curriculum in their own image, a phenomenon that often occurs in professional schools, where students seek something more applied than theoretical (or, in some cases, find the material as taught in the college of arts and science to be too difficult).

The results of the life adjustment movement, which Hofstadter deplores, are stark. In 1910 49 percent of high school students studied Latin, in 1949 a mere 7.8 percent. The modern foreign language numbers: from 84.1 percent to 22 percent; algebra, from 56.9 percent to 26.8 percent and geometry from 30.9 percent to 12.8 percent. Science enrollments (excluding so-called "general science") plummeted from 81.7 percent to 33.3 percent (1963, p. 341).

Progressive education and the life adjustment movement may not be in the ascendant or even on the radar screen today, but that does not mean that they have disappeared. They reappear in the student service professionals' pleas for "holistic education" and in their quiet desire to see their activities supplant those of the faculty; they exist in the advocacy for "student-centeredness," a euphemism for soft standards, student "success" at any cost and the depreciation of serious learning; they still live and move and have their being in the college of education's privileging of "skills" over content and pedagogy over substance. They exist in the encouragement of student "expression" that may or may not be informed by knowledge and in the ongoing replacement of liberal education by vocational training and utilitarian programming which trades in didactic instruction and repackages tired ideas with shiny new acronyms and catchphrases.

Hofstadter positions this succession of efforts within a far wider context, seeing it as evidence of the continuing power of *Romanticism*, and he draws a clear line between the attitudes embedded in it and the practices of the eighteenth century. As he puts it, great intellectuals up to and through the Enlightenment sought "the conjunction of knowledge and power and accepted its risks without optimism or naïveté. They hoped that knowledge would in fact be broadened by a conjunction with power, just as power might be civilized by its connection with knowledge " (1963, p. 427).

In short, the eighteenth century was comfortable with seeing the Treaty of Utrecht negotiated by a poet, Matthew Prior. Though he disagreed with some of its terms it became known as "Matt's Peace." Similarly, Goethe might play an important public role in Weimar while also studying theories of light, comparative anatomy, and working as a writer who produced one of the world's masterpieces and—in *Werther*—one of the most influential cultural works of its generation.

This is, of course, the ethos of our founding fathers. Society in the eighteenth century was unspecialized, while today, Hofstadter writes, "knowledge and power are differentiated functions" (1963, p. 428). Power now seeks expertise, not intellection. "The truth is," Hofstadter concludes, "that much of American education aims, simply and brazenly, to turn out experts who are not intellectuals or men of culture at all . . ." (1963, p. 428).

Again, however, there is reason to resist despair. Jonathan Cole's recent, weighty book, *The Great American University: Its Rise to Preeminence, Its Indispensable National Role: Why it Must be Protected* (2009) reminds us of some important facts. The highly specialized and seemingly fragmented work of American institutions of higher education has nevertheless resulted in a series of research accomplishments that have saved and enhanced lives in innumerable ways.

Since the 1930s Americans have won approximately 60 percent of the Nobel Prizes. Germany, the research university exemplar, has still not recovered from the rise and depredations of Hitler. Once the finest system in the world in certain regards, Cole argues that there is not one German university in the top fifty today (2009, p. 4). The preeminence of American universities in research and graduate education, however, does not solve the problems of undergraduate education. It actually draws attention away from it, since universities are measured by their top, German, portion more than by their foundational, English, undergraduate portion.

Cole identifies what he considers the elements of a great university (2009, pp. 110–16). Most research-institution faculty would agree with him:

1. faculty research productivity
2. the quality and impact of research
3. grant/contract support
4. honorific awards
5. access to highly qualified students
6. excellence in teaching
7. physical facilities and advanced information technology
8. large endowments and plentiful resources
9. large academic departments
10. free inquiry and academic freedom
11. location
12. contributions to the public good
13. excellent leadership

These are, almost exclusively, the hallmarks of a great graduate school. The focus is narrowed even further as he (again, I think, quite truthfully) homes in on the select institutions which offer the highest levels of quality. While we have (in 2007) approximately 260 research universities, only some 125 of them (Cole's number) contribute in meaningful ways to the growth of knowledge (2009, p. 6). He notes that roughly 10–15 percent of the people in any academic field account for more than 50 percent of all scholarly literature in that field (2009, p. 177) and he cites Nobel laureate Julius Axelrod's estimate that 99 percent of the discoveries have been made by 1 percent of the scientists (2009, pp. 177–78). Hence the so-called "arms race" for the top scholars and scientists.

Research in the physical and life sciences is not "applied" or "vocational"; it is what Cole terms "disinterested" and what others usually call "basic research," but it does, nevertheless, eventually have applications. Graduate training in those fields is not "vocational" per se, but many graduate students enter those fields with plans to work in industry rather than the academy.

The less-vocational (purer?) Humanities do things that are quite different, things that were once at the center of core curricula and general education/liberal arts studies. And there, Cole correctly sees problems (he is a sociologist, by training and—in administrative experience—the former provost and dean of faculties at Columbia).

He sees the changes in the Humanities and social sciences commonly associated with the spirit and impulses of the 1960s as ultimately a questioning of the Enlightenment and its rational models of thought (2009, pp. 151–52) and says that the ultimate upshot of high theory, counterculturalism, and race/class/gender thematics was a devaluation of the Humanities themselves. As this came at a time of increasing utilitarianism within our society and within our universities, the self-devaluation of the Humanities ("willing themselves to the periphery" in Giamatti's phrase) contributed to the problem rather than offering an alternative or possible solution to it (2009, p. 155). This all paralleled a corresponding, national reduction of financial support for the Humanities as the late John D'Arms—classicist, sometime graduate dean at Michigan and President of the American Council of Learned Societies—demonstrated in sad detail (in Kernan 1997).

As Humanities faculty questioned their own fields and often found them wanting, undergraduate students lost interest in them. Enjoying 18 percent of the majors in the late 1960s, by 2004 they had dwindled to 8 percent, a decline of nearly 60 percent. In fairness, many would argue that the decline in Humanities enrollments were a side effect of the growing vocationalism in higher education. That is doubtless true, to some degree, but a field that announces that its object of study has been the work of dead white males seeking cultural hegemony and, in the process, brutalizing women and minorities or that linguistic and, *a fortiori*, literary "meaning" is a will-of-the-wisp and always unattainable (what Hirsch termed "cognitive atheism") is not nearly as inviting to hopeful, idealistic and curious eighteen year-olds as the study of "great books," the "great tradition" or the examination of "the best that has been thought and said."

The 60s attack on the Enlightenment, as Cole, correctly, I think, sees it is actually a reassertion of some of the core beliefs of Romanticism, as we have seen with Hofstadter. While I will return to that issue later, I must comment here on the irony of the devaluation of the liberal arts in general, the Humanities in particular. While these fields help us to fashion a life they also facilitate the making of a living.

Remembering that many nurses and teachers leave their positions after a very small number of years, Bok mentions the fact (2008, p. 290) that approximately one-half of young lawyers leave their firms within three years. Many go to other firms, of course, but many utilize their law degree as a generalized credential and do a host of other things than practicing law. Many, of course, do not even take the bar exam.

In the first ten years of a career, Bok argues (2008, p. 295), vocational majors have the jump on graduates in the liberal arts and sciences, but after ten years the advantage goes to the liberally-educated students, in part, Bok says, because of their communication skills, their human relations skills, their creativity and their "big picture thinking." Among top management, he writes, neither has a clear advantage, but as Hacker and Dreifus (2010, pp. 104–5) point out, the CEO of Costco is a Sociology major, the CEO of Goldman Sachs an English major, the CEO's of IBM, Procter & Gamble, Union Pacific and Wyeth all History majors.

A 2014 report from the AAC&U and NCHEMS (the National Center for Higher Education Management Systems) notes that graduates with degrees in the Humanities achieved higher salaries in their peak earnings years (56–60) than graduates with professional or pre-professional degrees, who had initially enjoyed higher salaries. Allie Grasgreen comments that "employers consistently say they want to hire people who have a broad knowledge base and can work [collaboratively], debate, communicate and think critically . . . all skills that liberal arts programs aggressively . . . strive to teach" ("News," 2014, p. 57).

A recent study by the Social Science Research Council (Marklein 2012) looked at 925 takers of the CLA, the test that forms the basis for the Arum/Roksa study, and found that those possessing the skills most associated with a liberal arts education (thinking critically, reasoning analytically and writing effectively) were three times less likely to be unemployed than those who did not develop those skills to a comparable extent, half as likely to be living with their parents and far less likely to have amassed credit card debt (2012, p. 1).

This is perhaps a reflection of Bart Giamatti's frequent comment that a liberal arts education prepares its students to address and solve *the problems that have not yet arisen* or, indeed, *not yet even been imagined*. Churchill, as always, may have said it best when he stated that, "The first duty of a university is to teach wisdom, not a trade; character, not technicalities. We want a lot of engineers in the modern world, but we do not want a world of engineers." When we lament the results of a country run by lawyers, we need to remind ourselves that the Soviet Union was run, if that is the most precise word, by engineers.

My preference for education for life rather than for a living begins with a heartfelt love of the life of the *intellect* and its many blessings, but it ends with an unavoidably pragmatic argument based on the nature of contemporary life. If each of our students is indeed going to have *three or more careers* and many, many more jobs, why would we ever encourage the children that we love to spend their undergraduate years preparing for only one?

I would make exceptions for those who need specific training and are dead certain that they want to spend their lives doing nothing else—physical therapists, for example. Tendonitis is likely to always be with us and those who can help to cure it will be well- if not generously, compensated.

I remember my classmates at Notre Dame, however, who studied aeronautical engineering; the field was changing so fast that many decided to transfer to electrical engineering so that their educations would not quickly become obsolete. In graduate school at Illinois I had a neighbor in aeronautical engineering who had a standard invitation from Boeing to fly to Seattle, at any time, at his convenience, to work on a specific problem. He told me that a few years after the receipt of his Ph.D. he was likely to be obsolete and would have to teach general principles rather than solve emerging problems. Aircraft continue to change, shoulders, wrists and elbows not so much.

One of my college classmates, then both a pre-med and an English major, agonized over the issue. He said that one of his science instructors had told him that if he was stricken with disease, lying on a gurney and a masked man was standing above him with a scalpel in his hand he wouldn't care if the individual was capable of quoting Shakespeare. Fair enough, but what does the physician do when he is alone with his thoughts, reflecting on his life and experience and seeking meaning and purpose? My classmate, now a distinguished Boston cardiologist, reads Thomas Hardy.

Chapter Five

The New School of Mortuary Science

Alan Turing's colossus computer at Bletchley Park filled the better part of an entire room, with tape rolls running like segments of a complex roller coaster. The ENIAC computer, a second generation computer from the 1940s, occupied 1,800 square feet of floor space and had less power than a MacBook Pro. The first digital computer built and owned entirely by an educational institution was the ILLIAC I (1951–) at the University of Illinois. It weighed in at five tons and included 2,800 vacuum tubes.

I entered this world at West Point in 1968, when I took a (very elementary) computer science course. The computer system was a UNIVAC; it filled a large room. Ten years later, at the University of Wisconsin, I visited the university's Physical Sciences Laboratory, a facility that fabricates equipment and instrumentation for university research. The engineers showed us the newest development in computer chips—a piece the size of a stick of Dentyne gum that had more memory than the entire UNIVAC system at West Point.

While IT systems are enhanced and improved at amazing speeds (Gordon Moore's law: the capacity of computer chips doubles every two years [Cole 2009, pp. 176–77]), some *timeless* learning persists, viz. the first lesson inculcated in my computer class, a lesson that would apply as well to an Assyrian stone carver or a director of a medieval scriptorium—garbage in, garbage out. And the second: when you begin any task and have multiple instruments at your disposal, be sure to use the instrument(s) most appropriate to the task.

In universities we operate on both planes—that of science and engineering, with their ever-advancing development of cumulative knowledge, and the realm of non-cumulative knowledge, principally in the Humanities, where our knowledge may become richer and broader and deeper, but whose ultimate value or ultimate claims to truth cannot be inferred by simply looking at their publication date.

We also deal in what are sometimes misidentified as the "practical" and the "impractical." The practical/vocational are actually, in my judgment, ultimately impractical, while the impractical/liberal are ultimately the most practical of all. They enhance our lives as well as augment our income. When Carnegie thought about the knowledge that he prized most, it was his knowledge of Shakespeare. (And Carnegie was not an impractical man. Baker Hall at Carnegie-Mellon was so constructed that it could be converted to an assembly line, should the college project fail.)

As we conjure with multiple intellectual realms, we build curricula and structure programs. Some program planners, however, are tempted to focus upon certain elements of learning and intellectual processes to the exclusion of others. For-profits, for example, stress efficiency and utility.

"Traditional colleges with traditional classrooms operate within very expensive constraints, while for-profits operate online courses serving thousands of students." So goes the maxim, but it is not true. The officials of such for-profits as Capella, Kaplan and the University of Phoenix report that their average enrollment per course ranges from nine to eighteen students (Alva 2010, p. 2). In 2010 the University of Phoenix enrolled 470,800 students, utilizing 33,000 faculty, a (quite favorable) student-faculty ratio of just over 14 to 1 (Alva 2010, p. 2). The "efficiency" comes in other ways and that efficiency must provide for a sizeable investment in marketing and a sizeable yield in profit.

In 2009 the University of Phoenix enrolled more students than the University of California system—exceeding them by 150,000 (Christensen and Eyring 2011, p. 8). Their graduation rate was less than 27 percent. The for-profits' characteristic claim is that they serve an at-risk population in an impressive way (DeMillo 2011, p. 222), the community colleges' graduation rate being 20 percent (though the latter institutions have quite different missions and many students enroll in them for single courses or small groups of courses).

The for-profits are also more expensive than many public colleges; tuition of $15,000+ a year is a good average number; (current [2017–18] Berkeley tuition: $13,928; Mizzou tuition: $11,008; Ohio State tuition: $10,591). Their students are, correspondingly, financially needy. The for-profits depend on a disproportionately large share of federally-backed student aid for as much as 85 percent of their total revenue (DeMillo 2011, pp. 221–22).

Their leaders have exhibited considerable honesty in describing their operations. James Traub, a former president of the University of Phoenix, has said that "the people who are our students don't want an education. They want what the education provides for them—better jobs, moving up in their careers" (Donoghue 2008, p. 136).

The University of Phoenix's founder, John Sperling, is even more honest about his institution's purposes. The University of Phoenix, he states, "is a corporation, not a social entity. Coming here is not a rite of passage. We are not trying to develop . . . [students'] value systems or go in for that 'expand their minds' bullshit" (Washburn 2005, p. x). Take that, Sandy Astin. No statistics are offered on whether the University of Phoenix's students meditate with any degree of frequency.

Update: since beginning this study the University of Phoenix's enrollments (and stock) have plummeted, falling to 142,500 students by 2016. This can be attributed in part to the pressure brought on the for-profits by the Obama administration. For-profit education remains a large activity; in certain parts of the world it represents 70 percent of the education industry.

From a commercial point of view, one has to applaud or at least understand their efforts. The at-risk population is expanding. If business is about market share, the for-profits have seized upon a growing population and attracted their/federal funds—including the funds of the 73 percent who fail to graduate.

Another way of thinking about this is to say that many of those at risk should not be going to college in the first place and they should not be lured there by for-profit corporations. In fairness, however, one must remember the conscientious, hard-working, adult students, who seek to obtain a credential which will lead to a job or a promotion. For-profits offer them accessibility and ease of scheduling. They can, *if they succeed*, support their families at a higher level and give their children expanded opportunities.

These are generally not the students who seek a diploma so that they can drive a BMW rather than a KIA. These are students like my father, who supported himself by doing the unpleasant jobs in a Newport, KY butcher shop so that he could attend night law school at the Cincinnati YMCA (now the Salmon P. Chase College of Law at Northern Kentucky University). His classes were taught by practicing attorneys and judges. It was an all meat-and-potatoes law school and the pass rate on the bar examination was extraordinarily high. It also required "pre-law" courses, i.e., general education. He eventually became a partner in a firm whose original partners included the father of supreme court justice, Potter Stewart. As a result of his labors I was able to attend college in the daytime.

I am thus an ardent supporter of bootstrap education, but it should be at fair cost and with the chance of largely-positive results. And I would not be honest if I did not register some concern with regard to an enormous institution of putative higher education that has no patience with that "expand their minds" bullshit.

Within the not-for-profit modern university we offer a multiplicity of programs and the nature of those programs is very important, not just because of the opportunities that they offer, the traps, snares and illusions that they might include or the extremely important courses of study and research that they might embody, but because the choice of programming, the sustaining of programming and the abandonment of programming speak to the core values and purposes of the institution. What we do is what we are and what we start or stop doing indicates an alteration—sometimes a dramatic one—in who and what we believe that we should be.

Jary Pelikan once commented on the nature of programming and the danger of creating programs that distorted the core purposes of the university. He said that every time we consider approving a new program we should imagine ourselves as the founders of the university, in his case, Yale. We should assume that nothing yet exists, today, and that we are deciding what will exist, tomorrow. The question, then, is should this program be part of what would eventually be called Yale University?

While Jary did not enumerate the programs that should be at the heart of the college and then the university, he was clear on one point. "One thing we would never create is a School of Mortuary Science." For the curious, thirty states have such programs and we certainly need morticians and funeral directors. The question is, should the university be the locus for their training? And if it is and if such programming becomes widespread, what kind of university will result?

I was once asked to consult at a religious institution which sought to operate a traditional college and graduate school. Its most distinguished programs were in its school of theology but its essential operation was a cash-cow, multiple-degree program in aviation. At the very center of the campus was a landing strip, with a considerable volume of traffic. Needless to say, such programming involves messaging that makes traditional programming more difficult to sustain and enhance.

One of the results of this condition is that elite colleges and universities make the approval of new programming a complex and difficult process, involving the drafting of elaborate planning documents, the seeking of approval at multiple levels, including that of the institution's board of trustees. That is as it should be. You should think and plan very carefully before you undertake steps that will lead to the shaping of students' minds, hearts and lives. The corollary is the great danger involved when "entrepreneurial" institutions reduce the layers of planning and approval and, in effect, allow corporatists to construct programming that appears to offer what represents a (potentially momentary) market opportunity.

Shortly after I arrived at Georgetown we suspended nine graduate programs. This was not an easy thing to do; one of the corollaries to making the approval process difficult is the perceived "impossibility" of ever instituting a "closing" process.

My predecessor had positioned the graduate school as a supplier of cash rather than a sustainer of standards and the programming had become over-extended. At the same time, some of the doctoral programs had diminished in size to the point of near nonexistence. One modern foreign language and literature program had but two-thirds of *one* full-time-equivalent student actually enrolled.

When the review was completed no faculty positions were lost. Students within suspended programs were allowed to complete them and their financial aid was sustained until they graduated. A small number of faculty were asked to redirect their efforts to undergraduate instruction. With resources eventually reallocated, and additional resources provided (including the costs of reducing teaching loads), a number of our core programs improved significantly in the next round of national research council program rankings.

The key decisions turned on mission and purpose. Like many institutions with foreign affairs components, Georgetown had established a series of area studies programs, programs that have faded nationwide as the foundations which earlier encouraged them have moved on to other priorities. We suspended admission to our PhD program in Russian Area Studies, e.g., and concentrated instead on our master's program there and the doctoral programs within the contributing disciplines.

The decision came down to the determination that our doctoral programs should be academic programs that would lead to academic jobs, while our professional programs would lead to jobs in such entities as the Washington establishment and international nonprofits.

The decision turned on the judgment that academic hiring was done through departments and that departments were most likely to select individuals trained within their respective disciplines. Economists hired economists; historians hired historians; neither hired regional studies specialists. In some ways this is an academic truism and there is always a certain stigma attached to something like "American Studies" as opposed to the study of American history within History departments or the study of American literature within English departments.

The primacy of the disciplines over multidisciplinary programs is an academic fact of life as well as an academic principle. The clientele for an area studies program is different from that for a discipline-based/housed program. In the Russian Area Studies master's program, e.g., students would study history, economics, political science, language, literature, religion, culture and demography. They would become regional specialists rather than disciplinary scholars. In a (pre-1989) RASP economics course they would discuss *Soviet* economics; in the Economics department they would discuss *centrally-managed* economies with the Soviet Union as one example among many.

The contributing faculty were largely the same people, with the addition of an occasional adjunct. Still, the line is drawn between programs preparing scholars and programs preparing students for a multiplicity of jobs. Large programs with industrial connections make these separations clear. At USC, for example, there are programs for individuals who wish to make movies, programs for individuals who want to produce movies, individuals who want to work in related industries (cable television, e.g.) and individuals who want to study cinema, write books about it and teach in university film schools or film departments.

It is always to the advantage of every university to have one or more schools that are particularly distinguished. Rochester has the Eastman School of Music and Penn the Wharton School. These kinds of schools have very deep applicant pools which result in higher student profiles overall. They also bring to the university a large group of talented individuals who may then decide to major in other fields. A large number of the prominent Missouri graduates first came there as students in the School of Journalism.

At Georgetown the journalism "program" consisted of one adjunct professor; at Mizzou the J-school occupies multiple buildings, publishes a daily newspaper (separate from the "student newspaper"), operates a research institute and contributes to television and radio programming. It has awarded doctoral degrees since 1934.

As my administrative colleague Brian Foster is fond of saying, it is important to the AAU that a member institution contain a distinguished school (or more), but that school must be in an area respected by the AAU (in other words, an area that speaks to a traditional, established academic discipline). Journalism, unfortunately, falls on the cusp in that regard; we are more respected within the AAU for our extensive programs in the plant sciences or for our possession of the largest university-based research reactor.

In some ways the aggressive development of nontraditional programs marks an institution as one that is less serious than institutions which retain and enhance their traditional, foundational programs. When Oxford and Cambridge flirted with the establishment of (and actually did establish) schools of business it was a matter of international interest and, truly, international importance. (Both institutions' business programs offer doctoral degrees to train future college professors.) The line between academic and professional programming is a decisive one and the side of the line that dominates is an indicator of the fundamental nature of the institution.

I would be less than candid if I did not acknowledge that one of the reasons that we tightened and re-focused our graduate programming at Georgetown was to underscore the fact that we saw the graduate school as a sustainer of quality and standards (that offered some, solid professional programs) rather than a simple supplier of cash to the general purpose revenue coffers. We wanted to stress our academic core—the departments of Government, Economics, History, Linguistics, Spanish and Philosophy.

At the time there were even some suggestions that we abandon the arts and sciences altogether and become, as one faculty member put it, "the Caltech of the human sciences." That was not to be, since the undergraduate college (with soaring admission statistics) depended on its pre-medical students to raise its SAT averages, the pre-medical students depending on the existence of a core of science departments. The application/admission rates drove the university's bond ratings and enabled them to deal with the continual revenue shortfalls from the university medical center (which Fr. Tim Healy had wished to close).

Within the graduate school we had also wished to highlight our "academic" dimensions and differentiate ourselves from some of the financial temptations of Washington to which other District schools had sometimes succumbed. Metropolitan Washington is the destination of a highly-educated and ambitious populace. Once there, however, this populace settles in in an array of federal occupations whose health and retirement plans and, yes, whose salaries, exert a nearly irresistible centripetal force.

We capitalized on this by enhancing the country's largest liberal studies program. It was designed for "professionals who wished to read Plato" and there were many such professionals in the metropolitan area. The master's program was explicit in its mission: it would *not* offer a vocational credential and it would *not* lead to some new job. It offered study for the sheer love of study. Period. Eventually Dean Michael Collins and his colleagues developed an undergraduate track for serious adults with little prior college-level work. The general-education curriculum developed was rigorously historical, beginning in antiquity and coming up to the contemporary period over a course of two years, including summers. The students studied history, literature, art, political theory, philosophy and the history of science in what was the most integrated and coherent undergraduate general education sequence on the campus.

Other institutions, on the other hand, had often constructed programming that spoke directly to the local marketplace. They also sought to offer programming for specific government agencies at the same time that they hoped to secure research contracts from those agencies. The Georgetown faculty had little interest in such programs or "research" since they tended to be very applied and, often, pedestrian. We did not entirely ignore the District's opportunities and we did develop locationally-appropriate programs, the most prominent of which was a program in public policy which had remained dormant for years, suspended between the Government and Economics departments and attracting a small handful of students. It flourished instantly and should continue to do so; it received a $100,000,000 gift in 2013 that has turned the "program" into a school.

It will seem incredible to most readers that Georgetown did not have a sophisticated and heavily-enrolled graduate public policy program until the 1980s, but that is the case. While programming should emerge from faculty expertise and planning processes should begin there, it is the case that an occasional top-down approach is necessary. The operative word is *occasion-*

al and the operational planning must have the support of the faculty and the curricular planning be the prerogative of the faculty. Most important, all such planning and programming should be conducted with a careful eye on the university's academic core. The alternative is a so-called "donut university" in which the academic core is not as strong as one might wish, but the periphery is populated by a multiplicity of programs which attract the students.

While I do not wish to cast aspersions I feel that it is necessary to provide an example. The George Washington University currently offers over 200 degree and certificate programs, among them certificates in Campaign Strategy, Exhibit Design, Grief, Loss and Life Transitions and Sustainable Landscapes. It offers a master of science degree in Crime Scene Investigation.

There is the opportunity there to pursue an MPS (master of professional studies) in Publishing as well as an MPS in Law Firm Management. Another opportunity is the MSPM, a master of science program in Project Management. My personal favorite is their MTA program—a master's in Tourism Administration. Within the MTA one can concentrate on Event and Meeting Management, Hospitality Management, Sport Management and Sustainable Tourism Management with other individualized concentrations in Ecotourism and Cultural Heritage Tourism.

The proliferation of programs geared directly to the marketplace alters the university at its core. It further corporatizes the university and it inevitably distracts it from foundational concerns. A university is, in part, an administrative entity, and that entity's works and days are driven by the nature of its activities. To the extent that the university participates in a multiplicity of nontraditional programs it becomes a different university. Its resources are invested in different ways. It presents itself in different ways, organizes itself in different ways, and, most important, prioritizes its activities in different ways. If the focus of the university begins to fall on the transitory, it begins to embody and, ultimately, endorse a very different system of values. To the extent that such values displace traditional academic enterprises and principles, the university has become transformed into an emporium rather than a place of serious study, a marketplace or cafeteria rather than an entity designed to enable its students to know, to think, to position themselves within history and within society and to communicate with effectiveness and authority. It has become a service provider and a jobs bureau.

Update: Georgetown has recently acquired space on Massachusetts Avenue and is now offering a host of degree programs in such areas as real estate, sports industry management and hospitality management. Rather than differentiating themselves from the George Washington University they are now imitating it.

Arizona State University now terms itself "the New American University," part of the motto entailing the welcoming of a wealth of students rather than a select few, with programming that looks more to the future and the futuristic than to the traditional or the twelfth century.

ASU's president, Michael Crow, is a very nice man and a very intelligent man. He ran Columbia's research enterprise with exceptional skill; he is a forward-looking individual, driven to enhance Arizona State and make it an innovative, great university. I do not, however, agree with how he is attempting to do that, because I fear that his strategy is unsustainable and, ultimately, deleterious, not because the programs and structures which he has installed are of poor quality, but because I believe that dramatic proliferation redefines an institution in ways that are hazardous to core enterprises. With Giamatti, for example, I would rather see first-generation college students embracing the learning that was once the province of the elite. I would rather see them studying philosophy and chemistry rather than pursuing a vocational course with a temporal horizon.

At any rate, my concerns with regard to Arizona State are tempered by its utter uniqueness. Dartmouth is not going to become Arizona State; Lawrence and Carleton are not going to become Arizona State and, most noticeably, the University of Arizona is not going to become Arizona State.

Arizona State in its new incarnation has become possible because of an exploding growth in enrollments. Tens of thousands of new students appear at the university gates. Faculty who have long yearned for an activity that was less traditional or an activity that is "forward looking" in a way that squares with their individual interests and research agendas can be recruited to populate new institutes, centers, departments or, indeed, new schools. The revenue from the waves of new students provides the resources. *There is no need to suffer through the bloody process of redirecting funds from old programs to new.* The resources are available and no previously-existing oxen are gored. There are preexisting faculty delighted at the prospect of participating in and/or leading the new entities. The money is there; the cheerleaders are there and the shiny prospect of becoming "the New American University" raises spirits without frightening the traditionalists.

Without the thousands of new students, such a process is both financially impossible and politically unimaginable. In the face of looming demographic declines and the everyday reality of reduced support, most public universities are doing their best to simply sustain what already exists at a high enough level of quality to maintain public and collegial respect.

At Arizona State some of the "new" organizations represent reorganization. The College of Health Solutions, e.g., contains a number of traditional, previously-existing entities. There is also, however, a School of Sustainability and a College of Public Service & Community Solutions.

The latter includes a School of Criminology and Criminal Justice, a School of Public Affairs, a School of Social Work, a School of Community Resources & Development and ten+ centers, including the Center for Social Cohesion, the Center for Urban Innovation and the Center for Sustainable Tourism.

The Arts and Sciences entity looks quite different from cognate units at other institutions. It contains a College of Liberal Arts and Sciences, a New College of Interdisciplinary Arts and Sciences and a College of Letters and Sciences. It includes a School of Earth and Space Exploration (the latter interesting in that NASA has been pared back and Caltech is unlikely to relinquish its Jet Propulsion Laboratory). It includes a School of Human Evolution and Social Change, a School of International Letters and Cultures, a School of Social and Family Dynamics and a School of Social Transformation. Some of this, again, is nomenclature, but the proliferation is noteworthy. The only school within most Colleges of Arts and Sciences is the School of Music and, occasionally, a school of the Arts, Drama or Dance.

Proliferation is expensive. Proliferation requires infrastructure and it incurs administrative costs. Administrative costs do not add faculty and they do not increase student financial aid. Proliferation sometimes results in curiosities. Arizona State University does include a *Department* of English, for example, but it also includes a *School* of Transborder Studies. The *Department* of English has approximately 270 faculty, including graduate teaching assistants; the *School* of Transborder Studies has eleven core faculty, several dozen affiliated faculty and nine administrators.

I am not arguing against change or innovation, but much that appears to represent change in American higher education is actually further corporatization and proliferation, the changing of slogans and nomenclature. The instincts behind that change are often survival-related and we understand that. Meanwhile, the institutions which are not at risk of dissolution, focus on *brand* rather than *signature*.

"Signature" speaks to content. An institution's required curriculum indicates the breadth, depth and precise nature of the learning that one can expect its graduates to possess. In the past, "signature" also spoke to specific professors and specific courses. Harvard students took Bate's course on the Age of Johnson and many returned, as established academics, to audit it years later. Northwestern students took the courses of Bergen Evans. In the early American university, the institution's president taught the college's capstone course. In a later generation, Georgetown students took (and take) Bruce Douglass's courses in political theory. At Notre Dame students took the literature courses of Frank O'Malley.

One of Bruce Douglass's colleagues once described him as the "kind of person around whom you build a college." In other contexts, particular teachers taught thousands of students in the course of their careers, often in required, general-education classes. They became the subject of alumni/ae reminiscences—some loving, some, of course, humorous. On a more pragmatic note, the individuals best remembered by middle-aged alumni/ae are the people around whom one builds key segments of a development campaign. The people *were* the institution; their courses *were* the educational experience. *They* are what has been remembered.

"Brand" putatively speaks to quality and/or quality control. Publishing houses use different imprints for different types of books. Procter & Gamble's name on a product implies a product deemed acceptable for a respected line. Other branding may indicate different levels of quality—a Timex versus an Omega—or different facets of quality: Toyota's reliability, Jaguar's style.

In universities "brand" means something else. It means quality, of course, and a product that can be safely exploited, as when a commercial enterprise sells dvds of the lectures of teachers from "prominent universities" or when a distant outpost of a university is established that still carries that university's (or school's) name.

Most of all, the "brand" speaks to the quality of the club that your daughter or son may be about to join. It speaks to the quality of the "network," a word which is used more explicitly in professional programming than in academic, but a fact of life that colleges and universities consider of significant importance. "Come to us and you will study with these kinds of people. These kinds of people will be your classmates and lifelong friends. These kinds of people will help you in business. These kinds of people will afford you strategic advantages."

Consider the aestheticized description of *brand* by an anonymous admissions official: "It's a message architecture . . . that gives consistency to the mental impression an admissions committee wants to develop in the mind of a young person." Built "with color and images, not with words—though typefaces can serve as visual cues . . . color palette is key" (Ferguson 2011, p. 111). This, in part, is why the experience costs $60,000+ a year. Someone has to pay that message architect.

The careerism which "branding" undergirds is not confined to the student body. It is a truism that the professoriate was once more loyal to the institutions in which they worked; now, they are more loyal to their fields and to their professional associations, broadly considered. They are all independent businesspersons, prepared to take their wares elsewhere when the right offer is made. If the corporatists have exhibited disloyalty to them, they are prepared to return the favor. Meanwhile they shape their behavior accordingly. Where once the faculty might have hoped for a position of prominence within the curriculum they now negotiate for research leaves and reduced course loads. Nevertheless, these alterations in faculty behavior are dwarfed by the student careerism and vocationalism which have materially reshaped our colleges and universities.

Students believe they know what is best for them and we are prepared to accede to their wishes even if those wishes are misinformed or misguided. By the same token, as seventeen- or eighteen year-olds they have little sense of the actual nature or quality of an institution or of the quality of its discrete fields. They are most likely to respond positively to "brand," not knowing anything else.

Disciplines also tout their brands. One often hears the argument that "traditional" fields such as History, Chemistry and Economics trump ersatz fields and multidisciplinary configurations ("American Studies") because they are undergirded by specific theoretical frameworks. There is no "theory" behind American Studies, just the sum total of the work of fields that have distinct theoretical bases of their own.

There is some truth to that premise (a favorite of one of my former provosts), but I would be hard put to explain the "theory" behind the eclectic assemblage of activities that constitutes the modern department of "English." There are also a number of separate fields which share common techniques; both anthropology and folklore (or folkloristics) utilize ethnography, for example. Some fields are deeply riven—anthropology and philosophy, for example, and some universities have created separate departments from single fields (often with new nomenclature) to keep the peace or, as in the case of "Literature" and "English" at Duke to take the area in a different direction without riling the natives.

Our Counseling Psychology group left our Psychological Sciences department and joined the College of Education. The reason for their desire to do so was never made explicit, but the best guess is that the two entities (psych and counseling psych) had come to represent different cultures. Psychology, once a blend of science and the Humanities, is increasingly scientific and the standards of professional performance there have changed. Extramural grant support, for example, is expected and much research is driven by the availability of specific instrumentation. The ideological ways of "counseling psych" have come to be more like those of the ed school.

In the life sciences some of the divisions between "fields" have largely disappeared. There are different emphases and different subjects of investigation, of course, but we are a great distance from the days of Darwin on the Beagle, collecting and categorizing whole-organism specimens. "Biochemistry" is done in a multiplicity of departments, divisions, schools and centers.

Within this vast and diverse realm it falls on provosts and deans to allocate resources and the ways in which they do that are very instructive; budgets reveal values. The every-tub-on-its-own-bottom approach, which Harvard is rich enough to utilize is beyond the means of the vast majority of universities and even at the wealthiest institutions there will be marked "inequities," since the divinity school will fall far short of the capabilities of the schools of medicine and business to attract external funding.

Responsibility-based budgeting is often discussed and often more honored in the breach. Elaborate plans are erected to induce separate units to take responsibility for their own destinies and, in effect, to pull their own weight. If and when such plans are "put into place" they are usually immediately adjusted and tweaked with a long succession of separate arrangements and special exceptions.

Absent an endless series of rules and protocols, the actual effect of such budget models is the immediate reappearance of chaos and old night. The university is addicted to the massive income from general education courses taught in large lecture halls by junior or adjunct faculty, courses which are delivered inexpensively. If dollars suddenly flow to the departments housing such instruction they must flow *from somewhere else*. The reluctant donors would counter by instituting such courses themselves and, quite possibly, by lowering expectations in courses cognate with and countable toward general education requirements, thus drawing in the paying customers from other units. Depending on how the budgetary protocols are formulated, departments and schools would either attempt to drain students from other programs or (in the case of dollars flowing to "majors" rather than enrollees) erect barriers between themselves and their competitors, denying their competitors' students access to proprietary courses and programs. When Wisconsin made some efforts to encourage departments to develop coursework which would draw large numbers of students the Classics department promptly instituted a course in science fiction (including Aristophanes' *The Clouds)*, taught in translation. I have seen departmental legates posting course advertisements on other departments' bulletin boards and taking down their competitors' notices. University budgeting ultimately represents a very complex and delicate balancing act that is developed over time and is now very difficult to explain and very difficult to alter. "Clever," "entrepreneurial" alternatives are seldom successful.

When I interviewed for the arts and science deanship at Missouri the chancellor asked me to assess the college's strengths and weaknesses. After I had done that, he asked me what I would do first—address needs or build on strengths?

I had been asked the same thing by the faculty. It is an important question and a highly charged one, since the campus is replete with oxen and no one wants to see their own gored. At the same time, no one wants a time server who is unable to make decisions and everyone (hopefully) wants an individual whose decisions will be in the best interests of the institution.

The answer, of course, is that you must do several things simultaneously. Even if certain programs are weak, they may be necessary for a coordinated, integrated curriculum. The math department (ours was quite strong, fortunately) is essential for students in the college of engineering and the physical and life sciences. An institution can function (as most do) without a school of architecture, but no one can purport to do science well without simultaneously doing mathematics well.

One must also attend to student interest—not succumb to it or grovel before it—but pay attention to it. Our biological sciences division and our department of psychological sciences have over 1,000 majors each and, fortunately, both are very strong. Our political science department is on its way to joining them, with rapidly-growing numbers of majors and, fortunately, strong leadership and strong faculty.

I told the chancellor that I would shore up certain departments and maintain others at a sufficient level of strength, but that my primary task would be to build upon strengths. The fact that we were entering a state-funded "mission enhancement" exercise that would help us to do that made the response easier, but the response is an appropriate one for various reasons, reasons which I discussed with the chancellor.

Strong programs attract strong graduate students who enrich both the research and undergraduate teaching programs. Strong programs attract extramural support and raise the university's profile. An often overlooked benefit of strong programs is that they attract academic leadership, one of the greatest needs—if not *the* greatest—in the contemporary American university.

Strong departments have high expectations. When they recruit faculty and graduate students, but especially other faculty, they set standards which can raise the college's standards as a whole. Faculty serve on search committees for "higher" administrators. They serve on the university press board. They serve on deans' advisory councils. They make promotion and tenure recommendations within their departments but they also make them as members of college and campus promotion and tenure committees.

When a strong department puts up an individual for tenure and/or promotion, the other members of the college committee see the dossier. They see the accomplishments; they see the plaudits from distinguished external reviewers and they see the strong department's expectations. They know that the dean allocating resources sees them and they realize to what degree their own department's expectations meet, exceed or fall short of those of the strong department.

Strong faculty sit on panels that allocate internal support for research. They sit on panels that bestow awards and honors. Their personal research activities bring journals to campus and high-visibility conferences. They bring distinguished lecturers. They are also positioned to speak truth to corporatist power and are insulated by their personal accomplishments and positions from administrative reprisal. They are available, in some cases, to take on administrative responsibilities and they are consulted by the local and national press. The effects of their abilities and their actions reverberate throughout the institution.

Yes, there are *prima donnas* and yes, there are individuals who consume resources greedily, but the trick is not to hire such individuals. And even such individuals can say and do good things. If they are self-absorbed their avowed impatience with time-wasting tasks may serve to make an important point. Universities are filled with time-wasting tasks whose reduction would serve to focus all of our efforts and energy on more important ones.

My boss at Wisconsin had a strict policy with regard to graduate school faculty meetings. The agenda would be published well in advance of the meeting and it would never, absolutely never, be altered. Why? He said that faculty could then see the agenda, assess whether or not it was sufficiently important to take them away from their labs and then make the decision whether to attend or not, knowing that no secret or last-minute agenda items would be snuck in on them.

He was a biochemist doing very important work in genetics. In the war, as a young sergeant from Milwaukee, he had actually guarded the captured members of the German general staff. He knew the value of time and he knew what was important and what was not.

These kinds of principles and procedures speak to two major needs: quality and coherence. They are not ignorant of student interests and student vocationalism but they are not shaped by them exclusively. I was astounded when one of our local liberal arts colleges reshuffled its structure and its curriculum. The then-president announced that her college would highlight *professional opportunities for women*. She then closed the political science department. Obviously, one professional opportunity for women—attending law school—had been overlooked.

More than likely, enrollments in political science had been low and the "professional opportunities for women" theme was simply a slogan. Dance, after all, had been retained, and we all know that the nation is clammering for more professional dancers. The college's equestrian program was also retained, so that the future of dressage could be safeguarded.

The restructuring, of course, was a transparent survival mechanism and the equestrian program was reinforced by an alliance with our College of Agriculture, Food and Natural Resources. My best friend from graduate school days was a veterinary physiologist. He took a position at the University of Kentucky for a time because of the access to thoroughbred horses, whose genetic histories were as pristine as those of any large animals on the planet. Some ride horses; some bet on them; some study them for the advancement of scientific knowledge. The latter is the occupation of serious universities.

Our British colleagues are now wrestling with these same issues. We often fantasize that they have served as the keepers of the flame, preserving universities from the crassest forms of vocationalism. This is, unfortunately, not always the case. A recent issue of the *Daily Mail Online* carries the title:

"Ministers declare war on degrees without prospects as university fees are set to hit £9,000 a year" (Chapman 2010).

"Degrees without prospects." The ministers' concern—in the face of what they perceive to be very high tuition rates—is that students are incurring these costs while undertaking courses of study that will not lead to lucrative employment. David Willetts (until 2014, Universities Minister) wanted to evaluate degrees by the employment rates and salaries that they yielded. He would also flag the most successful programs, so that student/parent buyers could make informed choices.

A little context: the £9,000 fees were a considerable jump from the previous limit of £3,290. Those who borrow the full tuition for a three-year course, along with the cost of room and board, could then find themselves with £40,000 of debt, a considerable sum. From an American perspective, however, £9,000 equals a little over $12,000, the sort of tuition that at-risk students would here pay/borrow to enroll in for-profit institutions.

Granting the fact that British taxes are higher than American taxes and that students there are more likely to have to borrow than their American counterparts, the Minister's reservations are appreciated. My own concern here is that courses of study are being evaluated on purely vocational grounds, though the examples of weak programs provided in the article ("Soft Options?") seem to be open to the additional criticism that they lack academic challenge.

The four examples given: 1) a course in International Spa Management (master of arts) offered by Derby University. "Taught in a purpose-built spa, students learn massage techniques alongside 'financial decision making'." Course 2) a course in Surf Science and Technology (bachelor of science—honours) offered by Plymouth University. "The course is aimed at allowing those 'with an interest in surfing to pursue rigorous academic study of the scientific, technical and business aspects of the international surfing industry'. Students also 'get opportunities for practical surfing'." Course 3) a course in International Football Business Management (bachelor of arts—honours) offered by Bucks New University. "Students qualify as football coaches and learn about the commercial aspects of professional football." And, lest the arts be neglected, Course 4) a course in Theatre Practice: Puppetry (bachelor of arts—honours) offered by the Central School of Speech and Drama. "Course tutor Jessica Bowles claims it leads to 'very concrete career opportunities', citing leading roles in the West End play *War Horse*" (2010, p. 2).

While the courses do seem soft, a far cry from molecular genetics, epistemology or theoretical physics, they do seem to be quite vocational in their thrusts. The government concern is probably that there are few jobs in international football business management and that it is likely that they will be secured via different career paths. I take the point that borrowing money to study puppetry may not be the wisest of decisions.

The thrust of the article and of the Minister's concerns appears to be to reinforce the notion of *caveat emptor* and I can happily second that. What strikes me is that while some rudimentary knowledge would be helpful in some of the "careers" (bookkeeping, e.g.), the best preparation (and the one that one is most likely to encounter in the real world) is experience. The courses of study are targeted at narrowly-conceived occupations. If I am a manufacturer of surf boards, e.g., I am likely to have first been a surfer myself and I am likely to be familiar with a large number of surfers who can advise me (yes, and endorse my products). The expertise needed for success is likely to be hard-won knowledge, attained over time. As to puppetry, Jim Henson was working with puppets while he was still in high school. He later attended the University of Maryland (studying to be a commercial artist), but his career (inspired by Edgar Bergen and Burr Tillstrom) was largely self-created. He did take a puppetry class but technically graduated in Home Economics.

Jeff Dunham, the most successful current ventriloquist, attended Baylor, studying communications, but he began studying ventriloquism at the age of 8 and began attending ventriloquist conventions when he was in the 6th grade. He was already performing for audiences as a teenager. The educational model here (like the model for traditional liberal arts education) is far closer to that of apprenticing. You learn your craft from masters and then you hone it.

The British example raises another interesting point: should the government subsidize "impractical" courses of study? Identifying "soft" courses of study is politically difficult, since many voters are enrolled in them, but should the government require—in return for grants or subsidized loans—that the courses undertaken be likely to yield a credential that will lead to employment which will contribute to the public good in some recognizable way?

One often hears references to some poor unemployed alumnus/alumna with $100,000 of debt and a degree in Women's Studies (or something comparable, though that is a frequent example). The fact of the matter is that such examples are very, very few in number; they are more useful as eye-catching headlines than as significant statistical exemplars. What interests me are the principles—should the government tell us what to study and withhold support in certain areas? Should the government offer incentives for study in certain areas?

NDEA loans were forgiven, in part, if an individual was employed, for a given period of time, as a teacher (10 percent of the loan forgiven, per year of teaching, up to 50 percent of the loan's total). When I was in college, the Army would allow an ROTC graduate to go on delay status to pursue a graduate degree before reporting for duty. The Navy would not, unless the course of study bore directly on the young ensign's likely duties as a naval officer. The GI bill did *not* constrain student choice and a significant number who matriculated in colleges and universities elected to study the liberal arts.

For many interesting jobs there is no formal course of study, though institutions on the make sometimes create programs to lure students. Samuel Johnson thought that gifted individuals were intellectually ambidextrous. Isaac Newton, Johnson thought, could have written a fine epic poem if he had decided to do so. At West Point, cadets were observed by departments and records kept. A student who performed well, e.g., in the social sciences, might later—as a senior captain or junior major—be invited to attend graduate school at Army expense and then return to West Point to serve a three-year tour as an instructor. It was possible for different departments to be tracking the same individuals. A person might be invited to study any number of fields if he had shown aptitude for them.

In the case of particularly successful individuals there are multiple pathways. Some, such as Bill Gates, have good ideas and are at the precisely perfect point in time to develop them. Some, like Gordon Moore, accomplish great things in science and engineering and prepare themselves by doing PhD's (at Caltech, with a postdoc at Johns Hopkins)—thus following a more linear path. Others tailor their experience to their aspirations. A friend of mine who was a very successful insurance company CEO obtained a master's degree in economics after college and then worked for a time in state regulatory agencies and at the Federal Trade Commission. Insurance is a heavily-regulated industry and his specific experience prepared him to take on positions of leadership there.

Individuals who work in university advancement (and in development operations, generally) will tell you that there is no career path for that work; everyone falls into it in a different way. That is the case, of course (or should be) for all university line administrative positions. If someone told me that he or she had taken a master's degree in higher education administration and wanted to be my associate dean I would politely decline. Administrative details are simple; developing a career as a strong teacher-researcher (the pool from which I would wish to draw) is difficult.

The bottom line is that nearly all vocational programming is flawed in some way, in some cases in serious ways. It may delude students, for it will *not* lead to successful employment. It may lead to employment, but the student is likely to leave that employment after three to five years or less. It will involve "vocational" content but that content will soon become out-of-date. It will prepare students for forms of employment that will cease to exist. It will prepare them for one form of employment but not help to develop the transferable skills that will serve them as they aspire to promotion or as they are inclined (or forced) to move from one career to an entirely separate one.

Vocational programming is unlikely to prepare students for life, particularly at a time when general education programming has been depreciated and is treated as a distraction. My greatest concern, however, is that vocational programming is implicitly cruel and patronizing. The unspoken assumption is that there is a cohort of bright young people for whom we have no need to worry. They will attend elite institutions where they will have the opportunity to pursue their interests and enrich their lives. They will be fine. In most cases they come from wealth and they will promptly re-join the ranks of the wealthy when they graduate.

For the rest . . . well . . . we must do something. The English gave the poor small beer instead of French wine, English literature instead of the Greek and Roman classics. We will give them vocational training. Michigan President James Angell (1871–1909) may have argued for "an uncommon education for the common man" (Duderstadt 2007, p. 15), a bulwark against the aristocracy of wealth, but that was then and this is now. Everyone must now attend college but they cannot really "do" college, so we will create something that they *can* do and then call it "college." It is unlikely that they will ever join the ranks of the wealthy (never mind the ranks of the authentically-*educat*ed, the *intellect*ual, the curious, the personally-enriched) but they will achieve a tentative grasp on a lower rung of the ladder leading to the middle class and that will represent an improvement in their lot.

The corollaries are not articulated, but they are very real: they will vote for us; they will continue to pay tuition; they will enable *our* careers to flourish by expanding our voter base or by expanding the industry in which we seek to rise to higher administrative rank.

For me this all reprises (in slightly different, but still recognizable form) an eighteenth-century debate. The question was—should the poor be educated when their education might serve as a torment to them? Their education would enable them to see a wider world but they would be unable, ultimately, to enter that world. Their heads would be swirling with Latin quotations but they would still be forced to work with their hands. Hardy raises the issues, many years later, in *Jude the Obscure*. The question (among many, for Hardy) ultimately concerns the fixity of class lines. What are the personal results if they cannot, ultimately, be bridged?

For Johnson, they can be bridged, at least sometimes, and favoring education—authentic education—for all, as in his discussion with Boswell concerning the Thames waterman, he immediately sees the question's (should the poor be educated?) unstated, dark overtones.

In 1757 in the *Literary Magazine* he reviewed a book entitled *A Free Inquiry into the Nature and Origin of Evil* by a minor writer and politician named Soame Jenyns. The review is a harsh masterpiece, enlivened and energized by Johnson's personal feelings. His response to the question of the education of the poor must be quoted at length:

> Though it should be granted that those who are *born to poverty and drudgery* should not be *deprived by* an *improper education* of the *opiate* of *ignorance*; even this concession will not be of much use to direct our practice, unless it be determined who are those that are *born to poverty*. To entail irreversible poverty upon generation after generation only because the ancestor happened to be poor, is in itself cruel, if not unjust, and is wholly contrary to the maxims of a commercial nation, which always suppose and promote a rotation of property, and offer every individual a chance of mending his condition by his diligence. Those who communicate literature to the son of a poor man, consider him as one not born to poverty, but to the necessity of deriving a better fortune from himself. In this attempt, as in others, many fail, and many succeed. Those that fail will feel their misery more acutely; but since poverty is now confessed to be such a calamity as cannot be born without the opiate of insensibility, I hope the happiness of those whom education enables to escape from it, may turn the balance against that exacerbation which the others suffer. I am always afraid of determining on the side of envy or cruelty. The privileges of education may sometimes be improperly bestowed, but I shall always fear to with-hold them, lest I should be yielding to the suggestions of pride, while I persuade myself that I am following the maxims of policy; and under the appearance of salutary restraints, should be indulging the lust of dominion, and that malevolence which delights in seeing others depressed (Schwartz 1975, p. 103).

Our conditions and the eighteenth-century's may not be precisely cognate, but it is the case, as studies continue to show, that many of our current approaches to our condition tend to sustain the inequalities that characterize it. The nagging reality is that we cannot change the condition utterly, because we cannot alter the inequalities in talents and conditions with which we begin (though we could address the inequalities which result from specific, alterable behaviors).

What we have to face is the reality that only about half of the students who matriculate in institutions of postsecondary education complete their programs and of those—in these very difficult economic times, times which are likely to remain challenging, given globalization and international competition—only about half of that half are finding satisfactory employment. We must make our students' education more challenging and more authentic and we must stop deluding ourselves that all actually want this sort of education or can benefit from it.

I have no problem with vocational training. My problem is with the degradation of our educational system and standards and its replacement with often-inappropriate and misguided vocational training that we are falsely labeling "education."

My problem is with the unspoken assumption that vocational training should be, largely, the lot of the poor. One of my best friends from college (a scholarship student) was from Louisville. His father worked in a factory that was lined with thick walls to protect the workers from the frequent explosions there. He became the valedictorian of his class, received Woodrow Wilson and Danforth Fellowships, took a PhD at Yale, taught at Cornell, Northwestern and the University of California, Santa Barbara and authored or edited more than a dozen significant books.

My roommate's father was a tailor (not a fashion designer, an actual tailor); he took a doctoral degree in music education at the University of Illinois. My father worked his way through night law school; his father was a custodian, who had lost his previous job in the Great Depression. My mother's father was the foreman of the Newport Rolling Mill in northern Kentucky.

All three of us would, I think, find Johnson's comments to be resonant (I am the only one of the three still remaining). All three of us, I know, considered a traditional liberal arts education to be the only real option for both personal development and professional success. Our engineering classmates studied in a five-year program, designed to insure both the proper professional training and the receipt of a liberal arts general education. Seeing students, especially first-generation and working-class students shunted into vocational training represents, for me, a significant failure of our system.

When I began serving as arts and science dean it was reported to me that one of my professional-school colleagues had quietly said that he "hoped that I was not a liberal arts snob." He later commented that he was glad to see that I was not, though I am not sure that he should have been so comforted. I do not see myself as condescending, as snobs tend to be, but I do see myself as a vocal advocate for forms of education which I believe to be in our students' best interests.

When Johnson looked around at the men and women of his age he certainly saw the desperate poor and an aristocracy with vast, hereditary wealth. He saw the works of enormously-skilled craftsmen and artists like Sir Christopher Wren, Grinling Gibbons and Robert Adam. He saw industrialists and manufacturers like Josiah Wedgwood, Thomas Chippendale and George Hepplewhite and skilled entrepreneurs like Lancelot "Capability" Brown. His friend and patron, Hester Thrale, was married to a prominent London brewer. He counted successful and very wealthy artists like Joshua Reynolds among his friends, indeed among the members of his Club. Boswell was a lawyer, Burke a writer and politician. Johnson was surrounded with both wealth and success. (Boswell called himself "Baron" when he was on the continent.) Johnson himself had to leave Oxford after a year because of his inability to pay his fees. He tried, unsuccessfully, to be a village schoolmaster. He came to London as an aspiring writer with a half-finished play in his pocket, doing hackwork for magazines and newspapers and struggling to find his way.

He was arrested for debt and his house was a retreat for the ill, the poor and the now largely-unremembered. He edited the first English dictionary. He edited Shakespeare. He wrote one of the greatest of the essay serials, *The Rambler*. He wrote headnotes (some of monograph length) for a collected edition of the works of selected English poets. He wrote prefaces, dedications, reviews, successful verse and a philosophic tale entitled *Rasselas*, which is often compared with Voltaire's *Candide*. He was never very wealthy, though he was, eventually, comfortable. He gave away approximately two-thirds of his £300 government pension to the poor.

Referring to himself in very humble ways and often criticizing himself for failure to do what his talents enabled him to do, he spent his life doing what he began doing in his father's Lichfield bookshop—reading, sometimes voraciously, and writing—sometimes pieces which were then considered ephemeral—and involving himself in projects which advanced knowledge (editing the Harleian collection, e.g.) and are now forgotten. The public always seeks wealth to some degree and the public always appreciates material success. The public can be very pragmatic. Indeed, the English invented "utilitarianism" far earlier than the Americans' embrace of it, but when all is said and done the educated public looks to its deepest values and when it does it sees the second half of the eighteenth century in quite simple terms; it is the age of Johnson.

Chapter Six

Fever Dreams

Grades inflated, core curricula gutted, general education depreciated, graduation rates fallen, expectations lowered, tenure track faculty vanishing, students infantilized, public support diminished. . . . When we are ill it is fair to inquire concerning the etiology of the diseases that afflict us. With regard to the ills afflicting both K-12 and higher education, three causes have commonly been identified: the "tenured radicals" who have instituted and then sustained the educational demands of the student radicals of the 1960s, the pedagogies and programmatic "innovations" sponsored by colleges of education and their fellow travelers and, in some ways the most interesting of the common suggestions—a persistent but mistaken belief in the attitudes broadly associated with Romanticism.

The more closely one looks the more clear it becomes that certain elements of Romanticism are at the heart of the problem, that Romanticism and vulgar forms of utilitarianism drove the colleges of education's thinking, generations before the appearance of the 60s radicals. The administrators' response to the student radicals, despite the radicals' ultimate paucity of numbers and their programmatic incoherence (recognized quickly and now commonly acknowledged by left-leaning scholars) was tepid if not outright cowardly, so that they might bear some share of the responsibility for our current condition.

The "program" of the radicals contained elements that were greedily adopted by the emerging corporatists, among them the privileging of student choice and the resistance to traditional coursework. The individuals held in the greatest contempt by the student radicals—bottom-liners in gray suits—embraced parts of the once-radical agenda and oversaw its mutation into something that neither the traditionalists nor the radicals would have approved. That mutation has become the new normal.

Solutions have been proposed for the K-12 side of the problem, but while they are characterized by stark clarity they seem to many to be either too extreme or too difficult. The economist Thomas Sowell (1993, pp. 298–300), for example, states the case succinctly: close all of the colleges of education, thus removing their power to credential; do not award tenure to K-12 teachers; establish accountability metrics and monitor the results; offer students and parents "school choice"; return the curriculum to the basics and jettison the touchy/feely nonsense.

The resistance to the "conservatism" of these proposals is actually an indication of the inherent conservatism of both the populace and the academy. We know that in our global economy our schools are not competitive, and it has been remarked, again and again, that while our students consistently rank number one in self-esteem they rank far lower in all of the important subject areas. When we face a diagnosis of malignancy our personal response is generally to take aggressive counter-measures, but our public response to our educational shortcomings appears to be one of consistent denial. The methods underwritten by our colleges of education (augmented by a tripling of funding) have not proven to be successful and yet we continue to tolerate them.

Rita Kramer (1991) provided an extensive ethnographic study of more than a dozen colleges of education (from the most distinguished to the least, from the east to the west coast). She sat in on classes, sat in on meetings, met with deans, teacher/students and the "teachers of teachers" and allowed their words and actions to speak for themselves. The goal of ed schools is not the inculcation of learning. It is sociopolitical: to achieve equality of result (not opportunity) by dumbing down the curriculum to the point that all students can "succeed" and graduate. Their summum bonum is self-esteem, not the honing of skills and the acquisition of knowledge. Students are to feel good about themselves because of who they are, not because of what they have achieved. Nonjudgmentalism is paramount and relativism and multiculturalism are the order of the day. Expectations are systematically lowered and "content" is subordinated to pedagogy. In fact, "content" is considered to be of marginal importance and it is often treated with the same contempt that attends discussions of tracking, testing, and, of course, competition and meritocracy, which are seen to be hegemonic tools to solidify the position of the white establishment. Teachers are seen as facilitators, not instructors, and didactic instruction is treated with derision. Dewey is alive and well even though he died in 1952 and the institutionalized expressions of progressive education disappeared with him. The purpose of education is still "social change" not education per se (which could bring authentic social change) and the classroom is student-centered, privileging "expression" over the acquisition of knowledge. Education is seen as essentially therapeutic, not intellectual, and teachers are seen as social workers rather than, well, teachers.

The ethos which Rita Kramer investigated and revealed has now expanded significantly; its hegemony in the student affairs bureaucracy is apparent. The one unspoken point that stands out with crystalline clarity is that our K-12 (and increasingly our K-16) systems are riddled with failure. We are trounced by other industrial democracies in international tests and the educational establishment simply does not care. If it cared it would consider alternatives to our current methods of proceeding. Moreover, the students who suffer most from this situation are the minority students who are not expected to perform at the level of their actual capacity. A system designed to attack "racism" ends up being among the most "racist" in modern experience.

To recapitulate the statistics: the OECD Programme for International Student Assessment ('PISA') study for 2012 looked at forty-three developed countries. American students ranked 23rd in science literacy and 30th in mathematics; our long suit was reading, where we scored 19th. As the National Center for Education Statistics points out, this performance is "not measurably different from average scores in previous PISA assessment years" (IES>NCES 2012, par. 11).

As a first-semester freshman in college I was shocked to see that the work I was submitting was receiving B's and C's. In the second semester I began to study seriously. At the same time, I caught a glimpse of the new world on the horizon when I saw an English paper graded by Frank O'Malley with comments to the effect that his (undergraduate) student had not only been brilliant in his analysis of the text under consideration but had, in the process, made "a significant contribution to American Literature." This sort of nonsensical hyperbole is now commonplace. In reviewing letters of recommendation in job applications for assistant professorships one quickly discovers that the order of the day is often absurdist hype, the exorbitant praise of the faculty mentor(s) often coexisting with the most elementary grammatical errors in the applicants' cover letters. I remember one letter from a (household name) colleague at a prominent university, stating that her student (who had written an English dissertation on John Locke) was, in fact, a far greater philosopher than Locke, himself.

The psychologist John Rosemond explains the inflated-praise phenomenon and the responses which reinforce it: "Children don't know what they truly need. They only know what they want, and they believe that what they want they deserve to have, and no one has a right to deny them. That belief defines a child, in fact; therefore, lots of the children in question are much older than 21" (Cyr 2011, p. 2).

While the denial phase may persist for a long time, the moment of instant recognition for both B.A. and Ph.D. holders often comes when their in-boxes are filled with job application rejections. The valorization of childhood which often spawns both inflated praise and inflated grades, is vintage Romanticism, vintage ed school ideology and (on the surface) vintage 60s radicalism. The harsh Dr. Rosemond sounds like a person out of the eighteenth century (and the preceding two thousand+ years).

Sowell (writing in the early 1990s), states the issue with painful clarity: college of education students score either low or the lowest in standardized tests and they have done so since the 1920s and 1930s. They are the least qualified students in the university. They are taught by the least-qualified professors and they take the poorest courses. Low admission standards, poor professors and poor courses thus constitute the elements of the pipeline for the teachers to whom we entrust the education of our children (1993, pp. 24–25).

Outrageous, outrageous. I can hear the voices in the background, but Sowell is an economist dealing in large statistical aggregates. There are certainly many distinguished teachers in our public and private schools (though many in the latter have finessed credential requirements and teach in private schools with arts and science- rather than college of education preparation).

At Wisconsin, in the graduate school, there was a running joke concerning the unit within the university that was consistently the most inept in all of their administrative dealings; it was the group in the ed school specializing in *higher education administration*. That school's most distinguished faculty member, Carl Kaestle (now at Brown), was joint-appointed with the department of History; his undergraduate training was at Yale in English. The Wisconsin ed school was later put in the hands of a dean whose training was in linguistics and whose home was the department of English in the College of Letters and Science.

When one of our recent ed school deans at Missouri was hired she reassured her interviewers that her basic preparation had been in modern foreign languages in an arts and science college, not an ed school. At our graduate school commencement exercises one of the activities pursued to forestall somnolence is the counting of doctoral degree recipients mentored by one faculty member in the ed school. The excessive number (four, five or more in a given semester) bespeaks, it is felt, a significant absence of seriousness.

At Wisconsin I served on the graduate school Research Committee for ten years. We met every Wednesday afternoon and every Saturday morning throughout the fall semester, and for several weeks in the spring semester, evaluating faculty research proposals that would be supported (if approved) by WARF funds. In 45+ years in English departments I have seen the credentials of many faculty in English Education. For two summers in graduate school I worked for the National Council of Teachers of English, which includes high school teachers as well as college and university teachers in its membership. I worked for and with the leaders in the "English Ed" world—

people such as Jim Squire and Nick Hook—and I know how that world looks and feels.

While there are occasional, impressive exceptions, garden variety "research" in "education" tends to be voluminous, often autobiographical and largely trivial. At Missouri we have one of the most successful math ed groups in the country; it was the signature program of a long-serving dean. I have seen some of their bibliographies. They are lengthy in the extreme, and yet, one of my department of Mathematics friends said to me, "it is doubtful that they could even do differential equations."

The ed school posture privileges the student over the subject, the pedagogy over the content, student "skills" over student knowledge. The result is the predictable friction between ed school subject area specialists and their colleagues in cognate arts and science departments. The latter seek to engender a love of the subject and attempt to stimulate and satisfy curiosity concerning it. The self-esteem of the student is a subsidiary or tertiary concern. It is not that they are callous or uncaring; they simply see their job to be the teaching of, e.g., mathematics, not the burnishing of the student's self-image.

In a recent, important study, Frank Furedi has argued that the ed school model now pervades higher education and is the source of its infantilization. What Talcott Parsons called "permissive therapeutics" has moved from K-8 into our colleges and universities (Furedi 2017, p. 74). The "permissive therapeutics" watchword is *validation*. Where once students went to college to learn and be tested they now go to be "respected" and "heard." They want encouragement and approval; they want the equivalent of bluebird stickers and gold stars affixed to their papers. They want their identities (rather than their accomplishments) to be acknowledged and rewarded. They may be biological adults but they long for adult control and (unlike the 60s radicals) embrace the notion of *in loco parentis*. Hence Camille Paglia's longstanding characterization of the contemporary university as extended daycare.

The students' demands square with the identity politics of the contemporary left and the race/class/gender "victimology" obsessions of the Humanities and social science faculty. Since the corporatist administrators seek to collect the students' tuition and featherbed their own bureaucracies they quickly accede to student demands and expand the number of handholders and advocates, reducing the instructional budget and diluting (with student approval) the claims of academic freedom and free speech. This might seem to be an exaggeration until we remind ourselves of the post-election administrative offer of Play-Doh therapy to law students at the University of Michigan.

The key problem, of course, is that this infantilization vitiates the efforts of higher education and destroys its content, quality and integrity. While the student demand for "validation" may be honest it may also be a useful dodge. Let me offer a simple example. A teacher calls on a student in class. The student perceives that he or she is being oppressed and complains to a "bias report" officer. (Another student perceives that he or she is being oppressed because the professor did *not* call on them, but rather on someone of a different "identity.") Both students are "uncomfortable." The former student may also be unprepared for class and is seeking a way to block the professor from causing him or her embarrassment. If the student plays the discomfort card he or she can go to class without having to read the material. Once the professors (or, far more likely, the contingent instructors) undergo an encounter with the political correctness/identity politics apparatchiks and see themselves savaged on anonymous student evaluations (in some cases with their positions hanging in the balance) they take the path of least resistance and simply stop calling on students in class. Comfort is restored; the students learn less and no longer need to come to class prepared.

The shibboleths of American teacher training are not universal phenomena. Recently (March 8; March 22, 2012) Diane Ravitch published a two-part study of educational practices in Finland in the *New York Review of Books*. A moderate commentator; a left-leaning publication; the practices of a left-leaning Scandinavian society. This is not Tom Sowell speaking to us from the Hoover Institution. Why is the Finnish educational system so successful? The answer is not far to seek.

In America, no other profession has a higher rate of turnover; it is virtually a revolving door. Up to forty to fifty percent leave in the first five years; the turnover is highest in low-scoring urban districts. In Finland there is both greater longevity and a higher degree of professionalism (March 22, p. 17). Finnish teachers are far better prepared. Only one in ten is accepted into teacher's education programs and all subject matter teachers earn master's degrees from the academic departments, not the school of education divisions (March 8, p. 20).

Ken Bain echoes Ravitch's point. The key ingredient is knowledge, not validation. Irreducibly, the outstanding teachers know their subjects extremely well (2004, p. 15). He adds that college instructors who are particularly effective also have a keen sense of their disciplines' history, including the various controversies that, as he puts it, have swirled within them (2004, p. 25). In English studies, Gerald Graff has famously advised us to "teach the controversies." My view is that we need to have an overarching sense of our discipline, whatever it may be, and not just a narrow focus on a specific research area within it. The latter might be of interest to the most advanced students, but it will not enable us to communicate the nature and insights of our discipline, writ large, to students in general education and introductory courses, the settings in which, across the educational spectrum, faculty most commonly encounter them.

Many pedagogues believe that students who feel good about themselves are better positioned to learn. Fine, but unless they *voluntarily* and *spontane-*

ously dedicate themselves to learning (as the pedagogues seem to expect, following Rousseau), they *must* (the traditionalists such as Giamatti will argue) be *required* to do so. Unless they have infused knowledge, those who do not personally *choose* to learn will remain ignorant. Those who do not spontaneously and voluntarily learn and who are not *required* to learn—a taboo for the student radicals, the ed schools and the corporatists—are doomed to remain ignorant. High self-esteem that is not based on achievement is delusory. Self-esteem or, better, self-respect, that results from achievement may often be hard-won, but it is authentic. Why would we ever choose delusion over authenticity?

Since we *do* choose delusion, every day, we must consider it to have some redeeming value. But does it? In 2005 Professors Roy Baumeister, Jennifer Campbell, Joachim Krueger and Kathleen Vohs examined the self-esteem literature. Their study, conducted under the aegis of the American Psychological Society (now the Association for Psychological Science), resulted in an article entitled "Exploding the Self-Esteem Myth." Their summary conclusion: "Boosting people's sense of self-worth has become a national preoccupation. Yet surprisingly, research shows that such efforts are of little value in fostering academic progress or preventing undesirable behavior" (2005, p. 1).

They also conclude that while studies "certainly do not indicate that raising self-esteem offers students much benefit," there are other findings which "suggest that artificially boosting self-esteem may lower subsequent performance" (2005, p. 7). On a related issue, they conclude that "the results do not support the idea that low self-esteem predisposes young people to more or earlier sexual activity. If anything, those with high self-esteem are less inhibited, more willing to disregard risks and more prone to engage in sex" (2005, p. 10). In an earlier study, Roy Baumeister found that those who are perpetrators of aggression "generally hold favorable and perhaps even inflated views of themselves" (2005, p. 12).

Christopher Lasch associated "unseemly self-absorption" with "romanticism run rampant" (1979, p. 30). Janice Fiamengo has linked Dewey with Wordsworth in tracing the origins of the self-esteem movement and argued that its products "often arrive [in college] essentially unteachable, lacking the personal qualities necessary to respond to criticism" (2012, p. 1). Harvey Mansfield (the Harvard political scientist who famously gives his students two grades—the "Harvard grade" and the grade they actually earned) links the self-esteem movement directly to grade inflation. Many have traced the grade inflation trend to the 60s professoriate, protecting the draft deferments of their students (and the two grade-inflation blips do seem to correlate with both that phenomenon and the expansion of the numbers of contingent faculty, ca. 1990), but Mansfield's view is that we should look to the ed schools as the source: "Grade inflation has resulted from the emphasis in American education on the notion of self-esteem. According to that therapeutic notion, the purpose of education is to make students feel capable and empowered, so to grade them, or to grade them strictly, is cruel and dehumanizing. Grading creates stress. It encourages competition rather than harmony. It is judgmental" (Lewis 2006, p. 219).

The issue is clearly not a simple one. The ed schools bear some responsibility; the 60s professoriate bears some responsibility; consumerism and the corporatization of the university bear some responsibility (certainly in sustaining the practice); student pressure plays a role; the use of student evaluations in promotion and tenure decisions (and renewal decisions for contingent faculty) plays a role. Indeed, "society" plays a role, at least that segment of society that sees competition as harmful, the segment that encourages games in which scores are not kept and "participation trophies" are awarded, the segment that loathes spelling bees, the segment that seems to believe that a non-competitive childhood and a non-competitive system of education will somehow prepare our children for a global society in which competition has reached unforeseen levels of intensity.

Robert Hughes, in his book *Culture of Complaint: The Fraying of America*, cites the historian, Daniel J. Singal:

> The prevailing ideology holds that it is much better to give up the prospect of excellence than to take the chance of injuring any student's self-esteem. Instead of trying to spur children on to set high standards for themselves, teachers invest their energies in making sure that slow learners do not come to think of themselves as failures . . . one often senses a virtual prejudice against bright students (1993, p. 63).

Shortly after the ravages of 1968, Seymour Martin Lipset (once the national chairman of the Young People's Socialist League) and Gerald M. Schaflander published their book, *Passion and Politics: Student Activism in America* (1971). They found (and Todd Gitlin and Diane Ravitch have concurred in this) that most leftist students were children of leftist or at least, liberal parents—so-called "red diaper babies." They were generally from well-to-do backgrounds and those on the far left were more likely to be Jewish or have no religious affiliation (1971, pp. 80–84). They came, in short, from educated families, not the sort who needed, necessarily, to be targeted for self-esteem training, though perhaps the sort that might have been supportive of such phenomena as "progressive education."

Interestingly, Lipset and Schaflander do not find their inspiration in Rousseau when they set about to describe the youth who were, suddenly, to lead us. They turn instead to Aristotle, who saw the young do "things excessively and vehemently," the young who "have exalted notions, because they have not yet been humbled by life or learnt its necessary limitations" (1971, p. 16). They cite the psychologist Gordon Allport, noting that the young are inherently less able to handle ambiguity. They tend to overreact to stimuli and lack a high capacity for tolerance (1971, p. 17).

They may have lacked a high capacity for tolerance when their passionate beliefs were challenged or constrained, but that would eventually be trained out of their successors. The student services staff commonly talk about "channeling the idealism of the young," i.e. channeling it in ways that the staff find acceptable. For them, self-esteem might be important, but *tolerance* is among the highest of goods.

And tolerance is a very important characteristic, particularly in a diverse, democratic society. But what does it mean when *they* use that word? Are they implying that we should be tolerant of behaviors of which *they* disapprove? Ought we to be tolerant of attitudes which they consider troglodytic? Or is their "tolerance" a generalized feeling of undifferentiated bonhomie, kept within politically-correct constraints (but within an ethos of warmth and general sympathy)? How does "tolerance" accord with speech codes? How wide open are the gates of a "welcoming" university? Does an "inclusive" university truly include *everyone*? And how has "diversity" come to convey the restricted meaning which they assign to it?

To be "nonjudgmental" would appear to be a very good thing. Jesus tells us to avoid judging others so that we ourselves will not be judged and the Lord's prayer itself counsels us to forgive those who trespass against us.

The latter may represent Christian behavior, but anyone who has spent any time in a modern college or university and has seen programming that seems contradictory (counseling programs, e.g., that warn against being too "directive," i.e., that seem to be warning against actually *counseling* anyone) will know that some of our ideals have become confused and even—in their new "meaning"—destructive.

My wife once urged one of her classes to read Jane Austen's *Pride and Prejudice*. She was promptly challenged by a student, who asked, "Why would you ever tell us to read a book about prejudice?" The student's point was that prejudice is a bad thing and that a book with the word *prejudice* in its title must somehow be supportive of the practice. My wife gently told her that the book actually warns the reader concerning the damaging effects of prejudice, but the student remained frustrated and unconvinced. I was not there, but my guess is that the student did not expect a rational response, but rather what she had probably often received in the past—some vague form of emotional reinforcement. In this "nonjudgmental" world, a rational answer to an honestly, foolish question is rarely expected. The teacher's role is to encourage, not to teach.

Perhaps that seems cruel. It might not have been cruel in 1940, but it may well seem cruel now, because the self-esteem ideologues have sought to brainwash us for the last several generations. Being "judgmental" is very different from "exercising judgment" but the "nonjudgmental" ideology is now so deeply engrained that the two are often conflated and exercising judgment is perceived, perversely, to be judgmental.

There are multiple meanings to the word *discriminate*. One is very bad: "to make a difference in treatment or favor on a basis other than individual merit," viz. "The school is not allowed to *discriminate*." Another set of meanings is quite different. "Discriminating" in the sense of "making discriminations" is essential to intellectual life. It means "to use good judgment," "to make a distinction," "to mark or perceive the distinguishing or peculiar features of."

It is not, I believe, too great an exaggeration to say that the multiple meanings of the word are now frequently conflated. Discrimination is a bad thing. Well, yes, in one sense, but certainly not in others. Those who are unwilling to *discriminate* against others are probably good people; those who are unable or unwilling to *discriminate* by *drawing distinctions* are unable to decide, to evaluate, to prioritize, to plan, to reason, to . . . even . . . think.

As I argued earlier, faculty proceedings are far different now than two generations ago. There is a wariness, a fear that somehow, someone might be offended if an argument is pressed too insistently. Feelings appear to now trump principles, at least on the surface, and a universal preference for "tolerance" (no matter the cost) appears to be the ruling standard. The Enlightenment's defense of reason, logic and evidence has been supplanted by Romanticism's privileging of emotion.

I am not talking about good manners here. I am talking about a transition from an academy characterized by honest debate to one characterized by an unwillingness to cause discomfort. This is an academy that subscribes to the beliefs of a therapeutic society, one that has grown up with an acceptance of the necessity of "support groups," an academy in which Humanities researchers (long characterized by their ability to work in solitary settings) now form "writing groups."

Recently (June 3, 2012) the *Chronicle of Higher Education* ran a piece that posed the question, "Why Are Associate Professors So Unhappy?" (The answer is that they have competing claims on their time and, now tenured, they are asked to take on administrative responsibilities, particularly in small departments in small colleges. There is also a common, across-the-professions mid-career malaise and a questioning of prior choices and future prospects. The academy is not immune to it. A heavily-bureaucratized academy may, in fact, be more susceptible to it.)

The story goes on to report that one of these individuals (at a small, relatively elite college in Ohio) addressed these feelings by utilizing some (unspecified) part of her sabbatical year to form the "post-tenure action group," a support system for her and two other newly-promoted associate professors.

As a lost observer from another era I hardly know how to respond to this. Initially, I think of the contingent faculty out there who are scratching out an existence in an exploitative environment and how they would feel if they could trade places with the newly tenured group of three—receiving a dramatic raise, a dramatic reduction in teaching load, office space, support staff, fringe benefits, some recognition in the college's publications and job security for life. I cannot imagine that they would form a support group to help them through the many travails of that condition.

I can believe in support groups for individuals with children with a shared disease. I can think of support groups for individuals who have suddenly and unexpectedly lost their spouses or partners. I can think of support groups for a vast array of individuals with a multiplicity of conditions and situations. I cannot, however, think of a support group for people who have just been promoted and just been given a lifelong promise of job security. I cannot conceive of using *any* part of a treasured sabbatical *to form a support group*.

This is the therapeutic society. Sensitivity is the *summum bonum*, or perhaps Sandy Astin's *equanimity*, but it is not the society of passionate, all-consuming study. It is not the society of moments of great insight, of experiments successfully replicated with initial results confirmed, of those instants when the neurons are firing in a certain way and things are almost . . . finally . . . coming together and making sense. It is rather a world of *feelings*. Where the ed school sees the self-esteem of the student trumping the acquisition of knowledge (and a resulting, authentic, self-confidence), this therapeutic world sees the personal, emotional well-being of the faculty member trumping the activities of the determined scholar, the person fixated on his or her subject and utterly devoted to the life of the mind. (My Wisconsin colleagues Stuart Curran and Joe Wittreich used to say that the only people who should be given tenure were those who were *obsessed* with their scholarship.)

The goal in this therapeutic world is not to wrest secrets from a stubbornly-resistant Nature, but rather to keep depression at bay. The goal is not to change the course of scholarly thought and help direct an international discussion but rather to be at peace with one's feelings. It is the kind of world in which "judgment" and "discrimination" in their most positive senses may indeed feel dangerous and threatening.

It is not, however, the world of the student radicals of the 1960s. We cannot lay the responsibility for the therapeutic society at their feet. That does not, of course, absolve them of responsibility for other aspects of our condition. We can begin with the thoughts of someone who knew/knows them both as a fellow participant and as a serious scholar—Todd Gitlin.

Gitlin, sometime president of Students for a Democratic Society (the famous and notorious SDS), a distinguished sociologist and accomplished novelist, has written a definitive account of the Sixties (rev. ed., 1993).

Writing as both an insider and, simultaneously, as an objective observer, he identifies what he terms the nexi of the insurgencies: a) the desire for social equality (with regard to race, gender and sexuality); b) an interest in "lifestyles" (= sex, drugs and rock and roll); c) the curtailing of national violence and an increased care for the earth and, d) the spread of democratic activity.

Interestingly, the similarly distinguished sociologist Norman Birnbaum's conception of the counterculture's principal thrusts (1973) is somewhat different. He sees the counterculture issuing: a) "a comprehensible demand that *joie de vivre* become a general condition of existence" and advocating a program, b) that represents "a refusal of more ascetic values"; that represents, c) "a disinclination to accept bureaucratic and impersonal routines"; and includes, d) "a generalized familism which at times resembles a new tribalism" (1973, p. 212).

Birnbaum focuses upon the "let everything hang out" dimension and the us-against-them tribalism in defense of the romantic *natural* as opposed to the "established" and bureaucratic. Gitlin is more sensitive to the counterculture's varied political agendas, their splinter sects and their endless, internecine maneuvering, the latter of which he covers very expertly.

The bottom line, of course, is that there is both a bright side and a dark side to the counterculture. On the one hand, there is the advocacy of liberty and equality that in many respects represents an extension of the civil rights movement. Here, history has vindicated the counterculture's general aims (if not its sometimes strident tactics). On the other hand, there is the side involving self-indulgence, promiscuous sexuality and dramatic expansion of the drug culture. History is far less kind to the latter, since a national out-of-wedlock birth rate exceeding 40 percent and a now omnipresent set of drug-related phenomena (including property crime and large-scale incarceration) have contributed significantly to social decay. As always, of course, there are those who can manage their personal and pharmaceutical lives but also those who have been destroyed by their new-found freedoms.

Gitlin puts it succinctly. The student movement "started as a movement *for others*—a support for blacks, Cubans, and Vietnamese who were victims of privation and violence and whose revolt seemed elemental." However, "an impulse that began as altruism then spawned a movement *for itself,* a revolt of the white young who wanted to overcome their own alienation and shape their own lives . . ." (1993, p. 353).

Gitlin links this directly with an academic phenomenon: "A loose antiauthoritarianism was normalized . . . in the ease of unpunished cohabitation, as well as in the corrupt and sloppy grade inflation that became a regular feature of school and university life" (1993, p. 431), the ultimate prices paid including teenage pregnancy, STD's, especially AIDS, drugs and the damage done, and the undermining of family commitment (1993, pp. 431–32).

Though very far to my left, Gitlin characterizes the resulting ferment in the Humanities and social sciences as including "cant and intellectual masturbation, the academic equivalent of vanguard revolutionism" (1993, p. 432) and he concludes by acknowledging another dark side of "revolutionism," "the injuries done to human freedom and dignity not only by the Soviet Union but by Castro's Cuba and the Chinese Cultural Revolution . . . [as well as] the staggering carnage left by the Khmer Rouge" (1993, p. 437).

It is very important, I believe, to distinguish the positive and negative elements of the counterculture's program. The positive are now taken for granted, the negative a source of ongoing social dysfunction. The two, of course, are not unrelated within Romanticism. When one is throwing off shackles, the first shackles to go are those that constrain sexuality. They are the most obvious, in some ways the most personal, the most elemental. In *The Marriage of Heaven and Hell*, for example, Blake tells us that the covering cherub with his flaming sword who guards the tree of life in Eden will be commanded to leave. When he does, "the whole creation will be consumed and appear infinite and holy whereas it now appears finite & corrupt. *This will come to pass by an improvement of sensual enjoyment*" [my italics].

The valorization of youth, central to Romanticism and common (or apparently common) within the counterculture was an idea that was underscored but sometimes misrepresented by the media. For example, the key Berkeley slogan, "Don't trust anybody over thirty" was actually coined by a CORE organizer named Jack Weinberg, who had just returned from Mississippi Freedom Summer.

He was insisting that the Berkeley Free Speech Movement not follow a formulaic communist line, but, on the contrary, be suspicious of the thought of older communists. It did not represent some quintessential aspect of a warmed-over romantic neoplatonism, but rather a portion of an ideological struggle within leftist groups. Reporters, however, loved the line, took it out of context and repeated it endlessly (Gitlin, 1993, p. 161). What the left was actually saying was that one needed to create one's own movement, go it alone and not be trapped by such things as past compromises.

One fascinating aspect of Gitlin's history of student action and activity is its later sequence of results. Students rallied for good causes; they also rallied for self-indulgent ones. The first have generally been vindicated, while the second have resulted in social disaster. But not—as I editorialized earlier—*for all*. Charles Murray (2012) has recently described the dire social results of a bifurcated population. Confining himself to white America, he argues that there are now two Americas, one prospering as a result of, largely, "traditional" behaviors—marriage, religious commitment, respect for the law, a strong work ethic and the acceptance of civic responsibilities—while the other America, succumbing in many ways to the extremes of 60s self-indulgence, finds itself in poverty and, often, in personal ruin.

Blurbing the book (*Coming Apart*) for Amazon.com, David Brooks said that he would be shocked if any book would appear that year that would be more important than Murray's. And Brooks knows that territory well; twelve years earlier he had charted the lives of those previously on the (at least, social) left who had made their accommodations with capitalism and managed their self-indulgence in less destructive ways.

While some from the sixties became neocons, others became what Brooks terms *Bobos*. His book, *Bobos in Paradise,* studies the life of the *bohemian bourgeoisie* and the manner in which the countercultural sixties made one with the achieving eighties. In effect, the culture and counterculture coopted one another (2000, p. 43). And, once again, the ur-cause: "Strictly speaking, bohemianism is only the social manifestation of the romantic spirit" (2000, p. 67). Among the bobos, ideas and emotions are turned into products; artistes join capitalists, but in a revivified form of American transcendentalism, designed to transcend rationalism and materialism (at least certain forms of it) and penetrate the inner spirituality at each person's core (2000, p. 70).

Brooks reprises Malcolm Cowley's 1934 list of the bohemian's priorities:

a. salvation by the child
b. self-expression
c. paganism
d. living for the moment
e. liberty (shattering laws and conventions)
f. female equality
g. psychological adjustment (no repression allowed)
h. "changing place" [truth comes from the road or the "new"] (2000, p. 75).

The sixties ethos will be immediately recognizable, with the (heavily-romantic) valorization of childhood in primary position. Neocons, such as Gertrude Himmelfarb, looked at this program and saw the roots of social disaster. In Brooks's summary of the neocon's perception of likely results, egotism would take over our lives; fathers would abandon their families; the two-parent family would be delegitimized; children would slip into criminality and drug abuse; pop culture would become more vulgar and people would be recast as society's victims and not be asked to accept personal responsibility for their behavior (2000, p. 81).

Not a bad summary, and Brooks recounts Himmelfarb's note that throughout the horrors of the industrial age (1860–1970) the divorce rate remained relatively constant in both the U.S. and the U.K., but from 1970 on divorce skyrocketed, as did out-of-wedlock births, the crime rate and the rate of drug use. Thus, the assault on bourgeois values seems to have resulted in bona fide social disaster (2000, p. 50).

But not exactly, since some members of the avant-garde did not succumb to the more destructive blandishments of bohemianism but instead embraced the values of the bourgeoisie. It was the poor and the uneducated, principally, who were devastated. Murphy Brown (*pace* Dan Quayle) could have both her fashionable home and her child without finding herself in a trailer court or a drunk tank.

In education such bifurcated results arose from the broad implementation of theoretical structures rooted, ultimately, in Romanticism. Gifted and wealthy students were positioned (then as now) to survive the innovations but many others were not. In the 1920s and 1930s the ideology of "progressive education" was advanced. "Traditional" education was seen as old-fashioned. It was subject-centered, rigid and authoritarian. It featured a controlling, domineering presence at the head of the room, a presence whose authority needed to be systematically diminished. The modern system of education would be one that was child-centered rather than teacher-centered, a flexible, democratic, and yes, progressive system (Ravitch 1983, p. 44).

Its goals were both social and political, but its intellectual underpinnings were dubious. It was (like Rousseau) skeptical of the usefulness of books. It did not see the preservation and transmission of culture and learning as a significant goal. It favored the here and now over the past and it sought to empower students, focusing on their socialization rather than their intellectual life and their actual learning (1983, pp. 44–45).

The larger progressive movement, exemplified by forebears such as Riis, Steffens, Dewey and William James, et al. did not survive the first World War, but what Diane Ravitch terms a "bastardized version" of it persisted in American education, a version which, in some ways represented a betrayal of what Dewey had actually advocated. The school as a lever of social reform became the school as a mechanism to adjust the individual to society (1983, pp. 46–48).

The "progressive educators" believed that they had science on their side—in, e.g., their opposition to teaching reading through the use of phonics. As Ravitch notes (1983, p. 49), Hofstadter had scored their "misuse of experimental evidence" as "a major scandal in the history of educational thought."

They believed what can only be characterized as nonsense. For example, they thought that the teaching of material of educational substance did not lead to mental discipline. When you studied mathematics you did not enhance your ability to concentrate or your appreciation of the importance of precision. You simply learned mathematics. When you studied Latin you simply learned Latin.

The absurdity of this is immediately apparent. A student who studies Old English, for example, or any other heavily-inflected language will be far better prepared to do so if he or she has studied another such language (like

Latin) first. If he or she has not done so, the immediate result will be confusion over the fact that the words "are all out of order," the result of ignorance of the fact that in heavily-inflected languages endings determine meaning and word order is far less important than it is in a language such as modern English where most of the inflected endings have broken down or disappeared.

Similarly, a language such as modern English, which includes a vast number of borrowings will be far more intelligible to those with a knowledge of the source languages from which we have borrowed. Beyond the mental discipline of understanding the concept of declensions and conjugations, of strong verbs and weak verbs, or of gender, there are a host of specific details at issue. Why do some related English words begin with d and some with t (*decade/ten* or *dental/tooth*)? What kind of numbers are we talking about when we *decimate?*

The reader should forgive this elementary material, but it did not appear to be elementary to the progressive educators. The study of Latin not only enables you to study the Latin literature of antiquity but the Latin literature which dominated Europe until the end of the seventeenth century. Newton's *magnum opus* is called the *Principia*, not the *Principles*. The student who does not study Latin because it is only, after all, "Latin," is an individual condemned to a state of ignorance and dependency. "There, there, don't worry. The priest (or lawyer or doctor or professional historian) will tell you what you should think and what you can know." This is why we had the renaissance, the reformation and the enlightenment—to free "average" people from their control by elites.

The progressive educators wanted to prepare us to "live" and did not see traditional subject matter or traditional pedagogy contributing to that goal. Forget the Greek and Latin; bring on the dancing, dramatics and playing with dolls (Ravitch 1983, p. 51). "Since social utility was the guiding star of [progressive] curriculum revision, the college preparatory subjects served no function for the large majority who were not going to college" (Ravitch 1983, p. 56). Good-bye, Chemistry, hello driver's education. Textbooks were often eliminated; spelling, e.g., was taught through games and projects and even though teachers and parents resisted, the innovators marched on.

Such an approach to education privileges *vocational* goals and *utilitarian* litmus tests. It is associated, ultimately, with the thought of one Charles A. Prosser, a crusader for vocational education who thought that the principal purpose of schools was their responsibility to enable a student to get a job, hold it and advance to better jobs. Since traditional study was not, in his judgment, transferable, it had to be replaced with learning that was far more specific and immediately applicable.

Prosser estimated that 20 percent of high school students would go to college and 20 percent would enter skilled occupations. Hence, with the 60 percent majority headed elsewhere (and with an overriding love for utility) he reasoned that education should become *life adjustment* training. The first step would be to jettison the study of mathematics and foreign languages (Ravitch 1983, pp. 64–66).

Here we see what Hofstadter means when he says that consequential educational theorists were essentially know-nothing philistines who were fundamentally anti-intellectual. Prosser's ideal was "the well-adjusted student," not the *learned* student (Ravitch 1983, p. 68).

We can take heart in the knowledge that these beliefs and practices were excoriated by thinkers such as Hutchins and the University of Illinois historian, Arthur Bestor, but the bottom line is that in 1910 foreign language instruction was received by 83.3 percent of high school students. By 1955 (3 years after Prosser's death) the number had plummeted to 20.6 percent (Ravitch 1983, p. 68). The College Entrance Examination Board test had been based on a common, liberal arts curriculum; it was replaced in 1947 by the SAT, which was virtually curriculum-free (Ravitch 1983, p. 69).

Critics pointed to the progressive/vocational's failure to teach fundamentals, its failure to discipline, its squandering of resources on fads and frills, its erosion of individual freedom, enhancement of bureaucratic control and, ironically, its authoritarianism, which compelled conformity (Ravitch 1983, pp. 70–72).

In 1955 the Progressive Education Association went out of business; two years later the journal *Progressive Education* ceased publication. Bestor had driven in some exquisite coffin nails, arguing, as Diane Ravitch puts it, that "the very essence of democracy is that all citizens are entitled to receive the liberal education that was once reserved for the privileged few . . ." (1983, p. 76). And then there is my personal favorite—his argument that "The West was not settled by men and women who had taken courses in 'How to be a pioneer'."

Unfortunately, the damage had already been done and the results of nonsensical ideas and destructive policies continue today, in slightly altered form. The rich can survive them; they simply attend private schools, but those most in need are at the highest risk. Ravitch points out that progressive education died, in part, because it was unable to change with the world. Internationalization cried out for the study of foreign languages; the perceived rootlessness of society demanded the study of history; international tensions required the study of the history, literature, religion and political traditions of other cultures; a world of rapid technological change could not proceed without the study of science, engineering and mathematics; the lone individual alienated by the pressures of mass society needed to study literature.

What did foster some change was Sputnik and we awakened, at least momentarily, to the need of (and the government support for) the study of mathematics, science, and foreign languages and, with them, the application of higher standards and expanded expectations. Our situation today is cognate, but the effects of the global economy are just now being reflected in the actions of the electorate. Some acknowledge a "problem" but the education establishment has not taken the steps—the fairly obvious steps—to remedy it. We feel that something is radically wrong but we trudge through the same trenches.

Ravitch's reading of the condition is that the post-Sputnik call for standards was quickly displaced by a "new progressivism," a desire for racial equality that "grew out of a bitter reaction against the inadequacies of American public schools in educating minority children and a profound hostility to the typical public schools' commitment to such values as competition and order" (1983, p. 235). The current problems, in short, were blamed on *traditional* methods rather than the persistence of *failed* methods.

This led to the "open education" movement, particularly for younger children. With neo-Rousseauan books like A.S. Neill's *Summerhill* (1960) hovering in the background, the call rang out for "reforms" that ultimately looked very, very familiar: students should decide what they wanted to learn; curricular constraints should be shattered; there should be no competition, conformity, dullness or mindlessness; the classroom may be noisy; talking and playing are part of learning; the classroom should be child-centered rather than teacher-centered; there should be no grill-and-drill Gradgrindism (Ravitch 1983, p. 236).

I do not doubt that such a system could be successful under certain circumstances, with certain teachers and certain students. My concerns are both practical and theoretical. How do you assess? How do you obtain coherence? Results? How do you handle disruptives, the bored and the unmotivated? Some of these questions are answered when one recognizes that the "open" educators did not share the traditionalists' concerns; one of the system's key assumptions, e.g., was that there is *no* minimum body of knowledge which is essential for everyone to possess (Ravitch 1983, p. 149). No minimum body of knowledge? Nothing? The basic elements of civics? Of reproduction? Of economics, geography and mathematics? Of the most elementary elements of history or of the law?

These methods flew in the face of a contemporary Gallup poll (1969) of public opinion which highlighted the leading problem in American public education as the lack of discipline (Ravitch 1983, p. 251), a view that corresponded with the views of each of my wife's teaching and administrative colleagues. The "open" educator's response to this, presumably, was that the general public was troubled by the apparent lack of order and discipline in the open classroom because of their own biases and ignorance.

I dissent because of a fundamental disagreement with regard to the nature of human behavior. Every manager will tell you that the most difficult part of his or her position is handling people—motivating them, correcting them in a compassionate but effective way, minimizing friction among them, securing their best work without being dictatorial or autocratic, rewarding performance while minimizing jealousies, and so on. The notion that a group of individuals (including a group of children with varied abilities and personalities) will spontaneously, consistently and collaboratively pursue a task which is not always easy or pleasant and do it to the very best of their ability without any external controls or constraints strikes me as uncommonly idealistic. All argument may be for it, as Johnson would say, but all experience is against it.

I also have my doubts with regard to the core principle—the notion that rote learning (a phrase which biases the discussion from the outset) is necessarily always and everywhere deleterious. Robert Hughes, e.g., writes, "I have never agreed with the conventional belief that rote learning of texts destroys a pupil's 'creativity'; actually, it enriches it by filling the wells of memory" (1993, p. 94). (This attitude would certainly be reinforced by Daniel Willingham's findings.)

Commenting on Hirsch and early childhood instruction, Charles Murray writes that the ed schools consider the memorization of facts to be boring. It does not have to be, he argues. Children love stories; they love myths and they love facts. They love tales of great deeds. Memorizing is easier for them than it is for adults. It is easier than making inferences and deductions and a larger number of students are able to do it (2008, p. 77). This squares precisely with my own experience. When my students begin to drift off, I tell them stories. I tell them facts that they might find useful and that they are unlikely to forget (e.g., pilfered from Todd Gitlin—Jack Kerouac never learned to drive and he was a mama's boy [1993, pp. 46–47]).

The ed school model, the progressive ed model, life adjustment model and open school model all appear to be based on the notion that the teacher is necessarily a dictatorial monster, with a birch rod in his hand and a streak of sadism in his heart. This approach was already being abandoned in the eighteenth century, though, as Johnson opined, what the students sometimes gained at one end, they lost at the other. In America it is a model based on eighteenth-century experience in which the requirement of knowledge of classical languages was intended to produce disciplined, upstanding behavior that was reinforced by liberal use of the rod. Colleges of education and their reform-minded fellow travelers still appear to be lost in that world. They are offended by strong teachers, traditional curricula and the notion of transferable "learning." They must recognize that the stereotype against which they continue to war has long ceased to exist. The problem has now shifted to the opposite extreme. Rather than chalking up the rod so that the sadistic teacher can strike the children's bottoms in the same spot and inflict the maximum pain, the teacher is now an empowerment counselor, seeking kumbaya moments and encouraging student "expression," no matter how vapid or uninformed.

Having said all that, it is necessary that I offer some alternative model, some instance of demonstrable and dramatic academic success. The "Servicemen's Readjustment Act of 1944" is commonly called the GI Bill. It had multiple provisions, enabling, e.g., individuals to buy homes and farms or to start up businesses. The American Legion originally referred to it as the "Bill of Rights for GI Joe and GI Jane." It provided unemployment benefits of $20 a week for up to fifty-two weeks. The average number of weeks of benefits taken was 17; many refused to accept it, considering it to be welfare (Greenberg 1997, p. 18).

We now think of the GI Bill as a great provider of educational benefits, even though it provided much, much more. There were actually 15,750,000 veterans. Four million took VA loans, 8.3 million took unemployment benefits and 7.8 million—approximately 50 percent—used the educational benefit for graduate and professional study, undergraduate college study and pre-college education and training. Seventy-eight percent used one or more of the benefits (Altschuler and Blumin 2009, p. 8). The ultimate cost of the GI Bill was $14 billion. It is estimated that for every dollar spent on these veterans' benefits, the government recouped eight dollars in increased income taxes (Greenberg 1997, p. 37).

In the peak year, 1947, military veterans represented 49 percent of college admissions in America (Toby 2010, p. 299). Peter Drucker considered the enactment of the GI Bill to be the most important event of the twentieth century, because it signaled the shift to a knowledge society (Altschuler and Blumin 2009, p. 3). It also fundamentally changed the nature of American higher education.

The initial response to the Bill was one of apprehension. From the august vantage point of the Harvard president's office, Conant expressed skepticism. He argued for the admission of a very small number of individuals. He was later to admit that the veterans were "the most mature and promising students Harvard [had] ever had" (Greenberg 1997, p. 39). Hutchins is famously quoted as fearing that as a result of the Bill colleges would be turned into "educational hobo jungles."

The latter comment is frequently taken out of context. Hutchins' fears centered on the concern that colleges would be lured to a table covered with suddenly-available money and secure it by permitting their institutions to degenerate into providers of vocational training programs (Altschuler and Blumin 2009, pp. 76–77). In this, he was doubtless quite prescient, but his fears would not be realized completely for several generations. What he wished for, in fact, was that GI Joe and GI Jane would enter college and study traditional liberal arts subjects. And so, in fact, they did.

At the University of Wisconsin, for example, in the class of 1949, 38.1 percent of the veterans studied in the liberal arts, as opposed to 25.5 percent of their civilian classmates. Forty-four percent of the civilians studied business, but only 13.9 percent of the veterans. In engineering, only 16 percent of the civilians graduated but 27.6 percent of the veterans (Altschuler and Blumin 2009, p. 94).

The dropout rate was lower for veterans than for civilians. At the University of Minnesota, for example, in the spring semester of 1947, 35 of 6,010 veterans flunked out; this represented one-twentieth of the usual failure rate (Altschuler and Blumin 2009, p. 95).

When the veterans matriculated there was no reduction in standards for them. The predictions of dire results proved to be not only unfounded but 180 degrees in error. At the University of California the veterans were called "D.A.R.'s" or "damned average raisers." They "hogged" the honor rolls and the deans' lists (Altschuler and Blumin 2009, p. 95).

The benefits for servicemen were all identical; a general of the army received the same opportunities and dollars as the most junior private soldier. There were no means tests. Grants went directly to the individual veteran who could then choose (once admitted) the institution in which he or she chose to study. They chose the top institutions. A TIME article (3/18/46) posed the frequently-repeated question, "Why go to Podunk College, when the Government will send you to Yale?" (Bennett 1996, p. 243).

This accelerated the admission of the Irish, the Italians, the Poles, the Hungarians and the Jews to the nation's premier universities. Henry Rosovsky, who had served with Henry Kissinger, was one of those Jews. He later became an economics professor and dean of faculty at Harvard, the first Jewish member of the Harvard Corporation (Bennett 1996, pp. 245–56). The pressure on Harvard dormitory space (in which one section had previously been termed "kike's peak") was so intense that house masters stopped asking young gentlemen if they minded sharing rooms with Jews and Catholics (Bennett 1996, p. 19).

The expansion was incredible. In February, 1946, Harvard enrolled 2,750 students; by September that number had grown to 5,000. Purdue enrolled 5,628 in 1945, 11,462 in 1946; Syracuse had 4,391 in 1945, 15,228 a year later (Altschuler and Blumin 2009, p. 87). The government paid up to $500 for the veterans' tuition; Harvard's tuition at the end of the war was $400 (Bennett 1996, p. 18).

And they did not lack a distinguished faculty. American universities snapped up 1,684 faculty (including 5 Nobel laureates) who had been dismissed by the Nazis and they also began to hire American Jews, among them the superb Harvard historian, Oscar Handlin and the great Cornell literary scholar, M. H. Abrams.

The veterans were intensely serious with regard to their studies; this is why they earned the "D.A.R." title. They had little patience with fraternity parties or beanie wearing. Most were older; many were married. They were used to dealing with an absence of creature comforts. Contemporary photographs of crowded dormitories look like overpopulated prisons. In fact, the government converted 39 POW barracks from Weingarten, Missouri into 117 housing units for veterans at Notre Dame. Farley Hall, which was built to accommodate veterans, was a prominent dormitory when I arrived at Notre Dame, but the Quonset huts for veterans were also still very much in evidence, as they were at the University of Illinois when I moved there and as they still remain on College Avenue on the southeast corner of the University of Missouri campus.

What did the experience of the veterans utilizing the GI Bill demonstrate? It demonstrated that the colleges and universities of America could absorb millions of students who were expected to struggle but who, indeed, proved to be the institutions' best students. It demonstrated that students of multiple nationalities and ethnicities could prosper there and that prior forms of discrimination proved to be a glaring embarrassment. It demonstrated that, given the (quite unexpected) opportunity (World War I veterans had been treated shamefully), they would not only embrace it but embrace the liberal arts, face the existing academic standards, lead their classes and graduate at a significantly above-average rate. They responded to the question, "Who could go to college?" with the answer, "All."

They could also, as a matter of fact, study abroad, as Art Buchwald did (in Paris). And they demonstrated that African-American students could succeed along with their white classmates. (They had, of course, been subjected to the vilest forms of discrimination; the military was not desegregated until President Truman did so in 1948.) At Wayne State University, fully one-third of the veterans were black. Enrollments at historically black institutions grew from 1.08 percent of the total before the war to 3.6 percent by 1950. Many of the black GI's who had taken advantage of the educational benefits of the GI Bill became active in the civil rights movement (Altschuler and Blumin 2009, p. 138).

As a result of its investment, the United States received 450,000 engineers, 180,000 doctors, dentists and nurses, 360,000 teachers, 150,000 scientists, 243,000 accountants, 107,000 lawyers and 36,000 clergymen (Altschuler and Blumin 2009, p. 86). The GI's would go on to win ten Nobel prizes and represent 50 percent of the NASA engineers. And, no, athletics were not forgotten. Seventy percent of the 1947 Michigan football team were GI's; they won the Rose Bowl. The 1947 Heisman trophy went to Johnny Lujak at Notre Dame, who had previously served three years as a United States naval officer. And in the arts—the GI bill yielded a number of significant drama students, among them Tony Curtis, Harry Belafonte, Walter Matthau and Rod Steiger (Greenberg 1997, pp. 47–61).

These men and women demonstrated that our expectations with regard to those who could attend college successfully had been very, very shortsighted. Milton Greenberg puts it thus:

> The sons of unemployed depression victims, the sons of immigrants, the children of sharecroppers were just as smart as the children of wealthy and successful industrial leaders or descendants of those who arrived on the Mayflower. Older people could share classrooms with recent high school graduates and adults could go to school while married, raising children, and working at a job (1997, p. 51).

Most important, their experience vitiates the notion that college is only for the 10 percent. Put another way, they demonstrated that a vast and vastly diverse group of individuals could constitute an entire class of "ten percenters." I believe that they succeeded for fairly obvious reasons. First, they were given the resources to do so. Cost, as an issue, was taken off the table. The education that they received was of high quality, with high standards, but with few frills. They lived under what their modern counterparts would consider to be appalling conditions, but, of course, they had known far worse. After the Depression, the siege at Bastogne and the battle for Guadalcanal, how hard could general education requirements really be? They were serious, motivated and focused. Many had family responsibilities. They had no time for nonsense and they could not afford to fail. They had come from a world in which excuses were unacceptable and personal empowerment counselors were nonexistent.

I am not suggesting that we would achieve far greater academic success if we required our matriculants to have prior experience in both desperate economic and life-or-death battlefield situations. What I am suggesting is that focus, discipline, and motivation can lead to unimagined levels of success, that costs must be covered, but that those costs need not be excessive and entail frills and peripheral services. I am also suggesting that the GI Bill changed American life and American Higher Education by demonstrating that all can achieve academic success. Our current system, for all of our protestations with regard to openness and to diversity, most often perpetuates the economic inequalities which exist in our society and all too often offers those who are in greatest need of opportunity a debased product.

We believe, however, or at least seem to believe that we are doing the right thing, since we persist in turning our heads from our problems. From time to time we realize that the newest scheme from our colleges of education—whole-word reading, a focus on "skills" rather than content, replacing highly competent teaching with a "student-centered" environment, or some new crackbrained approach to the teaching of mathematics—is simply not working, that our children are lagging behind the children of countries far poorer than our own. We need "new ways," but the process of finding those new ways must include the appreciation of the problems inhering in the current ways.

Some of the blame can fall on the sixties radicals (or, more properly, the cowards who acceded, willy-nilly, to their demands and the corporatists who saw in their antiauthoritarian "program" a market opportunity) and some can fall on the ed schools, but their common influence remains certain aspects of what we broadly term Romanticism, a subject far too vast for this discussion, but one that requires at least some attention.

I noted Blake's comment in *The Marriage of Heaven and Hell* expressing the desire that the angel guarding the tree of life might be directed to leave, in which case the world would suddenly be seen as holy. What he is seeking, of course, is a return to the garden of Eden, to which we are now forbidden admittance. The return to the prelapsarian childhood of man, envisioned as a return to an unsullied garden, is at the heart of the romantic vision.

The fact that we are denied access to prelapsarian Nature (though we persist in seeking it) results in the profound sense of *loss* which would become an overarching romantic theme. Wordsworth seeks access through the memory of unique moments in childhood; others take a shorter route, seeking it, e.g., via the use of opium. The spiritual dream of a return to Eden is paralleled by the political dream of the creation of a new Eden. Hence the revolutionary impulses and linking of dreams of the distant, shadowy "past" with dreams of an idealized future. As Frye puts it, the romantic's *rejection of history* represents "a rejecting of social *reality* in favor of a social *ideal*" (1968, p. 37; my italics).

The descriptive term *romanticism* recalls the world of the chivalric romance (here I am adapting Frye, 1968, pp. 37–39 with the addition of some time-tested insights from M. H. Abrams, 1953, 1971). In that form a knight leaves the protection of a walled city ("civilization") and enters a forest, thus passing through a symbolic threshold (Springsteen—a full-fledged romantic—sings of the *darkness at the edge of town*) in preparation for exotic adventures. The town has butchers and bakers, while the far more interesting but far more dangerous forest has wizards, necromancers, dragons and captive damsels.

The world of the forest is separate from the world of the walled city and when the knight returns from it he will necessarily attempt to speak of occurrences of which the townfolk have no experience. Since the knight is exceptional and the townfolk are workaday people, the knight's task is to somehow, in some way, communicate exotic experiences to them. Thus, one of the pivotal works of Romanticism is Coleridge's *Rime of the Ancient Mariner*—the story of an individual who has entered special "space," had special experiences and is now doomed to endlessly seek to communicate those experiences, even if it means disrupting weddings. (This is why the bourgeois version—*Robinson Crusoe*—haunted the imaginations of thinkers, including Rousseau and Marx, for generations.)

The experience may be more than exotic; it may in fact be ineffable. Hence the sense of both transcendence and evanescence which often exist hand in hand. Although Conrad is not a romantic, he adopts Coleridge's model wholesale in *Heart of Darkness*, the story's primary narrator assuring us that Marlow's story will, ultimately, be inconclusive. They always are.

This poetic model represents a complete departure from what preceded it. In the preface to his edition of Shakespeare, Johnson writes that "nothing can please many and please long, but just representations of general nature." We may be delighted awhile, he says, by "the irregular combinations of fanciful invention," by "that novelty of which the common satiety of life sends us all in quest; but the pleasures of sudden wonder are soon exhausted, and the mind can only repose on the stability of truth." And, in this regard, Shakespeare is the writer who never fails to deliver.

The "pleasures of sudden wonder" are the romantic's stock in trade. Johnson does not seek the transcendently evanescent; he seeks insightful representations of what we would call the workings of the human mind and heart, representations that ring true. In other contexts he will also call for fresh approaches, fresh representations, linking what he terms the "just" with the "novel." Justness without novelty is hackneyed; novelty without justness is zany. What he calls for, ultimately, is something tried, true but, simultaneously, richly imagined and fresh. He wants, in short, what all of the Hollywood production companies say that they want, but seldom receive, for the essentially 2,000 year-old+ model which Johnson espouses survived Romanticism in our popular culture and dominates in cinema, television and novelistic fiction (at, of course, quite varying levels of quality).

The traditionalist such as Johnson, looking back to the thought of Sidney, Horace and, ultimately, Aristotle sees literary art as "pragmatic," in the sense that its test is its effect on the audience. Was the audience both instructed *and* entertained (the two existing in a necessary unity, since art which only teaches is dull and that which only entertains risks triviality)? The romantic, on the other hand, shifts the emphasis from the work's effect upon the audience to the work's creator. The poet is the hero of the piece and the piece is an account of *his* journey. It is not, ultimately, about *us*; it is about *him*.

This would appear strange, narcissistic and even comic to the eighteenth century. In the club of authors depicted in Goldsmith's *Citizen of the World* letters, a poet must pay the other members of the society to listen to him read his work. When he announces that he has written an epic poem and that the hero is . . . *himself* . . . the response is stifled laughter. This is 1760; the response to Wordsworth's *Prelude* will be quite different, in part because of Wordsworth's genius, but in part because Kant's *Critique of Judgment*

(1790) had taken the pragmatic test off the table. We were now to judge works of art purely on their own internal terms and not on their effects upon the audience. Farewell to two millennia of criticism.

In the *Critique of Pure Reason* Kant had earlier argued that the internal workings of the human mind constitute a unique way of seeing, but one that will never offer us access to things as they are in themselves. We see, in the common metaphor, with eyeglasses that cannot be removed. Hence (in a world of ultimate uncertainty, Kant following Hume) the privileging of the individual perspective. Hence the artwork in which the poet can pen an epic in which he has become the hero. Hence the desire for exotic experience. Hence the dangers of narcissism and self-indulgence. Hence the continual privileging of individual *expression*. Hence—given the sins and failures of postlapsarian man and the epistemological uncertainties with regard to postlapsarian man's representations—the farewell to history and all previous notions of traditional *wisdom* (which, in Old English, conflates two words, meaning *wise judgment*).

But what of the child? How does the child come to play such a dominant role in romantic thought? That is a more straightforward issue. We all may wish to return to Eden, to a Nature without storms, vermin and death (or vast natural disruptions such as the Lisbon earthquake of 1755, which devastated the European imagination), to perpetual spring, to a close relationship with God and archangels and an innocent but rich sexuality, but for the romantic the individual closest to that experience is the child. The child is closer because, as Rousseau would argue, the evils of society have not yet had their way with him or, as Shelley might put it, life with a capital L has not yet triumphed over him, but it goes deeper than that. One line that inevitably finds its way onto the blackboard or the PowerPoint screen in Romanticism 101 is that "Each romantic writer finds his or her personal path to some form of neoplatonism."

In the neoplatonist construct, each of us has come to this life from a preexisting state—an edenic state in the romanticist's view. We knew things and felt things there, great things, and we have been forced to abandon them when we entered this life. Hence we are closest to that joy and that wisdom when we are children, not when we are adults. Hence children should be our guides and not weary, befuddled, broken adults.

In the "Immortality Ode" Wordsworth makes this utterly explicit: "The things which I have seen I now can/see no more. . . . there hath past away a glory from the earth. . . . But there's a Tree, of many, one,/A single Field which I have looked upon,/Both of them speak of something that is/gone. . . . Our birth is but a sleep and a forgetting:/The Soul that rises with us, our life's Star,/Hath had elsewhere its setting,/And cometh from afar. . . . trailing clouds of glory do we come/From God, who is our home:/Heaven lies about us in our infancy! . . . . Delight and liberty, the simple creed/Of childhood.... Though nothing can bring back the/hour/Of splendour in the grass, of glory in the flower...."

Thus, Wordsworth can sometimes recapture those moments of childhood ("Though inland far we be,/Our Souls have sight of that immortal/sea/Which brought us hither,/Can in a moment travel thither,/And see the Children sport upon the/shore,/And hear the mighty waters rolling ever-/more") and revivify the present. He can look into a cradle and see a "Mighty Prophet! Seer blest!" where his eighteenth-century predecessors would have seen a cute, dependent, and sometimes tyrannical infant, who will hopefully grow up to become an interesting adult.

I love the "Immortality Ode" and I love Wordsworth's vision of children sporting upon the shore, a transcendent affirmation of human joy and divine presence in the face of a fallen world, but I cannot go from that image to an actual embrace of literal neoplatonism. I also share F.L. Lucas' nagging concern:

> One of the stages infants pass through, according to Freudian theory, is that of being in love with themselves. But of this infantile stage there remains an unconscious memory; there is always a risk of neurotic regression to it. The malady has been well named Narcissism. And it becomes a plague among the Romantics, broodingly withdrawn from the real world and their fellow-men (1937, p. 102).

"Romanticism," Goethe thought, "is disease; classicism is health" (Lucas 1937, p. 102). And again: "Epochs which are regressive, and in the process of dissolution, are always *subjective*, whereas the trend in all progressive epochs is *objective*" (my emphases; Hughes 1993, p. 10).

I will always take Goethe over Rousseau, a classicist but also, perhaps, the last Renaissance man. Goethe provides an image of Romanticism and romantic poesy in the second part of *Faust* in the character Euphorion, the son of Faust and Helen of Troy. He is frequently taken to be an image of Byron or at least the Byronic poetic hero. He leaps, he soars, he cannot be shackled by earthly boundaries but, a young man, he quickly crashes to earth and dies.

Rousseau, however, lives in the hearts of romantic educators and his influence continues to be felt. Johnson thought him "a rascal, who ought to be hunted out of society," as, of course, he had been. Napoleon lived to see that the revolution did *not* yield a new Eden. He perceived that the revolution would not have been possible without Rousseau and that without the revolution he, let us be honest—a military dictator—would not have been possible.

One cannot resist noting that the person who is often touted as the father of child-centered education turned his own five children over to foundling homes. That does not, of course, necessarily undercut his educational theories, but it is fair to consider an individual's thought within the context of his personality. Even his defenders, e.g., acknowledge that his turning on Hume after Hume had helped to provide him a British haven was an example of his demonstrable paranoia. Since his educational theories turn on his conception of the "natural" it is fair to ask how clear and how compelling *his* conception of the *natural* actually was.

E. D. Hirsch (an expert scholar of Romanticism) considers romantic ideas a curse. He finds romanticism's faith in the benefits of nature "complacent"; he challenges the romantic view that there is no boundary between the natural and the divine and the notion that sin came from civilization (Hirsch 2016, pp. 4–5).

Milton, of course, thought that sin appeared much earlier in our cosmic history, Satan having given birth to her. Satan sinned long before civilization came along to despoil childhood and he helped bring sin to Eve and to Adam before they were exiled from Eden and forced to find their way in a natural world that was forever changed by their actions. He was also, however, a figure who exerted enormous influence upon the romantics, Blake, e.g. feeling that Milton was really a member of the devil's party without realizing it (an idea later deflated by C. S. Lewis and others). Satan apparently earns the romantics' affection because of his powerful will and energy; it cannot be because of his "naturalness," since he is the quintessential embodiment—in Milton—of lies and calculation.

The bottom line is that the many lineaments of Romanticism are often difficult to reconcile with one another. If we are prepared to entertain a neoplatonist vision involving preexistent states with an explicitly (Judeo-Christian) Edenic vision as a crucial overlay and, simultaneously, the assertion of "civilization's" causation of our many troubles it would seem fair to entertain questions concerning the historical sequence (or at least the intellectual relatedness) of all of these alleged events and phenomena. In the Miltonic vision, the ultimate cause of our banishment from Eden is the pride and arrogance of an archangel. It is the narcissism of a member of the elite, whose sin leads to the temptation, and original sin, of previously-unfallen humans, their sin then resulting in the fallen nature which still affects our civilization and society.

Is the basis for failed but still-hegemonic educational programming the result of compelling facts and compelling empirical arguments or does it find its origins in a series of vague feelings anchored in little more than unconnected strands and incoherent metaphors? Perhaps we can ask the question in a more basic way: are the acquisition of reading and mathematics skills "natural" processes? Horace Mann thought, e.g., that whole-word reading was preferable to phonics because it was more *natural*; Hirsch, on the other hand, argues that reading and doing math are not *natural* developments at all (Hirsch 2016, pp. 5–6).

In *Heart of Darkness* when Marlow finds the Russian/Harlequin's copy of Towson's book on navigation he is delighted. Here is something palpable and real, something embodying Victorian conceptions of work and "civilization," but he sees the handwritten comments in the book as some kind of cipher. Only later does he realize, in conversation with the Russian, that they are in Cyrillic. Chomsky may be right (certainly all modern linguistics is betting with him) that each of us possesses, in our wired brains, a universal grammar, but we most certainly do not possess a universal alphabet, sound system and handwriting style. And while we may possess exquisite impulses and instincts with regard to art (some seeing the upper Paleolithic cave paintings for the first time have thought they might have been done by a modern figure such as Marc Chagall) we do not see, at Lascaux, Pech-Merle, Altamira or Chauvet, any differential equations, much less the fluxions of Newton and Leibniz.

The abandonment of history or at least its depreciation has been cataclysmic for both higher education and for the society populated by its graduates. Equally damaging, however, has been the invocation of "history" and "evidence" and "proof" in a muddled way, since the passionate allegation of evil or wrongheadedness clears the slate of alternatives and allows the special pleader to advocate ultimately indefensible but temporarily "new" ways of proceeding. The urging of what looks *eligible* in the earlier sense of the term—worthy of consideration and choice—and its reinforcement by argument that may be correct or, on the contrary, what may be what F. L. Lucas would call nothing more than "moonshine" can truly be dangerous and ultimately very destructive.

It is one thing to sell snake oil, quite another to sell the results of incoherent research. As children we all thought (for a moment) about buying X-ray Specs for $1.00 and each of our electronic in-boxes has been cluttered with offers of high-priced, natural-ingredient nostrums to enhance our manhood. We know what that represents and we promptly hit the *delete* button, but as a society we have been far more accepting of half-baked schemes to enhance our systems of education. So far they have put us in 19th, 23rd and 30th place.

There is a name for all this. In 1745 the bookseller John Newbery published a series of miniature volumes entitled *The Circle of the Sciences*. Designed for home instruction, they were enormously popular, so popular that few of the multiple reprintings are now available since they had literally been read to pieces. Hoping to build on Newbery's success, Robert Dodsley prepared a rival publication, entitled the *Preceptor*. To hype the publication he asked Johnson to write a *Preface*.

In discussing history and chronology (section IV), Johnson discusses the ways in which History can enable us to understand why things were done and why things were not done. It enables us to assign praise and blame to, e.g., the Prossers of history and the Arthur Bestors who exposed them. Absent a clear sense of the past we are condemned to repeat it, Santayana famously said, but Johnson's concern here is not with the ignorance of history but rather with a muddled sense of it, a reprise of Pope's concern that a *little* learning can be a *very* dangerous thing. We think we know something but our minds are cluttered with contradictions and incoherence. We believe we have visions when we only have the kinds of fantasies and delusions that manifest themselves in fever-induced dreams:

> It is not easy to live without finding in the Mind some Desire of being informed concerning the Generations of Mankind, that have been in Possession of the World before us, and whether they were better or worse than ourselves; or what good or evil has been derived to us from their Schemes, Practices, and Institutions. These are Enquiries which *History* alone can satisfy.... Accordingly, it should be diligently inculcated to the Scholar, that unless he fixes in his Mind some Idea of the Time in which each Man of Eminence lived, and each Action was performed, with some Part of the contemporary History of the rest of the World, he will consume his Life in useless reading, and darken his Mind with a Croud of unconnected Events, his Memory will be perplexed with distant Transactions resembling one another, and his Reflections be like a Dream in a Fever, busy and turbulent, but confused and indistinct (Hazen 1973, pp. 182–83).

There are other potential sources of silliness besides outright falsification and muddled thinking. Some, for example, think in purely theoretical terms and they have no reference points in experience against which to test their theories. Student-centered instruction? Well, of course. The students have to be at the center; we'd hardly put them at the periphery, would we? Open classrooms? Well, why not? How can we be welcoming if we have a closed-door policy? Instructional policies that accord with *nature*? Certainly. What is the alternative—unnatural practices? We have all encountered the bearers of ephemeral educational theories. Their mouths are full of plans and maxims and acronyms. They move from conference to conference and consultancy to consultancy. The most recent example: "Confuse Students to Help Them Learn" (Kolowich 2014). Its tagline: "Professors who present classroom material clearly and concisely may not be doing their students any favors."

The educational industry is filled with individuals whose livelihood depends on pedagogical "innovation." Commonsensical answers (we essentially need curious students, passionate faculty, substantive material and effective infrastructure) are always and everywhere insufficient for them, because they return us to our core activities rather than illuminating career paths that consist of second-guessing those activities.

This is not to suggest that we should suspend all research on human communication and cognition. On the contrary, we should accelerate it, but we are far more likely to acquire useful knowledge from our neuroscience laboratories than from commentators who advise us with regard to the senses and the brain without ever truly studying them. The increased understanding of how we actually learn and communicate and how we might facilitate and enhance those processes are among the most fascinating subjects of contemporary research. Authentic research on human cognition will undergird and extend our central activity—the development and dissemination of new knowledge.

Discovering new truths, new methods, new facts, new texts, new materials and new explanations and then "possessing," internalizing and integrating them is our central challenge; the communication of that learning is, by a wide margin, the easy part. Replacing the process of *discovery* and the preservation/transmittal of the resulting learning with a focus on the process of *communication* has undermined and, in some cases, even effaced our core enterprise. Doing so with failed or fanciful methods has compounded the problem. Leaving all of the work to the student and assuming that the student's personal "quest" will always and everywhere be equally serious and equally successful is, quite simply, delusional.

Chapter Seven

I Came to Cornell to Become an Engineer

In 2009, Attorney General Eric Holder commented that our nation has been cowardly with regard to the conducting of candid discussions on race. To an academic this is a very curious statement, since the consideration of issues of race/class/gender has been omnipresent on our campuses for decades. In some corners of the Humanities it seems that these are the only subjects one is permitted to discuss, though one is generally only permitted to discuss them in certain, prescribed ways.

    The key word is *candid*. Many people of good will share the same egalitarian goals for our society, but differ on the strategies to achieve those goals. Some of those strategies are never articulated because of fears that the strategizer will be charged with racism, sexism or homophobism.

    Suppressing ideological impulses and anxiously-held "feelings" and focusing instead upon *reason, logic* and *evidence* is also more difficult in a postmodern ethos which seeks to efface the achievements of the Enlightenment, in part by challenging all vestiges of empiricism. The situation on campus is further complicated by the existence of simple, entrenched interests who will meet what they perceive to be antagonistic challenges with the rallying of troops and the alignment of artillery batteries. As the faculty attend instruction on how to conduct "difficult discussions," the middle managers are placing mines and barbed wire around their turf; meanwhile, the "higher" administrators are attempting to channel and canalize student emotions, lest they morph into demonstrations and disruptions. The campus culture recalls the diplomats' common characterization of the middle east—a "problem" that must be "managed" but one that will never be "solved."

    In discussing beliefs, budgets and Balkanization, let us begin with a related phenomenon—campus "women's centers." We have had them for decades. They were installed for the purpose of offering support, providing advocacy and a physical locus for programming of various kinds. None are evil and all, presumably, have done good things.

They also require resources. Unless they are generously endowed (to cover overhead as well as staff and programming) they will inevitably draw resources from other purposes, including the hiring of faculty, the preservation and enhancement of academic programming and the provision of financial aid to students. A person making the argument that these kinds of facilities were once very important but that they have, increasingly, become less and less necessary, might offer certain types of information in support of that position.

Women have enjoyed spectacular recent success, both in the university and beyond. The historical reasons for this success are likely to accelerate it further. The large, historical causes are clear. The development of the pill and, a century earlier, the vulcanization of rubber which led to far more effective condoms and, thus, far more effective methods of birth control, freed women from what Kay Hymowitz calls their "default mental position—fatalism" (2011, p. 63). In the early 19th century white women had, on average, 7 children. By 1900 that number had decreased to 3.56 (Hymowitz 2011, p. 62). Market capitalism and modern technology brought labor-saving devices, antibiotics, blood banks, safe baby formula, central heating and indoor plumbing, all of which enhanced both women's lot and women's health.

In 1948 33 percent of women were in the labor force; by 1995 59 percent were, a number that remains more or less constant today (Hymowitz 2011, p. 66). While the first, second and third waves of the women's movement brought the franchise and a succession of other positive developments, women were the overwhelming beneficiaries of the so-called "knowledge society" and the array of jobs which it provided, jobs in which women particularly excelled. By the mid-1990s so-called "knowledge workers" represented fully one-third of the American workforce. From 1960-2000 the number of lawyers increased from 1 in 627 to 1 in 300; from 1974–2000 the number of MBA degrees increased 310 percent (Hymowitz 2011, pp. 25–26).

A McKinsey study (1998–2006) concluded that 85 percent of the *new jobs* in America involved "complex knowledge work." The physical strength necessary for the full array of, e.g., manufacturing jobs offered men a comparative advantage that is now significantly diminished, particularly to the degree that manufacturing jobs now employ robotics and other devices that require skill rather than strength for their operation.

In 1960 women represented 6 percent of the nation's doctors and 3 percent of the nation's lawyers; today those numbers are 49 percent and 47 percent respectively (Hymowitz 2011, p. 54). In 1970 4 percent of married women earned more than their husbands; by 2007 that number had increased by 550 percent (Hymowitz 2011, p. 158). Today, women's salaries are 117 percent of men's salaries in Manhattan and 120 percent of men's salaries in Dallas. In 2006 27.9 percent of men had a college degree, while 34.2 percent of women did.

On campuses, in 2008–2009, for the first time, women earned a majority of the doctoral degrees awarded in America. The percentage appears slight—50.4 percent—but as recently as 2000 that number was 44 percent. Women have the momentum; in 2008–2009 their numbers increased by 6.1 percent, the male numbers by only 1 percent. With regard to master's degrees, women are well ahead, at a whopping 60 percent (Jaschik, 2010, p. 1).

The downside has already been mentioned. Women are so successful as students and so numerous within the applicant pools that universities are now discriminating against them, in part, as I noted earlier, because they want their institutions to have the kind of male-female mix that will attract top female students. This comes with a price. Kay Hymowitz reports recent admission numbers at the College of William and Mary: 43 percent of men admitted, but only 29 percent of women.

The bottom line: women are prospering, particularly on the college campus and they would dominate the population on each college campus if their numbers were not artificially reduced. Hence, the question—given the other priorities on campus (to reduce tuition, enhance programs, increase financial aid and increase the number of tenure/track faculty)—priorities that should be important to the majority of students (who are, of course, women), is it now time to close the women's center and redirect the resources to more pressing, current needs?

The question, of course, is, in all honesty, disingenuous. No campus administrator would even dream of closing the women's center, not only because such individuals are inherently risk-averse, but because they are aware of the pain involved in being publicly flayed.

Still, it is important to have an honest discussion, if only because informed decisions are better than uninformed ones. In the 2003 Grutter v. Bollinger decision, Justice Sandra Day O'Connor famously suggested that race-conscious admission policies might not be necessary, twenty-five years hence, a highly flammable number that has occasioned a great deal of discussion. It is still fair to say (no matter how sensitive these kinds of issues might be) that decisions made to effect social change should be reexamined and reevaluated after a great deal of social change has occurred.

"How much," of course, is the issue up for debate and that debate is welcome. We should have it and its central focus should be those strategies that are most likely to insure student academic success. My cautionary reminders would be two in number; the first would concern the fact that universities have been extremely successful, in part because they have resisted the temptation to effect precipitous change (though corporatist "entrepreneurs" and true student/faculty radicals may call for it). How many businesses have been in existence as long as the University of Bologna?

At the same time, universities' largely-positive institutional conservatism has a downside, particularly in difficult economic times. Some units continue to exist long past their point of need or maximum effectiveness. Every organization should make the best use of its resources and those resources should be focused on the organization's central purposes. Whether unit A or unit B should be retained is always a fair question. When one of those units generates intense political pressures, it is still the responsible thing to do to avail yourself of the facts and air them in an honest discussion. We make such decisions all of the time within our own families and it would be irresponsible not to examine facts and issues in depth when it comes to other entities for which we hold responsibility.

Let me inch closer to the third rail of the academic enterprise and turn the discussion to, broadly, "race and ethnicity," in this case a series of decisions made recently by the University of California at San Diego. In March 2011 UCSD ceased offering a master's degree in electrical and computer engineering; it dropped a master's program in comparative literature and coursework in French, German, Spanish and English literature. In the midst of its budget challenges it had lost three top cancer researchers to Rice and, with them, their significant grant support and the indirect costs which those grants generated.

At the same time, UCSD was creating a new full-time vice chancellor for equity, diversity and inclusion. This appointment did not represent an initial foray into diversity administration. The university's already-existing diversity apparatus included the Chancellor's Diversity Office, the associate vice chancellor for faculty equity, the assistant vice chancellor for diversity, the faculty equity advisors, the graduate diversity coordinators, the staff diversity liaison, the undergraduate student diversity liaison, the graduate student diversity liaison, the chief diversity officer, the director of development for diversity initiatives, the Office of Academic Diversity and Equal Opportunity, the Committee on Gender Identity and Sexual Orientation issues, the Committee on the Status of Women, the Campus Council on Climate, Culture and Inclusion, the Diversity Council, and the directors of the Cross-Cultural Center, the Lesbian Gay Bisexual Transgender Resource Center and the Women's Center (MacDonald, July 18, 2011, p. 1).

UCSD is not an outlier in this particular realm. Berkeley's vice chancellor for equity and inclusion, for example, has a staff of seventeen just in his immediate office. In 2009 his salary was $194,000; at that time the starting salary for an assistant professor at UC-Berkeley (where the faculty no longer have office telephones) was approximately $53,000 (MacDonald, July 18, 2011, p. 1).

This raises a number of questions. First, the individuals targeted by UCSD's efforts, transgendered students, e.g., or ethnic minorities, cannot now take a master's degree in comp lit or electrical and computer engineering. In registering for literature courses in English or modern foreign languages they will experience curtailed options. Granting that there are goods attached to all of these activities, what is the proper *balance* between the funding of support programs and the funding of academic programs, the academics being the basis for students' attendance in the first place?

This is a difficult discussion to conduct, because the moment someone suggests that the diversity bureaucracy is inflated, that person risks being called a racist, sexist or homophobe. At the same time, of course, anyone who denies academic opportunities to black, female or gay students could also be called those names, though there the risks are much reduced, even though the results may be just as real.

The reason that the risks are reduced is that course offerings and degree programs are part of a vast, nearly unintelligible miasma of activity, while specific offices and administrative titles have human faces. Behind those human faces are supporters prepared to march to the battlements in support of operations which have benefited them (and which may be providing them internships or part-time employment). Who, on the other hand will take up arms to defend to the death a course in renaissance prose, intermediate Portuguese, or the proto-romantic *sturm und drang*?

My question is, where are the tipping points? Assuming the need for both academic programming and an administrative apparatus, how much of one or the other must we have for 'success'? How much of one or the other can we afford to lose without inflicting significant damage on our larger purposes and processes?

These are questions that deans must conjure with every day. Resources are limited; the needs are many; the tradeoffs are always painful. Avoiding decisions is not a responsible option.

With the diversity apparatus, on the other hand, the decisions are quite different. While deans control that portion of the budget which is assigned to them (in addition to that which they can personally raise), the central administration controls the entire budget. They can always expand the bureaucracy by simply retaining some or all of the money that would have gone to the deans and redirecting it to some new office or offices.

In the case of "diversity" issues, they can do that and, simultaneously, receive plaudits from the faculty for doing so. The faculty will grouse about the absence of raises and support the reduction of bureaucracy in the abstract, but *few* or *none* will suggest reducing the diversity bureaucracy. The administrators are all very well aware of that fact.

Why would they expand the diversity bureaucracy beyond some reasonable level? First, because they can; second, because it is potentially self-serving. Administrators tout their credentials in two ways—through the enumeration of their responsibilities and the enumeration of their accomplishments. The expansion of the bureaucracy increases the number of an administrator's "direct reports." When he or she is looking for that next, better-paying job with an enhanced title, the person can list the dizzying number of individuals whose work he or she effectively "supervised" in the past.

He or she can also list past accomplishments and a significant contribution to "diversity" (even if it only means creating an office within a bureaucracy) will be at the head of such brag points. Any list of the top questions asked a prospective provost or president will (always and everywhere) include at least one question on that individual's commitment to diversity. "I'm so glad you asked that. As a matter of fact, I developed the Office for . . . which received recognition from . . . as a model for the enhancement of diversity." (Smiles and warm feelings all around.)

There is a darker point here, one stressed by Professor Ginsberg (2011). Corporatists expand "diversity" and "civility" operations in order to accomplish a number of purposes, including the wresting of power from the faculty. Sometimes they feel that they *must* do so. They have very real problems with which they must deal (in addition to their desires for self-aggrandizement): their institution may be losing points in external evaluations because of their diversity numbers; they may be receiving pressure from the black caucus in the state legislature—"increase your numbers or face our opposition during the next round of budget talks." There may be a racial scandal in athletics or a negative story line in a local newspaper . . . something that might be countered by a "bold new initiative." There remains the perpetual Damoclean sword of student "unrest," unrest which can bring down presidencies and chancellorships.

The fundamental issue, however, is often more basic than that. The traditional model for university governance is that the administration controls the budget, the faculty control the programs. The faculty plan, approve and review academic programs, construct the curriculum, secure new colleagues, rule on their tenure and promotions (and the denial of same). These processes may then proceed "up the ladder," with administrators approving those decisions, but the locus for control is the faculty.

By the same token, the administration controls the budget, but it takes advice from the faculty and, if it is wise, it runs all major initiatives by the faculty in an honest and transparent way. There is give and take on both sides, but, fundamentally, the faculty cannot tell the administration what to do with the budget and the administration cannot override the faculty on central academic issues, though they may do so, from time to time.

(Very) occasionally, the president might overturn a tenure recommendation. At the top institutions it is understood that everyone—up the ladder—can say no. The conflict comes when a senior officer tenures or promotes someone who has been given a negative vote by the department and/or the college.

The bottom line remains: a division of responsibility for the budget on the one hand, the programs on the other. *Corporatist administrators want to breach that line.* They want to control academic processes. They want to initiate programs which they consider attractive in the marketplace. The greater their philistinism the greater their disregard for academic content and quality. They want to control hires and they want to control curricula.

Absent collegial motives, it is difficult for them to do so. What do I mean by *collegial motives*? Assume that an institution has aspirations for greatness but is not there yet. It has pockets of strength and pockets of weakness. It can institute policies that will enhance strengths. For example, many departments have weak areas. They mandate that every job search will include faculty (or a faculty member) from another area. When the weak area is hiring, the chair places a strong person from a strong area on the search committee to keep the weak faculty from hiring someone like themselves. That person can then speak up when the department convenes to make the final hiring decision.

It is common in graduate schools to have faculty from other departments sit on examination boards or dissertation committees (often an individual from the student's minor field). A number of institutions grant the dean the authority to place a faculty member from a cognate or related department (in the life sciences, e.g.) on such boards. While this "reduces power" in some senses, it enhances quality (or is at least designed to do so) and the measures are taken in house. The *faculty* are looking over the shoulders of the *faculty*.

That is not the kind of process that bothers Professor Ginsberg, whose concerns I share. We are talking about administrative self-aggrandizement, not the university's higher needs (though the latter claim is often made to achieve the former result). The easiest way for a corporatist administrator to breach lines of authority and control faculty processes is to do so in the name of *diversity*, since few faculty will have the courage to complain or confront.

Thus, we see faculty search committees constrained by elaborate reporting requirements. We see them forced to work with bureaucrats and undergo "training" in search procedures. As noted above, the faculty on a search committee are likely to know far more about race, ethnicity and gender issues than the bureaucrats do. Often, the search procedures involve fantasies and fictions. There simply are no minority faculty available in some areas or their numbers are so miniscule that the administrative superstructures and reporting requirements are out of all proportion to the likelihood of a hiring success.

There is also a fair and important question—does the administration truly believe that the modern university faculty (let us say, e.g., the *Berkeley* faculty) would actually obstruct the hiring of a woman or minority if that person were the most qualified for the position?

Perhaps not, but they might wish to hire the *most qualified person* instead of an individual who had threshold credentials but fell ten or twenty places below more qualified candidates on the search committee's list. In that case, what is the administration to do?

Simple enough. The administration creates a fund housed in one of the senior offices in the diversity bureaucracy and dangles the money before departmental eyes. "If you can successfully surface (*surface*, never *find*) a potential hire with acceptable credentials, we will do what we can to find the money for the hire."

The departments nearly always succumb, particularly in difficult financial times (which are perpetuated, in part, by bureaucratic expansion). In some cases, this may be the only way in which they can hire at all and who knows when they will have another opportunity? The kindly administrator with the helping hand is, of course, the person who captured money that would normally have gone to the college's departmental programs. *That* person then decides how the money will be used; in this case he or she controls hiring and, in the future, he or she can tout the manner in which he or she contributed to diversity. "Normally," deans (far closer to faculty and hence more accountable) decide which departments need support and the form that that support should take. When administrators capture the resources first they in effect remove that authority from the deans. Administrators then control both the macro level of the university's budget and the micro level.

This might seem to be a benevolent practice. How else will minority faculty or women in underrepresented fields be hired? The answer is that they will be hired at the institutions in which their names rise to the top of the search committees' lists, not those in which they hover at the middle.

Administrative preemption carries a subsidiary risk: hiring practices that involve explicit set-asides can stigmatize the resulting hirees. Some, of course, will embrace the opportunity to be hired by a "reach" institution. It is the case, however, that top minority faculty frequently tell universities that they will not accept positions that are the result of set-asides. They seek "regular" appointments. By the same token, faculty are enormously sensitive to the nature of the units in which they are being hired. Minority faculty and women, for example, will often say that they are happy to participate in the work of interdisciplinary program A or B, but that they will only come if they are appointed to the Political Science department or History department as their tenure home.

This part of academic culture applies to all faculty. When a colleague leaves to take a more lucrative position elsewhere, everyone looks at the "receiving department." It matters, for example, if a card-carrying psychologist accepts a position in a college of education ed-psych department or if a mathematician moves to math-ed, or a credentialed Film or English professor moves to some vague "media" construct. These units have to pay the candidate coming from a traditional field more, because these receiving units carry less cachet than established or basic disciplines.

A person hired under "other" circumstances (not just minority hires but, for example, spousal or partner accommodation hires) will still have to meet the department, college and university's tenure and promotion expectations. If they are not the best qualified person for the position that they hold, they may well face difficulties later. They may, in fact, have been set up for failure. Their personal lot, however, is not the concern of the corporatist administrator. He or she deals in statistics and numbers. He or she wishes to point to percentages, percentages within the time frame in which he or she was in office. If it is found that individuals hired under set-aside conditions are having difficulty attaining tenure ... well ... then ... the administrator's successor can establish a new task force to study the issue and, later, invent a new office to oversee the results of the task force's recommendations.

This is an issue which is often misunderstood by the general public. They sometimes believe that "a person with a PhD should be able to be a college professor," that a PhD is a PhD. "Why are those stuffy old professors wringing their hands and discriminating against people?"

Search committees will always contain members with different interests and different reactions to the same credentials. Irreducibly, however, there will be considerable overlap in their "first cut" takes on the dossiers before them. A large group of individuals will be eliminated promptly; a tiny handful of "reach" applicants will hover at the top (with doubts expressed as to whether or not they will actually come) and a small group, 10–15 perhaps, will be kept in the pool because they have some support from one or more members of the committee. That group will generate the most discussion as the search committee moves to an interview list, prior to the development of the short list. There are always disagreements, of course, and disappointed search committee members, but these committees—if they are skilled and operate under shared assumptions—will nearly always be able to establish a hierarchy among their applicants. The "best qualified applicant," i.e. the best qualified applicant who emerges in the course of a now *international* search process, is more likely to raise the quality of the hiring institution than an individual from the second or third tier.

Some Ivy-league institutions are very wary of tenuring their "own" faculty (i.e. previously-hired individuals now aspiring to tenure) and require them to submit to international, competitive searches, searches that will demonstrate that they are, indeed, the top people available, in the world, at that time, in those fields. Caltech calculates the likelihood of a prospective faculty member receiving a Nobel prize before it issues an offer. The bottom line is that while there will always be disagreements about certain details, the faculty will be able to establish a hierarchy of job applicants and hiring from the *top* of the list (assuming that the faculty has high standards and is acting in good faith) will enhance the institution academically, while hiring from the middle or bottom of the list may well not.

"Diversity" will be part of the calculation when search committees (or admission committees) are making their decisions. What, precisely, does "diversity" mean? What does it entail? Why is it a desideratum? Heather MacDonald points out that Berkeley's vice chancellor for equity and inclusion commands a $4,500,000 slice of the diversity bureaucracy there. In 2004 Harvard created a new senior vice provost for diversity and faculty development responsible for $50,000,000 in diversity funding. It also created six new diversity deanships (MacDonald, November 25, 2011, pp. 1–2). What are the results that such investments are intended to bring?

The question is not easily answered beyond the straightforward desire for an increased number of underrepresented minorities and (in certain fields) women. Peter Wood has studied the issue in depth and has reached interesting conclusions. "Affirmative Action" was born in 1965 in a speech by President Johnson which was followed by an executive order. That followed a 1961 executive action (Executive Order 10925) by President Kennedy in which the term was first introduced. "Diversity" as a concept was born in June, 1978, with Justice Powell's opinion in the Bakke case. Powell argued that college and university admissions programs could consider race in their deliberations because of the contribution to *diversity* which would result in the promotion of beneficial educational pluralism.

In short, "diversity" would help promote stronger academics. Since it also would permit the consideration of race in admission policies, those who wanted to consider race in those actions embraced the notion that it *would* promote enhanced academic outcomes. How do we insure that that will be the case, that a student, for example, will actually enrich the overarching academic enterprise by bringing authentic *diversity* to it, particularly in a system of higher education which tends to be politically and ideologically monolithic?

We do not test for it. How could we? We do not require it. How could we? We do not ask for any guarantees. How could we? Even if we actually sought political diversity, e.g., *should we* ask an applicant about his or her private political views? Can we depend on an applicant's personal statement as a guarantor of diversity? Such an approach could always be gamed. *Merlyn's Pen* or one of its competitors would probably help guide the student for an additional fee.

In some cases we find that a cohort of students with putatively-different "identities" is actually from the same community, the same socioeconomic group, indeed, the same set of high schools. This is certainly an issue for the University of Illinois, for example, which draws a substantial number of its students from the north shore of Chicago. We *assume* that they will contribute intellectual and social diversity because of *who* they are, but we cannot guarantee that or even, I would argue, safely infer that.

There are now a considerable number of conservative African-American academics, pundits and public intellectuals. Their views enrich the public debate within the country and within the African-American community. Having them visit universities with greater frequency would be instructive for our students, but unfortunately there are very few diversity programs *per se* that seek to increase conservative presence on college campuses. The University of Colorado's "visiting scholar in conservative thought and policy" position might be applauded as a step in the right direction but in the larger scheme of things it is a very, very small step (1 in ca. 8,000 faculty [in all categories], at one institution).

It should go without saying that the assumption that a certain "kind" of student will yield a certain type of diversity entails a process of not very subtle stereotyping. My wife's hairdresser in northern Virginia, for example, was gay but he was also a successful small businessman trying to maintain his shop in a competitive environment. He was a staunch conservative, whose every conversation revolved around such things as regulatory policies and governmental "intrusion." To the extent that we are "defined" by anything, many are defined by their professions more than by their race, gender or sexual orientation. The most integrated organization in our society—the military—contains a large number of individuals who think of themselves, first of all, as soldiers. At Georgetown in our liberal studies program we had a student who worked in the dental school. She did her thesis on men and women as dentists, trying to determine whether or not their separate genders led to separate practices or concerns. The result of her research was that dental school turned everyone into *dentists* and that gender proved to be of relatively little importance in the process.

For a time, "diversity" became a compelling concern for the business community. In 1987 the Hudson Institute issued its Workforce 2000 report whose numbers were badly muddled. It was claimed that there would be 25,000,000 entrants to the labor force by 2000 but by then only 15 percent would be native white males. Businesses began to panic and urge colleges to graduate more minorities so that business's needs could be met. Actually, the 15 percent sliver represented the number over and above those who replaced the number of white males already there. In other words, the actual percentage of native white males would drop from 47 percent to 45 percent (the actual number: 45.6 percent). However, the false number was reported endlessly, including by such putatively reliable papers as the *Boston Globe* and the *St. Louis Post-Dispatch* (Wood 2003, pp. 204–8).

In some ways, of course, the "diversity" categories can be completely devoid of meaning. Peter Wood offers the following example. We confidently speak of "Asian-Americans," but consider the possibility that we have three individuals applying to our college. One is originally from western India; his family speaks Gujarati, an Indo-European language, and he is a Hindu. The second is Japanese. Her family speaks Japanese, an Altaic language and they are Confucian-inflected Shintoists. The third comes from a family of Khmer-American fishermen. Her family speaks Mon-Khmer, an Austro-Asiatic language and they are Theravada Buddhists.

Western India, Japan and Cambodia were never part of a single empire; they never shared a single culture and they never experienced similar forms of colonialism or, for that matter, Western contact. And yet, we call them "Asian," while the only thing that the applicants really have in common is the fact that they are now American (Wood 2003, p. 24).

My wife's aunt recently passed away and in her last days, in discussions of her life and family, she commented on the fact that there had been Native American blood within the family heritage. No one had known that and, hence, no one had thought to so categorize themselves. Tiger Woods describes himself as "Cablinasian," since he is Caucasian, black, Indian and Asian. In the 2000 census 4 percent claimed a multiracial background; 21 residents of Columbus, Ohio claimed five different races (Wood 2003, pp. 26–27).

One of the injunctions of political correctness is the notion that thou shalt not judge, *judging* often being equated with ethnocentrism and not with making good judgments. The problem is that this disallows *positive* judgments. At the same time, we expect *positive* results from diverse individuals; we are simply not allowed to talk about them in any detail (except to recognize victimhood). This risks 'diversity' leading to uniformity rather than bona fide *diversity*.

The sometimes-assumed commonality of "victimhood" as that which characterizes those who bring "diversity" (with the corollary that those characterized by "victimhood" will require special advocates and special services) is a problematic step. It can suggest, for example, that the core of the individual's personality or the "meaning" of the person's life comes not from the individual himself or herself but from the source of their victimization. The oppressor determines who or what they are. This is why we left Europe. This is why Buster Kincaid in *The Killer Angels* says that he damns all gentlemen and why he asserts that there is only one aristocracy, the aristocracy of the mind. The people who hung their countrymen like dogs back in Ireland (and, presumably, those who discriminated against the Irish in America) are not going to be permitted to define him.

Sacks and Thiel put it like this:

> Multicultural victimology is so powerful because it taps into two base emotions that are not often found together—self-pity and self-importance. The self-pity comes from believing oneself a victim, the self-importance from cast-

ing oneself in a fantastical historical melodrama. But, however psychologically gratifying in the short term, the focus on victimization creates a double bind for multiculturalists in the long run: If they ever succeeded in their struggle to end oppression, then they would lose their identities (1998, p. 156).

There are other problems, of course. Wood, e.g., notes "the contradiction between the diversiphiles' insistence that the differences among cultural traditions are vast and irreconcilable, and their simultaneous assertion that diversity is a path to overcoming divisions and achieving national (or pan-national) unity" (2003, p. 96). The talk of community, oneness, and unity, as he puts it, are all articulated in the context of the celebration of *difference* (2003, p. 98). *E Pluribus Unum* without the melting pot (or the eighteenth-century focus on *commonality*) may be a bridge too far.

Wood has a series of other observations that might be worthy of consideration. Indian doctors, e.g., studied in schools that have no relation whatsoever to the demographic profiles of American institutions and yet they succeed in their American practices despite a lack of diversity in their training (2003, p. 120).

Many elite women's colleges tout their diversity, while they continue to exclude men (2003, pp. 274–76).

The historically-black colleges and universities have never exhibited very much interest in the diversity movement (2003, p. 274).

The unspoken message of "diversity" is that there are enough students like you in our college that you will be able to mingle with your own group (2003, p. 278).

Colleges do not offer the *diversity* that is found in the real world. They offer simulacra of diversity. They are like aquariums and aviaries (2003, p. 280).

The penultimate and final points are interesting ones. Skip Gates and Cornel West, for example, have pointed out the disappointing fact that many of the gains made by African-American students in colleges and universities have largely been confined to individuals in the middle or upper-middle class. Students in the inner cities have not participated to the same degree.

Thomas Sowell, writing in 1993, commented that at Harvard 70 percent of the black undergraduates had parents who were in professional or managerial positions. A majority of the non-white college students come from predominantly white high schools, two-thirds of the students, e.g., at Stanford. Sowell comments that "the separate racial and ethnic enclaves on many college campuses are the first segregation experienced by many minority students." He adds that in the 1950s, when there were virtually no role models and no critical mass of black students [and, I would add, no gutted curricula or grade inflation] the black students at predominantly white colleges did very well. Their grades were far closer to school averages than in the 1980s. At Amherst and Williams, for example, there were many black Phi Beta Kappas (1993, pp. 282–83).

Sowell compares their experience with that of the Jews and, later, the Vietnamese. That does not mean that we should return to the race relations of the 1950s in order for black students to achieve academic success; it suggests that students did very well under what we would now consider very, very difficult conditions. The question, in short, concerns the degrees of success achieved by our *contemporary* attitudes, structures, programs and procedures. Black students (including the GI Bill students) demonstrated their capacity for success in the absence of current support systems. The GI's did, however, have *full funding*. Perhaps we should consider redirecting the money from the "support" budget to the financial aid budget.

Parenthetically, Derek Bok has also questioned the advisability of black centers on campuses, noting that some have suggested that they enable people to avoid the contact and the positive experiences that were to result from "diversity" in the first place and that they make segregation appear natural (2008, p. 210). Many have added that the programs and institutions created by the middle-aged must seem very odd to today's eighteen year-old undergraduates, for whom many of these issues were faced and largely resolved in the distant past.

My own granddaughters, for example, now in their mid-late 20s, attended Missouri's primary feeder school, Parkway West, a public institution in St. Louis. I attended a significant number of their concerts, football games, graduations and family parties. The school is "diverse" with a noticeable international component. The students are completely comfortable with questions of race, gender and sexual orientation that might have occasioned comment a generation or two earlier. These are simply not matters of concern to them.

I do remember, however, the African mother of a neighborhood classmate expressing concern about the company in which her daughter might find herself. She sounded exactly like the middle-class parents of my generation. By the same token, while "diversity" often places people of similar *appearance* within the same categories, I remember the ongoing wars of words between the faculty in the African Languages and Literature department at Wisconsin and the department of Afro-American Studies. They often related to one another as beings from alternate universes with whom they had literally nothing in common.

Another issue on which Sowell has focused is "fit," a subject recently brought to the forefront by the research of UCLA law professor, Richard Sander. A long-term civil rights activist and father of an African-American son, Sander was troubled by bar exam passage/failure rates by African-American students. He concluded that admission policies had created mismatches between the students and the institutions to which they had been admitted. If the students who failed had matriculated in law schools more commensurate with their abilities many more would have succeeded and we would now have more black lawyers, 8 percent more in his calculation (McKee 2007, p. 1).

The research has been criticized, of course, but Sander is not the first person to look at the issue of fit. Clyde Summers of the Yale law school had raised the issue in 1969 and Thomas Sowell raised it again in 1993. In 1976 law school admission generally required a B+ average and a score of 650 or more on the LSAT. The number of African American students in the U.S. with a B+ average and 600 on the LSAT was 39. It is little surprise, Sowell argues, that the grades of black students in the top ten law schools were in the 8th percentile.

Sowell looked at SAT and graduation numbers at Berkeley. The Berkeley average SAT was 1181; the average for black students was 952. Seventy percent of the black students failed to graduate. How can these admission policies be characterized as "successful" or "positive" for black students? (Sowell 1993, pp. 140, 144).

Sowell points to the plight of the student who is always attempting to catch up and who, as a result, suffers from self-doubt. Remediation and strategies involving lower course loads only serve to further increase those feelings (1993, p. 137).

The issue turns on the question of whether or not material is generally pitched to the perceived "level" of the class. In some settings this is not likely to be the case. In Army Instruction, for example, the field manuals are the field manuals and a film on "field-stripping the M-16 rifle" or a film on "how to brush your teeth" are what they are—straightforward explanations in everyday (probably sixth grade) English with very little theoretical content.

Since I have not studied in a top (or any) law school I cannot evaluate this issue, but Sander knows this world and is a more reliable witness than I would be. I take the general point. Gail Heriot (2011) has constructed a scenario which makes sense to me. She asks what she would do if she lost her job and/or had secured a job in which she needed a familiarity with physics. She says that she could obtain that familiarity but that she would have to take a course in it. What she would *not* do is take the physics course at Caltech.

The question in general is an interesting one. Should any of us matriculate at stretch schools? Lynn O'Shaugnessy, who has written what I consider the best parent/student educational advice book (*The College Solution: A Guide for Everyone Looking for the Right School at the Right Price*, second ed., 2012) advises caution (2012, p. 75): "When looking for matches, teenagers should typically aim for colleges where they would be in the top 25 percent to 33 percent of the applicants." Why? Because the schools whose academic profile would be enhanced by the student are most likely to be more generous with financial aid. The students whose credentials are only average or below average would be less attractive to the school.

For decades I have given potential graduate students the same advice: go to the program at the school where you can be the top student. Why? Because the student's graduate-school faculty will be carrying the student through the first major phase of his or her career—securing the first postdoc or first job, securing the first grant and opening the door, through their own contacts, to a network of individuals who will provide support of various kinds for the near future.

The last kind of letter of recommendation that you want is one that says, "Ms. Smith was a very nice young woman. She did quite well in a highly-competitive environment. As I recall, she did a paper for me on . . . X . . . which I considered very thoughtful. . . ." You want the letter that says, "Ms. Smith was, far and away, our finest graduate student in recent memory. I continue to marvel at her dissertation, which will certainly be published by a major university press. My own mentor once commented that only fifty individuals will be remembered from a generation. Ms. Smith will be among that cohort and she will be among the top five individuals there. . . ." The bottom line is that it is better to be pushed by a group of distinguished academics who consider you to be very, very special than to fall in the vague middle of a higher-ranked department.

African-American students, on the other hand, are likely to be attractive to a plethora of institutions because of the paucity of their numbers at most institutions and their paucity of numbers in a multiplicity of disciplinary areas. Everyone or nearly everyone is likely to want them and many will be forthcoming with generous offers.

Nevertheless, African-American students are like all students. Each of them has different gifts. If they are pressed to enroll in institutions which do not correspond with those gifts the results may not be positive. The general statistics on graduation rates and loan defaults suggest that this has often been the case. The research on "fit" (e.g., Heriot 2015; Sander 2004; Sander/ Taylor 2012) seeks to provide greater opportunities for African-American student success. It notes that black students generally perform at the same level as other students with comparable GPA's and test scores, that "other" students given admissions preferences (legacies, progeny of development prospects, e.g.) also have academic difficulties commensurate with their "mismatches," that while the number of black students has been reduced at UCLA and Berkeley, they have moved to other great universities (UCSD, UC-Irvine, and UC-Riverside, e.g.) and done very well. It basically comes down to the numbers. The wider the disparity between a student's qualifications and the average qualifications of that student's institution's student body, the more difficult it is to achieve success.

Individuals who study these matters for a living say that the best predictor of success in college is the student's high school GPA (see, e.g., O'Shaugnessy 2012, p. 82). While I would seek assurances that the high school challenged the student and that the courses taken were substantive ones, my own inclination would be to agree; I generally estimate the possibility of future success by looking at the individual's past success. Good GPA then; probably a good GPA later.

I trust past performance more than I trust academic pedigree and I trust it more than I do standardized tests. One of the great evils of grade inflation, in my opinion, is the power that it has given to testing agencies which, in general (the Miller analogies test is an exception), do not test for content. Valorizing aptitude over achievement (including "aptitude" that has been enhanced by test-prep services) sickens me. Similarly, I do not find such tests trustworthy. I took the GRE's twice and my verbal/mathematical scores transposed by approximately thirty percentile points.

One-off content-based tests may also lack "objectivity." I took the GRE subject test once and received very middling scores, even though I had taken nearly forty credits of English as an undergraduate. The version I took had only one question on literature before the early modern period, but it had a large number of questions on the Irish renaissance, so that you could forget Homer, Aeschylus, Sophocles, Euripides, the Beowulf poet, the Pearl poet, Dante, Chaucer, et al. but woe be to you if you were not intimately familiar with such writers as John Millington Synge and Seán O'Casey.

Before we look at test scores and affirmative-action practices, we should keep in mind a number of related realities. First, any concern about underrepresented minorities benefiting from preferential admission standards should be seen in context. There are many so-called admission "hooks" and most of them significantly outweigh the attention given to minority students (for the numbers that follow, see Ferguson, 2011, p. 185). As much as 65 percent of a class might be pre-shaped by those various hooks—25–30 percent of the places going to legacies, for example, and 10 percent to development prospects. Fifteen percent may go to athletes or even more at a tiny college that seeks to field teams in a large number of sports. We must remember the 60/40 principle and the fact that it generally represents affirmative action for men. The number of slots targeted for underrepresented minorities may be in the range of 10–15 percent of the total and the decisions there are not, in general, excluding white students; they are generally excluding Asian students.

The percent admitted for athletics may be especially problematic, particularly for athletes who are marginal students but dream of professional careers. The bottom line is that there are 70,000 black doctors and lawyers in the United States, but only 1,400 black professional athletes (Deford in

Hersh and Merrow 2005, p. 152). Many play for a very short time, if they play at all.

The decisions affected by a student's eventual prospects as a donor (or his or her parents' current capacities) may be particularly egregious. One of the most controversial decisions in which I have been involved concerned the admission of a graduate student from a very wealthy family who had been suspended for academic dishonesty by Harvard. The program director in the student's area urged me to admit her as a special student so that she could complete the remaining course which she needed for graduation. I said that I would not do that; I would keep faith with the Harvard faculty and admit her (if she still wished to come rather than take the course at Harvard) after she had served out the period of her suspension. Then (not unexpectedly), much of hell broke loose and I was accused of a number of enormities, one of which was an "inability to understand the development demands of the modern university."

Fortunately, the provost agreed with me. He knew, of course, that I would resign my position if he overrode my decision. My relationship with the program director (who was actually a relative of a close friend of mine) was cool forever after. *C'est la guerre.* The student was admitted by MIT and completed her program without interruption. My guess (and it is only a guess) is that one of Harvard's deanlets called one of MIT's deanlings and struck a deal.

Contemporary "reverse-discrimination" is not always understood. A 2005 study cited by Chace (2006, p. 268n) suggested that ending preferential admissions for underrepresented minorities at elite schools would reduce acceptance rates for black and Hispanic students by one-half to two-thirds, with 80 percent of the vacated seats going to Asians.

O'Shaugnessy (2012, p. 121) reports the following admission rates for Asian-American students: Brown (12%), Dartmouth (14%), Cornell (15%), Harvard (15%), Yale (16%), Penn (17%), Princeton (18%), Columbia (19%). In the University of California system, on the other hand (where the use of race in admissions is no longer permitted), the numbers are quite different: UC-San Diego (50%), UC-Irvine (49%), UC-Berkeley (40%), UC-Santa Barbara (36%), UCLA (34%).

Ethan Epstein, in an article entitled "The New Jews," cites a Center for Equal Opportunity study of admissions results at the University of Michigan in 2005. Asian students had SAT scores that were fifty points higher than the median score of accepted white students, 140 points higher than the scores for Hispanics and 240 points higher than the scores for blacks. Using a 1240 SAT score and a 3.2 GPA as markers, the university accepted 10 percent of Asian Americans, 14 percent of whites, 88 percent of Hispanics and 92 percent of blacks with those numbers (2012, p. 14).

In 2009, Thomas Espenshade, a Princeton sociologist, looked at discrimination against Asian students in the Ivy league. According to his analysis, an Asian student would need to score 140 points higher than whites on the math/reading sections of the SAT, 270 points higher than Hispanics and 450 points higher than blacks in order to have an equal chance at admission to the nation's most elite schools (Epstein 2012, p. 14). Some have argued that the SAT's are culturally biased, but Andrew Ferguson (2011, p. 92) has noted that first-generation Asian immigrant females have routinely outperformed native-born white males on the test.

Many institutions have clearly tilted their admission policies to favor certain groups of students. The problem is that at least in large statistical terms one glaring problem remains. While the nationwide graduation rate—based on a six-year count—is 60 percent for white students, it is only 49 percent for Hispanic students and 40 percent for black students (O'Shaughnessy 2012, p. 118). Assuming that we all want the same outcome—high graduation rates for all—it is fair to ask what it is that we are doing wrong. We are giving admission advantages to students that are not correlating with graduation successes.

That does not necessarily mean that admission "advantages" do not work. It may be the case, for example, as Sowell has argued, that the advantage given should be in the form of financial aid, but to an institution that is a better fit for the student.

Entering the purely anecdotal realm now: Tim Healy once told me that when he was vice president for academic affairs in the CUNY system, it was the case that black women would travel to any school within the system but that black men tended to stay closer to home. Our graduate school recruiters at Wisconsin found the same thing. Black male students in Chicago, e.g., were likely to attend schools in the UW system that were closer to their homes; attracting them to Madison was more difficult.

We wrung our hands and touted the quality of the Madison campus, but it may be that many first-generation black male college students are more comfortable staying closer to home (or at least they were then). If that is the case, then my vote is for their academic success and personal happiness rather than for "my" institution's diversity profile. However important that profile may be, it is not so important that it should jeopardize the future of the student, whose personal success must be our highest priority.

I should also note that our recruitment program was then often considered the country's model. We had a separate fellowship fund (a sizeable, seven-figure one, paid for by Wisconsin taxpayers, though many beneficiaries would be out-of-state students), two full-time recruiters, one black, one Hispanic, and we were part of the CIC common application program. A minority student could fill out one set of graduate application forms and then tick off the boxes of any Big 10 school or the University of Chicago and his or her application would be forwarded to all of the schools that had been so marked. The results were still not to our satisfaction.

Whatever our own desires, we should always keep our focus on the students and faculty themselves because we always risk the danger of celebrating "diversity" while simultaneously depreciating it. Jonathan Cole, e.g. (2011, p. 2) studied the newest rankings of doctoral programs from the National Research Council and found them wanting. In some ways they are a reflection of our society in that these putative "rankings" now go out of their way to be nonjudgmental. "Political orthodoxy," Cole writes, "ran through the discussion of the report's results." In one case, the study attempted to correlate the racial diversity of a program's faculty with its overall quality. When it was discovered "that there was a slight negative correlation between the percentage of minorities and a program's assessed quality, an effort was made to play down the finding, essentially burying rather than analyzing it."

The negative correlation would not, of course, indicate that minorities are weak faculty. It could indicate, however, that they had been hired in an academic tier that represented a mismatch for their talents. Any faculty member who is hired by a mismatched institution could either raise or lower the "departmental average." This has nothing to do with race or ability; it has to do with hiring and personnel policies. Many university presidents, e.g., now lack terminal degrees or bring experience that is principally corporate, industrial or political. If any of them were to be removed by the trustees and placed within an academic department they would "pull down the departmental average." I could say the same about many white male (and female) administrators I have known, including those *with* terminal degrees. That is because the contemporary, corporatized university frequently hires administrators who lack the academic credentials of an entry-level faculty member in what would be their home departments.

The same situation can result with any number of non-standard hires. Spousal accommodations, for example, can go either way. The trailing spouse might pull down the departmental average or raise it significantly. A friend of mine recently took a provost position at a very good but not top-tier university. She pulled up her department's "average" and her husband—one of the top social scientists in America in his field—pulled his departmental average up dramatically. Again, this has nothing to do with race or gender. It has to do with personnel and hiring policies.

Anthony Kronman has suggested that race/gender/class and ethnicity have become subjects of interest in the Humanities curriculum because they reinforce Justice Powell's justification for affirmative action. Diversity is claimed to result in the enhancement of academics; hence diversity becomes the academic subject (2007, pp. 145–46). I do not believe that that is precisely the case (though it could be a contributing factor) because there was a great deal of interest in such issues long before 1978. It may be that interest in them accelerated because of the Powell decision and it may be that the tilt given their consideration has resulted in part from the political concerns and commitments of the faculty. It is the case, however, that identity-based programs were often instituted to both support women and minority students and to prevent activists' "demands" from escalating.

Lasch (1979, p. 145) described programs in black studies and women's studies as consciousness raising for the purpose of heading off political discontent. Sacks and Thiel are equally harsh. They suggest that the establishment of minority studies programs and LGBTQA centers represent the receipt of institutional power disproportionate to the students' actual numbers (1998, p. 73) and argue that the desire for "diversity" has resulted in the establishment of race and gender studies departments that bring to campus a group of faculty "almost monolithic in its thinking" (1998, p. 74).

Stanley Fish takes a different tack. He is concerned that such programs may advocate specific political positions. If so—if these programs represent an extension of a political agenda—they should be stopped by the institution's administration (2008, p. 150). This seems either naïve or disingenuous. Such programs generally *do* advocate a political agenda. His point is, presumably, that scholarship and teaching should always aspire to a dispassionate objectivity and that scholars should follow the evidence wherever it may lead. Anything less than that involves a falsification of the scholar's task.

While I agree with the principle, the counter argument is a commonplace: everything is political and those who believe that they are dispassionately objective are deluding themselves. Read your Gramsci and your Foucault. For that matter, read your Churchill. He said that history would be kind to him because he intended to write it.

Nevertheless, Fish's point should not be dismissed. While it is true that many academics will acknowledge the unspoken agendas that undergird much scholarly work, explicit advocacy, *advocacy that consciously distorts evidence*, will still receive harsh criticism. Thus, while many will acknowledge an advocacy role for identity-based programs they will do so with a slight twinge. These programs do not have the "purity" of such disciplines as mathematics and physics, for example, and that diminishes them. The diminution may be slight or it may be significant, but such programs are not, ultimately, seen to be on a par with the more "basic" disciplines that serve as the home bases for the faculty who serve as their joint-appointees. Many will disagree with that view, of course, and argue that these programs have matured and now represent disciplines in and of themselves, disciplines with their own theoretical bases. At the same time, there will be individuals who dispute that. In the area of women's studies, for example, Daphne Patai and Camille Paglia have been quite vocal in challenging the field's claims.

I do not propose to join their numbers because I lack the expertise to do so. It has always been my belief that these programs were established, in part, because the kind of work that they were doing was not being done elsewhere. I was, however, concerned that programs such as this were disproportionately represented by faculty from a small number of fields, faculty who may have been *bien pensant*, but not equipped (by their training) to take up the many complex issues which needed to be studied.

I articulated this by saying that "I am a great believer in the *study of women*, but I am not yet fully persuaded as to the appropriateness of *women's studies*." For example, if women's studies programs are going to look at such issues as the manner in which the male and female brain are wired I would be reassured by the presence of neuroscientists and not just faculty from the English, French and Sociology departments. On women's economic issues I would like to hear the opinions of trained economists, and so on. I have also been troubled to see blank slate/heavily constructivist models espoused by large numbers of humanists and social scientists that have been thoroughly denied and demolished by a writer such as Steven Pinker. I have been troubled by claims of male/female commonality that do not square with what I take to be state-of-the-art psychological research, as in, for example, the work of David Geary.

In short, I have had my doubts, but I am not a professional in this area. I do, however, worry that a position of "advocacy" and a position of *interdisciplinarity* rather than full *multidisciplinarity* risks diminishing the importance of something whose deep importance, for me, was never in doubt.

Back in the early 80s I published a book on eighteenth-century social history which was posted in the *Chronicle of Higher Education* booklist under the heading "History." I showed it to my History department chairman, a very nice man, and said, "Look, Emmett, I've finally become a historian." He smiled and then began to laugh, heartily. I could never, ever, be considered a historian; my degree was in English language and literature.

The privileging of academic *disciplines* is an institutional reality. Anything that remotely resembles something "secondary" is problematic, particularly when the purpose at hand is to bring certain subject matter to the fore. As I said, I am not an expert with regard to such programming, but John Guillory is and he addressed these issues with great rigor over two decades ago.

I find it interesting that Guillory relies on Gramsci, one of the most prominent twentieth-century communists, to make a point with which I would wholeheartedly agree. Gramsci saw, Guillory points out, that the proliferation of "tech" and "trade" curricula would end up perpetuating both economic inequality and social differences (1993, p. 48).

He then goes on to argue that we should stop seeing women's studies and black studies as special curricula for separate constituencies. On the contrary, they should be seen as *research areas*, pursued by *discipline-based* faculty, as, I would add parenthetically, they already are (1993, p. 52). In short, he is arguing (following Gramsci) for a unitary curriculum. Absent such a curriculum you have different curricula for different groups and the alternative curriculum will, irreducibly, be seen as secondary. It will, as he puts it, produce the same social stratification as separate institutions for different classes (1993, p. 53).

As reasonable as this might seem, it represents the administration of very strong and bitter medicine to those most likely to be reading Guillory's book. Nevertheless, his arguments command considerable respect. Skip Gates blurbed the book and described it as "a brilliant analysis . . . an intellectually severe and uncompromising study that will leave few of our comfortable commonplaces quite intact. This is, in short, a landmark work: one that will outrage and inform in equal measure."

I am personally haunted by a story told to me by a late friend. We had studied together at Notre Dame, then went off to graduate school and, four years later, found ourselves in upstate New York. I was teaching at West Point, completing my active-duty obligation and he was teaching at Cornell. He had a very bright black woman in one of his required English courses and he approached her one day, informing her that he was also going to teach an African-American literature course and that she might be interested in taking it.

She politely said to him (fifty years ago), "Thank you very much, Professor McConnell, but I already know what it means to be black. I came to Cornell to become an engineer." Of course, his class would have been taught in a very traditional way; it would not have involved advocacy and it would not have focused on identity politics. Nevertheless, given her answer, I would infer that she perceived that he was assuming an interest on her part based on her race rather than on her deeper academic focus. She is probably retired now (or about to be). Whatever she did with her life, I doubt very much that she was unsuccessful.

Another image haunts me. Several years ago we hosted a high school band competition and invited the bands to perform in our stadium. The odds-on favorite was one from the Kansas City suburbs. They clearly enjoyed great financial support. The band was huge and their luxurious uniforms might have brought an envious gaze from John Philip Sousa.

One of the bands, however, was from a rural area. They had no uniforms. All that they had were matching tee shirts. They were small in number but they performed very well. These are the students who are less likely to attend college in our country and that is a national tragedy. For all of our federal loan programs, our outreach programs and our student-service support programs, the vast majority of our students come from wealthy or at least comfortable families. When they do attend, however, their failure rate is high, far higher than it should be. When they do graduate they possess a credential that may represent little more than a certificate of attendance. In a difficult economy, which some claim represents the "new normal," approximately half are having difficulty securing jobs commensurate with their "education." The current system is simply not working; when will we face that fact? And when will we face the fact that our current strategies for increasing the number of first-generation college students are not working?

I am neither a psychologist nor a sociologist, but students will be best positioned to attend college when they are interested, curious and motivated. First and foremost, they must be readers. In 2005 a survey of high school students asked them how much time they spent reading for pleasure. The number responding "none" was 24.8 percent; the number responding "less than one hour" was 26.1 percent. The group answering "none" had actually increased by 26 percent from surveys done a decade earlier. Crunching the numbers, 74.7 percent read less than 17 minutes per day (Bauerlein 2009, p. 54).

Many enthuse over digital learning, but while digital activities help with such things as the perception of spatial relationships, problem solving and information retrieval, they are less successful than is widely believed in actually leading to knowledge formation. Johnson once said that there are two types of knowledge, knowing something and knowing how to find something. The latter might be enhanced by digital activities, but the former far less so. The young may be nimble, agile multi-taskers, but still not know very much (Bauerlein 2009, pp. 90–94).

Vocabulary building is key. A child who reads children's books encounters 50 percent more rare words than one who watches television. Vocabulary comes from home life and social life, reading skills from vocabulary skills. Interactions with family and friends are the root source of those skills, not interactions with teachers. Thus, the valorization of the media (as opposed to the valorization of books and family contact) hurts the poor and the culturally impoverished the most (Bauerlein 2009, pp. 127–30).

Reading proficiency, across racial and ethnic groups, is now a national scandal. Some 59 percent of white students fail to read at a reasonable level of proficiency, 85 percent of Hispanic students, 88 percent of black students. Reading proficiency should be the new civil rights frontier (Hirsch 2006, p. 3).

Mark Wertheimer, the principal of the Trout Core Knowledge school in Ft. Collins, Colorado, says that, "The most serious problem facing education is the breakdown of the family" (Brand 2010, p. 153). For all of the heroic actions of single parents, halving the number of adults in a family reduces the time and the resources that those adults can provide their children.

We need better teachers. Teachers are pivotal to students' academic success, but we also, Thomas Friedman argues, need better parents. The PISA or Program for International Student Assessment tests fifteen year-olds in the world's principal industrialized nations. The students are tested every three years for reading comprehension and the ability to utilize mathematical and scientific knowledge to solve real problems. We are consistently trounced in this competition by students from such places as Singapore, Hong Kong and Shanghai. We are not outpaced for the single reason that our K-12 system is in shambles. Starting with four countries in 2006 and adding fourteen more in 2009, the PISA officials interviewed the parents of 5,000 students and asked them about the manner in which they raised their children. The results were not surprising. The students whose parents read books with them during their first year of primary school did markedly better later than students whose parents read with them infrequently or simply not at all. The performance advantage is clear and it is evident *regardless of the family's socioeconomic background*. Parents need to read with their children, tell them stories and talk to them about their experiences. Simply playing with children results in far fewer positive effects.

Moreover, the parents' involvement with their children at home was shown to be far more effective in achieving success than the parents' involvement in their children's schools—whether as PTA members, classroom volunteers, fundraisers or faithful attendees of back-to-school nights (Friedman 2011, pp. 1–3).

The problems with our schools—at all levels—represent an ongoing challenge, but we can ameliorate those problems by addressing our practices as parents. The "nonjudgmental" injunction so common across our society is part of the problem; it is not part of the solution. Charles Murray's recent study of dysfunctionality among (largely, poor) whites, offers the suggestion that the successful be more vocal in their advocacy of "best practices" as opposed to dysfunctional ones. To many this may seem to be a recommendation for a revivified Puritanism, with the successful tsk-tsking the poor and poking arrogant fingers in their faces.

I understand that attitude, but I also understand the alternative. To remain "nonjudgmental" and reticent to identify the problems which hurt our fellow citizens and their children could be seen in another way (as Murray realizes): the successful are guarding their strategies and keeping them to themselves so that they might continue to enjoy their status as elites. How can we ever consider that acceptable?

Those who seek broader participation in both minority college attendance and employment within the professoriate often acknowledge the problem of a paucity of numbers. Hence, they argue that the colleges and the graduate schools take responsibility for increasing the potential numbers of minority students and minority faculty. Some institutions, Notre Dame, for example, have struggled mightily in this effort. Colleges have created summer programs for minority high school students, bringing them to campus laboratories, e.g., and introducing them to an array of career opportunities. Universities have created pre-doctoral fellowships in which minority doctoral students are brought to campus and given the opportunity to write their dissertations without the need to teach or worry about other claims on their time. The best of these students are then recruited to the university's faculty.

There have been attempts to recruit faculty from HBCU institutions as well as from largely-white schools. There are a multiplicity of strategies that have been attempted, most motivated by noble intent. Unfortunately there are certain things that colleges *cannot* do. They cannot alter the course of K-12 education with the wave of a wand. They cannot stop social promotion in the schools; they cannot inculcate discipline there. They cannot reduce out-of-wedlock births or force the teachers' unions to support school choice.

There are things that they can do, but they will face enormous political pushback in the process. They can, e.g., raise the matriculation requirements at public institutions, thus forcing the high schools to reshape their curricula and raise their expectations, placing the political burden on them when their graduates fail to be accepted at the institutions supported by their taxpaying parents. They can close colleges of education and put the responsibility for teacher preparation in more content-focused areas. They can even create their own preparatory schools and offer opportunities to a select number of promising students, including a significant number of minority students. Many interesting and potentially successful ideas might be discussed. The cost of such programs, however, would not be inconsiderable and nearly all public institutions now struggle with other budgetary challenges. Moreover, one could not fairly expect "higher education" to duplicate the efforts of K-12 without receiving a portion of the resources invested in K-12 now.

The only plausible solution to our current plight is for each element of the education establishment to address its problems and focus upon authentic student achievement. For that to occur, it will require not just overwhelming political pressure from society at large but also a reconsideration of the structure of family life and the family's responsibility for the education and well being of its children. We can offer some significant help but we cannot provide wholesale amelioration of our current condition when the students appear at our doors as (at least in years) adults; we must begin at the beginning.

Chapter Eight

Every Man His Own Carver

A recurring commonplace among commentators on higher education is that research has supplanted teaching, to the students' detriment. The American educational edifice is like an allegorical beast, with an English body and German head. The head directs the body, which produces the golden eggs.

While the undergraduate programs' tuition revenues provide the fiscal gold, the graduate programs and their distinguished faculty provide the reputational gold. Because our "product" is the generation and dissemination of new and existing knowledge, those who do that best are those who are most revered and most highly compensated (forgetting, of course, the orthopedic surgeon in the med school who makes millions and the football and basketball coaches).

For the faculty, research activities generate the higher salaries, the outside offers, the promotions, the named professorships and the personal acclaim. "A teaching reputation," a colleague of mine used to say, "is always a local reputation." Thus, the university reward system dictates the faculty's behavior. Research reputation undergirds the graduate programs and it is the graduate programs that are evaluated by the National Research Council. Meanwhile, we do what we must for the undergraduate programs to sustain good *US News* numbers, but our heart and resources are in the graduate programs, while the undergraduate majors get an occasional head pat and the general education courses are handed over to teaching assistants and contingent faculty. So goes the common narrative and while it may exaggerate a bit it is not without truth.

One of the self-evident but seldom-noticed issues here is that the undergraduates and graduate students are largely the same people, just a few years older or younger. Our treatment of them in their younger incarnation comes back to bite us when they matriculate as graduate students. Those "shorted" by the system earlier then appear on our doorsteps as graduate students who are underprepared for the new task at hand. Many faculty prefer to work in research universities but they like to admit undergraduates from top liberal arts colleges to their graduate programs (and often prefer to see their own children attend an Amherst or an Oberlin rather than a prominent research university). One of my colleagues in the Wisconsin graduate school visited a potential university with his son and commented, "I know it's a great place, but I saw a lot of teaching assistants hanging around there." (His son eventually attended Colby.)

The faculty reward system is straightforward. Other research issues are a bit more arcane. We "believe," for example, that sponsored research should be touted because it generates both the direct costs which support the research and the indirect costs which support the larger university enterprise. Thus, we are urged to increase those resources because they both help to balance the budget and contribute to the local, regional, state and national economies.

They may do that, of course, but the issue is not that simple. Indirect cost rates are negotiated with the federal government. The rate *negotiated* may not reflect a university's *actual* costs. Moreover, there are governmental divisions, private foundations and other institutions which do not pay *full* indirect costs, as well as entities which pay *no* indirect costs at all. Hence, the formal indirect cost rate might not equal actual costs and the *actually-recovered* indirect costs will—it is guaranteed—be less than actual costs. The bottom line is that a university's vaunted research enterprise may actually be losing money. More precisely, it is being subsidized by the armies of undergraduates taking Psych 101 in vast lecture halls, taught inexpensively by part-time faculty. (On this, see Newfield, 2008, who provides numbers for the California system, p. 212.)

The very modest grants received by humanists, however, might actually extend the curriculum though they might not always enhance it. For example, a professor in a humanities department receives a $45,000–$50,000 fellowship from a foundation or government agency to complete a book project. The faculty member's current salary is $80,000. The lower fellowship stipend does not represent a financial "loss" to the faculty member or the university. Through various forms of budgetary legerdemain, the faculty member will "keep" his or her regular salary and "turn over" to the department the fellowship money. Since the faculty member generally teaches four courses per year, the department can take the amount of the fellowship and hire a visitor who would be asked to teach six courses. Alternatively, it could pay out $2,500 per course to a group of contingent faculty and receive as many as twenty courses in return.

Thus, the curriculum is covered/extended. The quality of instruction, of course, might be either degraded or improved. If the faculty member is an exceptional teacher, the tradeoff (in the case of a visitor) could be "negative"; in the case of contingent faculty offering twenty courses in lieu of four, you will usually lose "upper division" courses but still gain many more sections. In any case, the tuition paid by undergraduates is the same—whether for a beautifully-taught seminar or an introductory, assembly-line course.

In structuring these arrangements the department chair will be driven by several needs—to cover the curriculum, to balance the budget, to uphold the department's reputation and to keep senior faculty content. At a research university with graduate programs, faculty will be heartily encouraged to obtain grants that generate research even though the faculty member's research leave will simultaneously reduce his or her participation in the instructional program. At many universities faculty will be forced to apply for external funding before they can even apply for internal support, so that the internal funds can be extended and the research output multiplied.

This is not necessarily as callous and calculating as it might sound. For example, the unspoken assumption at Wisconsin was that the instructional budget (generated by tuition and state subsidies) would simply not cover the faculty who were in place. A significant number had to be on leave—paid for by external or WARF grants—in order to sustain their total numbers. In other words, the students were studying with a faculty that might be as much as one-third larger than the university's instructional budget could actually afford. A third might be on leave every year, but over the course of four years (or more) the students had the opportunity to study with a wider range of individuals in a richer array of programs.

The forgotten element in all this is often the research itself. The dollar amounts are so large and the press announcements so punctuated with glittering images that we may forget the fundamental purposes of the exercise—the expansion of human knowledge, the curing of disease, the reduction of ignorance, the amelioration of the human condition. The limelight falls on the positioning of the decimal points, but we do this work (hopefully) for more noble and important reasons.

The question that should be asked—will the world actually benefit from this research?—is seldom asked, for it is widely assumed that we *will* benefit from the research conducted by scientists and engineers, particularly biomedical scientists, and that we can suspend our disbelief and tolerate the work of humanists and social scientists.

In this chapter I hope to provide a closer look at our condition. I will focus on the Humanities, not just because I know that area best, but because that area has been the principal cause of concern. Jonathan Cole (2009) has enumerated the vast successes of American research in the physical sciences, the life sciences, and engineering. When he describes the contributions of the Humanities and social sciences he has far less to say.

I will look at English in particular, because it is the largest of the Humanities fields. It influences departments of comparative literature and modern foreign languages. It also appropriates the research interests and foci of other fields. The heart of the medieval trivium and quadrivium are language and mathematics: grammar-logic-rhetoric/geometry-astronomy-arithmetic-music. In the beginning were the words and the words (language, literature, "letters") are still (or should be) at the heart of higher education. If we fail to get that part right, the negative effects are broad and deep.

What is the state of (broadly-considered) "literary" research? It may not be too extreme to characterize it as a welter of white noise. There is more "research" now than anyone can possibly be expected to read. Thus, most do not read any but a tiny portion of it and even so-called "cutting edge" or "state of the art" research will always be ignorant of a considerable amount of the research that preceded it. Research is a social activity in that it is evaluated based on common expectations and contemporary (often transitory) interests rather than on Platonic ideals. The adjective *learned* connotes very different things for different generations. Like a college diploma it now often certifies far less than one might expect.

Why is so much written and so little read? In the first place, the volume of scholarly research has increased by 500 percent over the last fifty years (dating from 2009). In the area of language and literature, the increase over that period has been from approximately 13,000 publications per year to 72,000 per year. In 2007 there were eighty-five publications on William Faulkner; from 1980–2006, 3,584 studies of one kind or another of his work. For Dickens: 3,437 studies, for Milton, 3,969 studies, for Shakespeare 21,674 studies, with an additional 569 in 2007 (Bauerlein 2009, pp. 5–11).

If one thinks of individual scholars as part of a field and not just students of a single author the prospect of "keeping up" becomes all the more daunting. One of the "recognition" assignments for faculty is to be asked to review the previous year's work in a particular field for *Studies in English Literature*. I did it in 1981 and even then it was a difficult task. Essentially you put everything else on hold and read seventy-five books or so (and major articles and major scholarly editions) and summarize "what happened" in the previous year. Many acknowledge that they were forced to overlook a substantial number of the materials that *SEL* sent them. Bottom line: "keeping up" each year means to read very, very selectively. And for the student entering the field as a newly-minted PhD? There are literally many thousands of primary and secondary works constituting a "field"; the student may actually have read and been tested on less than a few hundred of them.

If one were entering the profession in the mid twentieth century, however, the picture was very different. The expectations were higher; the volume of research was far smaller and the dissemination outlets more "clear." There were, e.g., fewer panel sections at scholarly meetings and more plenary sessions. At the MLA meeting there were literally hundreds of people in the room for a session on a given historical figure or period and young faculty were more easily exposed to the senior scholars in the area. Now we attempt to professionalize our graduate students by urging *them* to attend conventions and even to deliver papers there. We encourage them to create their own conventions, in fact, and develop their own journals so that they can prepare themselves to pursue this professional activity in earnest later. National conventions, however, have become, very often, simulacra of conventions rather than conventions. Everyone wants the professional credit for delivering papers there and thus individuals form small combines within microspecialties and ask their friends to deliver papers at their sessions, expecting their friends to do the same for them next year. The result is that there are sometimes sessions with *no attendees* beyond the presenters and conveners themselves (and their commandeered spouses and partners). This is not scholarly communication in any realistic sense of the term.

In a world of exploding microspecialties tenure reviews can be seriously compromised. The tenured departmental faculty reviewing their untenured junior colleagues feel that they are unable to review work in areas with which they are largely or completely unfamiliar. Hence, they are forced to depend upon the opinions of outside reviewers. With expanding microspecialties, however, the community of scholars, field-by-field, becomes smaller. The outside reviewers are increasingly likely to be friends and fellow logrollers of the candidates. Thus, the internal reviewers study the external *reviews* rather than the actual *work*, a practice which exacerbates their already problematic "nonjudgmentalism."

Fifty years ago field specialists read widely in the books that appeared in their broad area. As graduate students they had been tested on wider bodies of material and they then *taught* wider bodies of material. They bought books beyond their specific area(s) of research.

With the proliferation of new, often transient areas of study, the field continues to splinter (some of the resulting constructs having very little, if anything, to do with literature qua literature). In 1960 an English department might consist of approximately ten areas; now it can consist of as many as thirty or more (many social science departments consist of only four or five). When there is no recognizable discipline, in the sense of a given body of material to be mastered, the curriculum becomes more of a moving target than a definable core and it is more and more difficult to align areas of activity with parallel publishing outlets. The result is significant disruption and dislocation.

In the publication of serials, for example, there is a phenomenon known as "twigging." You begin with the roots and the trunk—the core—and then watch the branches spread. You start (to give a fictional example) with a journal of Restoration and eighteenth-century literature, then develop a journal of eighteenth-century poetry, then a journal for Dryden, a journal for Swift, a journal for Pope, et al. (Often these begin as newsletters and then, after multiple iterations, become full-fledged journals.) You develop a journal for rural poets and then a journal for rude, "natural," rural poets. Burns splits off and gets his own journal. Then you publish the Stephen Duck (the "thresher poet") newsletter and think about a *Stephen Duck Journal*, and so on.

The result: the number of journals doubles in less than a generation. In 1981 there were 74,000 journals, by 2003 there were 172,000 journals. Their pages fill in part because faculty wishing to extend their *vitae* write overlapping versions of the same articles, a process known as "shingling" (Trimble et al., 2010, pp. 277, 281).

Serials are out of control (a research library may subscribe to no more than one-tenth of them or less; Missouri subscribes to 53,400), but some are crucial to their fields and are thus seen as market opportunities for commercial publishers. When the commercial publishers enter, overall costs go up— 320 percent, from 1986–2006—and 7–11 percent each year (Bauerlein 2009, p. 10; Goldstein 2010, p. 2). As a result, library serials budgets eat the library monograph budgets. In 1986: 44 percent for books, 56 percent for journals. By 1988: 28 percent for books, 72 percent for journals (Chace 2006, p. 139).

The growth in microspecialties and the resulting volume of research leads to a reduction in book sales by university presses. Since individual scholars cannot "keep up" overall they only buy books in their microspecialties. University presses order smaller print runs and attempt to survive by selling monographs to libraries at inflated prices and publishing regional trade books. The libraries, however, have their budgets threatened by general resource shortfalls and their acquisitions budgets for monographs have largely been consumed by serial subscriptions. They thus reduce the number of monographs purchased, which further raises the price of monographs, since university presses publish a small number of books whose revenue must support each press's operation.

With university presses struggling, commercial/academic presses fill the gap, often by further inflating prices. I recently reviewed a 200 pp. scholarly monograph; the Mellen press charged $139.95 for the hardcover version, $49.95 for the paperback.

My first book, a revision of my dissertation, was published in 1971. It had a dust jacket, a frontispiece and recurring printer's devices. The print run— which largely sold out—was 3,000 copies. It cost $10 (which I considered very expensive). University press monographs in English studies now have print runs as small as 200–300 copies. A "best" seller would bring 800–900 sales. Library purchases in 1971 would guarantee approximately 1,500 sales; now that number is closer to 150.

Meanwhile, the librarians are conjuring with "bundle" sales of journals delivered electronically. Savings may be possible, but the overall cost is high and the packages are difficult to prune. The problem is comparable to that of the cable-television subscriber who may get things that he or she doesn't want, can't get things that he or she does want without getting other things as part of the bargain and can't delete surgically.

As literary scholars proliferate thematic microspecialties, the microspecialties enlarge their reach to raise their profile. Something that appears to be tiny in its proportions suddenly becomes the monster that ate Minneapolis. Such work is often claimed to be "interdisciplinary," but as Thomas Sowell observed in 1993, "interdisciplinary" often means *non-disciplinary*—"studies which require no mastery of the analytical methods of science, economics, logic, statistical analysis or other encumbrances to 'exciting' ideological discussions" (1993, p. 279).

An example: as graduate dean at Georgetown I interviewed a candidate for a position in the English department. Her specialty was "literature and food." I asked her about her research and likely teaching and it appeared to be largely thematic. She would look at works or "texts" in which food played a significant role and then attempt to draw points of connection. (Think of such films as *Tampopo*, *Like Water for Chocolate*, *Babette's Feast*, or *Eat Drink Man Woman*.) There are many other possibilities, of course—the inscribing of race or gender in such iconic images as Aunt Jemima, Uncle Ben or Betty Crocker, or the inscribing of race or gender in specific types of food.

The possibilities are endless, in a very real sense, but by the same token, the more "endless" the possibilities the greater the number of areas to be investigated in which an English PhD has little or no true professional expertise. Film is a huge subject; Japanese film is a huge subject. The cultural importance of food—historically, sociologically, psychologically, physiologically, biochemically, economically, and so on—is an enormous subject. Nutrition alone is often an academic department in schools of human environmental sciences and scholar-scientists in that field are often serious biochemists.

Cultural phenomena can and should be studied, of course, but the greater their importance the greater the need for trained professionals to do so. English PhD's are not actually trained in "food" in the way that serious food scientists are. They may take a course or two, develop some independent interests and produce some interesting work, but that work is likely to be closer to journalism than to science.

Nevertheless, the "literature and food" specialist can now find a home in an expanded world where nearly everything can be studied from nearly every perspective. On January 26-29, 2012 a conference on "Food Networks: Gender and Foodways" was held at the University of Notre Dame. The focus was on "food and gender" though that did not connote the specificity that some might expect. The general call for papers was as follows:

> This conference seeks to address gender issues as they relate to food. We welcome papers from all disciplines—Anthropology, Literary Studies, Film Studies, Sociology, Theology, Cultural Studies, Visual Culture, Gender Studies, Food Studies, American Studies, Ethnic Studies, History, Agriculture, and more. We seek a wide range of papers dealing with food in all its variety and complexity, as it relates to gender, sex and sexuality. Possible topics and areas of interest include:
>
>> *Gender and food figures*: the gourmet chef, the housewife, the family, the writer, the food critic . . . .
>> *Gendered food spaces*: the kitchen, the grocery store, the dining room, the farmers [sic] market . . . .
>> *Gendered representations of food*: in literature, in film, in television, in magazines, in ephemera, in metaphor . . . .
>> *Food and Gender/Sex Identities*: queer food, feminist food, masculine food, food and family, food and singles culture . . . .
>> *Gender and*: eating, diets, starvation, foodies, localism, sustainability, cookbooks, fat, sexuality, gastro-porn, disgust, shame, pleasure, sensuality, food communities, slow food, raw food . . . .

It is fair to say that the conference lacked a sharp focus. On the other hand, it was not designed to focus. It was designed to represent a research area as "God's plenty" and hype its importance by demonstrating its many-sidedness, but this raises a serious concern. Since disciplines tend to professionalize themselves (in part) by developing recondite vocabulary, nomenclature and taxonomy, one wonders how serious anthropologists, e.g., could talk (with full scholarly rigor) to serious students of film at such a conference.

If anyone doubts the sophistication of some of these areas of study, I would invite them to check out, e.g., David Bordwell's personal website on film. When David speaks about film to a literate but non-professional audience—at a film festival such as Roger Ebert's, e.g.—he is both learned and lucid, but when he speaks with full-fledged film professionals (such as his wife, Kristin Thompson, who seems to have seen every film ever produced) the discussion is at a totally different level of sophistication. Common knowledge is assumed that is far from "common knowledge"; theoretical issues are raised that are totally unfamiliar to lay people; examples are adduced that would be completely unfamiliar to even the most serious of moviegoers.

In a world of academic white noise, one of the great challenges to scholarship is to be able to contribute new knowledge, to materially advance the field, and to do so in important, not minor or peripheral ways. At the same time, the person who is able to do this must also be able to take all of the obscure material and field "lore," the major scholarship and the minor, and present it in sophisticated but clear, intelligible form to the larger culture. If it does not find its way into the larger culture, of what use is it? Why should the taxpayers subsidize private, arcane hobbies? Einstein famously said that, "You do not really understand something unless you can explain it to your grandmother" (Hacker and Dreifus 2011, p. 3). David and Kristin are able to do just that and individuals such as them should be our models.

The thematic commentary, on the other hand, the kind of discourse that blurs lines that serve to establish disciplines, the omnivorous expansion of, e.g., literary studies into area after area that is ultimately beyond its ken is something quite different. This is why Anthony Kronman can say, "Today, the humanities are not merely in a crisis. They are in danger of becoming a laughingstock, both within the academy and outside it" (2007, p. 139).

I would disagree with the use of such a broad brush, however. History (if one considers it part of the Humanities, as I do) has maintained its academic standards to a higher degree than literary studies have done, though it has sometimes been diverted in its emphases. From the relative absence of social history, for example, we moved to a point where social history became the all-consuming interest of departments of History to the exclusion of nearly all else, but that has since moderated.

Among professors of Philosophy there is a marked trend to dissociate themselves from the ills affecting the Humanities and a tendency to associate themselves instead with the culture, purposes and rigor of the natural sciences. When Richard Rorty left Virginia to go to Stanford he did not join the department of Philosophy; he joined the department of Comparative Literature. Similarly, the French Nietzscheans had far greater impact on literary studies than on their native disciplines. Derrida commanded some respect in departments of Philosophy, but you will generally hear very little about Lacan in the nearby department of Psychological Sciences. A distinguished historian once described Foucault to me as an individual who practiced "history without facts."

The twenty years or so in which high theory dominated literary studies are now often seen as a lost period; contemporary graduate students express relief that they were fortunate to have escaped it. A tiny (and shrinking) percentage of graduate applicants now express interest in it.

Menand's mini-history of the field (2010, p. 92) identifies three periods of modern literary studies: the "interpretive turn" (the 60s and 70s), the "diversity turn" (the 80s and 90s) and the current period of eclecticism, in which we pursue, as he says, an ongoing inquiry into the limits of inquiry.

Some traditionalists would label the "interpretive turn" as the period in which we systematically indulged in what Hirsch calls "cognitive atheism," the "diversity turn" as the period in which we enshrined identity politics. The noteworthy dimension to these "turns" is that they represent a good bit of churning, of searching for the next big thing. Bauerlein comments that "despite the breakdown of literary study as a *discipline*, it has survived as a *profession*" (my emphases, 1997, p. 141).

The precipitous drop in English majors over this period (from 7.6% of graduates in 1970 to 4% in 2001 [Donoghue 2008, p. 91]) is sometimes attributed to the profession's embrace of new, often tangential or even nonrelated subject matter. The drop would have been far more dramatic had it not been for the expansion of creative writing programs, a growth industry which can now account for as many as half of a department's registrations—an area which valorizes literature as art and, of course, pays significant attention to genre and to literary history. Some of my creative writing colleagues would argue that creative writing programs have not only saved literature departments; they have saved literary *study* itself.

The overarching statistical reality, however, is that the last academic year in which 50 percent of students graduated with traditional liberal arts majors was 1969–70 (Donoghue 2008, p. 91). From 1970–2001, Mathematics graduates (to return to the quadrivium for a moment) dwindled from 3 percent of the total to 1 percent, the social sciences and History from 18.4 percent to 10 percent. Meanwhile, graduates in business administration grew from 13.6 percent of the total to a whopping 21.7 percent, while such for-profits as the University of Phoenix and DeVry prospered, enrolling hundreds of thousands of students though graduating a small proportion of them and serving them with an instructional staff, only 26 percent of whom had been there for four or more years (Donoghue 2008, pp. 91–104). The "vocational turn" had arrived and triumphed.

What is seldom discussed within this historical narrative is the systematic reduction in expectations for the training of doctoral students in English accompanied by the seemingly inexplicable fact that requirements have been demonstrably eroded without achieving the expected reduction in what the graduate deans term "time to degree."

I noted earlier that Alvin Kernan's studies for an Oxford *baccalaureate* degree in English (1949–51) required twenty-seven hours of formal, final examinations. William Chace took his PhD in English at UC-Berkeley in 1968. It took him seven years to complete his graduate studies. At that time a student needed to demonstrate a knowledge of three foreign languages in order to receive a Berkeley PhD in English. There were three batteries of exams: a ninety-minute oral on all of English and American literature (roughly = an MA exam), a three-hour oral on six periods of English and American literature (roughly = "comps") and a written examination on a foreign or ancient literature. Then, the student wrote the dissertation.

At Wisconsin, Mert Sealts, the great Melville scholar, frequently spoke of the benefits of "possessing another literature" as in the case of the third Berkeley exam, but the practice was not widespread at the time. At Illinois the pattern was slightly different and it had, indeed, been reduced since the time when my college teachers who were Illinois alumni (Sy Gross, Jim Robinson, et al.) studied there.

We were only required to do two foreign languages, but the exams were challenging. One was required for the MA, a second for the PhD. I had had multiple years of French in high school and multiple years of French in college, but I failed the first Illinois French exam. It was actually relatively easy, but it was graded stringently. I misconstrued one sentence and lost a point for every word in that sentence. One native speaker of French was failed on the exam, but his results were reversed when he presented himself at the examiners' office and swore at them in fluent, idiomatic French for a period of forty-five minutes. I had left the first exam more than thirty minutes early, but took the next test, which was far more difficult, and passed, using every available second of the three hours available to us.

There was an MA exam that covered all of English and American literature. It was three hours in duration. In addition to the major and minor coursework (I studied the history of science with Bob Kargon, who later moved to Johns Hopkins), we were also required to complete a three-course philology requirement (Old English, Beowulf, History of the English Language). If you received grades of B or better in all three you were relieved of the responsibility to take a written philology "prelim" (prelims or preliminary examinations = Illinois comprehensive exams).

Four written literature prelims were required. Each covered approximately a 100-year period and each was four hours in duration. If you had A's in both a survey course and a seminar within a given field you could postpone examination on that area (one such area and only one) until the three-hour oral exam which followed the (then) twelve hours of writtens. I was examined on the sixteenth, seventeenth and eighteenth centuries, postponing the examination on the nineteenth until the oral examination.

These policies represented a significant relaxation of degree requirements. When Sy Gross and Jim Robinson were at Illinois, for example, they had to complete all four written literature prelims and they had to do the written philology prelim. (We were also examined on our minor field, but not until the three-hour dissertation oral, at the end of the program.)

The prelims were very difficult but they were not quirky. You did not need to fear far-out-of-left-field questions. On the other hand, you had to prepare a vast amount of material, knowing that it would be very difficult to "evade" questions. The questions were flatfooted but comprehensive and nearly all were generally required to be answered. (On the seventeenth-century prelim, for example, there was always a question on Milton. One example: "It is sometimes said that Milton 'changed' significantly over the course of his life. Taking a work from his early period and a work from his later period, assess the degree of 'change', taking into account relevant works—in prose and verse—written in between.") To prepare for the "Milton question," one of six or seven on each of the 3–4 prelims, students would generally take a course in which Milton figured prominently, then be sure to have read all of his major and most of his minor works. They then virtually memorized Hanford's *Milton Handbook*, to cover the biographical and historical materials and, at a minimum, read the essays in Arthur Barker's anthology of modern commentators on Milton. A familiarity with other standard texts would be expected, e.g., C. S. Lewis' *A Preface to "Paradise Lost,"* Douglas Bush's Oxford history of early seventeenth-century literature, et al. It would be especially prudent to know Barker's *Milton and the Puritan Dilemma*, since he was making up the questions.

Most students asked for copies of past prelims when they entered the program, so that they would have a sense of what they needed to learn in order to pass and graduate. The challenge was very clear: learn this stuff and then take the exam. If you tried to finesse an exam you were almost certain to fail it. The separate reading for each prelim complemented two-three formal courses in each of the fields. Students generally completed their coursework and then spent a year doing the reading to prepare them for the exams. One of my fellow graduate students—then well into his thirties—took eighteen months to prepare. I pressed myself and took 8 months.

When I took the exams the two American literature prelims were particularly difficult. On one of the two exams every student (of approximately fifteen) failed but two. Of the two who passed, one failed the other American lit prelim; the second who passed had been taking the exam for the second time.

All of the testing was done anonymously and all of the tests were of equal difficulty, in the sense that no allowance was made for the student's intended "field." I would be writing a dissertation in the eighteenth century, but I was required to pass the same sixteenth- and seventeenth-century exams as the students who would be writing dissertations in those areas.

This resulted in interesting phenomena. While most would take prelims in the fields prior to and after their area of ultimate specialization, other patterns were permitted if one could justify them. Jim Robinson, for example, had been a specialist in Elizabethan drama, but he took one of the American literature prelims. He was, we might say now, an "Atlantic studies" specialist before the research area had been institutionalized. Later, when he taught at Notre Dame, he had been asked to fill in for an American lit professor who was on leave. He could do that quite easily because he had had the proper preparation in graduate school. He then continued to teach American literature throughout his career.

The bottom line was that with the bearish MA exam (Wisconsin's was even harder), the philology requirement and four hundred years of prelim coverage, Illinois PhD's were said to be able to teach virtually anything. This gave them a comparative advantage in the job market.

While Illinois remains a great university (receiving two Nobel prizes in 2003, e.g.) its expectations have changed. For example, as noted above, when I taught Freshman composition the students wrote every week in the first semester; in the second semester they wrote twelve papers and then produced a term paper. The comparable courses today require only 11,000 words of writing in two semesters (forty-four pages of writing, more or less, over thirty weeks).

The English PhD program is also quite different. There is now only one foreign language required. The master's exam is no longer required. The philology courses are no longer required. The four-field prelims are no longer required. The student is examined in only one field, a field essentially constructed by the student, with faculty approval.

This is not a gut program. It is comparable to other doctoral programs in English at top American universities. It may even be a bit more demanding, in that the field exam is described as being just that. At other universities, for example, the single "comprehensive" exam or "field exam" is shaped to some degree (sometimes to a considerable degree) by the student's dissertation topic. In other words, the student can be tested on a chosen body of material which looks, in part (or in large part), toward the dissertation research, thus executing two birds with a single stone. The test then looks at the student's preparation to write the dissertation more than the student's ability to teach and do research in a broad field, i.e. a period of approximately 100 years.

Such coverage-light/dissertation-heavy programs are more like old Oxford D.Phil's than like traditional American PhD's (although the British students would have specialized earlier than their American counterparts and achieved much of the coverage as undergraduates). The "graduate program" under this model becomes the preparation for and the writing of a dissertation rather than broad preparation within a discipline followed by specialization within a single field and then specialized dissertation research within that field.

This is problematic in a number of ways. First and foremost, contemporary English PhD's are no longer prepared to teach across the discipline. Back in the day, of course, they would not have been expected to teach in the same depth across the entire corpus of English and American literature. They could, however, offer survey courses across that corpus and, in a pinch, they could teach upper division undergraduate courses in a number of fields. At Wisconsin I taught a course in Chaucer, Spenser and Milton in addition to multiple courses in the eighteenth century. At Georgetown I taught the undergraduate Milton course, my regular eighteenth-century courses and a course in American fiction.

At Wisconsin, John Shawcross, the great Miltonist, taught both Milton and modern fiction. Joe Wittreich was at home in both the seventeenth century and the nineteenth. In some ways, you have to be. You cannot understand the romantic poets without knowing Milton in depth, since he influenced them to such a considerable degree. You cannot understand Johnson without understanding both Milton and Shakespeare, because each influenced him profoundly.

Fields cannot be tidily separated and isolated from one another. African-American literature, e.g., draws on a multiplicity of literary traditions and it cannot be "narrowed" without falsifying it; the "Atlantic studies" field is an authentic one. To give but a single example: Nancy Armstrong has written about the "American origins of the *English* novel." We often say, for example, that Defoe is the "first novelist," but Defoe was influenced by such things as American captivity narratives, so the "influences" go in both directions and are far more complex than first meets the eye. Hence, you cannot neglect American writing that preceded Defoe, even though you might choose to present yourself as an "English" rather than "American" specialist.

The bottom line is that English scholars study the work of very sophisticated people. The broader the knowledge of the English language, English literature, American literature, world literature, the literature of antiquity and the middle ages, history, mythology and the Bible (for starters) that you possess, the more likely it is that you will be able to do historiography and analysis that has a chance of being of some significance. In short, you need the "broad preparation" in order to do the focused scholarship.

In some ways the programs of the 1960s and earlier are caricatured and thought of as depreciating the importance of research, while focusing on a hopelessly broad range of material, the vast majority of which would be of little interest to contemporary undergraduates. This misstates the reality to a considerable degree. The traditional programs focused heavily upon research, but only after one was certified as a disciplinary professional. You got your union card when you passed your comprehensive exams, the saying went; then you wrote your dissertation and got your degree.

My comments should not be applied to other doctoral programs in the Humanities and social sciences. While my colleagues in other fields (Political Science, Music, Anthropology, et al.) inform me that requirements have been relaxed significantly since the 1960s, the common pattern is nowhere near the magnitude of relaxation that one sees in English. To offer a quick, local example: our department of History's PhD program requires comprehensive examinations, both written and oral, in five substantial fields.

This absence of broad coverage is particularly problematic now, in a world where fewer and fewer students attend elite liberal arts colleges and serious research universities. The growth in enrollments and, hence, in teaching jobs are elsewhere and the students in those other institutions (principally regional publics and community colleges) have a crying need to understand broad ranges of material to which they have not yet been introduced.

But then, to a considerable degree, it has always been that way. A study of Berkeley English PhDs looked at the careers of students from the early 1980s. By the mid-1990s 53 percent had tenure, but less than twenty percent of them were in research universities (Menand 2010, p. 147). Note that this is one of the top English PhD programs in the country, frequently the top such program. What is unspoken in the statistics is the fact that at least half of the students probably dropped out along the way, so that a number closer to (a scant) 10 percent of the original cohort ended up teaching in research institutions, the kinds of institutions for which their training had been designed.

In the 1960s (when the programs were far more demanding) the average time for *registration* in a graduate program in the Humanities was six years; it is now (2010) nine years, with the median total time to degree (including 'stop time') at 11.3 years (Menand 2010, p. 148).

When Chace began his program at Berkeley in the 1960s there were 120 other English graduate students. Only twelve eventually got PhDs (Chace 2006, p. 60). This is a very high attrition rate; the norm is 45–50 percent in the Humanities (and those who leave, interestingly enough, tend to have higher undergraduate GPA's and higher GRE scores). By comparison, the attrition rates in law schools and medical schools are low, in the range of 5–10 percent (Donoghue 2008, pp. 27–28).

The general justification for the "streamlining" of English PhD programs has been the desire to reduce the time to degree, but this attempt has clearly failed. The programs have certainly been "streamlined," but ten to eleven year completion rates remain common. Why? Menand echoes the thoughts of Bowen and Rudenstine (Menand 2010, p. 149) and suggests that graduate students in English take so long to complete their programs because "the paradigms for scholarship in the humanities have become less clear." This is a very polite way of saying that the "discipline" of English is now marked by chaos and confusion and students have difficulty developing a research agenda that will have both resonance and longevity.

This is clearly a contributing factor. There is also the desire to stand out in a world of white noise. It used to be said that capital-T theorists (whose work often sounded radical and revolutionary but actually consisted of the endless confirmation of the same theories) needed to raise the level of their rhetoric and enlarge the nature of their claims because they needed to increase the metaphoric volume in order, simply, *to be heard*. We might call this the Nigel Tufnel principle: "This one goes up to eleven."

Theory is now largely passé, but the need to rise above the din is not. Thus, many dissertators develop topics that appear to advance bold new theories and claims—redefining whole periods, uncovering momentous cultural movements, and so on. That is not easy to do, particularly when they are not trained broadly, and it takes time. Most of the results are, at best, half-baked.

In addition, the programs now appear to be far more bureaucratized than in the past. There are endless deadlines and protocols, due-dates and procedural steps. My own preferences are always Thoreauvian. I prefer the "learn this stuff; then take the exam" approach because it places the emphasis on learning and not on endless energy transactions and the need for charts, timelines and professional advisers. Such approaches are designed to keep students on track and keep them moving steadily through their programs, but they require significant administrative oversight and often result in endless "extensions" and other bureaucratic fixes.

I see the same kind of bureaucratization in course syllabi. There are seemingly endless small requirements with writing assignments and re-writing assignments, due dates and deadlines (but comparatively few actual challenges) and elaborate, complex point-methods for grading which sometimes defy comprehension. Perhaps the complexity of the requirements substitutes for the previous complexity of the content, just as college curricula now often manage to be both vacuous and maze-like.

The principal reason for the extended enrollments in graduate programs is the field's chosen response to a constricted job market. Rather than expand the students' required knowledge, which would enable them to teach more broadly (and, in many cases, more appropriately), we have required them (it is said) to already have a "career" in place before they begin their careers. They are expected to publish a handful of articles and present at a number of scholarly conferences while they are still graduate students. Many now begin their careers as assistant professors with a published dissertation in hand, work that was completed during the period in which they held a succession of non-tenure track, "visiting" positions.

With such expectations, reducing the time to degree in Humanities doctoral programs now appears to be impossible. In 1991 the Mellon Foundation developed the GEI (the Graduate Education Initiative) in an effort to shorten the time to degree in top Humanities programs. The target was to reduce their duration to six years. (Note that catalogue descriptions often state that programs are designed to be completed in four to five years.) The foundation selected fifty-four departments at ten elite institutions and, over a period of ten years, threw $85,000,000 at the problem, and, basically, failed. There was an occasional victory here and there and some non-counterintuitive results. For example, if you give a student a summer grant to take coursework or work on a dissertation he or she *will* make more progress than if he or she was forced to work outside the university during that same period, but the overarching results were disappointing in the extreme (for a full account of the saga, see Ehrenberg et al., 2010).

Note that the foundation program also included the proviso that departmental programs be "streamlined," i.e., their expectations and requirements be reduced. In addition to the above-suggested reasons for protracted doctoral study, the Mellon initiative suggests that students may have proceeded slowly for other reasons—because they were being funded generously, because they had health insurance and because they lived in subsidized housing. I have also heard, for decades, the sad explanation that, for many, this will be their only teaching job (or their only teaching job in an elite institution) and they seek to prolong the experience.

An additional reason may be that the contemporary reliance on coursework in lieu of exams does not work when the coursework is less challenging than it once was. In a recent piece in the *Chronicle of Higher Education*, Leonard Cassuto discusses the various reasons adduced for requiring doctoral comprehensive exams and finds them largely unpersuasive. He echoes Cary Nelson and Stephen Watt in asking, "What do such exams accomplish that the twelve to sixteen courses doctoral students take don't?" (2012, p. 3).

The question assumes that advanced coursework in graduate programs covers a broad range of material and could thus substitute for the reading previously required for comprehensive exams. This is seldom the case. Most such coursework, particularly seminar work, is narrowly focused. It often corresponds with the research interests of the individual offering the course rather than with some larger vision of a period's *oeuvre* and the works with which a student should become familiar.

The actual *content* of specific courses is not only *narrower* than it once was; there is also much less of it. I was introduced to Johnson in a serious way in Bob Haig's course, English 349. An 'over/under' course, it was open to both junior and senior Illinois English majors and graduate students. It surveyed the second half of the eighteenth-century, the so-called "Age of Johnson" or, as it was sometimes described, "Johnson and his circle."

When I appeared at the registration table in the old Armory I was handed a note that came from the instructor. The note indicated that we would begin the course by reading Boswell's Life of Johnson. Since that is a long book, we were urged to begin reading it promptly, so that we would be ready to discuss it on the first day of class. The full text in the Oxford edition was approximately 1,400 pages in length. And so we read it. I do not remember any students complaining about that assignment, though most (approximately fifty in all) were undergraduates.

It is now simply unimaginable to assign the complete Boswell life unless it would be the only text in a course. In English 349, however, we also read Boswell's London Journal, approximately 600 pages of Johnson's writings, perhaps 500 pages of Goldsmith, Gibbon's autobiography, multiple plays by Sheridan, multiple works of Burke's, including the full *Reflections on the Revolution in France*, several of Sir Joshua Reynolds' *Discourses on Art*,

David Garrick's *The Clandestine Marriage* and a large amount of mid and late eighteenth-century poetry.

When I offered my own version of the course twenty years later at Georgetown I asked the students to read approximately one-third of that amount of material. I would not offer the course now, because I would have to require even less than that amount and I could not teach the period credibly and intelligibly with so few readings. When I taught the course at Georgetown I shamefully asked the students to read an abridged Life of Johnson, but the abridged version was still 400 or 500 pages in length and—as frequently happens now—the students simply did not read it.

In my college and graduate school departments, drama courses and novel courses generally covered one play or one novel per week. Now, four to six novels per semester, rather than thirteen to fifteen, would be expected and perhaps six to seven plays. The claims are sometimes made that the material is now studied in greater depth. That may be true and that may be good, but there are still massive gaps in knowledge which must be filled later, if at all.

Doctoral students in English are now, by and large, examined on a list of materials which they develop in tandem with their faculty advisor(s). The size of that list will vary from student to student, but a common number that one hears is in the area of 150 titles (approximately one-quarter of the readings required for Illinois prelims). At the University of Chicago, not very long ago, students were required to take a qualifying exam (not their doctoral comprehensives) that covered 100 titles. This was simply to determine if they could handle a significant amount of material and discuss it intelligently. Such expectations are a thing of the past.

A related problem with today's English doctoral programs is that of quality control. Current programs, e.g., enable students to avoid familiarity with a great deal of material. If they are canny and remain beneath the radar they can pass their exams and complete a doctoral program with vast gaps in their training.

The best way to get a feel for "coverage" issues is to examine actual cases. One might consult, for example, the online orals (i.e., comprehensive exam) reading lists at Columbia, a traditionally difficult program.

The lists include student samples of such lists, i.e., the lists that past students presented as subjects for examination and evidence of mastery. One student reading list for a minor in Shakespeare includes only twenty of Shakespeare's plays. We are not talking about a master's exam reading list or a full Elizabethan/Jacobean specialty-area reading list, but rather a reading list that would constitute the material for a full "minor" in Shakespeare alone.

Astoundingly, the reading list for a minor in Shakespeare does not include Shakespeare's sonnets. We can all probably get through life with a single reading of *Venus and Adonis* and *The Phoenix and the Turtle* and it is not likely that any but the most advanced students of Shakespeare will need to study *The Two Noble Kinsmen*, but Shakespeare's *sonnets*? Not only are they among the greatest in the language, they include some of Shakespeare's most famous lines and they have long been considered (in one way or another) a door to understanding certain aspects of his private life, something about which we know all too little. The sonnets alone have been the subject of, literally, thousands of studies. To omit them, while certifying high competency in the knowledge of their author, is to me unimaginable.

A Columbia student's reading list on the restoration and eighteenth century conceives of the period in thematic terms (i.e., as a set of categories such as "ladies, wives, women: the debate") and thus excludes everything that fails to fall within the artificial boundaries of these themes. For example, Johnson is represented by a small handful of works and Hume's major works are excluded. A *major field list* prepared by another student of "Imperial Modernism" includes fewer than sixty titles and omits the relevant, indisputable masterpiece by Joseph Conrad, *Nostromo*.

How does this all affect the job market? Actually, it is often geared to the job market. Illinois, e.g., invites students to propose special subjects for examination if they can demonstrate that their proposed "specialty" is reinforced by job ads calling for individuals with such expertise.

The dispersion within the field is mirrored in the job ads. Hiring departments list multiple desiderata with regard to the expertise (hopefully) possessed by potential candidates ("Victorian literature, post-colonialism, women and gender studies, and, ideally, skills with regard to the digital humanities") and applicants respond by dredging up as much plausible material as they can to demonstrate their ability to fit each particular template.

Since the fields are now many and the hires in difficult economic times relatively few, the hiring departments hope to cover multiple fields with each appointment. Correspondingly, the applicants spread themselves thinner and thinner to enhance their chances of being hired. However, many of the subspecialties or microspecialties are not broad, historical periods but rather themes of contemporary interest. These can be very transient, of course, and the more exotic they are the less "relevant" they may be for a first-generation college student with shaky high school preparation, enrolled in a third- or fourth-tier regional public institution. Experts on "performance studies" suddenly find themselves at the front of a classroom filled with students who are unaware of the difference between the present and past tenses.

The situation is now so serious that one recent president of the Modern Language Association proclaimed in her presidential address that the English profession essentially had no common body of learning that would certify its members as experts of a particular kind. This is Marjorie Perloff, a distinguished scholar, speaking in 2006: "Whereas economists or physicists, geologists or climatologists, physicians or lawyers must master a body of knowledge before they can even think of being licensed to practice, we literary scholars, it is tacitly assumed, have no definable expertise" (Chace 2009, p. 7).

Cardiologists cannot study the right ventricle and overlook the left, but English teachers can now define "the field" for themselves, bringing in whatever previously-foreign material they choose and leaving out whatever previously-central material they wish.

Citing Marjorie Perloff's comments, William Chace writes that "Perhaps the most telling sign of the near bankruptcy of the discipline is the silence from within its ranks." No one has come forward to counter Professor Perloff's observation and argue that the field does in fact possess some form, however modest, of observable coherence. "Such silence strongly suggests," Chace writes, "a complicity of understanding, with the practitioners in agreement that to teach English today is to do, intellectually, what one pleases" (2009, p. 7).

The Harvard department of English, to which many still turn in search of an academic model, has removed the requirement of a survey of English literature for undergraduates and has put in place four "affinity groups," including such categories as "Arrivals" and "Diffusions." There is no single book or group of books that one can now assume a Harvard English major will have read. As Stephen Greenblatt puts it, students are now to craft their own literary "journeys" (Chase 2009, p. 8).

On the other hand, they do have at least one remaining option, but it is open to only a few. Greenblatt notes that he and his colleague Louis Menand actually offer a survey course that begins with Homer and ends with Joyce. "The pressure on enrollment is huge," he acknowledges, "because it turns out that many students—without the compulsion of their teachers—feel that they really shouldn't go through their undergraduate years without reading the great imaginative works of the past" (Abrams and Greenblatt 2012, p. 2).

The fact that there is student demand for such courses is unlikely to result in an increase in their numbers, in part because the only people capable of teaching them are individuals such as Greenblatt and Menand, people at the very top of the English profession.

At Missouri we offer old-school survey courses through our honors college; they are, in effect, reserved for the very best students, even though it is the least-prepared students who most need them. These kinds of programs carry an unacknowledged subtext: there is still an authentic education available, if you want it, but it will be reserved for elites and access will be carefully controlled. This is the sort of discrimination which one would expect academics to decry, but they do not. They want to do what they want to do and they do not want to be pressed to offer survey courses which they, in all likelihood, are unable to teach anyway.

The Greenblatt quote comes from an interesting piece in the *New York Times* in which Greenblatt and M. H. Abrams discuss the fiftieth anniversary of the *Norton Anthology of English Literature*. Abrams, then 100, was the founding general editor, Greenblatt the current general editor.

Abrams observes that this time-honored collection was designed for undergraduates, "but it's used [now] by graduate students in preparing for their oral examinations" (Abrams and Greenblatt 2012, p. 2). Pause and read that again. An anthology *originally designed to be used in freshman and sophomore survey courses is now used by doctoral students* to prepare for their comprehensive examinations.

My eldest granddaughter recently graduated from the University of Rochester, an excellent, AAU, private institution, with high standards and a strong reputation. She majored in Molecular Genetics, but she was required to take an English course along the way. It was not a survey course covering the major works of English or American literature. It was a course on satire—presumably the interest of the graduate student who taught it.

English and American literature both include masterpieces of satire, but satire is not a major form, considered in the context of the epic/lyric/dramatic designations of antiquity. There is no shelf for "satire" at Barnes & Noble. It is not so minor as to be safely overlooked, but it is safe to say that it is a bit off the beaten track if a course in it is the only course to which an undergraduate student will be exposed. Kudos, however, to Rochester, for not asking her to take a course in Teenage Paranormal Romance or something on Gendered Food Spaces. Nevertheless, the driving force behind the curriculum remains faculty choice rather than student need.

Swift's greatest satire is a book entitled *A Tale of a Tub*. It is seldom taught today to undergraduates because its materials are too recondite for modern students and the instructor is put in the position (as one of my teachers once put it) of "trying to make a dinosaur dance." For those sufficiently immersed in the historical period and in Swift's ways it is a brilliant, even riveting work, dense with ideas, wit and wisdom.

The "tale" is told by a "projector," an individual who dreams up crackbrained proposals. Johnson's second definition of *projector* is "one who forms wild impracticable schemes." The term was associated at the time with quackery in science and with what we would now term "public policy." Swift's "modest proposer" who suggests the harvesting of infant and teenage flesh as an interesting market opportunity for an Ireland riven by economic challenges is of the same ilk.

The tale is told in alternating sections—an allegorical narrative concerning three brothers which satirizes the excesses within the interplay of Catholicism, Calvinism and Lutheranism and a series of digressions that broadly satirize contemporary "learning." In Section V, "A Digression in the Modern Kind," the persona/projector mentions several of his other works: "my 'New Help of Smatterers, or the Art of being Deep Learned and Shallow Read,' 'A Curious Invention about Mouse-traps,' 'A Universal Rule of Reason, or Every Man his own Carver,' together with a most useful engine for catching of owls."

"Every Man his own Carver" suggests Swift's view of rationalism detached from an anchoring reality. Swift casts his lot with evidence and experience and decries deductive approaches which begin with a bizarre theory (Descartes' system of vortices comes to mind) and then search for the data (or bend the data) to confirm it. Swift here imagines a generalized "intellectual" scene in which everyone dreams his own dreams, forms his own schemes and creates his own concept of knowledge and learning. It is not too distant from our current reality.

And who would have thought that the person to chart a way out of this thicket would be the Prince of Wales? Dismayed by the reduction of expectations with regard to core learning and (with E. D. Hirsch) by the "trendy" teaching which puts more focus on "skills" than knowledge, Prince Charles has established a charity—The Prince's Teaching Institute—to protect traditional subjects by bringing secondary school teachers under the wings of Cambridge history/literature dons in a two-year master's degree program in advanced subject teaching.

The full program, which has just begun (2012), focuses on those areas of the school curriculum that have somehow fallen out of favor, such as the works of Chaucer or the history of the Crusades. The program was developed by Adrian Barlow, the recently-retired Cambridge International Examinations director. The program began in 2002, with summer-session versions. Since then more than 3,000 teachers from more than 20 percent of England's secondary schools have participated, the instruction also encompassing science, geography, mathematics and modern foreign languages. Bernice McCabe, the institute's co-director and headmistress of a private girls school in Edgware says that "One of the key aims is to promote the idea that subject *knowledge*, subject *rigour* and the enthusiasm for communicating them are essential requirements for effective teaching to children *of all abilities*" (Henry 2011, p. 3, my emphases).

Prince Charles's comment is interesting and his final lines are memorable: "All of a sudden, in the 1960s, anything which might conceivably be described as a timeless principle was abandoned on the basis that all we had known and learned had suddenly become irrelevant, old-fashioned, out-of-date and definitely not modern. Frankly, I thought this was bonkers and likely to end in tears" (Henry 2011, p. 3).

The crucial line for me is Ms. McCabe's observation that knowledge, rigor and enthusiasm are *necessary for students of all abilities*. The "do whatever I wish" approach does not lead to the kind of coherent learning which might meet the needs and enhance the lives of the poor and previously-marginalized. Moreover, reserving such material for a select few such as the students in a special track in an elite institution is likely to perpetuate the inequalities between those who are prepared to do college work and those who are not.

There may be a strategy here, however. If students continue to demonstrate an interest in authentic, traditional learning, the corporatists' dollars might follow them and such programs might be expanded. The ways which brought success to the GI Bill generation might be "rebranded" as something new and fresh or "cutting-edge," something that would reinforce the vision of the institution's mission statement and strategic plan and, perhaps most important, attract additional recruiters from industry.

It will not happen in literary study, however, without some external event or sequence of events. The graduate schools will not be inclined (or able) to dictate to powerful English departments and urge them to restore breadth and depth to their doctoral programs. A national task force study will not do it. When the president of the Modern Language Association tells the membership that their field has no there, there and their response is one of silence, that form of leadership is also likely to be unsuccessful.

Leading departments and leading faculty will have to find the way and their imitators and ephebes will have to be encouraged to follow them. It will take leaders—individuals associated with a significant body of work—and it will take some administrative urging. It will also take time. However, if and when more demanding programs are installed, *their graduates will land the top positions*. Others will then take note and follow in short order.

Such programs can be completed and they can be completed within a relatively short period of time. My dear friend, Walt Pritchard, with whom I taught at West Point was, then, an Armor major. His interests were primarily in engineering and he had studied for a year at Rensselaer before obtaining his appointment to West Point.

As a member of the class of 1957 he had done well enough in the handful of English courses then offered to be pulled from the ranks years later and sent to graduate school for two years to prepare him to teach at West Point. The time elapsed between his taking the scant, West Point English courses and his matriculation in graduate school would have been in the neighborhood of eight to nine years, during which time he would have been leading Armor troops, going to jump school, and generally leading the life of a junior officer preparing to become a field-grade officer.

He was sent to Columbia. In two years there (with nothing approaching a prior major in English) he passed his language exams, completed his master's degree, completed his doctoral coursework, passed his doctoral comprehensive exams and was able to begin work on his dissertation.

The subject of his dissertation was Oliver St. John Gogarty, the "Buck Mulligan" figure in Joyce's *Ulysses*. His dissertation director was William York Tindall, one of the world's leading Joyce scholars. Walt had the advantage of full Army funding during his graduate program, but he also had to conjure with a complex Manhattan commute. The bottom line is that a great deal can be accomplished in a short period of time if you have curiosity, discipline and tenacity. He never completed his dissertation because he was killed in Vietnam after a two-year tour at West Point, but he was working on it during the time that his wife Maryellen visited him in Hawaii for his R&R leave.

Walt's determination was reminiscent of that of the students who matriculated with the help of the GI Bill. We need such individuals today and we need them in serious numbers. Students can accomplish what they are asked to accomplish. There is no need to accede to a failed status quo. Some might say that we have now simply gone soft, that there was a greatest generation in scholarship as well as in other areas of our national experience. There may be some truth to that, but we will never know what our students can accomplish unless and until we ask more of them. We must simply join hands and step off the cliff together. It is not so great a distance to the solid ground.

Chapter Nine

Physics for Poets

In the contemporary American research university, scientific study is the principal measure of accomplishment, the central source of reputation and acclaim. At the same time, its students are comparatively few in number and often, as we once said, *foreign*. Science *is* international, but it continues to be perceived as exotic, a subject for the few, despite its centrality to our lives, our health and our economies. Science is now largely divorced from the Humanities, the Humanities having failed to "theorize" and relativize it in order to reduce its truth claims and dissolve its dominion. How can we begin to enhance scientific literacy, integrate scientific study within the curriculum and foster an ethos in which the Humanities and the sciences might work in concert? We can begin by noting that science's place of privilege is a very recent one.

In the hymn to light which opens Book III of *Paradise Lost*, Milton speaks of his own blindness, pairing that reality with a by-then religious and scientific commonplace:

> . . . and ever-during dark
> Surrounds me, from the cheerful ways of men
> Cut off, and for the Book of knowledge fair
> Presented with a Universal blanc
> Of Nature's works to me expung'd and ras'd,
> And wisdom at one entrance quite shut out (ll. 45-50).

The notion is that God reveals Himself to man in two ways—through the book of His *word* and the book of His *works*, scriptural revelation in the first case, the created universe in the second. While the first form of revelation is long-acknowledged and broadly accepted, the latter implies that the individual best positioned to understand God's revelation of Himself—through His *works*—is the scientist, the natural philosopher, as he (and sometimes she) was termed, a descriptive title echoing with associations and implications.

This represents not just a considerable change in cultural perception but one that was effected very rapidly. Earlier in the century, as James VI of Scotland succeeded Elizabeth, he was warned by Robert Cecil concerning possible political opposition. That opposition included Henry Brooke, Sir Walter Raleigh and Henry Percy, ninth Earl of Northumberland. Raleigh and Percy were linked intellectually as well as politically; both were interested in science.

In *Love's Labour's Lost* Shakespeare's King of Navarre states that "Black is the badge of hell/The hue of dungeons and the school of night." From this reference and other inferences it has been suggested that there actually was a "school of night," a group centered on Raleigh but including Christopher Marlowe, George Chapman, the astronomer and mathematician Thomas Harriot and Percy. Robert Persons, a contemporary Jesuit, referred to the school of night as the "school of atheism," atheism being associated with the black arts and also considered tantamount to treason in the sense that the monarch was the head of the church as well as the state.

Percy was not burned at the stake, like Giordano Bruno (persecuted primarily for religious heterodoxy rather than for his studies of astronomy), but he was imprisoned in the Tower for seventeen years and fined £30,000 (perhaps $140,000,000 in purchasing power today). His wealth insulated him within the Tower and the so-called "Wizard Earl" was able to acquire additional space, establish a laboratory and meet with Raleigh, with Harriot and with the astrologer John Dee. Despite his personal comforts, the position of the renaissance scientist was still such that random charges of atheism and treason could still, to a considerable degree, stick.

Milton, writing three generations later, was safely ensconced in what Whitehead would term the century of genius, a century that included the work of William Gilbert, William Harvey, Marin Mersenne, Johannes Kepler, Christiaan Huygens, John Flamsteed, Pierre Gassendi, the astronomer, mathematician, physicist (and, yes, architect) Christopher Wren, Bacon, Hobbes, Descartes, Pascal, Galileo, Spinoza, Leibniz and Newton.

Galileo's contretemps with Rome reminds us that science could still be suspect, as does the Royal Society's decision to steer clear of both religion and politics in its proceedings. The selection of *Bishop* Thomas Sprat to write the Royal Society's History (1667) is another indication of the scientists' desire to protect their flanks in the face of potential ideological opposition.

By the early eighteenth century the scientist moved from being a suspicious person in the dark and on the margins to playing the triumphal role of intellectual model and leader. Pope penned an epitaph for Newton, intended for his site in the Abbey: "Nature, and Nature's Laws lay hid in Night./God said, *Let Newton be!* and All was *Light*" (1730).

Pope argues, indirectly, that one might consider the birth of Newton and the publication of the *Principia* as events parallel in importance to the very creation of the universe itself. Pope's epitaph was not used, but Newton's official inscription characterizes him as having "a strength of mind almost divine."

In our own time and within the walls of the university the scientist's position is both dominant and secure. Not only do the women and men of science obtain a significant portion of the resources which support the university's overall operation, they also receive research support from the federal and state governments, industry, foundations and individuals. Because they achieve discoveries which lead eventually (and sometimes directly) to the amelioration of the human condition and the security and growth of the national life and economy they carry a large measure of the university's reputation.

In arguing for the indispensability of the American research university, Jonathan Cole summarizes a number of the modern research successes in engineering and the physical and life sciences. This necessarily-brief summary occupies nearly 100 pp. of text. Among those achievements are the following: Barbara McClintock's research on maize and her discovery of transposition and "jumping genes" (a subject of great interest to my boss at Madison, Bob Bock) which led to the discovery of the molecular structure of DNA, which in turn led to recombinant DNA technology that proved useful in the treatment of heart disease, stroke, hemophilia, rheumatoid arthritis, thyroid cancer, asthma and non-Hodgkins lymphoma (Cole 2009, pp. 209–11).

The isolation of the gene for insulin aided in the treatment of diabetes, which puts millions of individuals at increased risk of heart attack, stroke, hearing loss, colon cancer, a host of autoimmune diseases, thyroid problems, celiac disease and Addison's disease (pp. 213–14). Studies of oncogenes, oncogenesis and an oncogenic virus have aided physicians in the treatment of cancer. An enhanced understanding of the biochemical basis for cancer led to the invention of Gleevac, a powerful and effective anticancer drug (2009, pp. 218–19).

We now are often able to cure childhood leukemia and we can detect cervical cancer with the use of the pap smear (2009, pp. 220–21). Sequencers and synthesizers have enabled us to achieve success with the human genome project and have led, in turn, to the establishment of a series of commercial entities (2009, pp. 222–23). We have the nicotine skin patch and artificial joints and we can now offer the deaf cochlear implants (2009, pp. 223–25). We can treat and prevent Hepatitis B (2009, pp. 227–28).

Between 15,000,000 and 25,000,000 Americans, including 10,000,000 children are afflicted by head lice. Purdue's Dr. Jerry McLaughlin identified substances in the bark of the pawpaw tree which can be processed and marketed and result in a 100 percent effectiveness rate for both their removal and the removal of their nits (2009, p. 230). Worldwide, annually, more than 50,000,000 people now receive organ transplants. (2009, p. 231); kidney dialysis now offers an alternative to kidney failure (2009, pp. 232–33). Louis Pasteur and Alexander Fleming were able to accelerate the use of molds to cure human disease, so that antibiotics are now taken for granted (2009, p. 233), as are stem cell technology, cardiopulmonary resuscitation and the treatment of HIV/AIDS (2009, pp. 235–40).

Agricultural production, storage and transport have been revolutionized (2009, pp. 240–43) and at a time when Darwin's stock has never been higher we have seen the birth of sociobiology, evolutionary psychology and a host of parallel applications of evolutionary science to human life and experience (2009, pp. 243–44).

Quantum mechanics have changed our understanding of the laws of physics operating on the atomic level while the theory of relativity has altered it on the macro level. With all of Pope's (deserved) praise of Newton, Newton's mechanics were already being refined in the eighteenth century by Laplace and Lagrange. In the twentieth century came Einstein and Heisenberg to further the discussion, both of whose ideas have been used to underwrite specific aspects of religious faith.

And now we have the laser. And LED's. And bar codes. And radar. And the transistor. We study superconductivity, develop new medical diagnostics, employ MRI technology, and utilize the applications made possible by biomedical engineering. We have computers and smart phones, tablets, the internet, World Wide Web and GPS navigation systems. We have neuroscience and we are beginning to understand the immensely-complex workings of the human brain.

In the late renaissance and eighteenth century we saw the beginnings of what we would now call demography, urban planning and sophisticated statistical analysis, developments associated with such figures as Descartes and Sir William Petty. Adam Smith taught economics (as well as logic, moral philosophy and rhetoric and belles-lettres). Political theory made significant leaps, as did historiography. Cole gives the social sciences—already established in the eighteenth century—approximately one-third the space he accords the natural sciences and engineering and highlights such notions as David Reisman's "lonely crowd," Robert Merton's elaborations of the phenomena of unintended consequences and the many, important developments in contemporary economics. The study of linguistics has led to significant conclusions concerning the wiring of the human brain. John Rawls's notions of distributive justice have, for many, constituted a landmark in the area of social contract theory.

Despite the achievements of the social sciences, their position is often perceived to be tenuous. We frequently hear invocations of Auden's injunction that "thou shalt not commit a social science." Many feel that the thoroughgoing quantification of economics has marginalized it. Anthropology departments, as I noted earlier, are often riven. Norman Birnbaum considered the possibility that Sociology had come to an end as early as 1975. Departments of Psychological Sciences have essentially abandoned their affiliations with the Humanities and relocated, to the degree possible, among the life sciences.

The challenge of the social sciences is the challenge of studying something as rash, mercurial and unpredictable as human behavior. Animal behavior studies—employed to elucidate human experience—are sometimes of help, sometimes not. Johnson's *Rasselas* ends with a "conclusion in which nothing is concluded," but so do, it often seems, the social sciences. C. S. Lewis thought that the existence of the natural law could be demonstrated by seating 5 individuals around a table and then cutting a pie in four slices. The cries of injustice would be heard everywhere, in all societies, in all places and at all times. Perhaps that is true, but the study of human and animal behavior beyond the simplest aspects of "distributive justice" quickly become complicated. Some animals *do*, routinely, eat their young. Some *do* mate promiscuously, while some *do* mate for life. Some human societies rigorously identify certain behaviors as taboo; others do not. Some are violent, others more peaceful. Politically (assuming that political postures flow, to some degree, from different conceptions of "human nature" [humans are irreparably fallen; humans are demonstrably perfectible]), we are now split more or less right down the middle and our attitudes and behaviors with regard to such practices as divorce and out-of-wedlock births have altered dramatically within an exceptionally brief period of time and in the face of statistical evidence demonstrating their social and economic cost.

The social scientist is perforce obliged to deal in large statistical aggregates while the voices in the deep background echo the Twain-popularized mantra that there are three types of lies: "lies, damned lies, and statistics." The amount of labor and intelligence invested in the prediction of election outcomes is staggering; at the same time we will regularly be told that one of the best predictors of electoral success involves the quality of that year's Beaujolais harvest. Harry Truman's desire for a one-armed economist (who could never say, with the pertinent gesture, "on the other hand . . .") is not an indictment of economics but a reflection on the object of its study, a society that will include "rational actors" as well as individuals anxious to purchase expensive "pet rocks" rather than simply adopting strays.

Given the nature of the human component and the human capacity for bias and special pleading, the social sciences begin at a significant disadvantage vis `a vis the natural sciences, but that does not mean that their work is unimportant. Obviously, from what has preceded in this study, I consider Christopher Lasch's and Richard Hofstadter's work—to give two examples—of consummate importance and interest, but their "conclusions" are quite different from the notion that force equals mass times acceleration or that for every action there is an equal and opposite reaction.

The same is true, *a fortiori*, in the Humanities. Several years ago I read an exchange in which two titans of literary criticism were engaged in a debate. One opined that the problem with his opponent was that "he simply did not know how to read." That did not imply that he was illiterate, but rather that, given the Everest of theoretical and practical texts that comprised the backdrop for their dialogue, one individual came to the task of interpretation from a slightly different direction wherein some minute distinction might constitute a definitive difference. This happens constantly amid the higher reaches of the Humanities while one would never see a serious chemist charged with ignorance of the existence of hydrogen or oxygen. The "certainties" within their respective disciplines are different in kind, though that does not imply that they do not draw upon one another. Sometimes the appropriations are metaphoric; sometimes they involve the actual use of principles: a) "State houses, like nature, abhor vacuums"; b) "Your syllogism fails because of its undistributed middle."

While each has its theories, the bottom line is that science actually does (in some ways) *work*. *Scientific* theory, as George Steiner says (1989, p. 71), *applies*. We notice when the Caltech Jet Propulsion Lab's rover sends images from Mars. We notice when a friend's non-Hodgkins lymphoma death sentence is postponed for a decade or when our Camry engine is still humming steadily after 250,000 miles of service.

Science has been dealt some high cards. "Correct" and "incorrect" are notions with which humanists conjure; in the sciences they are notions with which one must deal. Fortunately, that "correctness" is not absolute. While the scientist is engaged in a process whose results are both replicable and falsifiable he or she enjoys the advantage that a discovery or application might be either erroneous or inexplicable but still possess heuristic value.

The eighteenth century believed that fire occurred because of the release of a substance called phlogiston. This, we can now say definitively, was not true. Nevertheless, chemistry did not stand still during the eighteenth century. Lavoisier was able to serve as the so-called father of modern chemistry not just by overturning the phlogiston theory but by accelerating a succession of changes and redirecting its study from a qualitative science to a quantitative one.

We now take Lyrica (Pregabalin) to treat seizures and relieve fibromyalgia, diabetic nerve pain, spinal cord injury nerve pain, and the pain resulting from shingles. The FAQ section of its official website includes the question, "How is Lyrica believed to work?" The largely-tautological answer:

LYRICA is believed to work within your body to calm the damaged or overactive nerves that cause pain. Although *the exact mechanism of action is unknown*, results from animal studies suggest that LYRICA works by calming damaged or overactive nerves that cause pain or seizures. The implication of these studies in humans is not known (my italics).

Neurontin (Gabapentin) is similar in activity to Lyrica though it binds to a different site. Its mode of action is also not yet understood. Such examples could be multiplied. While pharmaceutical companies warn you that a particular drug "is not for everyone"—the opening line on the Lyrica site—there will *still* be gratitude from those whose pain is reduced and whose condition is ameliorated. Science studies the real world (or aspires to) and it does so in largely-material ways rather than largely-abstract ones. The interaction between science and physical reality *grounds* it in such a way that any results that follow are potentially instructive and, as such, potentially useful. Absent proven cures we welcome experimental ones, particularly if our illness is a desperate one.

Absent full understanding (so-called "causal" explanations would never be possible, the early members of the Royal Society thought, because they were the province of the Divine) we embrace partial understanding and while the levels of understanding are proportional to the depths of the scientist's knowledge there is truth or falsehood within each of those levels.

For example, atomic activity is understood at ever-increasing levels of subtlety, but the elementary model must include electrons. Neuroscience must begin with neurons, axons, synapses, dendrites and neurotransmitters. There is room for cabbages and room for kings in poetry but not within subatomic activity.

The Higgs boson was theorized two generations ago; its discovery was announced on July 4, 2012. One could once talk about the *likelihood* of its existence; now one *must* talk about its existence, but while the levels of understanding vary at different times and among different individuals there are standards of precision expected at each level—from the level of a high school junior to the level of a senior investigator at CERN.

The truth claims of science should not be romanticized, though we fully understand the *cri de coeur* of the humanist whose students challenge his grading: "in science *there are true and false answers* . . . if only there were *here*." (This is exacerbated by the nonjudgmentalists who see "true and false answers" in, e.g., rules of grammar and spelling as hegemonic tools of oppression.)

In the *Timaeus* Plato suggests that we should not see scientific explanations of phenomena in our world as anything more than "likely stories." Although this is anchored in his view of the profound difference between our world of change and the eternal, changeless world of ideas, his statement can be seen to parallel the Royal Society's view that we will never achieve causal explanations. It also accords with the history of science. Even an accomplishment as dazzling as Newton's requires additional study and, ultimately, fundamental reevaluation.

This is not to say, however, that the "likely stories" are postmodern "narratives" of purely relative authority. There remain the palpable heuristic measures, the demonstrable falsehoods and the overriding method. That method is so straightforward as to be applicable to "systematic" activities within the Humanities.

The method is anchored in modesty. We follow our initial observations with very tentative hypotheses, test them by experiment, refine them, re-test them, confirm or abandon them, conduct more experiments, polish and tweak them; we listen to other voices, voices prepared to confirm, reinforce or falsify our work. We expect setbacks and blind alleys; we hope for elegant explanations and the successful utilization of Occam's razor, even as we deal with outliers and exceptions.

As a member of the Wisconsin Research Committee one of the earliest projects I recommended for funding was Elliott Sober's now-celebrated study, *Simplicity*. The book deals with the principle of "simplicity" in the evaluation of scientific theory. Given the sophistication and rigor of its arguments, it may be one of the most ironically-titled books in the history and philosophy of science. Every good scientist knows, however, that to achieve that treasured simplicity one might well invest a lifetime of effort. A senior medical official once introduced me to one of his investigators, a man who had spent decades in the study of a single phenomenon. "This is how we learn," he said.

There are parallels within the Humanities. A biographer, for example, will begin with a notion of the core of the biographical subject, an "image" or "concept" we might say, or the person's "character" as the eighteenth century would. The biographer expands the base of information, finding, exploring and studying documents. She or he listens to other voices and entertains other perspectives, looking for essential points of contact with other studies and examines the experiences, pronouncements and private letters that confirm (or undercut) the validity of the overarching conception of the biographee which has since been sharpened, polished, tweaked and clarified.

The biographer will labor to insure that the overarching conception—necessarily a partial one because the *totality* of potential evidence is never available—will be confirmed when some new evidence comes to life. There will be an ongoing interaction between "theory" and evidence. Ultimately the biographer will be superseded because a process utilizing the scientific method will always be superseded. The capability of being superseded is part and parcel of science. This is how it succeeds and this is why it must be understood historically and, in part, why it is taught sequentially.

The physicist's subject and the biographer's are, in the end, quite different. There is greater latitude within the Humanities for subjective (but still valuable) judgment. As George Steiner puts it, Copernicus supersedes Ptolemy but the Aristotelian conception of *mimesis* is not superseded by Lessing or Bergson. There is a Sophoclean Oedipus, an Aristotelian Oedipus and a Freudian Oedipus but there is only one second law of thermodynamics (1989, pp. 76–77).

The humanist's likely ignorance of that law was one of the points of combat in the F. R. Leavis/C. P. Snow debate. Five years before Leavis' 1962 volley, Northrop Frye attempted to bridge the humanist/scientist divide by making literary study more "systematic," the result (*Anatomy of Criticism: Four Essays*) being a grand experiment in interpretation and, principally, taxonomy. Much later, some of the postmodernists hoped to "theorize" science in such a way as to relativize it. Rather than mimic science they would absorb, neutralize and paralyze it. This effort failed. It encouraged Alan Sokal's notorious 1996 hoax in which he published a nonsensical article on science—replete with the recondite jargon of contemporary theory—in the journal, *Social Text*. The objects of the hoax were not amused, but their enthusiastic publication of rubbish constituted a cultural moment. Later, one of the most trenchant and searching critiques of postmodernism came from the Humanities, the philosopher Paul Boghossian's *Fear of Knowledge: Against Relativism and Constructivism (2006)*.

For me, a pivotal rejoinder came in Daphne Patai and Will H. Corral's 2005 "anthology of dissent," *Theory's Empire*. A 700 pp.+ doorstop, the book assembles oppositional statements from a galaxy of such important commentators as René Wellek, Tzvetan Todorov, Morris Dickstein, John M. Ellis, Denis Donoghue, John Searle, M. H. Abrams, Frederick Crews, Brian Vickers, Mark Bauerlein, Todd Gitlin, William C. Dowling, Elaine Marks, Kwame Anthony Appiah, Russell Jacoby, Eugene Goodheart, Thomas Nagel, David Bromwich, Frank Kermode, Marjorie Perloff and Wayne Booth.

The ultimate coffin nail is driven in by Chomsky. If he followed the postmodern urgings and recognized that "scientific endeavor is also in the world of story and myth creation," no better or worse than other "stories and myths" . . . [it] would help solve [his] problems. "If I can just tell stories about the questions that I've been struggling with for many years," he writes, "life will indeed be easier; the proposal 'has all the advantages of theft over honest toil,' as Bertrand Russell once said in a similar connection" (Patai and Corral 2005, p. 534). Ultimately, Chomsky argues, we have only one way to proceed: "by assuming the legitimacy of rational inquiry" (2005, p. 529).

The rational inquiry embodied in the scientific method stands as an institutional monument and that monument is undergirded by significant resources. In fiscal 2011, federal research and development dollars exceeded $40B, government support constituting 60 percent of university R&D budgets. Johns Hopkins alone (the perennial leader) received $1.88B in federal support (87.8% of Hopkins' total support). Wisconsin (coming in at #9) received $594M from the government, 53.4 percent of their total support.

We should not think of universities as awash in oceans of money that make possible an endless latitude for error and waste. On the contrary, the federal contracts may be with the universities, but the vast bulk of the proposals come from individual investigators and the responsibility for the work falls on their shoulders. The universities may capture and utilize the indirect costs of the individuals' research, but the individuals handle the direct costs. If they fail, the federal spigot is turned off and the flow ceases. Selecting those investigators and providing them the initial support which will lead to long-term funding is the crucial decision point and it is not an inexpensive one. If the hiring of each scientist requires a $1,000,000 investment (a good rule-of-thumb number for instrumentation and appropriate space) there is virtually no latitude for error.

My successor-dean, Mike O'Brien, recently met with departments and noted the experience of Caltech. Regularly ranked as the top university in the world, Caltech has only 330 professorial faculty. Each hiring decision is enormous because the intellectual and financial stakes are immense. Approximately 20 percent of federal R&D funds go to only ten universities. Membership in the AAU, the Association of American Universities, turns on the magnitude of such support. The AAU consists of only sixty U.S. institutions (+2 Canadian institutions). Membership is highly prized; the principal decision points for membership include the amount of federal research funding, the number of faculty elected to the National Academies, the number of faculty awards (principally nationally-competitive fellowships and elected memberships in learned societies) and the number of scholarly citations of the faculty's research.

Other things are considered: the number of doctorates awarded, the number of postdocs, the research funding from other sources, principally the Department of Agriculture, industry and the individual states and, finally, the quality of undergraduate education. The "Phase 1 indicators," however, are those that matter the most.

Doing "big science" ultimately determines the weight and quality of a university's reputation. The achievements are impossible without the initial investments. A pivotal element is (if it has one) the university's medical center. Such elements can prove to be both enormously productive and highly problematic. Medical Center budgets can represent 50–60 percent or more of the university's total budget. These centers are magnets for litigation. Their cultural traditions are more hierarchical and autocratic than collegial or democratic. They have "separatist" impulses (nearly always and nearly everywhere) and they seek their own governance structures separate from the normal lines of traditional university authority. They nearly always, e.g., *require* separate Human Resources, Advancement and IT operations.

Their budgeting is volatile and, as with intercollegiate athletics, a single "issue" or scandal there can paralyze the entire university. At the least, their budgetary weight automatically consumes a significant portion of the time and resources of the upper administration. Their temptations (e.g. to approach a tobacco company for support for the study of carcinogens) are legion.

At a university such as Georgetown a 10 percent medical center budgetary shortfall could represent the entire budget of its distinguished (and the nation's largest) law center or the entire instructional budget of the university's "Main Campus"—the totality of the undergraduate colleges and the graduate school. Policies with regard to university hospitals also automatically draw the attention of mayors and archbishops; the external pressures applied to them can be extreme. For these reasons it is essential that their operations be of the highest quality.

Some institutions put that quality at the forefront of what they do (Johns Hopkins, Washington University in St. Louis, e.g.) while others (Missouri, e.g.) do their best to integrate medical center research with that of the veterinary school (if they have one; we do), the college of agriculture, school of natural resources, the nutrition program in the College of Human Environmental Sciences and the research in the basic sciences, particularly the life sciences within the College of Arts and Science. The medical center, in effect, becomes one of several, potential *primus inter pares* sources of synergy.

This all occurs with the ongoing risk that the medical center will, at every turn, attempt to wag the rest of the university. Thus we have universities with medical centers and medical centers with undergraduate colleges attached. The old quip is that the university president has a nightmare that he is in hell and has just been put in charge of a university with two medical centers. The medical school corollary is the nightmare of a medical school dean who finds himself in hell, responsible for a medical school with two departments of surgery.

All of these risks are magnified in a world in which medical care is increasingly buffeted by external forces. As the interim medical center vice president at Georgetown once said at a faculty convocation, "When we were able to charge a dollar and a half for a dollar's service we didn't have all of these problems."

One of the challenges and advantages of research in the life sciences is the convergence and collaboration which such work necessarily involves. When we were in the final stages of constructing our Life Sciences Center and were about to begin the search for its director, the question was raised concerning the departments and divisions that would be appropriate to approach. One of the search committee members sighed and said that in writing to colleagues at Wisconsin we might find ourselves sending letters to as many as fifty different departments, divisions and centers. "Convergence" is a major concern of journalism schools these days, but it has been common in the life sciences for generations. One of the ongoing internecine battles at Wisconsin in the 1970s involved the life science departments' jockeying for position in representing themselves to potential graduate students as *the* unit doing "biochemistry." The 40+ "converging" scientists in our Life Sciences Center have also included individuals from the social sciences; two of the recent individuals were from the Department of Psychological Sciences. Common areas within the structure are characterized as "collision space."

This internal collaboration mirrors the larger pattern of collaboration that involves industrial laboratories, government laboratories and such transnational entities as CERN. The Synchrotron Radiation Center at Wisconsin is now being decommissioned. When I visited it in the late 1970s there were individuals from multiple entities, including small universities in the Midwest, stationed around the accelerator, doing research of various kinds, a tiny microcosm of a larger model for research. (Classic announcement at the beginning of our visit: "Yes, we have *beam*.")

This pattern of collaborative activity carries over into grant competitions, where requests for instrumentation will be met with initial skepticism from peer reviewers. "X in Department Y already has an earlier model which she would be willing to share." "A used model of that apparatus would be perfectly adequate." "That could be leased rather than purchased." "He can have it, but he must agree to share it with A, B and C." Big science carries big price tags, but every dollar is precious. In many cases scientists manage very large enterprises and they are constantly forced to make difficult decisions—e.g., to support postdocs or graduate students from their grant(s), the former generally being more productive but the latter representing the next generation of investigators.

How does the investment in big science affect undergraduate education? The answer is that it might have no effect on undergraduate students at all or it might radically alter their lives and offer them an unparalleled experience. Let me give an example. In the psychological sciences, one of the most important and most rapidly-progressing research enterprises is the study of the human brain. One way to study the functioning of the brain in real space and time is through the use of large MRI instruments. Medical centers commonly have them; their costs can be offset through clinical charges. Medical centers, however, are protective of their instruments and while they are unlikely to refuse to share those instruments with colleagues in the arts and sciences they will certainly require that other users meet their costs and utilize the instrument during "down," i.e., *far less favorable*, times.

A top Psychology department will require its own instrument and will develop strategies for funding it. It will need to have a sufficient number of researchers, with grants, capable of amortizing the "mortgage" offered by the university for the purchase of the instrument, as well as the renovation and maintenance costs of the facilities to house it, the technician(s) to operate it and the faculty member to direct the overall enterprise. Our fMRI instrument and imaging program came with an overall price tag of approximately $5,000,000. I was able to secure an endowed chair for the faculty position and the faculty are now handling the other costs. If one wants to study the human brain, such instruments as this are indispensable. An institution either does big science or it does not and if it does or does not, the opportunities for students are either expanded or contracted. The student who takes an introductory course in "psych" with hundreds of other freshmen and then goes on to major in Sociology does not need such an instrument and may not even be aware of its existence on campus. On the other hand, the student who wants to study the human brain and takes the necessary steps to become a part of the research enterprise doing so, will have a superb opportunity, an opportunity that simply will not exist at the great majority (95–99%) of institutions.

The obvious problem, of course, is that the technology for such studies changes constantly. "Brain imaging" has been conducted for years using various devices with various qualities of result. Remaining at the forefront of such studies is enormously expensive because they generally do not end. Funding science is comparable to maintaining dental health. It is not the "solution to a problem"; it is an ongoing journey.

But is it all worth it? First, we must acknowledge that the study of science is essential and, in nearly all cases, costly. Then we must remember that the money spent on research and development by the federal government is, in some ways, a trifle. This investment constitutes a little less than four days of government spending. To solidify the case for federal spending on R&D, construct a simple Benjamin Franklin T-chart. On the left list such items as were enumerated earlier: the development of the transistor, the computer, the internet, the kidney dialysis machine, the Salk vaccine, the capacity for organ transplants, the cochlear implant, and so on.

On the right list some government "investments" that *all* should find galling—duplicative programs, for example. A quick Google search would reveal, e.g., that the 2008 farm bill mandated catfish inspections that were conducted by three separate agencies. Foreign-language support for the Department of Defense entailed the use of 159 separate contracting organizations. The article that I seized upon (from *The Washington Post*'s Josh Hicks, April 9, 2013) suggested that we could save "tens of billions of dollars each year by trimming duplicative programs." That we do not may be explicable but it is no less scandalous. By reducing this particular form of waste we could expand the federal contribution to science and mitigate the inflation of tuition (without incurring increased taxation).

Nor does the federal government alone have to carry the cost of scientific research. States, industries, foundations and individuals all share in the effort. In some cases the faculty themselves provide the resources. At Wisconsin, for example, we benefited, every day, from the patent income from Harry Steenbock's discovery that irradiating milk with ultraviolet light would increase its vitamin D content and eradicate rickets. (James Lee Burke's recent historical novel, *House of the Rising Sun* [2015], depicts a jarring and compelling world in which an individual walking through early twentieth-century Mexican streets continually encounters children with rickets.) Karl Paul Link developed warfarin (which many now take as Coumadin), a substance that thins blood, kills rats and reduces heart attacks. The name parallels "WARF"—the Wisconsin Alumni Research Foundation, whose research support has both improved and extended human life and helped make Wisconsin the great university that it is. It was WARF that served as the model undergirding the Bayh-Dole Act of 1980, a pivotally-important law that allowed universities to keep the intellectual property rights to the results of research which had been funded by the federal government. Because of Bayh-Dole, universities now continually seek ways to exploit the results of research. Tech transfer offices, life science business incubators and interdisciplinary life science centers are now commonplace on research-intensive campuses. The government can help, not just with explicit resources, but with such policies as Bayh-Dole that encourage individual effort and entrepreneurship.

Within an eight to ten minute walk from my office I have colleagues and friends who are trying to reduce the personal, social and economic impact of human addictions, individuals who are laboring to find alternative fuels for personal and commercial vehicles, individuals who are working on organ transplant technologies and the cure of specific forms of cancer. They are developing molecules which will deliver medications to specific sites within the body without creating systemic side effects. They are working to expand the food supply for a hungry world by developing insect-resistant and disease-resistant plants. They are developing the capacities for supplementing foods with vitamins and vaccines (and, yes, colleagues studying the scientific, ethical and public policy implications of practices such as the latter).

By and large these individuals are not handsomely compensated, certainly not in comparison with those in white shoe law firms and Wall Street financial concerns, positions which the scientists' intellectual skills would easily enable them to hold. They do what they do because of their curiosity, their passion and their desire to effect positive change. They are worth every penny of our investments in them.

That does not, however, suggest that we are utilizing their talents and learning to the extent that we might. The sciences have sustained standards to the degree that they could while some of their colleagues in other divisions have acceded to the overall reduction in expectations, but no discipline can sustain past practices when administrators admit unprepared and underprepared students. Colleagues in STEM fields tell me that the pace of instruction has now slowed; they cannot cover the material as rapidly as they did in the past. As a result they cover less material.

For the prospective medical student, the MCAT's remain as a control. They are indifferent to the pace at which you studied as well as the venue in which you studied. The expectation remains that in order to pass them at a satisfactory level you need to have covered a specific range of material.

The MCAT's and the medical school places that sit beyond them are much on the minds of many students. This is why, in part, there are a thousand majors in biology; in other science fields the number of majors is far smaller. In some departments the actual number of majors is miniscule. At the same time, what Milton would have termed a "fit audience though few" may actually have the most intense and satisfying experience within the university. The tiny number of physics majors, for example, very often finds itself deeply involved in the work and research of the faculty, participating directly in the life of the department and understanding, at a sophisticated level, the manner in which research is conducted and knowledge developed. (One thinks of Richard Feynman's Caltech course, "Physics X," in which any undergraduate student could gather one afternoon a week with him and pose any scientific questions they wished [Gleick 1992, p. 398].)

The sciences teach a great number of service courses, but the sequential nature of the instruction results in many of those courses being delivered by the most junior instructors. It would be wasteful to employ a serious mathematician and then ask him or her to teach college algebra. While it requires a breadth of knowledge to teach certain survey courses in the Humanities we would hesitate to ask a senior chemist to introduce entry-level students to the rudiments of the discipline (though some do, to impressive effect).

Because one must begin with the rudiments many do not continue further. Any student can, potentially, walk into an introductory Humanities course and say something interesting. It is far more difficult for a student in the sciences to do so. As a result, the material grows ever more interesting as you negotiate the initial phases of study, but since those phases are challenging and, for many, difficult, many decide not to continue. This leads to the misconception that only a small number of students can actually *do* science. We do find, of course, that a very large number of international students *can* do science, in part because that is what their governments need and what they are willing to support.

These problems are, in some ways, recalcitrant, given the nature of science and the nature of sequential instruction. Few or no English departments will now do what mine did at Notre Dame—require, as a first course for majors, Chaucer in Middle English. This was done because knowledge of the language is indeed foundational and because the requirement was a test of the student's seriousness. The sciences, on the other hand, do not have the latitude to simply reduce standards and let students take whatever they might want whenever they might want it.

The subject of science is no less than the world that we inhabit and the manner in which we articulate with it. In a society where nearly 60 percent fail to read at grade level and many cannot even identify the branches of our government, the absence of scientific study or the grudging acceptance of it at the most elementary levels leads to a condition in which scientists are seen as wizards or otherworldly beings with whom mere mortals are unable to converse, but without a populace familiar with the strengths and limits of such scientific techniques as, e.g., computer modeling, climatologists with whose opinions we think we disagree will simply be labeled biased ideologues chasing research dollars or troglodyte reactionaries, in which case we will vote based upon political shibboleths rather than confirmable/falsifiable scientific evidence.

How can we increase our students' knowledge of science without expanding the existing rift between the sciences and the Humanities? At Georgetown in the early 1990s the provost decided that it was time to reexamine the undergraduate curriculum. Potentially a step of great consequence, such enterprises usually entail a large expenditure of time with little likelihood of positive change. Fears of the latter were confirmed when the committee chair announced that we would not be able to proceed until *all* members of the committee could first agree on the purposes of an undergraduate education.

Such discussions perforce entail consideration of both purposes and content. I suggested that we float models of content and debate them, with our sometimes-not-articulated "purposes" surfacing in the course of the discussion. Using that technique we would have models on the table for consideration from the outset and we would be more likely to achieve progress in our proceedings. The chair considered that method to be impossible; principles and purposes would have to be established first. The result was eighteen months of floundering and threats by senior faculty to resign from the committee.

When we finally got down to cases and proposed models, I suggested something that I knew would be unlikely to succeed there, even though I believed in it sincerely and passionately. I suggested that we require all undergraduate students to take a two-semester sequence in the history of science.

I arrived at my suggestion based on personal experience—my own work in the history of science as my doctoral minor and my positive interactions with colleagues in the history and philosophy of science at Wisconsin. Indeed, Wisconsin even had a discrete department studying the History of Medicine.

It was years later that I saw George Steiner's earlier comment that "the absence of the history of science and technology from the school syllabus is a scandal" (1971, p. 133). The reasons for its inclusion are compelling. Aside from the fact that science and technology involve nothing less than the understanding of the world we inhabit and our attempts to protect ourselves from it and utilize it for survival and happiness, the history of science, broadly considered, integrates nearly every element of our intellectual, spiritual and material experience.

Science is inextricable from religion, from philosophy, politics, literature, language, mating, health, nutrition, clothing and shelter. It determines the dimensions of our economies; it saves and extends our lives as well as taking them with an efficiency characteristically described as *ruthless*. It enables us to pose both first questions and last.

I noted earlier that the world of our founding fathers was one in which poets could negotiate treaties. It was also a world in which such figures as Jefferson and Franklin could freely indulge their scientific interests. At one level, Johnson conducted his own chemical experiments and indulged his curiosity by such activities as shaving the hair on his arm and measuring the time for its regrowth. At quite another level, Goethe studied optics and independently discovered the intermaxillary bone. He was the first to prove its peculiarity to all mammals. Locke, Goldsmith, Smollett and George Crabbe were also physicians, as was Keats.

Absent a knowledge of the history of science (and its Humanities element, philology) we are unable, really, to understand a significant portion of English and American literature and we talk oversimplified nonsense when we discuss such pressing issues as the relationship between Darwinian evolution and faith. We are now immersed in extensive, path-breaking studies of the human brain and the Humanities have barely taken notice, while a small group of literary scholars (Joseph Carroll, Brian Boyd, et al.) are now applying the insights of neoDarwinian research to the study of literature. Much of this work is inchoate but it is also extremely promising.

Our curricular world is now bifurcated. Science, which can so powerfully serve as an integrator, often remains separate. In the physics department at Wisconsin Bob March taught a course entitled Physics for Poets. Offered for students from non-scientific fields, it was designed to give them a sophisticated awareness of the nature and achievements of, principally, twentieth-century physics.

Bob's course was accompanied by a successful book that has reappeared in successive editions. The Wisconsin students quickly called Bob's course Physics for Freaks, *freak* being the *nom de guerre* of the hippie and the activist. Our initial impulse with regard to science seems to be to divide and diminish. STEM-field students are labeled geeks and techies. At Georgetown the School of Foreign Service's acronym—SFS—was regularly translated as "safe from science," since it avoided such requirements and, thus, served a clientele that was automatically separated from the students in Georgetown College.

We do not need such divisiveness; we need integration. We need an educated populace that is conversant with science and we need patterns and traditions of research in all disciplines that are suffused with knowledge of the natural world and its inhabitants. Campuses are divided, in part because of the space needed for laboratories and the synergies that are achieved by grouping disciplines. At Missouri we have the "red campus" and the "white campus"—the 19thc red brick quadrangle and the Missouri limestone-encased extension. Some science remains (Geological Sciences) on the red campus and there are social science incursions (History [considered a social science at Missouri], Geography) on the white, but the cultural division remains. That division is happily bridged every moment of the day, but the descriptors are suggestive of underlying realities that we have never been able to afford.

It is clear to me that science should play a far larger role in the undergraduate curriculum than it is presently permitted to do, but that role could be played in part within the department of History or in a separate department of the History of Science and Technology. The sciences would not be "theorized" and "relativized" within the postmodern project but they would be considered utilizing the historical and philosophic methods and protocols of what for me are essential parts of the Humanities.

The relationships between the two—science and the arts and Humanities—have been considered at length by George Steiner. A contemporary polymath, Steiner operates in a succession of languages, literatures and other disciplines, including mathematics and music. He has thought at length of the relationship between science and the arts and Humanities. A humanist by training, he is tormented by the Humanities' status and limits. He discusses the ways in which science might usefully supplant humanistic culture, but in doing so he can never really part with some of the arts and Humanities' essential characteristics. In considering some of his discrete observations we can advance our own discussion.

In Bluebeard's Castle (1971) takes as its central metaphor a one-act opera by Bartók. Bluebeard and his wife Judith have eloped and she is coming home to her husband's castle for the first time. There are seven locked doors in the darkened castle and Judith wants the doors opened so that their home can be filled with light. There are both terrible and wonderful things behind the doors. When she reaches the seventh, Bluebeard asks that she leave it locked and simply agree to love him.

She fears that the bodies of his ex-wives may be entombed there, but when he gives her the key she finds that the three ex-wives are all alive, bedecked in crowns and jewelry. He falls at their feet and praises the first three wives as well as the fourth, Judith. Now weighed down with jewelry she follows the three ex-wives along a beam of moonlight through the seventh door. It closes behind her and Bluebeard is left alone, plunged into total darkness.

This endlessly-suggestive psychosexual folk tale essentially asks the question, "what awaits us?" and do we dare attempt to seek an answer to that question. The historical context, Steiner's real-world preoccupation, is the holocaust and its aftermath. Where do we go from here? After such knowledge, what forgiveness?

We see "a great garden of civility now ravaged" (1971, p. 7) and Steiner wonders if that civilization was itself somehow complicit in its rape. He offers a series of thoughtful and insightful suggestions of the holocaust's etiology, beginning with the French Revolution and moving forward. They are too rich and complex to summarize briefly, but he concludes that the holocaust was a second Fall, "a voluntary exit from the Garden and a programmatic attempt to burn the Garden behind us" (1971, p. 46). He sees "the malignant energies released by the decay of natural religious forms" (1971, p. 53) and the concentration camps as "hell made immanent" (1971, p. 54).

Now our dominant culture feels guilt over its dominance and "seeking to placate the furies of the present, we demean the past" (1971, p. 66). We have lost our sense of centrality, abandoned or seen the fracturing of the idea of progress and experienced the failure or at least inadequacy of knowledge and humanism in the face of social reality (1971, p. 81). These represent "irreparables."

Our desire to be remembered, to create art and science and find immortality in our work is, at base, a religious impulse and it is now gone or at least it has significantly diminished (1971, p. 91). He will return to this issue with a renewed spirit in his book *Real Presences*.

And now the sadness: "The major part of Western literature . . . is now passing quickly out of reach." It is "modulating from active presence into the inertness of scholarly conservation" (1971, p. 99). As proof positive he offers a discussion of Milton's *Lycidas*. The Victorian author and academic, Mark Pattison, thought it "the high-water mark of English Poesy and of Milton's own production." As Steiner examines it he traces each of its echoes, references and allusions, contextualizing it within classical and contemporary examples of the pastoral elegy. He demonstrates the elements which a fully literate reader would recognize, suggesting, of course, that no one now is really capable of examining and internalizing the poem within the contexts present to Milton at the time of its composition. Here, in short, is a great work of art that we can no longer read or understand.

And he is quite right, though one doubts that few could *ever* read Milton at Steiner's level of sophistication. At the same time we must remind ourselves that Johnson detested *Lycidas* and found its artifice and leveraging of conventions cloying. He refuses to suspend his disbelief, just as in his savaging of Gray's odes. "Criticism disdains," he says, "to chase a schoolboy to his common-places."

Milton is no schoolboy, of course, but Johnson is exhibiting more than his characteristic mischievousness. He is expressing his taste and his taste is for the real and the authentic rather than the artificial. When he writes of the death of one of *his* friends (Robert Levet, e.g.) he does so personally and historically; he does not speak of their battening their flocks together. He is exhibiting the attitude which he expressed when he said that he would prefer to see a portrait of a pet he actually knew over all allegorical painting.

Times and tastes change and we must be careful not to equate those changes with willful ignorance or associate them, reflexively, with cultural collapse. Many years ago I saw a piece by Ben DeMott on a student's record (i.e., vinyl) collection. In effect, DeMott lamented the fact that the student was a discographer rather than a bibliographer. The student spoke of his records the way the master bibliographer Fredson Bowers would speak of Elizabethan drama texts. He knew the editions, the variants, the jacket tweaks, exclusions, inclusions, textual alterations and piracies. Of course, the student *did* have the bibliographer's skills and dedication, but with regard to a different medium. My students may not be able to read *Lycidas* in the manner that I might prefer, but neither can I read Japanese anime in the way that they can.

There is no question that we have seen a great deal of cultural loss, but we have also seen a great deal of cultural change. When I follow (or attempt to follow) my students into their own cultural byways and along their superhighways I am often reassured by their degree of passion as well as their degree of persistence.

I take Steiner's powerful point and I understand the weight of the holocaust on his vision, but I believe that we must be careful in attributing the fact of the holocaust to, in part, the palpable weakness of humane culture. The points are several: the enormity of the holocaust reveals the capacity for evil as much as or, perhaps, much more than the weakness of art, literature and all that is encompassed in the word *civilization*.

Greece is the cradle of democracy; Greece offered Socrates hemlock. The Romans brought roads, aqueducts, law and crucifixion. The holocaust, in all of its horror, still stands amid the killing fields of Cambodia, the Soviet gulag, the depredations of the Cultural Revolution, the Iraqi rape rooms and the Rwandan genocide. Indeed, in the age of Enlightenment we can witness the genocide that followed Culloden and remember that the image of Matthew Prior negotiating the Treaty of Utrecht is forever tarnished by the British desire to there secure the sole right to the slave trade with Spanish America.

We can leave *In Bluebeard's Castle* with two of Steiner's comments on science and the humanities. The last first: "It is not only that the humanities have been arrogant in their assertions of centrality. It is that they have often been silly. We need no poet more urgently than Lucretius" (1971, pp. 133–34). And a hint of what is to come in *Real Presences*: "our current inroads on the human cortex dwarf all previous images of exploration" (1971, p. 126).

The pivotal question is, should the Humanities be eclipsed by the sciences or is there some possibility of rapprochement? *Real Presences* follows *In Bluebeard's Castle* by a period of just under two decades. Steiner returns to an issue which he had raised earlier—human creativity and the necessity for its divine underwriting, the notion that a transcendent reality grounds all genuine art and all human communication.

He begins with a notion that appears to be tangential, but it becomes clear that his point reinforces a significant contrast between art and criticism. He writes that "the best readings of art are art" (1991, p. 17). James's *The Portrait of a Lady* is, among other things, a reading of Eliot's *Middlemarch*. Joyce's *Ulysses* is a reading of the *Odyssey*. I would agree that all too often we choose the commentary of academic critics over that of practicing artists, but Steiner is going a step further, stressing the notion that the artists' *art* is itself the most significant form of commentary, a form of commentary different in kind and importance from criticism.

Why? Because nature cooperates with science and validates the scientific method. It *works*. Theory *applies*. Aesthetic theory and criticism *do not*. Aesthetic theory does not extend to the external reality; it is "bound to the language circle" and cannot transcend the medium of its own saying (1991, pp. 71–75). Hence, there is no *real* aesthetic *theory* because it is neither verifiable nor falsifiable through experiment and predictive application (1991, p. 75).

Art, on the other hand, shares with science the underlying belief (at least on behalf of such figures as Descartes, Newton, Pascal, Galileo, and Heisenberg, et al.) in the notion that God serves as a divine underwriter, animating the cosmos (and not, as Einstein famously said, playing dice with it). Thus, there is aesthetic creation because there is *creation*: "The core of our human identity is nothing more or less than the fitful apprehension of the radically inexplicable presence, facticity and perceptible substantiality of the created. It is; we are. This is the rudimentary grammar of the unfathomable" (1991, p. 201).

As he puts it, the *imitatio* is a replication of the first *fiat*. The rival poet in Shakespeare's sonnets is, ultimately, God, for "a theology . . . underwrites the presumption of creativity" (1991, pp. 206, 216).

Criticism, including all academic humanistic criticism, is thus circumscribed within its own universe of discourse and, ultimately, *unscientific*. This is not to say that it does not have contact beyond that language circle, but its contacts can prove to be deleterious:

> The esoteric impulse in twentieth-century music, literature and the arts reflects calculation. It looks to the flattery of academic and hermeneutic notice. Reciprocally, the academy turns towards that which appears to require its exegetic, cryptographic skills. The text solicits adoption by the university syllabus and reading list. The term is revealing; for the paternity thus obtained is, indeed, a false one (1991, p. 38).

Thus, the academy sometimes seeks the bizarre and recondite on which to exert its skills and a portion of the practicing artists in the world beyond detach themselves further from their "lay" audience to curry favor with the academic cognoscenti to mutual advantage. The academic world/art world come into further congruence as the academy offers an actual refuge from a world with a shrinking audience. The academic institutionalization of the arts provides not just shelter and salary; it offers a different domain—one with itself as audience, itself as publisher and promulgator and itself as validator, judge and awarder of tenure. The academy consumes the arts and renders the necessity for an external audience largely unnecessary.

As these realities swirl in our heads, along with lingering suspicions of the arts and Humanities' flaccidity in the face of National Socialist evil we can begin to wonder if these activities are, truly, doomed. With a shrinking literate audience, even within expanded university rolls, we can wonder if the foundational texts, thoughts and images created by the arts and Humanities now exist only as fading ghosts whose existence and importance is defended by a dwindling number of nostalgic traditionalists.

Before we court despair we should remind ourselves of certain realities. The texts, conventions and methods of the arts and Humanities can be used as tools, for good or ill. Leni Riefenstahl might use them to brilliant effect in the interest of Nazi propaganda, but Churchill might simultaneously find his core inspiration and resolve in language, literature and history, memorizing, at the age of thirteen, lines from Macaulay's *Lays of Ancient Rome*:

> Then out spake brave Horatius,
> The Captain of the Gate:
> To every man upon this earth
> Death cometh soon or late.
> And how can man die better
> Than facing fearful odds,

> For the ashes of his fathers,
> And the temples of his gods. . . .

We can also find solace in the fact that while the academy may have consumed much of modern poetry it has been unable to absorb drama and fiction. The plastic arts continue to find a public audience and not always in hothouse forms. For Steiner, hope remains particularly in music, in which "form is content, content form. Music is at once cerebral in the highest degree. . . ." (1991, p. 217).

Finally, for Steiner, there is another source of hope, one anticipated in his prescient reference to modern neuroscience some 45+ years ago. If we can no longer turn to the Humanities as a bulwark we can turn to the realities of the natural world themselves, whose exploration and depiction expand perception and stir the imagination in the same manner as the great texts of the Humanities. We can, in short, find our poetry in our physics, in our mathematics, in the miraculous but curious efficiency of our organs of perception and the still-echoing, perceptible and *measurable* results of the moment some fourteen billion years ago when the cosmos came into existence.

We cannot do that, however, without the *voice* of the poet and brush of the artist. Science may be the *subject* of art but to the degree that it is depicted with skill and beauty it is dependent on the language and techniques of the arts and Humanities. It always has been. Steiner invokes the name of Lucretius. We might turn to Shakespeare's discussions of flora, fauna and cosmology, to the illustrations in Vesalius' *De Humani Corporis Fabrica*, the Godzilla-level insects in Hooke's *Micrographia*, to Sir Thomas Browne's reflections on diuturnity, Virgil's enumeration of the weather signs in his Georgics, Pynchon's screaming, that comes across the sky or his recent evocation of Silicon Alley in *Bleeding Edge*.

Science fiction has bridged these worlds since (in some perspectives) Aristophanes, while steampunk fiction now points to the subgenres and hybrid genres which endlessly captivate our students' and some of our colleagues' imaginations. Mystery and detective fiction, it has been argued, finds its birth and momentum in a reaction against the waning powers of the aristocracy and institutional Church. Gothic romances featured evil monks and aristocrats abusing English maidens. The emerging force for justice in the genre that followed was a middle-class individual of common sense and uncommon abilities, sometimes a man, sometimes a woman, utilizing the weapons of science and the instruments of technology. Those figures still stand at the center of our popular culture.

I would like to close with a single example of the sort of material that illustrates the interaction of science and the Humanities both in practice and, potentially, within the university curriculum. One of my favorite biographies is Barbara Shapiro's life of Bishop John Wilkins, the warden of Wadham

College during the Interregnum, an individual whose work at Oxford combined with other contemporary efforts that led directly to the formation of the Royal Society. A great (and I do not use the word easily) university administrator, he refused to allow his personal relationship with Cromwell (he was married to Cromwell's sister, Robina) to obstruct his desire to bring together people of good will, regardless of their religion and regardless of their politics—people whose shared love was the study of science. Himself a brilliant thinker, advancing notions with regard to the creation of submarines and the facilitation of heavier-than-air flight, he also had an uncommon sense of humor which he utilized within what could be very dark times. Installing a talking statue on the grounds beyond his lodgings at Wadham, he used an underground tube to issue special revelations to the overtly pious. He is the kind of individual who has materially advanced civilization and Professor Shapiro's depiction of him is a lovely example of the manner in which the Humanities, the history of science and the nearly-scientific biographical method can combine to kindle our spirits, extend our imaginative reach and enrich our knowledge. We simply need to remind ourselves of such opportunities and we must systematically expand them for our current and future students.

Chapter Ten

Out of the Dark

A university has two central responsibilities—the hiring of faculty and the admission of students. Both are crucial to its foundational purposes. If we do not choose wisely in securing the essential parties to the academic enterprise the long-term results are likely to be damaging. Each faculty hire, in particular, should raise the university's intellectual level and professional expectations. Every middling hire is both a missed opportunity and a step backward.

An even more important decision, however, concerns the manner in which our universities and colleges select the individuals who hire our chancellors and presidents, for many later successes and failures begin with their choices. Trustees . . . Directors . . . Visitors . . . Overseers . . . Curators . . . Regents . . . we sometimes tend to overlook their activities because they visit so seldom and generally do so little. "Gratefully, gratefully," Conrad's Marlow might have added. When they do act, however, their decisions can range from benign neglect to the destructive and even the cataclysmic.

They carry the primary responsibility for the governance of the institution though they often have precious little understanding of its purposes, its strategies, the markers of its true success and the endlessly-complex nature of its many operations. It is hard to know which method for selecting trustees is the worst. Political selection is common among public institutions and it is predictably problematic. (How would we like something truly important—the board certification of pediatric oncologists, e.g., run politically?) Selection based solely on past and (potential) future financial support is common but it carries no guarantee that the appointee will be wise or effective. Such donors can be accorded significant recognition without handing over to them the control of an entity of whose culture, purposes and operational details they may be largely ignorant.

Selection of prominent alumni/ae is common and sensible, given the importance of institutional loyalty. At the same time, all should remember that the institution such appointees attended existed twenty, thirty or forty years ago. That could be a good thing or a bad thing, depending on whether or not the university needs to return to first principles or move beyond a leaden past.

The Jesuits like to put fellow Jesuits on their boards, even if those individuals might actually be their competitors. They believe that there remains such a thing as a "Jesuit education" and that their fellow priests are the most qualified individuals to exemplify and reinforce it. Those priests are increasingly in very short supply.

Some individuals are sought because of their personal prominence; their appointment provides a good headline, even if their future attendance is likely to be sporadic. Some are appointed because of their public or professional positions; they can serve the institution as uncompensated lobbyists. Some might be appointed because they possess expertise (in hospital management, e.g., or investment strategy) which is required by a university with specific challenges at specific moments in time. Whatever the reason, the individuals who *rarely* appear on such boards are highly-qualified *educators*, even though such individuals begin with a profound knowledge of the enterprise and are positioned to offer wise counsel concerning its governance and enhancement.

Boards do a number of things, many in the realm of general oversight, but the one area in which they make consequential decisions is the selection and termination of chief executives. Their behavior in this regard tends to follow a common course; their preference is nearly always for external candidates. Duderstadt (2007, pp. 91–92) notes that they make such choices approximately 80 percent of the time. Why? Some might argue that it is a natural human impulse to prefer a potential archangel to the slightly tarnished angels with whom we are already familiar, though the traditional maxim is to prefer the known devil to the unknown one. Duderstadt argues that they do this because external candidates are more easily controlled; they come without an internal base of support.

And why would boards want to control rather than simply supervise? Because they truly believe that they have a better understanding of the institution than an academic professional (assuming they have appointed an academic professional)? Because it boosts their own egos? Because they covet power for its own sake?

It is difficult to say, since we cannot enter their hearts and minds, but it is obvious that current methods are frequently unsuccessful. The issue may not be "internal vs. external" candidacies so much as it is that the selectors simply lack the competence to perform their task, but the bottom line is that the average tenure of a university president at a major public university is now a mere five years (Duderstadt 2007, p. 115). In my twenty years at Missouri I have seen six chancellors and seven system presidents (including interims). Meanwhile, the plaintive cries for authentic *academic leadership* at all institutions continue unabated. When we look back to the nearly lifelong tenure of nineteenth- and early twentieth-century presidents we often draw the conclusion that it was "easier" then. If so, then why have *we* (and that certainly includes the trustees) made the job so difficult that no one will remain in it long enough to bring significant improvement to the institution? Or, to put it another way, why have we constructed academic jobs in such a way that they will often only prove attractive to self-interested careerists who see them as stepping stones rather than sacred trusts? (In many cases, private institutions are more successful with their presidential choices, but the vast majority of students attend public institutions now, so that their successes and failures are particularly pertinent.)

I firmly believe that senior administrators should be held accountable, but holding them accountable is different from hamstringing them. It is different from frustrating their efforts to do things that are clearly in the best interests of the institution.

The University of Notre Dame occupies 1,250 acres, the University of Missouri, Columbia 1,400 (not counting its tens of thousands of acres of experimental farms and other external research sites); Georgetown sits on 100 acres and in that circumscribed space it operates its undergraduate programs, its graduate programs, its student recreational facilities, dormitories, food services, its medical school and hospital. (The law school occupies a set of buildings near Capitol Hill.) Prior to my arrival there in 1981 a large parcel of land became available that was contiguous to the campus. The president wished to purchase it; the board refused to permit him to do so. That land is now occupied by 138 townhouses, the approximate cost of two of which (decades ago) represented the price tag for the entire piece of land. This was not a trivial decision with temporary financial implications such as the campus contract for drink of choice—Coke or Pepsi? It was a decision that has permanently reduced the university's opportunities.

By the time that I was in a position to address that board they were wringing their hands over deferred maintenance concerns. The current academic headline concerned Yale's $1B deferred-maintenance problem. "We certainly don't want to end up *like them*," one of the directors commented. In as polite and deferential a manner as I could muster, I noted that Yale then sat atop the *US News* rankings—not something that represented the Platonic ideal of academic absolutes, but something that most responsible boards of directors might be expected to notice.

I recognize the fact that business people do (and should) focus on the equity represented by a university's physical plant, but since that equity is generally not liquid and since strong students and faculty tend to choose schools on more substantive academic grounds, it is fair to expect them to have a more expansive view of academic reality. The simple (and obvious) truth is that great universities all have problems of one kind or another with their physical plants. Some have row upon row of cinder-block dormitories, key departments in former apartment buildings, academic buildings with gothic basements, bat-ridden attics, and so on. My friend Jerry Atwood once worked at Imperial College, London, the Caltech/MIT of Britain. He said it was a wonderful experience even though they never washed the windows. The dirtiest classrooms I have ever seen in my life (and the narrowest, nearly impassable hallways) were at the London School of Economics. Every competent academic leader knows that institutions must prioritize and that they sometimes choose to purchase instrumentation, hire faculty and fund students who will advance the heart of the enterprise, saving certain maintenance issues for another day. That is why they are great and why they are considered to be great.

The last time I was at Caltech and walked through one of their laboratory buildings I saw equipment standing in the hallways (some might say "cluttering" the hallways). This might offend the sensibilities of a business-oriented trustee, but a university whose physical plant is not packed to the gunwales with instrumentation, books, journals, computers and, most of all, human activity, is a university that is either mediocre to begin with or now in observable decline.

Notre Dame once followed a strategy that would have been more to the liking of the Georgetown board. For years they focused their resources on budgetary "responsibility." They had no deferred maintenance whatsoever. None. In nearly every case they put endowed professorships under existing individuals (saving the endowment pay-out portion of their salaries) rather than expanding and enriching their faculty. They were the very model of budgetary discipline and probity. And they were decidedly mediocre. Now they are emerging as a significant research institution because they are investing in academic essentials.

Recently we have seen the University of Virginia discombobulated by a vocal rector who appears to have believed that the principles and practices of the world of real estate development are transferable to the governance of one of the nation's great public universities. Crusading overseers are the most dangerous of all. Frequently, they have read a book, often a polemic, and have then become self-appointed experts on higher education. Sometimes they recommend "business practices"; often they ride a single hobby horse, believing, for example, in the all-powerful opportunities offered by the internet.

So what is the solution? There is *no* solution unless the individuals carrying fiduciary responsibility for the institution are intelligent, informed and prepared to act in the best interests of that institution. There are, however, some useful strategies.

The average board size is twenty-nine members, with eight separate committees (Fain 2010, p. 1). That is much too large. The Harvard Corporation actually runs Harvard. It has recently been expanded from six members (plus the president) to twelve members (plus the president).

Harvard also has a thirty-member Board of Overseers which provides "strategic direction and counsel" (Fain 2010, p. 1). Georgetown had a tiny, nearly secret corporation, plus the board of directors, the board of regents and the (alumni) board of governors. Since boards have multiple and often quite different responsibilities, tiering them can be a useful strategy. The GU board of directors carried the principal responsibility for governance while the board of regents served as a launching pad for emerging leaders and emerging development prospects. The alumni board was largely ceremonial and consisted of faithful contributors to the annual fund and individuals appreciated for their many contributions of "sweat equity."

My own preference would be for a two-tiered system, one for ultimate governance, the second for fundraising, counsel and public representation. The governance group would be small. They would be skilled; their decision-making processes would be transparent and their numbers would include prominent academics, i.e. fine scholars, scientists and teachers who have had significant administrative experience. Bureaucrats and corporatists need not apply. In "my generation" or a little earlier I would think of such individuals as Jary Pelikan, Bart Giamatti, or Jacques Barzun, more recently of a David Baltimore, Judith Rodin or Mark Wrighton.

The larger board would be utilized to recognize supporters, successful alumni/ae and other individuals who would exemplify the quality and values of the institution. That board would include serious academics, diversity appointees (including individuals who represented intellectual diversity, a Robbie George or Niall Ferguson, for example), and "conscience" appointees such as Marian Wright Edelman or Michael Walzer.

I disagree with James Garland that trustees should be paid (2009, p. 129). Their compensation should come from the opportunity to become acquainted and work with serious, interesting people in a cause of high importance. The difference between non-profits and for-profits should be underscored at every opportunity.

The principal tasks of primary boards should be, first, to do no harm, and second, to appoint and then support presidents. The hiring of presidents should involve a two-step process. There should be a board search committee and a faculty search committee. No one should reach the board search committee who has not been vetted and approved by the faculty first.

The board could always ask the faculty to start over, if it believed that action to be in the best interests of the institution, but it could not hire someone independently of the faculty. These systems work best if the leadership of each committee is a highly-respected individual of significant accomplishment whose devotion to the institution is ongoing and unquestionable. True quality seeks quality.

The best way to increase quality in an institution of higher education is to seek it in every single hire. Those who exemplify it and are passionate in its support provide the best leadership for such activities, while the structures of the majority of contemporary search committees are more likely to result in mediocrity.

Such groups are frequently selected based on their ability to represent constituencies, their deliberations then tending to result in lowest-common-denominator decisions. They seek out individuals who are acceptable to all. What that often means is that the successful person is the one who will ruffle no feathers, soothe all egos and accomplish comparatively little. Garland puts it this way: "The traditional search committee gravitates toward consensus builders, because its members do not want to risk hiring a leader who might step on the toes of their constituents—even if doing so is what the institution needs to solve its problems and move forward" (2009, p. 155).

Constituency-based search committees all ask the same question: "As president, will you support my constituency and advance its interests?" (Garland 2009, p. 154). And the candidate's answer: "Yes, I certainly will, and did I happen to mention my prior (very successful) efforts on behalf of diversity?"

Garland's courageous book, which should be must-reading for all interested in the contemporary college presidency, particularly at public institutions, makes other points. He argues, for example, that it is a bad idea to hire a woman or minority as president *simply to make a point*. Universities should hire the person who can really lead the institution in the most effective manner, regardless of ethnicity or gender (2009, p. 153).

Corollary: if some personal characteristic will help the person lead the institution in the most effective manner, that personal characteristic should be accorded significant attention. Leading a niche institution such as Gallaudet, for example, might well require a president who has a deep, personal understanding of and experience with deafness and hearing impairment.

Constituency-based search committees have trouble assessing decisiveness, planning skills, the ability to identify and motivate strong people, to understand finances and exploit opportunities. They tend to gravitate toward people with egalitarian but unrealistic philosophies of collegiality. Essentially, they opt for those with an attractive demeanor, choosing image over substance (Garland 2009, p. 154). Two tactical points: make the search committee small, because "large committees encourage the campus to parse itself into an even finer grid of interest groups" (2009, pp. 156–57) and do not put stalled associate professors on such important committees. Their presence there sends the wrong message to the institution's assistant professors (2009, p. 168).

The provost position (or dean of the college, in liberal arts colleges) is of enormous importance. In many cases the position is significantly compromised because of the manner in which the president's cabinet is structured. Enter the room, look at the big table with the name cards, the bottled water and hard candies in silver-plated bowls and who do you see?

You see the president, his/her aide or aides (sitting behind him/her), the director of athletics, the treasurer, the head of the alumni association, the dean of students, the vice president for buildings and grounds, the head of advancement, the university counsel, the vice president (unless he has a more honorific title) of the medical center, in some cases the secretary of the board (of directors), potentially the chief information officer, potentially the vice president for research, potentially the vice president for diversity, the chief operating officer and, oh yes, the provost.

The chief academic officer is only one voice among many and this typifies the importance of academics in the modern university. The symbolism and social dynamics say it all: this is not an educational institution; it is a city. Academics are only one thing that we do and they may, after all, not be the most important thing that we do. The rest of us can outtalk the provost, outvote the provost and monopolize the president's time and, hence, the president's agenda.

In an optimal situation the support staff should all report to the provost, who would also serve as chief operating officer, and the president should meet with his line *academic* officers—the provost and deans—rather than with the miscellaneous administrators. That sounds like a tall order and a difficult pill for the university warrant officers and bureaucrats to swallow, but it is one way to insure that the president will have time for his many representational duties while the academic center of the university is protected.

Some use a modified version of this model. At Michigan, for example, the provost has veto authority over every other executive officer on issues that have implications for the university's academic activities (Duderstadt 2007, p. 136). Some large research institutions, Harvard, for example, involve the president directly and in detail in the tenuring of faculty and elevate the position of the dean of the faculty of arts and sciences. There are many strategies but one principal goal: keeping academics at the center of the institution's activities.

At Georgetown there were three vice presidents for academics, one for the law center, one for the medical center and the third, called the provost, for the "main campus." Under Tim Healy, the provost was a fellow Jesuit priest and—always—the acting president in Tim's absence. The provost, Don Freeze, served as *primus inter pares* with the other vice presidents, but the signals were all clear: Don was Tim's number two and he was not to be messed with. When he was acting president he was not a placeholder but a person prepared to make significant decisions.

They complemented one another in several ways. Tim was the visionary, the Helen Gardner-trained Oxford D.Phil. Don was the details person (later the money man for the Maryland province). Ted Hesburgh followed a similar pattern. He was the outside person, his provost the inside person. They communicated constantly so that the president was free to pursue representational duties and fundraising. Hesburgh raised the profile of the university by his prominent activities in Washington and beyond; he still holds the record for the highest number of honorary degrees received. Thus, the Notre Dame joke: What is the difference between God and Fr. Hesburgh? God is everywhere; Fr. Hesburgh is everywhere but Notre Dame.

The resistance to a strong provost (or any other title or format that keeps the academic function in charge of the overall operation) is strong. There is first the protestation that the president is also an academic officer (and a damned good one!), so he or she can look after the other members of the cabinet and keep them on the straight and narrow.

They say that, knowing that the president's schedule is, in many ways, a plan or a dream, not a fixed document. A single event, either good or bad, consumes time that cannot, ultimately, be controlled. A donor calls from Geneva, saying that he is prepared to make a nine-figure gift, but has a few remaining questions on the university's proposal. Can the president meet with him, in Paris, on Thursday? A student athlete has died of an overdose; his parents, the press, the head of the board of directors, the head of the conference and the head of the NCAA have called so far; it is only 9:10 a.m. The governor's assistant has just called the president's legislative liaison; a budgetary shortfall at the capitol means that the university will likely sustain a mid-year budget cut of $27,000,000. How would the campus absorb the cut?

There are too many issues such as this that cannot be handled by assistants. In certain cases (many that involve the president) delegation represents weakness and the interests of the university could be damaged. Hence the need for a strong provost to protect the university in the president's absence.

Not so fast, the other executive officers respond; *no one person can realistically supervise so many different offices*. On the face of it, that is absurd, because it is arguing, essentially, for lone-wolfery writ large. No one *could* possibly supervise all of us, so no one *should* supervise us, except, of course, the president (who can't, because he is, necessarily, not here).

In some ways, the bureaucracy is speaking *its* truth, but that "truth" is only persuasive when you accept their assumptions and their methods of proceeding. In most cases (certainly not in every case; there are, after all, many good and conscientious administrators) their lives *are* enormously complicated, but largely because they have made them so.

They have constructed a world of endless, formulaic meetings, of organizational tables with lines, dotted lines, bold lines, and criss-crossed lines, of endless systems of review, with written reviews, oral reviews, formal memoranda of record, words to the wise and forms with ticked boxes. Every day there is a retirement party or a "welcome aboard" reception. They have filled every available moment with what Chaucer terms *bisinesse* and they assume that anyone who would supervise them would do the same thing.

Every academic has had the experience of seeing an administrator, perhaps at the faculty club—his hair thinning, his eyes ringed with black lines, his shoulders lurching forward. You ask him how he is doing. He shakes his head and says, "I'm very, very busy" or "You have no idea. . . ." And yet, from all available indications it is really not clear what that person actually *does*, if anything. I can tell you what he does. He attends meetings in which little of importance happens. He writes reports that are seldom if ever read. He plays telephone tag. He tries to effect forms of "collaboration" that would never happen naturally, for a number of obvious reasons (principally, unequal partnerships). He tries to interpret, translate and explain things to some other bureaucrat who is either thick or simply too inexperienced to understand. He has been updating the strategic plan, tweaking the vision-and-goals statement or investigating ways in which to enhance his office's website. He is battling with his counterpart in Human Resources over a job description that is preventing him from giving a promotion and raise to a favored toady. He is making off-the-record phone calls to other administrators, speculating on the results of a possible restructuring that could reduce the size of his operation. He is trying to write his introductions of the three speakers on his panel discussion at his next professional meeting. One has promised to email his c.v. but has neglected to do so. A second simply sent a brief, cryptic entry from a knockoff version of *Who's Who*, while the third sent one that had not been updated in the last month and has yet to send the new and improved version because he has been laboring intently over his review of *his own* university's mission statement.

This is why we need a strong provost—not just to keep us focused on core activities, but to minimize the kinds of activities which tend to displace them. The old truism is that if you want something done you give it to a busy person to do. Unfortunately, that is not always the university's way. In many cases the task is handed off to someone with very little else to do, for there are always individuals whose research accomplishments are behind them and who long for the pseudo-prominence which certain forms of "service" bring. Hence, the easy proliferation of committees, task forces, commissions and blue ribbon panels.

Unfortunately, heavily "democratic" procedures are often deleterious to the institution. In managing our home budgets we know that it is much more important to cut back the cable TV subscription or forego the planting of hydrangeas rather than allow water to fall through a hole in the roof or toilets to overflow. In the university, however, we routinely cut budgets across the board because any more selective procedure would result in either insurrection or endless process. (As a former Bennington president once quipped, university governance is like a basketball game in which the purpose of the game is not to score but rather to take timeouts.)

The simple fact is that in universities we do not believe that time equals money (or at least we do not behave as if we believe it). Covington and Burling account for their time in 6-minute increments (Garland 2009, p. 97); we meet endlessly, not worrying whether the bovines will ever return home. Garland (2009, pp. 100-1) calculated that a six-person committee meeting for two hours cost his university (Miami of Ohio) over $1,000. The university senate cost $13,400 per meeting, nearly $54,000 per month. The calculation is based on an estimate of $87 per hour for each member of the faculty or staff (salary + fringe benefits + overhead/indirect costs).

This is not to suggest that universities should suspend their democratic processes. It is simply to remind us all that those processes entail significant costs, costs that could be used for other good purposes, and that a bureaucratized university tends to increase those costs rather than diminish them. Similarly, a truly *academic* officer will do what he or she can to minimize administrivia and focus our attention on teaching and research.

Planning is fine and important but it should not be formulaic. (I have already reinforced Professor Ginsberg's trenchant criticisms of "strategic planning.") It should have clear goals, clear timelines and clear, intended results. For example, at Georgetown we realized that we had a (good) problem. The high teaching load had forced the university to promptly replace faculty whenever positions came open. The tight job market everywhere meant that Georgetown often got its first choices, despite the high teaching load. (The great scholar of Russian social history, Richard Stites, had been teaching at Ohio State-Lima when he was hired.) Once at Georgetown, however, these individuals wanted to pursue their research agendas in earnest and were frustrated by the high teaching load.

Thus, we planned. We knew what the additional faculty would cost if we were to reduce the teaching load. We realized that the hiring of a large number of additional faculty would create a significant problem with regard to office space. We also knew that the highest priority for the faculty was the reduction in load and the enhancement of research. Hence, they would cooperate with us in effecting a transition that might involve office-sharing and phased-in teaching load reductions. This was a big step for the university, one well worth taking, but inevitably the work of several years. Don Freeze, the deans and the faculty enjoyed sufficient mutual trust that we were all ready to sit down together and address the issue.

The plan was conceptualized by Dan Martire, a professor of Chemistry. Hence the "Martire Plan." We determined costs, prepared for the budgetary impact, created a timeline for the full accomplishment of the plan and then proceeded. The goal was important; there was full consultation, a bump or two along the way, principally with regard to space, and, at the end, a very positive result. We also enhanced our internal support for research at the same time that the course load reductions enabled us to raise our expectations with regard to its production. Georgetown became a research institution in reality as well as in name.

The elasticity of time within the university is one of its great advantages and one of its most significant threats. One disaffected faculty member can invest all of his or her spare time (which can be a *lot* of time) in hamstringing an entire department with a lawsuit. One alienated faculty senate voice can divert an entire body from more important work. As our system administration at Missouri learned, one ill-advised decision—summarily closing the university press without proper consultation and announcing the decision when the faculty were away from campus—resulted in a reaction which essentially paralyzed the system administration and the leadership of the Columbia campus for five months.

Deliberative decision making is one of the beauties of the university, of course, and this is one of the reasons for its persistence, for centuries. The long view is essential, because there is significant lag time between the making of a decision (to expand or to contract, to initiate or to terminate) and the preparation of the next generation's professoriate and the retirement of the current one. Abrupt and peremptory decisions can be very destructive and the ultimate success of "innovative" activity is very difficult to predict. The bottom line is that we need to think and plan, to proceed cautiously and thoughtfully, but we need to do that efficiently, without wasting time in formulaic meetings, diverting ourselves and our energies from more important tasks. Hence the need for *academic* officers who understand the trade, know its culture and its challenges, and who can keep those who do not really understand it at bay so that we can do our work.

We need efficiency but we also need the space for creativity. James Watson famously said, "To encourage real creativity, you need to have a good deal of slack" (Bok 2003, p. 31), a crucial insight that corporatists often fail to grasp.

One of the reasons that the University of Illinois is a great university is that it has a library that is great in every sense of the word. Second only to Harvard in the size of its collections, it was also, in my time, a truly ideal place in which to work. It was filled with the kind of "slack" that Watson advocates, though I don't believe that a single dollar of its budget was wasted.

The "English library," a branch library within the main library building itself, was a collection of 60,000 volumes with a display shelf for new books, a reading room, periodicals section (so that you could sit at one table and both run bibliographies and check journal articles without going to a separate location), faculty office space for those doing library-intensive projects (Gwynne Evans, preparing the Riverside Shakespeare, for example), and, at the end of a hallway, a classroom, so that students and faculty could stop in for a class and then promptly return to the reading room.

Faculty carrels in the library were designed on two explicit principles: they would not contain telephones and they would be difficult to locate, thus discouraging and minimizing interruptions. The library contained a "Bibliography Room" which was actually a duplication of central portions of the reference collection, open only to faculty and graduate students. This minimized theft and misshelving and maximized efficiency: key research tools were always readily available.

The Rare Book Room served individuals who needed single volumes for a brief period of time, but it contained other facilities as well. It housed, for example, a Hinman Collator—a large optical device facilitating complex editorial work. The Rare Book room contained library tables for those doing long-term projects. On those tables the librarians would leave the materials that the individual investigator was using on an ongoing basis. The librarians put me in a position adjoining that of a graduate scholar from France who was writing his dissertation for a *doctorat d'État*. I was writing a dissertation on Johnson and science; he was writing a book on literature and science in the eighteenth century. This enabled us to get to know one another and, as necessary, share materials.

At one point in my work I reached an impasse. I needed to see Dr. Robert James's *Medicinal Dictionary*, whose three folio volumes contained medical biographies that had been attributed to Johnson. It would have been both inconvenient and expensive to travel to one or more distant repositories, so I asked the acquisition librarian for help.

She got back to me in a matter of days, telling me that there were actually a small number of duplicate copies available from several other research libraries, including the University of Pennsylvania. She asked me if I thought the university should purchase them. After offering her my thanks, I said yes. The library acquired them and I was able to proceed with my work. Never in my professional life has a librarian been prepared to invest significant resources in a set of rare eighteenth-century books, simply on my say-so. I was then a graduate student, not a member of the faculty or a dean.

The last time I visited the Illinois library I was shown ten stack levels of rare books. This kind of investment costs money, but this kind of investment generates greatness. It also generates efficiency. When I was studying Johnson's reviews of now very obscure books in the *Literary Magazine* I could consult the books firsthand, since the Illinois library had copies of all of them. One of the reasons that we could complete our graduate work in a timely fashion was that the university was structured and funded to protect and produce scholarship. That praise comes from an individual in the Humanities, not in the physical sciences or engineering, where the University of Illinois excels to an even greater degree.

Writing as Thomas Hart Benton, William Pannapacker has recently recommended a series of steps to return us to an ethos supportive of serious academic study. "Hemmed in by barbarians on every side," he writes, "it's time for academe to get medieval" (2011, p. 1). In short, it is time to jettison the corporatist university and return to a secular-monastic model:

> Why not bring together a core group of serious-minded but underemployed academics—who already have adopted a life of poverty, more or less—to form a college that has none of the superfluities that have made higher education the equivalent of a four-year Carnival cruise? No more millionaire vice presidents and coaches, no more gargantuan stadiums with double-Jumbotrons, no more dorms and dining centers that look like Disney World resorts, no more exploited adjuncts who fear displeasing their student-customers. Instead, this college would have full-time, resident professors, recreational athletics, and basic dormitories that the students maintained themselves. In time, a few administrators could be chosen from the faculty (2011, p. 3).

As attractive as the suggestion sounds, I can assure everyone that it is not going to occur. Each year a few colleges go out of business and a few are opened, but this is not the way that it happens. On the other hand, nearly all of his suggestions *could* be adopted—the reduction of superfluities, the shedding of overpaid administrators and bureaucrats, the de-emphasis of athletics, the development of simple, clean but not luxurious dormitories and food services (with a commensurate reduction in price) and a policy of (largely) full-time professors. On the last point, it would be imprudent to rule out all adjuncts and part-timers, because there are individuals with great skills who do not wish to be full-time faculty but who can significantly enrich students' educational experiences.

The fear of displeasing student-customers is a particularly compelling issue, one that puts junior faculty in a tenuous position when the students anonymously evaluate them. It is easily solved: give students a good deal of latitude in transferring from one course to another or one section to another; make it be known that students with bona fide complaints concerning the faculty can always (personally, not anonymously) bring them to the department chair and/or dean; and, then, stop requiring student evaluation of instruction. The practice is fatuous, expensive and potentially deleterious, particularly in the case of vulnerable, untenured or non-tenure track faculty who are tempted to reduce requirements and raise grades in order to curry favor.

Why fatuous? Let me first say that I served on the committee to design the inaugural evaluation instrument in English, at Wisconsin, some forty-five+ years ago. I have read such forms each year ever since in a multiplicity of fora and I have listened to the debates on their usefulness. The one area in which they are marginally useful is in the development of a case for a teaching award or a negative decision (i.e. a denial of tenure, promotion or salary raise). Simply put, they provide some documentary backup in the case of a challenge.

The problems with them are palpable. They never, ever measure student learning and learning, not entertainment, is our fundamental purpose. Their ultimate results always skew upward. Why? The only students who fill out the forms are the students who signed up for the class in the first place, did not drop out of the class in the course of the semester and showed up for class on the day—at the end of the term, when all are preoccupied and busy—that the forms were completed. By the same token, they skew down for required classes rather than electives because the students are in required classes, to some degree, against their will. They skew up for smaller classes. Hence, the system can be gamed: whenever possible, teach small-class electives.

Student evaluations commonly ask students to do something that they are not positioned to do, at least at the undergraduate level—evaluate the teacher's professional competence. That too can easily be gamed. One tried and true practice in the sciences is to require a textbook with problems and limitations. Then, quietly consulting a parallel textbook, the instructor critiques the class's book at every turn (in genial, positive ways, of course). "*You* should have written the book, Dr. Hadley." (Smiling) "Thanks, Gerald. Perhaps some day I will."

Humanities students, in nearly every case, will be unaware of secondary scholarship. A lecturer can stroll into class and fill the board with brilliant insights and nomenclature, pilfered from previous scholarship, while acting as if they are his or her own.

Most important, student evaluations inevitably focus on aspects of personality. Studies have been conducted in which students have been shown 30 seconds of video, without sound. The students do not know the subject of the lecture. The research confirms that student evaluations of the thirty, silent seconds of the taped instructor correlate highly with the actual evaluations of the instructor given at the end of the term. In other words, the key is to look good, look "nice" and exude optimism and confidence (Lewis 2006, p. 83). You could be offering up little but inanity, but so long as you do it "well" you should be OK. By the same token, even if you are caring, brilliant, and knowledgeable you could be penalized if you are shy, homely, have a speech impediment or a foreign accent. Bottom line: it should all be about education, not entertainment. There may be a performance aspect to it, but that should be less important than the learning that is imparted but never measured by evaluation instruments. I had instructors both in college and in graduate school who were appalling teachers in many technical respects, but I still learned far more from them than I ever did from showmen.

Professor Pannapacker's proposal for the restoration of monasticism, at this late hour, is more of a *cri de coeur* than a realistic suggestion, but the "de-churching" of higher education, as Gaye Tuchman calls it, has had other significant ramifications. De-churching, she argues, has recast universities' ideological justification in terms of corporatization and commodification, the latter subject to serious state surveillance. Instead of more "spiritual" purposes—leading students to grasp truth, grapple with intellectual positions or appreciate art and music, the university's function now is to prepare students for jobs—not to *educate* but to *train* (Tuchman 2009, p. 41).

By the same token, the tendency to bureaucratize and control has reduced what used to be considered "professionals"—lawyers and medical doctors, e.g.—to "*managed* professionals." (Cf. Vladimir Putin's preferred expression, "managed democracy" [Kasparov 2015, p. 128].) The same is true of university professors. The number of things which they no longer control grows daily (Tuchman 2009, p. 42). An audit culture emerges when trust breaks down and an audit culture represents "coercive accountability" (Tuchman 2009, p. 45). Higher education becomes an "industry" rather than a social institution (Tuchman 2009, p. 49).

Hence we get the serial nonsense. management by objectives, zero-based budgeting, strategic planning, benchmarking, metrics, total quality management, continuous quality improvement and the injunction to "work smarter" (Tuchman 2009, p. 50). And the next step: the sending in of the consultants. Consultants are individuals who are said to be overpaid but easily fired. I doubt that they were prominent at the University of Bologna in the eleventh century.

This variety of absurdity reached its apogee/nadir for me at Georgetown in the 1990s, after Tim Healy's departure for the directorship of the New York Public Library. His pale-reflection successor was floundering and his installation of a "university vice president" as official *éminence gris* (the man actually introduced himself as "the president's son-of-a-bitch") was not working out. At one point the budgetary crises were so daunting that a "management tool" was utilized to, as Bacon might have said, bring home to our minds and bosoms the enormity of the situation.

The strategy selected was the construction of paper airplanes. Each office within the university was directed to use a set of simple materials such as paper, glue, rubber bands and popsicle sticks to make the miniature aircraft. Particularly nice examples were recognized as such and (as God is my judge) displayed prominently on the president's desk. Then, just as the halos were appearing and the ticker tape was settling around the necks and shoulders, the aeronautical contractors were informed that they would have to continue making planes but, unfortunately, without some of the materials they had previously considered indispensable.

As the selected materials continued to vanish while the production lines were being kept open, the staff of the university would learn one of the master lessons of the ages: there are times when you must continue to do your best, even though you must work with diminished resources. The genius of the activity, however, was that it rose above the level of the simple articulation of that weighty maxim. In our case, the maxim was truly reified. Individuals actually saw with their eyes, felt with their hands and experienced in their hearts the reality of the managerial message.

My office did not have to learn the lesson in so vivid a manner because I refused to participate in the exercise. The problems had arisen in the first place because of financial shortfalls in the medical center, a medical center which Tim Healy had wanted to close, but was not permitted to do so by his board. Tim had even used a businessman's argument: excising the medical center piece of the university budget would have brought our existing endowment into direct parallel with our new operating budget—a common desideratum among the benchmarking set. It was to no avail. The university then reaped the whirlwind and the staff were forced to fly through the storm with paper airplanes that, day by day, became progressively less structurally sound.

Suddenly the monastery looks very attractive; absent its immediate reappearance, how are we to *sustain* the funding of its alternative—the modern, hyperextended university? The elite privates simply raise their tuition. So too do the publics, but they are constrained by their governors and legislatures. Only five states permit their public universities to set their own tuition; thirteen others do so but within explicit guidelines. In an ethos in which state support continues, inexorably, to shrink, there are some models which have emerged.

The University of Oregon, e.g., has proposed a plan in which the state would borrow money on the bond market to create an endowment which would provide a steady, predictable flow of support. Chancellor Biddy Martin at the University of Wisconsin proposed an arrangement in which the Madison campus would enjoy certain degrees of autonomy from the rest of the UW system. It is a palpable reality that the bulk of the institutions therein have totally different missions than the Madison campus, but the plan was opposed on several fronts (though not by the governor's office) and Biddy Martin is now the president of Amherst College. Public institutions in Colorado have been funded with a voucher system, one designed to break the political stranglehold on higher education and give the universities a greater degree of independence.

In general, however, politicians tend to construct scenarios in which the universities are forced to deal with frozen or reduced subsidies and simultaneous pressures to increase "access," while the politicians withhold the authority which would permit the universities to establish their own tuition levels.

It is true, of course, that the universities could also cut frills and services but as the bulk of the instructional budget now often comes from students rather than from the state, they are reticent to do so. They are especially reluctant to cut remediation and tutorial services because they would risk being attacked for elitism.

One possible model to consider is that instituted by Miami University of Ohio. A once-private institution that became state-assisted, it faced the same budgetary constraints as other quality publics. Its president, James Garland, proposed a plan that was accepted by the state's (then conservative) politicians.

The Miami plan was to raise resident tuition ($8,350 in 2003) to nonresident levels ($18,100), but then give need-based scholarships to state residents with a guaranteed minimum. The plan highlighted the fact that current tuition was heavily subsidized and, hence, a bargain, particularly for the wealthy. It pointed out that students were paying far less than their educations actually cost. It made the institution look more like a private institution, in which tuition is high(er) but in which there are conscious efforts to make education more affordable for the needy.

In the first year enrollments from first-generation college students rose 40 percent. Enrollments of minority students jumped 25 percent. Nonresident applications climbed 15 percent and applications from Ohio residents rose 8 percent (Garland 2009, p. xvii). As much as I dislike admitting it, this may actually have to do with "branding." Miami was highlighting both its academic reputation and its generosity.

The bottom line, in Garland's formulation, is that "institutional *quality* goes hand in hand with *campus autonomy*" (2009, p. 116, my emphases), two things that distinguished public universities will continue to seek. Politicians, one can be reasonably certain, will continue to resist their efforts. Absent the universities' cutting of remediation and student services (a short-term solution carrying liabilities) and absent an *increase* in state subsidies the result will be a balancing act between the raising of tuition and the further degrading of the educational enterprise. My university's solution—the continual increasing of enrollments (by 12,000 in seventeen years) is also a short-term solution and not a sustainable one.

Ultimately, of course, these are all stopgaps. Solving one piece of the puzzle alone is insufficient. Absent quality K-12 education which brings student skills up to grade levels we will have difficulty challenging college students. Until we can raise expectations in college courses we will continue to have credential creep. Until we reduce the number of unprepared and underprepared college students we will continue to see extensive remediation, tutors, counselors and handholders. We could, however, control the costs of room and board, make certain services and recreational facilities available on an elective, fee-driven base, reduce the duplication of services already available in the surrounding community and restrict athletics to club sports and intercollegiate teams that pay their own way through ticket and licensing revenue. We could make the dimensions of the instructional budget a key metric for accreditation, external evaluation and executive compensation and develop new methods of institutional categorization which would stigmatize vocational programming, particularly that which borders on huxterism.

We could challenge presidential, chief academic officer and decanal professional organizations to curtail chardonnay-and-canapé receptions and strategy sessions for securing federal largesse and instead begin to collaborate seriously on ways to reduce grade inflation, revivify liberal arts education and reinstall core curricula. We could expect such organizations to collaborate fiscally and, e.g., develop software systems that would serve academic needs at a reduced price. Instead of incurring costs separately for systems that were designed for corporate organizations, each could contribute to the construction of systems that would serve all.

We could close schools of education and develop new methods for training teachers, methods which would immerse them in disciplinary areas and focus on the development of curiosity rather than deluded self-esteem. In terms of both pedagogy and curriculum we could begin by looking at the practices of the countries that rank above us (significantly) in international testing.

We could reduce the size of oversight organizations, depoliticize them, require them to include a preponderance of senior, academic professionals and then expect them to hire chief executives who are bona fide academic leaders. We could stigmatize the hiring of the uncredentialed and celebrate excellence rather than simple survival. We could expect academic "signatures" and recognize "brand" for what it is—the cliché de jour that should embarrass those who speak it. We could reduce the hiring of contingent faculty in lieu of tenure-ladder faculty and restore the faculty's responsibilities beyond the classroom by making nearly all administrative roles part-time, faculty positions. Most important, we could cease acceding and start acting. We could assert the need for the kinds of standards and expectations which our students desperately require and increase the respect that the general public would like to invest in us.

How could we better prepare our students for life? Harry Lewis, the former dean of Harvard College has some suggestions. Like Dean Kronman at Yale, he is dismayed by the erosion of the liberal arts and the examination of significant questions which their study entails.

His first principles include the following: professors are now rewarded for their research excellence but not for helping students to find meaning in their lives and a sense of their place in society. The curriculum no longer has any identifiable ideals. Entry-level college students are teenagers; college's purpose is to help them become 21/22 year olds. Universities should act on what students need, not on what the students, myopically, claim to want (2006, pp. xi, xiv, xvi, 6).

The curriculum is central. Harvard's original curriculum, the first in America, "was long on purpose and short on choice" (2006, p. 25). Lewis speaks approvingly of the curriculum embodied in the Harvard 'red book'—*General Education in a Free Society* (1945). Prepared by a committee, but mostly the work of a Professor of Greek, John Finley, the red book sought to shape students' lives as responsible human beings and citizens and inculcate an appreciation for the shared values of a diverse people. It brought students into contact with those fields in which value judgments are of prime importance. Six of the curriculum's sixteen courses were specifically designed as elements within the general education curriculum. They focused on three areas: the Humanities, the social sciences and the natural sciences. The study of major literary texts and the principal elements of western thought and institutions were required for all. Lewis describes it as commensurate with "the postwar ideal of a common experience for a diverse student body united by citizenship in a democracy" (2006, pp. 52–54).

It was destroyed, he argues, by the late 1960s, which judged it "a hopeless anachronism," and as "chauvinistic and dated." The sixties did not see the educated man as an introspective gentleman, but rather as a socially perceptive activist (2006, p. 55). Echoing a report by the Student Council, he notes that the curriculum was very hard to sustain in times of prosperity and materialistic values. It had been made possible, in the past, by our narrow escape from totalitarianism (2006, p. 55). It was designed for a society whose thoughts and ideals were seen as bulwarks against genocide and enslavement; it fared less well in a society of self-regarding comfort. Perhaps more to the point, these courses were ultimately abandoned because they were very difficult for a later professoriate to teach (2006, p. 56).

In some ways, Lewis' story is a familiar one. The transmission of knowledge of the past is less favored than the imagining of an idealized future. "Value judgments" exemplify a "judgmentalism" which is potentially hurtful. Western institutions got us into our current, reduced circumstances, so why should we celebrate them? And—on the other side—the culture has become soft and self-indulgent. The old ways, the old expectations and the old constraints are too hard of a sell.

Lewis calls for a curriculum "so simple that the faculty can explain it to the students" (2006, p. 96) and an educational program that helps them to grow up rather than remain in childhood (2006, p. 147). The therapeutic, politically-correct university "is more interested in making students happier than in making them better" and it "indulges students' belief that they should not bear any responsibility for their genuine misfortunes" (2006, pp. 149, 161, 148).

He notes the "dependency" of contemporary students and comments that these are the first children principally raised in daycare. Their lives have been planned, scheduled and regulated for them and they are unskilled in addressing problems without adult supervision (2006, p. 141).

While I share his views, I would argue more vigorously against the notion that the teaching of western traditions, institutions, culture and art is necessarily chauvinistic or dated. The briefest look at contemporary popular culture demonstrates an abiding interest in the "dated." We have recently seen Caesar (again) cross the Rubicon in HBO's *Rome* and Brad Pitt playing Achilles to Eric Bana's Hector in *Troy*. *Beowulf* (though, admittedly, with a wildly-distorted plot) has been available to modern audiences in IMAX 3-D. At the moment there are at least three separate representations of Conan Doyle's Sherlock Holmes figure in production. One cannot count the adaptations of the works of Jane Austen, but note that she frequently has her own table at Barnes & Noble. Bram Stoker would be astounded at the contemporary interest in vampires, while Shakespeare, Shaw, et al. continue to be performed in recurring festivals. Literary stock rises and falls based on contemporary interests, as both Eliot and Frye said that it would, but the "traditional" is still "contemporary" in demonstrable, compelling ways.

Moreover, the traditions that are of the past but not passé are essential for an understanding of the newer traditions that are in current favor. The "new" is never really new. There has only been one true creator, as the old maxim states. One of the earliest recorded literary comments is the complaint that all has already been done. J. K. Rowling did not achieve her success by being radically new; her work was initially rejected because it was felt that there were already *too many* stories about schoolboys.

The teaching of western institutions can hardly be considered chauvinistic unless they are taught in a "we are the best" and "we are the only model" spirit. This is a straw man. When were they ever consistently so taught by American academics? Why have we established the field of "*Comparative Government*" in political science departments? How can we understand, analyze, utilize, reform, alter or discard traditional institutions if we do not first know what they actually *are*?

The assault on the traditional curriculum was not mounted because there was a coherent alternative to be substituted for it. The instincts behind the assault were essentially antiauthoritarian and the alternative proposed was little more than the *absence* of authority.

My counter proposal is not based on a defense of the west as all that is good and true and holy. It is based on the question raised earlier, "how much ignorance can we tolerate, particularly for those most lacking in cultural literacy and, hence, most in need of it?" If the response is that of the educational reformer who says that there is, literally, no knowledge that an "educated" individual must have, I am at a loss to respond. I cannot conceive of that position as a rational one and so I cannot offer a rational rejoinder. Even the most flatfootedly pragmatic of the reformers should agree that we need to understand the functioning of our bodies, our governments, our natural world and—at the most rudimentary level—our languages.

The core curricula of the past may have been portrayed as "fashioning gentlemen" or "people of leisure," but the core curricula of the GI Bill generation—the core curricula assailed by the sixties' activists—were nothing of the sort. (We had moved well beyond the images of Elizabethan gentlemen circulating their poetry in manuscript among their peers.) They were designed more to fashion functioning citizens and individuals (including the previously-marginalized) who would give a good account of themselves when engaged with educated elites. They were designed to free students from ignorance and introduce them to the world of mature, educated adults. They were designed to help rebuild a world that had been despoiled by fascism and genocide.

Lewis' educational ideal is quite straightforward. He writes that "a good university should help its students understand the complexities of the human condition—or at least what others, men and women of acknowledged wisdom, have thought about the difficulties of living an examined life" (2006, p. 255). That works for me, though in some ways, I prefer Frank Rhodes's formulation since it is so close to Johnson's argument in the *Preface* to the *Preceptor*—that a college education should provide "freedom from the isolation of one's own self, time and place" (Lewis 2006, p. 212).

This is another way of satisfying Dean Kronman's desire for the discussion of larger questions and his dismay at the prospect of endless vocationalism rather than the study of the liberal arts that both raise ultimate questions and attempt to address them. Rhodes's formulation personalizes it; it imagines an individual at a point in time who is, in a very real sense, imprisoned. To be ignorant is to be in thrall; it is to be in a state of moral and mental servitude. The liberal arts do not liberate you to be a gentleman or lady; they liberate you so that you may be a free man or woman.

"Traditional" should not be equated with "conservative" except in the sense that traditional education studies *traditions*; it forms and transmits bodies of material, thus conserving them. They may, of course, be bodies of thought which are not politically conservative at all. That education is *tradi-*

tional which charts and maps conversations, debates, movements and occurrences, lines of argument, influences, sequences, "interventions" and ruptures—the lineaments of thought and history in which we now find ourselves situated. Such education helps to satisfy curiosity by reducing the fear, confusion and sense of personal, spatial or temporal isolation that create that desire for clarification and understanding. It does not promise final or tidy answers, but rather an enhanced sense of the complexities of our condition. It takes us to a higher level of certitude that is not, finally, certainty. It helps us, in short, to see the world through the eyes of an intellectual adult.

Even so, some do not seek such a perspective. Some lack that curiosity. They may seek other things, things which the liberal arts are not designed to address or satisfy. We now make them go to college whether they desire to do so or not. Ask any current faculty member and he or she will tell you that they have students in class who simply do not wish to be there. Should they be? Should we seek to find a college place for every high school student in America?

I believe that we are asking the wrong question. The previous question offers advocacy for a failed circumstance into which we have slowly but deliberately devolved. Someone observes that college graduates earn more money than high school graduates and deduces that going to college earns you more money. Thus, we urge more to go to college. We then learn, however, that many students do not really want to go to college; they simply want to earn more money. By that time, however, we have become addicted to their tuition and so we change the nature of college and make it "college," a new place with fewer requirements, lower expectations, higher grades and utilitarian programs. Even then, however, the graduation rates are poor, but the number in "college" is still so high that it becomes necessary to go to "college" in order to make *some* money, even if it is not the money of which the attendees dreamed.

The issue is not college, but money. When I look at students I see some who have passion, curiosity, energy and interest. They want to learn—and not just required material; they want to learn anything and everything. I see other students who are detached and disinterested; they wish they were somewhere else. I would hire the first set, but not the second, not because the first set are "in college" but because they have passion, curiosity, energy and interest. It is not the "college" that makes the difference; it is the person.

We have attempted to use higher education to equalize income, but people are hired and people prosper because of what they are and what they can do. A contemporary college diploma does not certify knowledge, passion, curiosity, energy, interest and skill; it certifies attendance. The more who have such a diploma, the less such a diploma is worth.

In 2004 forty million Americans were illiterate. Two-thirds of school children could not read at grade level. In 1992, 72 percent of fourth graders could do third grade math, 20 percent of eighth graders could do seventh grade math and 6 percent of twelfth graders were prepared to do college-level math (Black 2004, pp. xiv, 88). The longer you are in school in America the more you fall behind.

This is the problem. Grammar school education and high school education have become significantly less meaningful. The jobs that were obtained in the past with a high school education are unavailable to high school graduates now because such graduates lack the skills and knowledge that their great-grandparents had. Our solution to that situation has not been to restore an effective system of primary and secondary education. It has been to require all students to go to college. The next step—with college in disarray—has been to require them to have a graduate degree.

The fiscal tragedy here is that we require many students to secure a second- or third-rate "college" education that forces them to incur debt. When they fail to succeed in their studies, the debts remain. Grammar school and high school are *free* (in the sense that their full costs are shared by all of the taxpayers, not just those with children in the public schools) and if they were as effective now as they were in the past, students would have the skills and knowledge to do a multiplicity of jobs.

While we have watched the continuing erosion of our K-12 system (accompanied by a tripling of its funding) we have also overlooked other potential strategies. In Germany, for example, 97 percent of the students graduate from high school, but only a third attend college. The remaining students enter training and apprenticeship programs, some of which begin while they are still in secondary school. Their apprenticeships result in training that is comparable in value to an American technical degree. The same is true in other countries (Austria, Denmark, Finland, the Netherlands, Norway, Switzerland): between 40 and 70 percent of the students opt for an educational program that involves both classroom instruction and workplace learning.

These programs are rigorous. The training is *paid for by the employers*, who see the apprentices as a pivotal part of their current and future work forces. The students receive high-skill technical training and are simultaneously *paid*, not *charged*. There is a further cultural benefit in that teenagers are taken from the often counterproductive realm of teenagerdom and brought into an adult world where positive skills, practices and attitudes yield successful careers (Tabarrok 2012, p. 3). Dean Lewis has argued that the therapeutic, nanny-state American system does exactly the opposite; it continues and encourages dependency and immaturity—college as extended daycare.

I would also revisit Charles Murray's suggestion that we increase the number of vocational opportunities that could be accessed by examination, opportunities that would not require students to take formal courses and incur debt. The for-profits play to their students' desire to study at home and on their own schedules. With materials increasingly available *gratis* on the internet, we should be multiplying the opportunities for students to acquire knowledge independently and then securing positions by demonstrating their knowledge through the passing of examinations.

I sometimes hear individuals arguing that we now need a "college" education because jobs that were once more straightforward now require technical skills. For example, the mechanics of yesteryear simply handled wrenches. Now they must utilize computers. I believe this is largely rubbish. In many ways it is now easier to fix a car when the computer identifies the problem. At the same time, I have seen many slackers who are unable to find their way through the thickets of English grammar or, for that matter, simple logic or basic mathematics, but who are able to play electronic devices in the way that Chopin could play the piano (and in vehicular traffic and on pedestrian walkways).

It is all quite remarkable. We downplayed honors programs, labeling them elitist, when we should have been expanding honors programs, in effect displacing downgraded programs with honors programs and making them available to all. The Directed Studies program at Yale . . . the Harvard survey courses offered by Greenblatt and Menand . . . Robbie George's Madison program at Princeton . . . these are for the select few and most probably for a highly-gifted, highly-motivated few. They should be available to all.

One strategy for offering core courses that the modern professoriate finds difficult to teach would be to create an entity for such offerings and hire individuals interested in providing them. When I interviewed for my first position in 1969, for example, Michigan State had a Humanities program which offered multidisciplinary survey courses. They were cognate with the kind of courses which we offered in the undergraduate liberal studies program at Georgetown—surveys of a period which looked at that period's literature, history, philosophy, art, political theory and science. The Michigan State courses had a broader range, however—moving from antiquity to modernity more quickly.

The problems with that program were obvious: faculty hired specifically for that program would be offering the same sequence of courses over and over and over again. There would also be potential issues with regard to their faculty's research when it came time to review them for tenure and promotion. The problems are not insurmountable, however. We now have positions in women's studies, e.g., and we joint-appoint the faculty therein to traditional departments. We could follow the same model in creating entities whose responsibility it was to offer certain kinds of general education courses with a wide sweep. These would attract faculty drawn to such areas as, e.g., intellectual history, faculty who would also be appointed to a traditional department as tenure home.

This would be a simple mechanism for expanding the honors college model while addressing a series of current problems—the tendency to fob off general education courses on adjuncts and teaching assistants, the problem of finding highly-specialized regular faculty simultaneously able to teach broad-based courses, the problem of constructing a general education curriculum with specific courses—designed directly to meet general education goals—rather than taking the easy path of offering a smorgasbord of already-existing courses and inviting the students to pick several from different columns.

There are faculty who feel constrained by a world of microspecialties who would welcome the opportunity to teach a broader range of material. At the same time, to the extent that a succession of universities instituted such programs and requirements, the number of people prepared to teach in them would grow. This would represent a gradualist, non-threatening way to reinstitute challenging and interesting core curricula. If taught well, such courses would have a massive appeal to students, as the examples indicated above suggest. Students may not have an interest in motorcycle-ride-through-the-Louvre surveys, but ambitious courses that seek to elucidate and integrate broad swaths of material in multiple disciplines can be utterly fascinating. They are, in fact, the academic version of the kinds of popularized historical programming so effective in television documentaries or programs such as James Burke's *Connections*.

Departmental restructuring can address other issues. Duke developed a program in literature to succeed "comparative literature" as traditionally understood. "Literature" now provides space for those who do theory, cultural studies and other things broadly related to but often very different from "English language and literature." It includes individuals joint-appointed with other departments. We could do the same thing to streamline English departments and reduce the multiplication of microspecialties. The English department could again focus (broadly) upon literature as art and (a key portion of) intellectual history. A separate unit (call it "cultural studies" or whatever) could do other things. Creative writing faculty—whose interests are principally aesthetic—could be included in the English department, as would the composition program, since expository writing qua student expression is very close to what we now call "creative nonfiction" in creative writing programs. I would include the expectation that cultural studies be challenging and sophisticated, tilting away from the largely journalistic or explicitly political and more toward the work of a distinguished, more pluralist enterprise such as the Committee on Social Thought at the University of Chicago.

I know that some of the things that I have said in this book will be considered outrageous, but there is very little in this book that has not been suggested by others in the comparatively recent and even, in some cases, distant past, many of them to my left. Indeed, I concur with Thorstein Veblen on the university's proper stress of the disinterested search for knowledge, on the deleterious use of businessmen on boards of trustees, on the valorizing of vocational education and on the grotesque overemphasis on athletics, notions firmly articulated in 1918.

My answers to the criticisms that may come are likely to take a common form. The current system is simply not working. It is broken. In many ways, it is absurd. I suggest that we look to the recent past, not to Plato's academy, and tease out those principles and strategies which worked. I was the beneficiary of a system which was quite imperfect but, I believe, far superior to the system which we are now, hopelessly, I believe, attempting to sustain. We need change and we need significant leadership to effect it. Our students deserve it, whether they are prepared for it or not and whether they wish it or not. Previously-marginalized students need it even more.

I think of Frank McConnell's African-American student at Cornell who came to Ithaca to become an engineer; I think of the students from the Missouri boondocks who came to our stadium to play their instruments in their tee shirts. I want to see them doing research in cognition on our fMRI instrument; I want to see them creating art in our studios and graphic design lab, studying plant sciences in one of our many, state-of-the-art greenhouses. I want to see them among the women and men from our medical, veterinary, agricultural, arts and science and human environmental science faculties working together in our life sciences building. I want to see them read Shakespeare and Jane Austen, study regressions, do physical chemistry and harmonic analysis and encounter Wittgenstein.

I do not want them to huddle in a safe space, manipulating Play-Doh and agonizing over their victimhood; nor do I want to see them sitting in a hot tub or at the shallow end of a swimming pool, bored, confused, anticipating free pizza and tee shirts at some manufactured social event, wondering how much a new BMW costs and wondering why on earth they are there in the first place. We did not create the greatest system of higher education in the world to infantilize our students and see our world-renowned enterprise reduced to a tiny handful of successes in a general morass of failure and mediocrity.

Bibliography

Abrams, M. H. *Natural Supernaturalism: Tradition and Revolution in Romantic Literature.* New York: Norton, 1971.
_____. *The Mirror and the Lamp: Romantic Theory and the Critical Tradition.* New York: Oxford University Press, 1953.
Abrams, M. H. and Stephen Greenblatt. "Built to Last." *The New York Times* (August 23, 2012). https://www.nytimes.com/2012/08/26/books/review/norton-anthology-of-english-literature-turns-50.html.
Adelman, Clifford. *Tourists in Our Own Land: Cultural Literacies and the College Curriculum.* Washington, D.C.: United States Office of Education, 1992.
Aeschliman, M. D. "Suffer the Little Children." *The Intercollegiate Review* (Fall 2010): 44–48.
Agresto, John. "The Liberal Arts Bubble." *Academic Questions* (Winter 2011): 392–402.
Allen, Charlotte. "Boondoggle U." *The Weekly Standard* (April 23, 2012): 21–29.
Allitt, Patrick. *I'm the Teacher, You're the Student: A Semester in the University Classroom.* Philadelphia: University of Pennsylvania Press, 2005.
Altschuler, Glenn C. and Stuart M. Blumin. *The GI Bill: A New Deal for Veterans.* New York, Oxford University Press, 2009.
Alva, Jorge Klor de. "For-Profit Learning is Always Cheaper, and Other Myths." *The Chronicle of Higher Education* (October 31, 2010). https://www.chronicle.com/article/4-Myths-About-For-Profit/125116.
Applebaum, Yoni. "Why America's Business Majors Are in Desperate Need of a Liberal-Arts Education." *The Atlantic* (June 28, 2016). https://www.theatlantic.com/business/archive/2016/06/why-americas-business-majors-are-in-desperate-need-of-a-liberal-arts-education/489209/.
Archibald, Robert B. and David H. Feldman. *Why Does College Cost So Much?* New York: Oxford University Press, 2011.
Arum, Richard and Josipa Roksa. *Academically Adrift: Limited Learning on College Campuses.* Chicago: University of Chicago Press, 2011.
_____. "Are Undergraduates Actually Learning Anything?" *The Chronicle of Higher Education* (January 18, 2011). https://www.chronicle.com/article/Are-Undergraduates-Actually/125979.
Asher, Lyell. "How Ed Schools Became a Menace." *The Chronicle of Higher Education* (April 10, 2018). https://www.chronicle.com/article/How-Ed-Schools-Became-a-Menace/243062.
Associated Press. "Cheating, Forging, Falsifying . . . How U.S. College Recruiters Waive English Tests and Write Phony Applications for Unqualified Chinese Students." *Mail Online* (November 26, 2011). http://www.dailymail.co.uk/news/article-2066443/Cheating-

forging-falsifying--How-US-college-recruiters-waive-English-tests-write-phony-applications-unqualified-Chinese-students.html.
Astin, Alexander W., Helen S. Astin and Jennifer A. Lindholm. *Cultivating the Spirit: How College Can Enhance Students' Inner Lives*. San Francisco: Jossey-Bass, 2011.
Babcock, Philip and Mindy Marks, *Leisure College, USA: The Decline in Student Study Time*. Washington, D.C.: AEI Education Outlook, no. 7, August, 2010.
Bain, Ken. *What the Best College Teachers Do*. Cambridge: Harvard University Press, 2004.
Barone, Michael. "The Higher Education Bubble: Ready to Burst?" *RealClearPolitics* (September 6, 2010). https://www.realclearpolitics.com/articles/2010/09/06/the_higher_education_bubble_ready_to_burst_107029.html.
———. "Will College Bubble Burst From Public Subsidies?" *Townhall.com* (July 21, 2011). http://newsofthefree.blogspot.com/2011/07/will-college-bubble-burst-from-public.html.
Barr, Margaret J. *The Jossey-Bass Academic Administrator's Guide to Budgets and Financial Management*. San Francisco: Jossey-Bass, 2002.
Barzun, Jacques. *The Culture We Deserve*. Ed. Arthur Krystal. Middletown, CT: Wesleyan University Press, 1989.
Baty, Phil. "Caltech: Secrets of the World's Number One University." *Times Higher Education* (February 6, 2014). https://www.timeshighereducation.com/features/caltech-secrets-of-the-worlds-number-one-university/2011008.article.
Bauerlein, Mark. *Literary Criticism: An Autopsy*. Philadelphia: University of Pennsylvania Press, 1997.
———. "Oh, the Humanities! They Have Seen the Enemy, and it Isn't Who You Think." *The Weekly Standard* (May 16, 2011): 37–38.
———. "Postgraduate Wrath." *The Chronicle of Higher Education* (May 13, 2010), with link to craigslist.org letter, "Dear University Alumni Office." https://www.chronicle.com/blogs/brainstorm/postgraduate-wrath/23971.
———. *Professors on the Production Line, Students on Their Own*. Washington, D.C.: AEI Future of American Education Project, Working Paper 2009-01.
———. *The Dumbest Generation: How the Digital Age Stupefies Young Americans and Jeopardizes Our Future*. New York: Tarcher/Penguin, 2009.
Bauerlein, Mark and Adam Bellow, eds. *The State of the American Mind*. West Conshohocken, PA: Templeton Press, 2015.
Baumeister, Roy F., Jennifer D. Campbell, Joachim I. Krueger, Kathleen D. Vohs. "Exploding the Self-Esteem Myth." *Scientific American* (January 2005). https://www.scientificamerican.com/article/exploding-the-self-esteem-2005-12/.
Bennett, Michael J. *When Dreams Came True: The GI Bill and the Making of Modern America*. Washington: Brassey's, 1996.
Bennett, William J., with David Wilezol. *Is College Worth It?* Nashville: Thomas Nelson, 2013.
———. *To Reclaim a Legacy: A Report on the Humanities in Higher Education*. Washington, D.C.: National Endowment for the Humanities, 1984.
"Benton, Thomas Hart" (William Pannapacker). "A Perfect Storm in Undergraduate Education, Part I." *The Chronicle of Higher Education* (February 20, 2011). https://www.chronicle.com/article/A-Perfect-Storm-in/126451.
———. "A Perfect Storm in Undergraduate Education, Part II." *The Chronicle of Higher Education* (April 3, 2011). https://www.chronicle.com/article/A-Perfect-Storm-in/126969.
———. "Getting Medieval on Higher Education." *The Chronicle of Higher Education* (January 23, 2011). https://www.chronicle.com/article/Getting-Medieval-on-Higher/126008.
———. "Why Do They Hate Us?" *The Chronicle of Higher Education* (September 28, 2010). https://www.chronicle.com/article/Why-Do-They-Hate-Us-/124608.
Berrett, Dan. "Which Core Matters More? Differences in Definitions of Quality Lead to New Debates Over the Importance of Teaching Practical Skills Versus Specific Knowledge." *The Chronicle of Higher Education* (September 25, 2011). https://www.chronicle.com/article/In-Improving-Higher-Education/129134.

Birnbaum, Norman. "An End to Sociology?" (1975), in *Searching for the Light: Essays on Thought and Culture*. New York: Oxford University Press, 1993.

———. "Students, Professors and Philosopher Kings" (1973), in *Searching for the Light: Essays on Thought and Culture*. New York: Oxford University Press, 1993.

Black, Jim Nelson. *Freefall of the American University: How Our Colleges Are Corrupting The Minds and Morals of the Next Generation*. Nashville, TN: WND Books, 2004.

Bloom, Allan. *The Closing of the American Mind: How Higher Education Has Failed Democracy and Impoverished the Souls of Today's Students*. New York: Simon & Schuster, 1987.

Boghossian, Paul. *Fear of Knowledge: Against Relativism and Constructivism*. Oxford: Clarendon, 2006.

Bok, Derek. *Our Underachieving Colleges: A Candid Look at How Much Students Learn and Why They Should Be Learning More*. Princeton, NJ: Princeton University Press, 2008.

———. *Universities in the Marketplace: The Commercialization of Higher Education*. Princeton, NJ: Princeton University Press, 2003.

Bousquet, Marc. *How the University Works: Higher Education and the Low-Wage Nation*. New York: New York University Press, 2008.

Bowen, William G. *Lessons Learned: Reflections of a University President*. Princeton: Princeton University Press, 2011.

Boyd, Brian. *On the Origin of Stories: Evolution, Cognition, and Fiction*. Cambridge: Harvard University Press, 2009.

Brand, Philip. *The Neighbor's Kid: A Cross-Country Journey in Search of What Education Means to Americans*. Washington, D.C.: Capital Research Center, 2010.

———. "Women on Top, Men at the Bottom." *RealClearBooks* (December 11, 2011). https://www.realclearbooks.com/articles/2011/12/11/women_on_top_men_at_the_bottom_5.html.

Brandon, Craig. *The Five-Year Party: How Colleges Have Given Up On Educating Your Child And What You Can Do About It*. Dallas, TX: Benbella Books, 2010.

Breneman, David W. "National Goals for College Education Depend on the States." *The Chronicle of Higher Education* (February 19, 2012). https://www.chronicle.com/article/National-Goals-for-College/130858.

Bromwich, David. *Politics By Other Means: Higher Education and Group Thinking*. New Haven, CT: Yale University Press, 1992.

Brooks, David. *Bobos in Paradise: The New Upper Class and How They Got There*. New York: Simon & Schuster, 2000.

Brooks, Peter. "Our Universities: How Bad? How Good?" *The New York Review of Books* (March 24, 2011): 10–13.

Burke, James Lee. *House of the Rising Sun*. New York: Simon & Schuster, 2015.

Burke, Kenneth. "Literature as Equipment for Living." In *Critical Theory Since Plato*, ed. Hazard Adams. New York: Harcourt, Brace, Jovanovich, 1971.

Burns, James MacGregor. *Fire and Light: How the Enlightenment Transformed Our World*. New York: Thomas Dunne Books/St. Martin's, 2013.

Caplan, Bryan. *The Case Against Education: Why the Education System Is a Waste of Time and Money*. Princeton, NJ: Princeton University Press, 2018.

Carey, Kevin. "'Academically Adrift': The News Gets Worse and Worse." *The Chronicle of Higher Education* (February 12, 2012).https://www.chronicle.com/article/Academically-Adrift-The/130743.

———. "College Grad Rates Stay Exactly the Same." *The Chronicle of Higher Education* (December 2, 2010). https://www.chronicle.com/blogs/brainstorm/college-grad-rates-stay-exactly-the-same/29394.

Carnevale, Anthony P. and Jeff Strohl. "Our Economically Polarized College System: Separate and Unequal." *The Chronicle of Higher Education* (September 25, 2011). https://www.chronicle.com/article/Our-Economically-Polarized/129094.

Carnochan, W. B. *The Battleground of the Curriculum: Liberal Education and American Experience*. Stanford, CA: Stanford University Press, 1993.

Cassuto, Leonard. "The Comprehensive Exam: Make It Relevant." *The Chronicle of Higher Education* (March 4, 2012). https://www.chronicle.com/article/The-Comprehensive-Exam-Make/131012.

Chace, William M. "Affirmative Inaction." *The American Scholar* (Winter 2011). https://theamericanscholar.org/affirmative-inaction/#.WvR5rUKxvoM.

_____. *100 Semesters: My Adventures as Student, Professor, and University President, and What I Learned Along the Way*. Princeton, NJ: Princeton University Press, 2006.

_____. "The Decline of the English Department." *The American Scholar* (Autumn 2009). https://theamericanscholar.org/the-decline-of-the-english-department/#.WvR5-EKxvoM.

Chapman, James. "Ministers Declare War on Degrees Without Prospects as University Fees are Set to Hit £9,000 a Year." *MailOnline* (November 3, 2010). https://www.highbeam.com/doc/1G1-241158592.html.

Chavez, Linda. "The College Racket: This Bubble Needs to Burst." *New York Post* (January 19, 2012). https://nypost.com/2012/01/20/the-college-racket/.

Christensen, Clayton M. and Henry J. Eyring. *The Innovative University: Changing the DNA of Higher Education From the Inside Out.* San Francisco: Jossey-Bass, 2011.

Chronicle of Higher Education, The. "Average Faculty Salaries by Field and Rank at 4-Year Colleges and Universities, 2010-11." *The Chronicle of Higher Education* (March 7, 2011). https://www.chronicle.com/article/Average-Faculty-Salaries-by/126586.

_____. "College Completion: Who graduates from college, who doesn't, and why it matters." *The Chronicle of Higher Education* (March 5, 2012). https://collegecompletion.chronicle.com.

Clegg, Roger. "Affirmative Discrimination and the Bubble." *Academic Questions* (Winter 2011): 403–411.

Clotfelter, Charles T. *Buying the Best: Cost Escalation in Elite Higher Education.* Princeton, NJ: Princeton University Press, 1996.

_____. "Is Sports in Your Mission Statement?" *The Chronicle of Higher Education* (October 24, 2010). https://www.chronicle.com/article/Is-Sports-in-Your-Mission/125038.

Cole, Jonathan R. *The Great American University: Its Rise to Preeminence, Its Indispensable National Role; Why it Must be Protected.* New York: PublicAffairs, 2009.

_____. "Too Big to Fail: How 'better than nothing' defined the National Research Council's graduate rankings." *The Chronicle of Higher Education* (April 24, 2011). https://www.chronicle.com/article/Too-Big-to-Fail/127212.

Cyr, Marc D. "Do Them No Favors, Tell Them No Lies." *The Chronicle of Higher Education* (August 14, 2011). https://www.chronicle.com/article/Do-Them-No-Favors-Tell-Them/128583.

Daily Mail Reporter. "Sarah Lawrence College Named America's Most Expensive School for Fifth Time in a Row at Over $61,000 a Year." *Mail Online* (October 12, 2012). http://www.dailymail.co.uk/news/article-2217097/Sarah-Lawrence-College-named-Americas-expensive-college-fifth-time-row-61-000-YEAR.html.

Damrosch, David. *We Scholars: Changing the Culture of the University*. Cambridge: Harvard University Press, 1995.

Delbanco, Andrew. "College at Risk." *The Chronicle of Higher Education* (February 26, 2012). https://www.chronicle.com/article/College-at-Risk/130893.

_____. *College: What It Was, Is, and Should Be*. Princeton: Princeton University Press, 2012.

_____. *The Death of Satan: How Americans Have Lost The Sense Of Evil*. New York: Farrar, Straus and Giroux, 1995.

Delworth, Ursula, Gary R. Hanson and Associates. *Student Services: A Handbook for the Profession*. 2nd ed. San Francisco: Jossey-Bass, 1989.

DeMillo, Richard A. *Abelard to Apple: The Fate of American Colleges and Universities*. Cambridge, MA: MIT Press, 2011.

Department of Education, U.S. (National Center for Education Statistics). "Fastest-Declining Academic Fields at 4-Year Colleges." *The Chronicle of Higher Education* (February 14, 2011). https://www.chronicle.com/article/Fastest-Declining-Academic/126360.

Deresiewicz, William. *Excellent Sheep: The Miseducation of the American Elite and the Way to a Meaningful Life*. New York: Free Press, 2014.

Dickstein, Morris. *Gates of Eden: American Culture in the Sixties: With a New Introduction by the Author*. Cambridge, MA: Harvard University Press, 1997.

Dillon, Sam. "Share of College Spending for Recreation Is Rising." *The New York Times*. (July 9, 2010). https://www.nytimes.com/2010/07/10/education/10education.html.

Donoghue, Frank. "Can the Humanities Survive the 21st Century?" *The Chronicle of Higher Education* (September 5, 2010). https://www.chronicle.com/article/Can-the-Humanities-Survive-the/124222.

———. *The Last Professors: The Corporate University and the Fate of the Humanities*. New York: Fordham University Press, 2008.

D'Souza, Dinesh. *Illiberal Education: The Politics of Race and Sex on Campus*. New York: Free Press, 1991.

Duderstadt, James J. *The View from the Helm: Leading the American University During an Era of Change*. Ann Arbor: University of Michigan Press, 2007.

Editors, The. "Can 'Neuro Lit Crit' Save the Humanities?" *The New York Times* (April 5, 2010). https://roomfordebate.blogs.nytimes.com/2010/04/05/can-neuro-lit-crit-save-the-humanities/.

Ehrenberg, Ronald G. *Tuition Rising: Why College Costs So Much*. Cambridge, MA: Harvard University Press, 2002.

———, Harriet Zuckerman, Jeffrey A. Groen, and Sharon M. Brucker. *Educating Scholars: Doctoral Education in the Humanities*. Princeton: Princeton University Press, 2010.

Ellis, Blake. "Class of 2013 Grads Average $35,200 in Total Debt." *CNN Money* (May 17, 2013). http://money.cnn.com/2013/05/17/pf/college/student-debt.

Epstein, Ethan. "The New Jews: They're Asian Americans." *The Weekly Standard* (June 11, 2012): 14, 16.

ESPN. "NCAA report: Economy Cuts into Sports." *ESPN* (August 23, 2010). http://www.espn.com/college-football/news/story?id=5490686.

Fain, Paul. "Harvard U. Overhauls Governing Board in Recession's Wake, a First After 360 Years." *The Chronicle of Higher Education* (December 6, 2010). http://www.fulbright.fi/sites/default/files/Liitetiedostot/Palvelut-asiantuntijoille/Opintomatka-alumni/harvard-university.pdf.

Farrell, Christopher. "On the Payoff to Attending an Elite College." *National Bureau of Economic Research* (December 2, 2010).www.nber.org/digest/dec99/w7322.html.

Ferguson, Andrew. *Crazy U: One Dad's Crash Course in Getting His Kid into College*. New York: Simon & Schuster, 2011.

———. "The Great Tuition Pander: Obama Versus the Bursars." *The Weekly Standard* (February 6, 2012): 10–11.

———. "The Quotas Everyone Ignores: Why Universities Are Quietly Favoring White Males Once Again." *The Weekly Standard* (March 28, 2011): 18, 20, 22.

Ferguson, Christopher J. "Narcissism Run Rampant? Let's Not Flatter Ourselves." *The Chronicle of Higher Education* (August 1, 2010). https://www.chronicle.com/article/Narcissism-Run-Rampant-Lets/123705.

Fertig, Jason. "Success without College." *Academic Questions* (Fall 2011): 291–99.

Fiamengo, Janice. "The Unteachables: A Generation that Cannot Learn." *PJ Media* (May 20, 2012). https://pjmedia.com/blog/the-unteachables-a-generation-that-cannot-learn/.

Fish, Stanley. *Save the World on Your Own Time*. New York: Oxford University Press, 2008.

———. "We're All Conservatives Now." *The New York Times* (December 12, 2010). https://opinionator.blogs.nytimes.com/2010/12/20/were-all-conservatives-now/.

Fitzhugh, Will. "High School Flight From Reading and Writing." *Academic Questions* (Winter 2011): 412–18.

Fonte, Richard. "The Community College Alternative." *Academic Questions* (Winter 2011): 419–28.

FoxNews. "Rutgers Parents Outraged by Snooki Speech." from *The New York Post* (April 3, 2011). https://lostinthe21stcentury.com/2011/04/04/rutgers-parents-outraged-by-snooki-speech-foxnews-com/.

Frezza, Bill. "The Root Cause of Market Failure in Higher Education." *RealClearMarkets* (November 28, 2011). https://www.realclearmarkets.com/articles/2011/11/28/the_root_cause_of_market_failure_in_higher_education_99387.html.
Friedman, Thomas L. "How About Better Parents?" *The New York Times* (November 19, 2011). https://www.nytimes.com/2011/11/20/opinion/sunday/friedman-how-about-better-parents.html.
Frye, Northrop. *A Study of English Romanticism*. New York: Random House, 1968.
Furedi, Frank. *What's Happened To The University: A sociological exploration of its infantilisation*. London and New York: Routledge, 2017.
Garland, James C. *Saving Alma Mater: A Rescue Plan for America's Public Universities*. Chicago: University of Chicago Press, 2009.
Geary, David C. *Male, Female: The Evolution of Human Sex Differences*. Washington, D.C.: American Psychological Association, 1998.
Gelernter, David. *America-Lite: How Imperial Academia Dismantled Our Culture (and Ushered In the Obamacrats)*. New York: Encounter Books, 2012.
Giamatti, A. Bartlett. *A Free and Ordered Space: The Real World of the University*. New York: Norton, 1990.
Gilley, Wade. "Is Higher Education America's Next Financial Bubble?" *Richmond Times-Dispatch* (April 15, 2012). http://www.richmond.com/news/is-higher-education-america-s-next-financial-bubble/article_4ab53ada-f730-5066-ad70-4c9d087fc1bc.html
Ginsberg, Benjamin. *The Fall of the Faculty: The Rise of the All-Administrative University and Why it Matters*. New York: Oxford University Press, 2011.
_____. "The Strategic Plan: Neither Strategy Nor Plan, But a Waste of Time." *The Chronicle of Higher Education* (July 17, 2011). https://www.chronicle.com/article/The-Strategic-Plan-Neither/128227.
Gitlin, Todd. *The Sixties: Years of Hope, Days of Rage*. Rev. ed. New York: Bantam Books, 1993.
_____. *The Twilight of Common Dreams: Why America Is Wracked by Culture Wars*. New York: Metropolitan Books, 1995.
Glassner, Barry. "Yes, College is Worth the Price of Admission." *USAToday* (September 28, 2010). https://usatoday30.usatoday.com/news/opinion/forum/2010-09-28-column28_ST_N.htm.
Gleick, James. *Genius: The Life and Science of Richard Feynman*. New York: Pantheon, 1992.
Glenn, David. "New Book Lays Failure to Learn on Colleges' Doorsteps." *The Chronicle of Higher Education* (January 18, 2011). https://www.chronicle.com/article/New-Book-Lays-Failure-to-Learn/125983.
_____. "Traditional Language Programs Have Declined Steadily Over Decades." *The Chronicle of Higher Education* (February 14, 2011). https://www.chronicle.com/article/Traditional-Language-Programs/126368.
_____. "Public Higher Education is 'Eroding From All Sides' Warn Political Scientists." *The Chronicle of Higher Education* (September 2, 2010). https://www.chronicle.com/article/Public-Higher-Education-Is/124292.
Goldstein, Daniel. "Library Inc." *The Chronicle of Higher Education* (October 17, 2010). https://www.chronicle.com/article/Library-Inc/124915.
Gonzalez, Liza, Michelle Stallone Brown and John R. Slate. "Teachers Who Left the Teaching Profession: A Qualitative Understanding." *The Qualitative Report* (March, 2008). www.nova.edu/ssss/QR/QR13-1/gonzalez.pdf.
Graff, Gerald. *Professing Literature: An Institutional History*. Chicago: University of Chicago Press, 1987.
Grafton, Anthony. "Our Universities: Why Are They Failing?" *The New York Review of Books* (November 24, 2011): 38–39, 42.
Greenberg, Milton. *The GI Bill: The Law That Changed America*. New York: Lickle, 1997.
Greene, Jay P., Brian Kisida and Jonathan Mills. *Administrative Bloat At American Universities: The Real Reason for High Costs in Higher Education*. Phoenix: the Goldwater Institute, Policy Report No. 239, August 17, 2010.
Guggenheim, Davis, dir. *Waiting for 'Superman'*. Paramount Vantage, 2010.

Guillory, John. *Cultural Capital: The Problem of Literary Canon Formation.* Chicago: University of Chicago Press, 1993.
Hacker, Andrew and Claudia Dreifus. *Higher Education? How Colleges Are Wasting our Money and Failing Our Kids—And What We Can Do About It.* New York: Times Books, 2010.
_____. "Take Back the Liberal Arts." *Los Angeles Times* (August 17, 2011). http://articles.latimes.com/2011/aug/17/opinion/la-oe-hacker-college-courses-20110817.
Hamrick, Florence A., Nancy J. Evans, and John H. Schuh. *Foundations of Student Affairs Practice: How Philosophy, Theory, and Research Strengthen Educational Outcomes.* San Francisco: Jossey-Bass, 2002.
Harris, Sarah. "Tougher GCSE Courses on the Way This Year to Counter Dumbing Down Fear." *Mail Online* (January 28, 2012). http://www.dailymail.co.uk/news/article-2092978/Tougher-GCSE-courses-way-year-counter-dumbing-fear.html.
Hazen, Allen T., ed. *Samuel Johnson's Prefaces & Dedications.* New Haven: Yale University Press, 1937, rpt. Port Washington, NY: Kennikat Press, 1973.
Henry, Julie. "Prince Charles's Elite Teachers Will Bring Back Chaucer and the Crusades." *The Telegraph* (November 6, 2011). https://www.telegraph.co.uk/news/uknews/prince-charles/8872095/Prince-Charless-elite-teachers-will-bring-back-Chaucer-and-the-Crusades.html.
Heriot, Gale. *A "Dubious Expediency": How Race-Preferential Admissions Policies on Campus Hurt Minority Students.* Washington, D.C.: The Heritage Foundation, Special Report No. 167. August 31, 2015.
_____. "Just Say No to Affirmative Action," *Academic Questions* (Winter 2011): 449–66.
Hersh, Richard H. and John Merrow, eds. *Declining by Degrees: Higher Education at Risk.* New York: Palgrave/Macmillan, 2005.
Hirsch, E. D., Jr. *Cultural Literacy: What Every American Needs to Know.* Boston: Houghton-Mifflin, 1987.
_____. *The Knowledge Deficit: Closing the Shocking Education Gap for American Children.* Boston: Houghton Mifflin, 2007.
_____. *The Making of Americans: Democracy and Our Schools.* New Haven: Yale University Press, 2009.
Hirsch, E. D., Jr. and Robert Pondiscio. "There's No Such Thing as a Reading Test." *The American Prospect* (June 13, 2010). http://prospect.org/article/theres-no-such-thing-reading-test.
_____. *Why Knowledge Matters: Rescuing Our Children from Failed Educational Theories.* Cambridge, MA: Harvard Education Press, 2016.
Hofstadter, Richard. *Anti-intellectualism in American Life.* New York: Vintage, 1963.
Holland, Elizabethe. "Furor at Washington U. nixes Bristol Palin Appearance." *St. Louis Post-Dispatch* (January 28, 2011). http://www.stltoday.com/news/local/metro/furor-at-washington-u-nixes-bristol-palin-appearance/article_ce74697f-8e28-57b3-9af0-cc0cb4c76733.html.
Horowitz, Helen Lefkowitz. *Campus Life: Undergraduate Cultures From the End of the Eighteenth Century to the Present.* Chicago: University of Chicago Press, 1987.
Howard, Jennifer. "4 Very Different Futures are Imagined for Research Libraries." *The Chronicle of Higher Education* (October 19, 2010). https://www.chronicle.com/article/4-Very-Different-Futures-Are/125011.
_____. "Threats to the Liberal Arts Worry Scholars in the Humanities." *The Chronicle of Higher Education* (May 8, 2011). https://www.chronicle.com/article/Threats-to-the-Liberal-Arts/127443.
Hoxby, Caroline M., ed. *College Choices: The Economics of Where to Go, When to Go, and How to Pay for It.* Chicago: The University of Chicago Press, 2004 (National Bureau of Economic Research Conference Report).
_____. "The Changing Selectivity of American Colleges." *National Bureau of Economic Research Working Papers 15446* (2009). http://citeseerx.ist.psu.edu/viewdoc/download?doi=10.1.1.378.6516&rep=rep1&type=pdf.

Hughes, Robert. *Culture of Complaint: The Fraying of America*. New York: The New York Public Library/Oxford University Press, 1993.

Hulme, T. E. "Romanticism and Classicism," (1924; written 1913-14), rpt. in *Critical Theory Since Plato*, ed. Hazard Adams. New York: Harcourt, Brace, Jovanovich, 1971.

Hymowitz, Kay S. *Manning Up: How the Rise of Women Has Turned Men into Boys*. New York: Basic Books, 2011.

Iannone, Carol. "Bubble Trouble." *Academic Questions* (Fall 2011): 258–61.

IES>NCES. "Selected Findings from PISA 2012." https://nces.ed.gov/surveys/pisa/pisa2012/pisa2012highlights_1.asp.

Indiviglio, Daniel. "The Importance of College: A Self-Fulfilling Prophecy." *The Atlantic* (June 2011). https://www.theatlantic.com/business/archive/2011/06/the-importance-of-college-a-self-fulfilling-prophecy/241092/.

Jacobs, Alan. "We Can't Teach Students to Love Reading." *The Chronicle of Higher Education* (July 31, 2011). https://www.chronicle.com/article/We-Cant-Teach-Students-to/128400.

Jacobs, Lynn F. and Jeremy S. Hyman. *The Secrets of College Success: Over 600 Tips & Tricks Revealed*. San Francisco: Jossey-Bass, 2010.

Jacoby, Jeff. "Don't Know Much About History." *The Boston Globe* (June 19, 2011). http://archive.boston.com/bostonglobe/editorial_opinion/oped/articles/2011/06/19/don't_know_much_about_history/.

Jacoby, Russell. *Dogmatic Wisdom: How the Culture Wars Divert Education and Distract America*. New York: Doubleday, 1994.

_____. *The Last Intellectuals: American Culture in the Age of Academe*. New York: Basic Books, 1987.

Jaschik, Scott. "Easy A." *Inside Higher Ed/USA Today* (July 14, 2011). https://www.insidehighered.com/news/2011/07/14/researchers_publish_new_analysis_of_grade_inflation.

_____. "Women Lead in Doctorates." *Inside Higher Ed/USA Today* (September 14, 2010). https://www.insidehighered.com/news/2010/09/14/doctorates.

Jennings, M. Kent and Richard G. Niemi. *The Political Character of Adolescence: The Influence of Families and Schools*. Princeton: Princeton University Press, 1974.

_____. *Generations and Politics: A Panel Study of Young Adults and Their Parents*. Princeton, NJ: Princeton University Press, 1981.

Johnson, Paul. *Intellectuals*. New York: Harper & Row, 1988.

Kahlenberg, Richard. "A Way Out of the Merit-Aid Mess?" *The Chronicle of Higher Education* (October 24, 2011). https://www.chronicle.com/blogs/innovations/a-way-out-of-the-merit-aid-mess/30633.

_____. "Restoring LBJ's Original Version of Affirmative Action." *The Chronicle of Higher Education* (May 26, 2011). https://www.chronicle.com/blogs/innovations/restoring-lbj's-origional-vision-of-affirmative-action/29527.

Kandel, Eric R. *In Search of Memory: The Emergence of a New Science of Mind*. New York: Norton, 2007.

Kasparov, Garry, with Mig Greengard. *Winter is Coming: Why Vladimir Putin and the Enemies of the Free World Must Be Stopped*. New York: PublicAffairs, 2015.

Keeling, Richard P. and Richard H. Hersh. *We're Losing Our Minds: Rethinking American Higher Education*. New York: Palgrave Macmillan, 2011.

Keohane, Nannerl O. "The Liberal Arts as Guideposts in the 21st Century." *The Chronicle of Higher Education* (January 29, 2012). https://www.chronicle.com/article/The-Liberal-Arts-as-Guideposts/130475.

Kernan, Alvin. *In Plato's Cave*. New Haven: Yale University Press, 1999.

_____, ed. *What's Happened to the Humanities?* Princeton: Princeton University Press, 1997.

Khan, Salman. *The One World SchoolHouse: Education Reimagined*. New York: Twelve, 2012.

Kimball, Roger. *Tenured Radicals: How Politics Has Corrupted Our Higher Education*. New York: Harper & Row, 1990.

Kirp, David L. *Shakespeare, Einstein, and the Bottom Line: The Marketing Of Higher Education*. Cambridge, MA: Harvard University Press, 2003.

Kissel, Adam. "Under the Green Thumb: Totalitarian Sustainability on Campus," *Academic Questions* (Spring, 2010): 57–69.

———. "Will Universities Rediscover Their Core Mission as They Shrink?" *Academic Questions* (Winter 2011): 429–37.

Koba, Mark. "Ivy League Diplomas Still Worth Price of Admission?" *USAToday* (March 5, 2011). http://english6p.com/2011/03/07/ivy-league-diplomas-still-worth-price-of-admission/.

Kolowich, Steve. "Confuse Students to Help Them Learn," *The Chronicle of Higher Education* (August 14, 2014). https://www.chronicle.com/article/Confuse-Students-to-Help-Them/148385.

Kramer, Rita. *Ed School Follies: The Miseducation of America's Teachers*. New York: Free Press, 1991.

Kronman, Anthony T. *Education's End: Why Our Colleges and Universities Have Given Up on the Meaning of Life*. New Haven, CT: Yale University Press, 2007.

Lasch, Christopher. *Haven in a Heartless World: The Family Besieged*. New York: Basic Books, 1977.

———. *The Culture of Narcissism: American Life in an Age of Diminishing Expectations*. New York: W. W. Norton, 1979.

Lazerson, Marvin. "The Making of Corporate U.: How We Got Here." *The Chronicle of Higher Education* (October 17, 2010). https://www.chronicle.com/article/The-Making-of-Corporate-U/124913.

Lehman, David. *Signs of the Times: Deconstruction and the Fall of Paul de Man*. New York: Poseidon, 1991.

Lewin, Tamar. "As Interest Fades in the Humanities, Colleges Worry." *The New York Times* (October 30, 2013). https://www.nytimes.com/2013/10/31/education/as-interest-fades-in-the-humanities-collegesworry.html.

Lewis, Harry R. *Excellence Without a Soul: Does Liberal Education Have a Future?* New York: Public Affairs, 2006.

Lipka, Sara. "Engineering Majors Hit the Books More Than Business Majors Do, Survey Finds." *The Chronicle of Higher Education* (November 17, 2011). https://www.chronicle.com/article/Who-Hits-the-Books-More-Study/129806.

Lipman, Joanne. "Why Tough Teachers Get Good Results." *The Wall Street Journal* (September 27, 2013). https://www.wsj.com/articles/why-tough-teachers-get-good-results-1380323772.

Lipset, Seymour Martin and Gerald M. Schaflander. *Passion and Politics: Student Activism in America*. Boston: Little, Brown, 1971.

Lucas, F. L. *The Decline and Fall of the Romantic Ideal*. New York: Macmillan, 1937.

Mamet, David. *The Secret Knowledge: On the Dismantling of American Culture*. New York: Sentinel/Penguin, 2011.

Mangan, Katherine. "Texas Board Requires the Phasing Out of 64 Degree Programs With Low Enrollments." *The Chronicle of Higher Education* (October 27, 2011). https://www.chronicle.com/article/Texas-Board-Requires-the/129562.

MacDonald, Heather. "Less Academics, More Narcissism." *City Journal* (July 18, 2011). https://www.city-journal.org/html/less-academics-more-narcissism-10885.html.

———. "Pepper-Spraying Taxpayers: 'Diversity' Boondoggles are the Real Scandal." *National Review Online* (November 25, 2011). https://www.nationalreview.com/2011/11/pepper-spraying-taxpayers-heather-mac-donald/.

McGurn, William. "What's Your Kid Getting From College?" *The Wall Street Journal* (November 1, 2011). https://www.wsj.com/articles/SB10001424052970204394804577010080547122646.

McKee, Mike. "UCLA Prof Wants to Test Affirmative Action Theory, but Can't Get Bar's Help." *The Recorder* (September 19, 2007). https://forum.bodybuilding.com/showthread.php?t=4810403.

Mead, Walter Russell. "The Crisis of the American Intellectual." *The American Interest* (December 8, 2010). www. blogs.the-american- interest.com/wrm/2010/12/08/the-crisis-of-the-american-intellectual.
Menand, Louis. *The Marketplace of Ideas: Reform and Resistance in the American University.* New York: Norton, 2010.
_____. "Live and Learn: Why we have college." *The New Yorker* (June 6, 2011). https://www.newyorker.com/magazine/2011/06/06/live-and-learn-louis-menand.
Murray, Charles. *Coming Apart: The State of White America 1960-2010.* New York: Crown Forum, 2012.
_____. *Real Education: Four Simple Truths for Bringing America's Schools Back to Reality.* New York: Three Rivers Press, 2008.
Nathan, Rebekah (Cathy Small). *My Freshman Year: What a Professor Learned by Becoming a Student.* Ithaca, NY: Cornell University Press, 2005.
Nelson, Cary. "Parents: Your Children Need Professors With Tenure." *The Chronicle of Higher Education* (October 3, 2010). https://www.chronicle.com/article/Parents-Your-Children-Need/124776.
Newfield, Christopher. *Unmaking the Public University: The Forty-Year Assault on the Middle Class.* Cambridge: Harvard University Press, 2008.
"News." "Liberal Arts Majors Succeed Over Long Term," *The Writer's Chronicle* (March/April, 2014): 57.
Nguyen, Mary. "Degreeless in Debt: What Happens to Borrowers Who Drop Out." *Education Sector* (February, 2012). https://www.air.org/edsector-archives/publications/degreeless-debt-what-happens-borrowers-who-drop-out.
Nieli, Russell K. *Wounds That Will Not Heal: Affirmative Action and Our Continuing Racial Divide.* New York: Encounter Books, 2012.
Ohmann, Richard. *English in America: A Radical View of the Profession.* New York: Oxford University Press, 1976.
O'Leary, Brian. "Tuition Over Time, 1999-2010." *The Chronicle of Higher Education* (October 28, 2010). https://www.chronicle.com/article/Interactive-Tool-Tuition-Over/125043.
Olsen, Florence. "Delays, Bugs and Cost Overruns Plague PeopleSoft's Services." *The Chronicle of Higher Education* (September 24, 1999). https://www.chronicle.com/article/Delays-BugsCost/15768.
Olson, Gary A. "How Not to Reform Humanities Scholarship." *The Chronicle of Higher Education* (February 9, 2012). https://www.chronicle.com/article/How-Not-to-Reform-Humanities/130675.
O'Shaughnessy, Lynn. *The College Solution: A Guide for Everyone Looking for the Right School at the Right Price.* 2nd ed. Upper Saddle River, NJ: FT Press, 2012.
Padilla, Art. "States Can Reap Rewards by Supporting Research." *The Chronicle of Higher Education* (January 30, 2011). https://www.chronicle.com/article/States-Can-Reap-Rewards-by/126076.
Paglia, Camille. "Academe Has to Recover Its Spiritual Roots and Overthrow the Ossified Political Establishment of Invested Self-Interest." *The Chronicle of Higher Education*, 37 (1991): B1–B2.
_____. *Free Women Free Men: Sex Gender Feminism.* New York: Pantheon Books, 2017.
_____. "Revalorizing the Trades." *The Chronicle of Higher Education* (August 29, 2010). https://www.chronicle.com/article/Revalorizing-the-Trades/124130.
Palmer, D. J. *The Rise of English Studies: An Account of the Study of English Language and Literature from Its Origins to the Making of the Oxford English School.* London: Oxford University Press, 1965.
Parker, Kathleen. "Colleges Come Up Short on What Students Need to Know." *The Washington Post* (August 15, 2010). http://www.washingtonpost.com/wpdyn/content/article/2010/08/13/AR2010081304468.html.
Patai, Daphne. *Heterophobia: Sexual Harassment and the Future of Feminism.* Lanham, MD: Rowman & Littlefield, 1998.

———. *What Price Utopia? Essays on Ideological Policing, Feminism, and Academic Affairs.* Lanham, MD: Rowman & Littlefield, 2008.
Patai, Daphne and Will H. Corral, eds. *Theory's Empire: An Anthology of Dissent.* New York: Columbia University Press, 2005.
Pelikan, Jaroslav. *Scholarship and Its Survival: Questions on the Idea of Graduate Education.* N. p.: The Carnegie Foundation for the Advancement of Teaching, n.d.
———. *The Vindication of Tradition.* New Haven and London: Yale University Press, 1984.
Pennington, Hilary. "For Student Success, Stop Debating and Start Improving." *The Chronicle of Higher Education* (April 8, 2012). https://www.chronicle.com/article/For-Student-Success-Stop/131451.
Pinker, Steven. *The Blank Slate: The Modern Denial of Human Nature.* New York: Penguin, 2003.
Pope, Loren. *Colleges That Change Lives: 40 Schools That Will Change the Way You Think About Colleges.* New York: Penguin, 2006.
Ravitch, Diane. *The Troubled Crusade: American Education, 1945-1980.* New York: Basic Books, 1983.
———. "How, and How Not, to Improve the Schools." *The New York Review of Books* (March 22, 2012): 17–19.
———. "Schools We Can Envy." *The New York Review of Books* (March 8, 2012): 19–20.
Readings, Bill. *The University in Ruins.* Cambridge: Harvard University Press, 1996.
Reilly, Kevin P. and Sheila A. Murdick, eds. *Teaching and Beyond: Nonacademic Career Programs for Ph.D.'s: Selected Descriptions and Comments.* Albany: The University of the State of New York, 1984.
Reynolds, Glenn Harlan. "Sunday Reflection: The Higher Ed Bubble is Bursting, So What Comes Next?" *The Examiner* (December 3, 2011). https://www.washingtonexaminer.com/sunday-reflection-the-higher-ed-bubble-is-bursting-so-what-comes-next.
———. *The Higher Education Bubble.* New York: Encounter Books (Broadside No. 29), 2012.
Richards, Alex and Ron Coddington. "30 Ways to Rate a College." *The Chronicle of Higher Education* (August 29, 2010). https://www.chronicle.com/article/30-Ways-to-Rate-a-College/124160.
Ricketts, Glenn M. "The Roots of Sustainability." *Academic Questions* (Spring 2010): 20-53.
Riley, Naomi Schaefer. *The Faculty Lounges and Other Reasons Why You Won't Get the College Education You Paid For.* Chicago: Ivan R. Dee, 2011.
———. "What is a College Education Really Worth?" *The Washington Post* (June 3, 2011). https://www.washingtonpost.com/opinions/what-is-a-college-education-really-worth/2011/06/02/AGzIO4HH_story.html.
Rosen, Andrew S. *Change.edu: Rebooting for the New Talent Economy.* New York: Kaplan, 2011.
Rosovsky, Henry. *The University: An Owner's Manual.* New York: Norton, 1990.
Ross, Andrew "The Corporate Analogy Unravels." *The Chronicle of Higher Education* (October 17, 2010). https://www.chronicle.com/article/Farewell-to-the-Corporate/124919.
Sacks, David O. and Peter A. Thiel. *The Diversity Myth: Multiculturalism and Political Intolerance on Campus.* Oakland, CA: The Independent Institute, 1998.
Samuelson, Robert. "Scrapping College for All (Part 2)." *RealClearPolitics* (June 14, 2012). https://www.realclearpolitics.com/articles/2012/06/14/scrapping_college_for_all_part_2_114477.html.
———. "The Schools and 'Competitiveness'." *RealClearPolitics* (January 10, 2011). https://www.realclearpolitics.com/articles/2011/01/10/the_schools_and_competitiveness_108478.html.
Sander, Libby. "22 Elite College Sports Programs Turned a Profit in 2010, but Gaps Remain, NCAA Reports Says." *The Chronicle of Higher Education* (June 15, 2011). https://www.chronicle.com/article/22-Elite-College-Sports/127921.

Sander, Richard. "A Systemic Analysis of Affirmative Action in American Law Schools." *Stanford Law Review* 57, no. 2 (November, 2004): 367–483.

Sander, Richard and Stuart Taylor, Jr. *Mismatch: How Affirmative Action Hurts Students It's Intended to Help, and Why Universities Won't Admit It.* New York: Basic Books, 2012.

Saul, Stephanie. "Meal Plan Costs Tick Upward as Students Pay for More Than Food." *The New York Times* (December 5, 2015). https://www.nytimes.com/2015/12/06/us/meal-plan-costs-tick-upward-as-students-pay-for-more-than-food.html.

Saunders, Debra. "Student Loans—Forgive and Forget." *RealClearPolitics* (October 30, 2011). https://www.realclearpolitics.com/articles/2011/10/30/student_loans_--_forgive_and_forget_111860.html.

Scholes, Robert. *The Rise and Fall of English: Reconstructing English as a Discipline.* New Haven, CT: Yale University Press, 1998.

Schwartz, Howard S. *Society Against Itself: Political Correctness and Organizational Self-Destruction.* London: Karnac, 2010.

Schwartz, Richard B. *Samuel Johnson and the Problem of Evil.* Madison: The University of Wisconsin Press, 1975.

Shapiro, Barbara J. *John Wilkins, 1614–1672: An Intellectual Biography.* Berkeley and Los Angeles: The University of California Press, 1969.

Shaw, Jane S. "What Will Colleges Do When the Bubble Bursts?" *Academic Questions* (Winter 2011): 438–48.

Shudak, Nicholas J. "Diversity in Teacher Education: A Double Helix." *Academic Questions* (Fall 2010): 348–55.

Sieben, Lauren. "Counseling Directors See More Students With Severe Psychological Problems." *The Chronicle of Higher Education* (April 3, 2011). https://www.chronicle.com/article/Counseling-Directors-See-More/126990.

———. "Nearly a Third of College Students Have Had Mental-Health Counseling, Study Finds. *The Chronicle of Higher Education* (March 14, 2011). https://www.chronicle.com/article/Nearly-a-Third-of-College/126726.

Smith, Christian. "Higher Education Is Drowning in BS And it's mortally corrosive to society." *The Chronicle of Higher Education* (January 9, 2018). https://www.chronicle.com/article/Higher-Education-Is-Drowning/242195.

Smith, Rodney K. "Yes, A College Education is Worth the Costs." *USA Today* (December 6, 2011). https://usatoday30.usatoday.com/news/opinion/forum/story/2011-12-06/college-education-debt-jobs/51680176/1.

Sokal, Alan and Jean Bricmont. *Fashionable Nonsense: Postmodern Intellectuals' Abuse of Science.* New York: Picador, 1998.

Sommer, John W., ed. *The Academy in Crisis: The Political Economy of Higher Education*, foreword by Nathan Glazer. Oakland: The Independent Institute; New Brunswick, NJ: Transaction Publishers, 1995.

Sowell, Thomas. *Inside American Education: The Decline, the Deception, the Dogmas.* New York: The Free Press, 1993.

Springsteen, Bruce. *Born to Run.* New York: Simon & Schuster, 2016.

State Higher Education Executive Officers (SHEEO). *State Higher Education Finance, FY 2009.* College Board. https://www.immagic.com/eLibrary/ARCHIVES/GENERAL/SHEEO_US/S100209F.pdf.

Stein, Harry. *Why We Won't Talk Honestly About Race.* New York: Encounter Books, 2013.

Steiner, George. *In Bluebeard's Castle: Some Notes Towards the Redefinition Of Culture.* New Haven: Yale University Press, 1974.

———. *Real Presences.* Chicago: University of Chicago Press, 1991.

Stossel, John. "The College Scam." *RealClearPolitics* (July 6, 2011). https://www.realclearpolitics.com/articles/2011/07/06/the_college_scam_110470-2.html.

Stripling, Jack, "Flagships Just Want to Be Alone: Hard Times Strain Relations Between Big Public Research Universities and Their States," *The Chronicle of Higher Education* (March 18, 2011): A1, A3–A4.

Supiano, Beckie. "How Liberal-Arts Majors Fare Over the Long Haul." *The Chronicle of Higher Education* (January 22, 2014). https://www.chronicle.com/article/How-Liberal-Arts-Majors-Fare/144133.

———. "What Are You Going to Do With That? For the First Time, Researchers Analyze Earnings Based on 171 College Majors." *The Chronicle of Higher Education* (May 24, 2011). https://www.chronicle.com/article/Whats-a-Degree-Worth-Report/127612.

———. "When it Comes to Earnings, Higher Education Isn't the Whole Story." *The Chronicle of Higher Education* (August 4, 2011). https://www.chronicle.com/article/Education-Pays-but-So-Does/128526.

Tabarrok, Alex. "Tuning In to Dropping Out." *The Chronicle of Higher Education* (March 4, 2012). https://www.chronicle.com/article/Tuning-In-to-Dropping-Out/130967.

Tang, Didi. "Universities Turn to Outsourced Instructors." *USA Today* (June 28, 2011). https://hollymccracken.wordpress.com/2011/06/.

Texter, Douglas W. "Academic English Is Not a Club I Want to Join." *The Chronicle of Higher Education* (July 31, 2011). https://www.chronicle.com/article/Academic-English-Is-Not-a-Club/128405.

Tierney, John. "Social Scientist Sees Bias Within." *The New York Times* (February 7, 2011). https://www.nytimes.com/2011/02/08/science/08tier.html.

———. "The Left-Leaning Tower." *The New York Times* (July 22, 2011). https://www.nytimes.com/2011/07/24/education/edl-24notebook-t.html.

Toby, Jackson, "How Scholarships Morphed into Financial Aid," *Academic Questions* (Fall 2010): 298–310.

———. *The Lowering of Higher Education in America: Why Financial Aid Should Be Based on Student Performance*. Santa Barbara, CA: Praeger, 2010.

Trimble, Stanley W., Wayne W. Grody, Bill McKelvey and Mohamed Gad-el-Hak. "The Glut of Academic Publishing: A Call for a New Culture." *Academic Questions* (Fall 2010): 276–86.

Trinko, Katrina. "When Did College Become About Simply Landing A Fat Job?" *USA Today* (June 2, 2011). https://usatoday30.usatoday.com/news/opinion/forum/2011-05-31-Value-of-college-is-more-than-just-a-paycheck_n.htm.

Tuchman, Gaye. "The Future of Wannabe U.: How the Accountability Regime Leads Us Astray." *The Chronicle of Higher Education* (October 17, 2010). https://www.chronicle.com/article/The-Future-of-Wannabe-U/124917.

———. *Wannabe U: Inside the Corporate University*. Chicago: University of Chicago Press, 2009.

Veblen, Thorstein. *The Higher Learning in America: A Memorandum on the Conduct of Universities by Business Men*, ed. Richard F. Teichgraeber III. Baltimore: Johns Hopkins University Press, 2015.

Vedder, Richard. *Going Broke by Degree: Why College Costs Too Much*. Washington, D.C.: AEI Press, 2004.

———, and Andrew Gillen. "Cost Versus Enrollment Bubbles." *Academic Questions* (Fall 2011): 282–90.

VerBruggen, Robert. "Racial Gaps in Testing and Scholastic Achievement." *Academic Questions* (Winter 2011): 499–505.

Washburn, Jennifer. *University, Inc.: The Corporate Corruption of American Higher Education*. New York: Basic Books, 2005.

Wax, Amy L. *Race, Wrongs, and Remedies: Group Justice in the 21st Century*. Hoover Studies in Politics, Economics, and Society. Lanham, MD: Rowman & Littlefield, 2009.

Wellek, René. *The Attack on Literature and Other Essays*. Chapel Hill: University of North Carolina Press, 1982.

Wente, Margaret. "We're Ripe for a Great Disruption in Higher Education." *The Globe and Mail* (February 4, 2012). https://www.theglobeandmail.com/opinion/were-ripe-for-a-great-disruption-in-higher-education/article543479/.

Wieberg, Steve. "NCAA Football Grad Rates at All-Time High, but Top Schools Falter." *USAToday* (October 27, 2010). https://usatoday30.usatoday.com/sports/college/2010-10-27-ncaa-graduation-rates-study_N.htm.

Wilhelm, Ian. "Caltech Retains Top Position in Latest World University Rankings." *The Chronicle of Higher Education* (October 3, 2013). https://www.chronicle.com/blogs/ticker/caltech-retains-top-position-in-latest-world-university-rankings/67193.

Williams, Jeffrey J. and Heather Steffen, eds. *The Critical Pulse: Thirty-Six Credos of Contemporary Critics.* New York: Columbia University Press, 2012.

Willingham, Daniel T. *Why Don't Students Like School? A Cognitive Scientist Answers Questions About How The Mind Works And What It Means For The Classroom.* San Francisco: Jossey-Bass, 2009.

Wilshire, Bruce. *The Moral Collapse of the University: Professionalism, Purity, and Alienation.* Albany: State University of New York Press, 1990.

Wilson, Robin. "Colleges Spend Far Less on Educating Students Than They Claim, Report Says." *The Chronicle of Higher Education* (April 7, 2011). https://www.chronicle.com/article/Colleges-Spend-Far-Less-on/127040.

──────. "Syracuse's Slide: As Chancellor Focuses on the 'Public Good,' Syracuse's Reputation Slides." *The Chronicle of Higher Education* (October 2, 2011). https://www.chronicle.com/article/Syracuses-Slide/129238.

──────. "Why Are Associate Professors So Unhappy?" *The Chronicle of Higher Education* (June 3, 2012). https://www.chronicle.com/article/Why-Are-Associate-Professors/132071.

Windschuttle, Keith. *The Killing of History: How Literary Critics and Social Theorists are Murdering our Past.* Sam Francisco: Encounter Books, 1996.

Wood, Peter. *Diversity: The Invention of a Concept.* San Francisco: Encounter Books, 2003.

──────. "Higher Education's Precarious Hold on Consumer Confidence." *Academic Questions* (Fall 2011): 262–81.

Woodhill, Louis. "Solyndras In the Classroom: How We Vastly Overrate Education." *Forbes* (February 15, 2012). https://www.forbes.com/sites/louiswoodhill/2012/02/15/solyndras-in-the-classroom-how-we-vastly-overrate-education/.

Wootton, David. *The Invention of Science: A New History of the Scientific Revolution.* New York: Harper, 2015.

X, Professor. "An Anti-College Backlash?" *The Atlantic* (March 31, 2011). https://www.theatlantic.com/national/archive/2011/03/an-anti-college-backlash/73214/.

──────. *In the Basement of the Ivory Tower: Confessions of an Accidental Academic.* New York: Viking, 2011.

Young, R. V. "Liberal Learning Confronts the Composition Despots." *The Intercollegiate Review* (Spring 2011): 3–11.

Zou, Jie Jenny. "Cornell U. Student Leads Petition Against Bandwidth Cap." *The Chronicle of Higher Education* (August 15, 2011). https://www.chronicle.com/blogs/wiredcampus/cornell-u-student-leads-petition-against- bandwidth-cap/32856.

Zunshine, Lisa. *Why We Read Fiction: Theory of Mind and the Novel.* Columbus: The Ohio State University Press, 2006.

Index

AAU (Association of American Universities), 98, 206
Abrams, M. H., 135, 138, 192–193, 205
Adam, Robert, 113
Adelman, Clifford, 51
Aeschylus, 163
Alabama, University of, 11
Albany, University at SUNY, 38
Allport, Gordon, 122
American Idol, 60
Amherst College, 159, 173, 236
Angell, James, 82, 111
Appiah, Kwame Anthony, 205
The Apprentice, 60
Aristophanes, 105, 219
Aristotle, 67, 71, 122, 205
Arizona State University, 101–102
Arizona, University of, 101
Arkansas, University of, 54
arms race for faculty, 6, 89
Armstrong, Nancy, 186
Arnold, Matthew, 73
Arum, Richard, 57–61
Astin, Alexander W., 74–76, 95, 125
Atwood, Jerry, 223
Auden, W. H., 200
Aunt Jemima, 179
Austen, Jane, 123, 240, 246

Babette's Feast, 179
Bacon, Francis, 76, 198, 235

Bain, Ken, 120
Bakke, Allan, 156
Baltimore, David, 28, 225
Bana, Eric, 240
Bandura, Albert, 41
Barker, Arthur, 183
Barnes & Noble, 46
Barr, Margaret, 44
Bartók, Béla, 214
Barzun, Jacques, 225
Bate, Walter Jackson, 102
Bauerlein, Mark, 170, 205
Baumeister, Roy, 121
Bayh-Dole Act, 210
Baylor University, 54
Beauvoir, Simone de, 42
Belafonte, Harry, 136
Bennett, William J., 20, 82–83
Bennington College, 230
Beowulf, 163, 240
Bergen, Edgar, 109
Bergson, Henri-Louis, 205
Berkeley, University of California, 54, 94, 127, 135, 150, 153, 161, 162, 164, 182, 187
Berrett, Dan, 62
Bestor, Arthur, xiii, 131, 143
Bettelheim, Bruno, 46
Betty Crocker, 179
biography and the scientific method, 204–205

Birnbaum, Norman, 126, 200
Blake, William, 127, 138, 142
Bloom, Allan, 63, 82
Bock, Robert, 7, 28, 107, 199
Boghossian, Paul, 205
Bohr, Niels, 29
Bok, Derek, ix, 40, 68, 78–79, 91, 160
Bologna, University of, 149, 235
Bonaparte, Napoleon, 141
Booth, Wayne, 205
Bordwell, David, 180
Boswell, James, 56, 84, 111, 113, 189
Bousquet, Marc, 26
Bowdoin College, 11
Bowen, William G., ix, 187
Bowers, Fredson, 216
Bowles, Jessica, 108
Boyd, Brian, 213
branding, 57, 103–104
Bromwich, David, 205
Bronfenbrenner, Urie, 41
Brooke, Henry, 198
Brooklyn College, CUNY, 54
Brooks, David, 35, 128
Brown, Lancelot "Capability," 113
Browne, Sir Thomas, 219
Brown University, 3, 5, 54, 118, 164
Bruno, Giordano, 198
Buchwald, Art, 136
Bucks New University, 108
budgeting, responsibility-based, 104–105
Burke, Edmund, 82, 113, 189
Burke, James, 245
Burke, James Lee, 210
Burke, Kenneth, 67
Burns, Robert, 177
Bush, Douglas, 183
Byron, George Gordon, Lord, 141

Caesar, Julius, 240
California State University System, 49
California, University of, System, 8, 94, 174
Caltech, 28, 72, 98, 110, 155, 161, 202, 206, 211, 223–224
Cambridge University, 72
Campbell, Jennifer, 121
Capital Times (Madison, Wisconsin), 16
Carhart, Tom, 78

Carleton College, 101
Carnegie, Andrew, 85, 94
Carnegie-Mellon University, 94
Carnochan, W. B., 73
Carroll, Joseph, 213
Cassuto, Leonard, 189
Castro, Fidel, 33
Cecil, Robert, 198
Central School of Speech and Drama, UK, 108
CERN, 208
Chace, William M., 164, 182, 187, 192
Chagall, Marc, 143
Chandler, Raymond, 54
chaplains for secularists, 39
Chapman, George, 198
Charles, Prince of Wales, 194
Chaucer, Geoffrey, 67, 163, 185, 194, 212, 229
Chicago, University of, 28, 54, 66, 68, 79, 87, 165, 190, 245
Chippendale, Thomas, 113
Chomsky, Noam, 143, 205
Chopin, Frédéric, 244
Churchill, Winston S., 76, 91, 167, 218
CLA exam (Collegiate Learning Assessment), 58–59, 91
Clancy, Tom, 39
Clausewitz, Carl von, 78
Clifford, James L., x
COFHE (Consortium on Financing Higher Education), x, 4
Cohen, Katherine, 18
Colby College, 173
Cole, Jonathan, x, 88–90, 166, 175, 199–200
Coleridge, Samuel Taylor, 138
Collins, Michael, 99
Colorado, University of, 157, 236
Columbia Teachers College, 87
Columbia University, 28, 54, 72, 87, 101, 164, 190, 195
Committee on Social Thought (University of Chicago), 245
Conant, James B., 3, 18, 66, 134
Connections, 245
Conrad, Joseph, 139, 143, 191, 221
Coolidge, Calvin, 85
Copernicus, Nicolaus, 205

Cornell University, ix, 9–10, 10, 112, 164, 169
Corral, Will H., 205
Covington and Burling, 6, 230
Cowley, Malcolm, 128
Crabbe, George, 213
Crane, R. S., 66
Crews, Frederick, 205
Cromwell, Oliver, 219
Cromwell, Robina, 219
Crouch, Eric, 79
Crow, Michael, 101
Cummings, Larry, 29
CUNY system, 165
curiosity, importance of, 57
Curran, Emmett, 168
Curran, Stuart, 125
Curtis, Tony, 136

D'Alembert, Jean Le Rond, 56
Dante, 67, 163
Darden School, 74
D'Arms, John, 90
Dartmouth College, 101, 164
Darwin, Charles, 104, 200
Dee, John, 198
Defoe, Daniel, 138, 186
Delbanco, Andrew, xii, 72–73
DeLillo, Don, 35
DeMott, Benjamin, 216
Derby University, 108
Derrida, Jacques, xiii, 181
Descartes, René, 194, 198, 200, 217
DeVry University, 182
Dewey, John, 35, 43, 63, 64, 65, 85–86, 116, 121, 129
dialing for dollars, 4
DiBianco, Douglas, 113
Dickens, Charles, 176
Dickstein, Morris, 205
Diderot, Denis, 56
disciplines, primacy of, 97, 104, 168
diversity, 31–32, 151–152, 157–166
Dodsley, Robert, 143
Donoghue, Denis, 205
Douglass, R. Bruce, 102
Dowling, William C., 205
Doyle, Arthur Conan, 240
Dreifus, Claudia, 91

Drucker, Peter, 134
Dryden, John, 177
Duck, Stephen, 177
Duderstadt, James J., ix, 12, 19, 222
Duke University, 78, 104, 245
Dunham, Jeff, 109

Eastman School of Music, 72, 98
Eat Drink Man Woman, 179
Ebel, Marvin, 29
Ebert, Roger, 180
Edelman, Marian Wright, 225
edifice complexes, 27
Edman, Irwin, 87
education, higher: academic professional staff, 17, 34; admission rates, 3; attendance rates, 3; colleges of education, 116–117; contingent faculty, 26; core curricula, 49, 54; corporatization and bureaucratization, 14, 27, 152–153; credential creep, 22; exercise facilities, 10; faculty, reduced role of, 29–30; faculty salaries, 6; federal regulations, 12; for-profits, 20, 94–95; general education, 52–53; graduation rates, 2; holistic education, 34; information technology, 9–10; instructional budget, 8, 26, 32; litigiousness, 13; percent who should attend college, 22–23; PILOTS (payments in lieu of taxation), 16; political pressures, 13; preserves of the wealthy, 18; remediation, 32; sameness, 28; startup costs for scientists, 7; strategic planning, 30–31; student debt, 23; student life staff, 17; student services, 41–44; student support staff, 20, 45; subsidized athletics, 11–12; sunshine laws, 16; tenure, 25; tuition bubble, 24; universities as cities, 18; value, 21
Ehrenberg, Ronald G., ix, 188
Einstein, Albert, 180, 200
Eliot, Charles W., 18, 50, 53, 66, 67, 68, 86
Eliot, George, 67, 217
Eliot, T. S., 240
Elizabeth I, 198
Ellis, John M., 205
Ellmann, Mary, 42

Emerson, Ralph Waldo, 74
Emory University, 8, 40
Encyclopedia, French, 56
Epstein, Ethan, 164
Erikson, Erik, 41
Espenshade, Thomas, 165
Evans, Bergen, 102
Evans, G. Blakemore, 232
Ewing, J. R., 24

Faulkner, William, 176
Ferguson, Andrew, 165
Ferguson, Niall, 225
Feynman, Richard, 211
Fiamengo, Janice, 121
Finland, educational practices of, 120
Finley, John, 239
Fish, Stanley, 167
Flamsteed, John, 198
Fleming, Alexander, 199
Florida, University of, 11
Foster, Brian, 98
Foucault, Michel, 167, 181
Franklin, Benjamin, 213
Frasier, 67
Frederick, John T., 32
Freeze, Donald J., S.J., 227–228, 230
Freud, Sigmund, 68, 205
Friedan, Betty, 42
Friedman, Thomas, 170
Frye, Northrop, 138, 205, 240
Furedi, Frank, 119

Galileo Galilei, 198, 217
Gallaudet University, 226
Gardner, Helen, 228
Garland, James, 225, 226, 237
Garrick, David, 189
Gassendi, Pierre, 198
Gates, Bill, 110
Gates, Henry L., Jr., 159, 169
Geary, David, 168
GEI (Graduate Education Institute, Mellon Foundation), 188
Gelernter, David, 65–66, 69
George, Robert P., 225, 244
Georgetown University, ix, x, 3, 6, 8, 11, 13, 16, 18, 40, 53, 54, 56, 65, 74, 80, 96–97, 98, 98–99, 100, 102, 179, 185, 190, 207, 212–213, 214, 223, 224, 225, 227–228, 230, 244
The George Washington University, 100
Gesell, Arnold, 41
Giamatti, A. Bartlett, 72, 80–83, 90, 91, 101, 120, 225
Gibbon, Edward, 189
Gibbons, Grinling, 113
GI Bill, 47, 109, 134–137, 160, 195, 196, 241
Gilbert, William, 198
Ginsberg, Benjamin, 29–32, 152, 230
Gitlin, Todd, 122, 125–127, 133, 205
Goethe, Johann Wolfgang von, 67, 88, 141, 213
Goldsmith, Oliver, 139, 189, 213
Goodheart, Eugene, 205
Gradgrind, Mr., 70, 132
Graff, Gerald, 120
Gramsci, Antonio, 167, 168
Grasgreen, Allie, 91
Gray, Thomas, 216
Greenberg, Milton, 137
Greenblatt, Stephen, 192, 244
Greene, Donald J., x
Greer, Germaine, 42
Gregorian, Vartan, 76
Gross, Seymour L., 182, 183
Grutter v. Bollinger, 149
Guillory, John, 168–169

Hacker, Andrew, 91
Hagstrum, Jean, x
Haig, Robert L., 189
Handlin, Oscar, 135
Hanford, James Holly, 183
Hardy, Thomas, 92, 111
Harper, George M., 49
Harper, William Rainey, 79
Harrington, Joey, 79
Harriot, Thomas, 198
Harvard University, ix, x, 3, 7, 10, 28, 40, 50, 51, 54, 59, 72, 78, 79, 86, 102, 121, 134, 135, 159, 164, 225, 227, 231, 238, 244
Harvey Mudd College, 78
Harvey, William, 198
Healy, Timothy S., S.J., 6, 98, 165, 227–228, 235, 236

Heisenberg, Werner, 200, 217
Henson, Jim, 109
Hepplewhite, George, 113
Heriot, Gail, 161
Herlihy, David, 53
Hesburgh, Theodore M., CSC, 228
Hicks, Josh, 209
Higgs boson, 203
Highet, Gilbert, 34
High Point University, 10
Himmelfarb, Gertrude, 128
Hinman, Charlton, 232
Hirsch, E. D., Jr., 63–64, 69, 82–83, 90, 133, 142, 181, 194
Hobbes, Thomas, 198
Hofstadter, Richard, xiii, 34, 46, 65, 76, 84–88, 129, 201
Holder, Eric, 147
Homer, 163, 192, 217
Hooke, Robert, 219
Hook, J. N., 118
hooks, admission, 163
Hoover, J. Edgar, 64
Horace, 139
Houston, University of, 10
Hoxby, Caroline, 21
Hughes, Robert, 122, 133
Hume, David, 140, 141, 191
Hunter, J. Paul, 82
Hutchins, Robert Maynard, 18, 35, 43, 131, 134
Huygens, Christiaan, 198
Hymowitz, Kay, 148–149

Idaho State University, 2
identity programming, 166
Illinois, University of, Urbana-Champaign, ix, 54, 59, 63, 93, 113, 131, 136, 156, 182, 231–232
illiteracy rate, USA, 242
Imperial College, London, 223
Indiana University of Pennsylvania, 10
indirect cost rates, 174
Irvine, University of California, 162, 164

Jackson, Andrew, 84
Jacoby, Russell, 205
James, Henry, 217
James, P. D., 67

James, Robert, Dr., 232
James VI, 198
James, William, 129
Jefferson, Thomas, 213
Jenyns, Soame, 111
Johns Hopkins University, x, 43, 69, 80, 110, 183, 205, 207
Johnson, Lyndon B., 156
Johnson, Samuel, 19, 56–57, 63, 67, 76, 84, 110, 111–112, 113–114, 132, 139, 141, 143–144, 186, 189, 191, 201, 216, 232, 241
Joyce, James, 192, 195, 217

Kaestle, Carl, 118
Kant, Immanuel, 65, 139–140
Kargon, Robert H., 183
Kazin, Alfred, 34
Keats, John, 213
Kennedy, John F., 156
Kentucky, University of, 107
Kenyon College, 54
Kepler, Johannes, 198
Kermode, Frank, 205
Kernan, Alvin, 55, 182
Kerouac, Jack, 133
Kerr, Clark, 18
Khorana, Har Gobind, 7
Kidd, Julie Johnson, 40
Kissinger, Henry, 135
Kittredge, George Lyman, x
Kohlberg, Lawrence, 41
Kramer, Rita, 116–117
Kronman, Anthony, 166, 181, 238, 241
Krueger, Joachim, 121
K-16, 40
Kubrick, Stanley, 34
Kuhn, Thomas, 52

Lacan, Jacques, 181
Lagrange, Joseph-Louis, 200
Lang, Francis J., 22
Laplace, Pierre-Simon, 200
Lasch, Christopher, 46–47, 121, 167, 201
Lavoisier, Antoine, 202
Lawrence University, 101
Leavis, F. R., 205
Lecter, Hannibal, 71
Lee, Robert E., 78

Leibniz, Gottfried Wilhelm, 198
Lessing, Gotthold Ephraim, 205
Lewis, C. S., 142, 183, 201
Lewis, Harry, 238–240, 241, 243
life adjustment training, 34, 86–87, 130
Like Water for Chocolate, 179
Link, Karl Paul, 210
Lipset, Seymour Martin, 122
Locke, John, 117, 213
London School of Economics, 223
Loram, Ian, 28
Lucas, F. L., 141, 143
Lucretius, 217, 219
Lujak, Johnny, 136

Macaulay, Thomas Babington, 218–219
McCabe, Bernice, 194
McClintock, Barbara, 199
Maccoby, Eleanor, 41
McConnell, Frank D., 112, 169, 246
MacDonald, Heather, 156
McLaughlin, Jerry, 199
Malone, Kemp, x
Mamet, David, 45
Mann, Horace, 142
Mansfield, Harvey, 121
March, Robert, 213–214
Marcus Aurelius, 71
Marks, Elaine, 205
Marlowe, Christopher, 198
Martin, Carolyn "Biddy," 236
Martire, Daniel, 231
Marx, Karl, 138
Maryland, University of, 80, 109
Matthau, Walter, 136
Medgar Evers, CUNY, 2
Melville, Herman, 182
Menand, Louis, 66, 71–72, 181, 187, 192, 244
Merlyn's Pen, 18, 156
Mersenne, Marin, 198
Merton, Robert, 200
Miami University (Ohio), 230, 237
Michigan State University, 244
Michigan, University of, ix, 11, 12, 19, 28, 78, 119, 136, 164, 227
Miller Analogies Test, 163
Milton, John, 67, 142, 176, 183, 185–186, 197, 198, 211, 215

Minnesota, University of, 29, 135
Missouri State University, 24
Missouri, University of, Columbia, ix, x, 8, 10, 11, 35–38, 54, 94, 98, 104, 105–106, 118, 136, 178, 192, 207, 214, 222, 223, 231
MIT, 29, 72–77, 164, 223
Moore, Gordon, 93, 110
Morgan, Donald O., 107
Murphy Brown, 129
Murray, Charles, 23, 127, 133, 171, 243

Nagel, Thomas, 205
National Research Council rankings, 166, 173
NCTE (National Council of Teachers of English), 118
Nebraska, University of, 79
Neill, A. S., 132
Nelson, Cary, 189
Nemerov, Howard, 34
Nevada, University of, Las Vegas, 11
Newbery, John, 143
Newfield, Christopher, 174
Newman, John Henry, Cardinal, 73, 81
Newton, Isaac, 110, 130, 198, 200, 203, 217
New York Public Library, 235
nonjudgmentalism, 116, 123, 177
Northern Kentucky University, 95
Northwestern University, 11, 29, 102, 112
Notre Dame, University of, ix, 2, 10, 19, 23, 32–33, 49, 54, 68, 92, 102, 136, 169, 171, 179, 212, 223, 224

Oberlin College, 173
O'Brien, Michael J., 206
O'Casey, Seán, 163
Occam's razor, 204
O'Connor, Sandra Day, 69, 149
The Ohio State University, 10, 11, 15, 94
Ohio State University, Lima, 230
O'Malley, Frank, 102, 117
open classroom movement, 34
open education movement, 132
Oregon, University of, 79, 236
Osborn, June, 29
O'Shaughnessy, Lynn, 21, 161, 164
Oxbridge, 19, 55, 98

Oxford University, 72, 113, 182, 185, 219

Paglia, Camille, 41, 119, 167
Pannapacker William ("Thomas Hart Benton"), 233, 235
Parkway West High School, St. Louis, 39, 160
Parsons, Talcott, 119
Pascal, Blaise, 198, 217
Pasteur, Louis, 199
Patai, Daphne, 167, 205
Pattison, Mark, 215
Pearl poet, 163
Pelikan, Jaroslav, 52, 57, 96, 225
Pembroke College, Oxford, 19
Pennsylvania State University, 78
Pennsylvania, University of, 98, 164, 232
PeopleSoft, 15
Percy, Henry, 9th Earl of Northumberland, 198
Perloff, Marjorie, 191, 205
permissive therapeutics, 119
Persons, Robert, 198
Petty, Sir William, 200
Phoenix, University of, 2, 94, 182
Piaget, Jean, 41
Pieper, Josef, 84
Pinker, Steven, 168
PISA study (OECD Programme for International Student Assessment), 117, 170
Pitt, Brad, 240
Plato, 67, 68, 203, 246
Plymouth University, 108
Pope, Alexander, 143, 177, 198–199, 200
Portland State University, 62
Powell, Lewis F., Jr., 156, 166
Princeton University, ix, 10, 28, 40, 54, 164, 165, 244
Prior, Matthew, 88, 216
Pritchard, Walter, LTC, 195
progressive education, 86, 129–132
Prosser, Charles A., 130–131, 143
provost, role of, 227–228
Ptolemy, Claudius, 205
Purdue University, 135
Putin, Vladimir, 235
Pynchon, Thomas, 219

Quayle, Dan, 129

Raleigh, Sir Walter, 198
Ravitch, Diane, 35, 120, 122, 129–132
Rawls, John, 200
Red Book, Harvard, 66, 239
Reisman, David, 200
Reynolds, Joshua, 113, 189
Rhodes, Frank, 241
Rice University, 150
Riefenstahl, Leni, 218
Riis, Jacob, 129
Riley, Naomi Schaefer, 25
Riverside, University of California, 162
Robinson, James, 182, 183, 184
Rochester, University of, 98, 193
Rodin, Judith, 225
Roksa, Josipa, 57–61, 62
Romanticism, 47, 53, 85, 88, 90, 115, 126, 138–142
Rome, 240
Rorty, Richard, 181
Rosemond, John, 117
Rosovsky, Henry, 135
Rousseau, Jean-Jacques, 85–86, 120, 122, 129, 132, 138, 140, 141
Rowling, J. K., 240
Rudenstine, Neil L., 187
Russell, Bertrand, 205
Rutgers University, 11

Sacks, David O., 158, 167
Salmon P. Chase College of Law, 95
Sander, Richard, 160
San Diego, University of California, 29, 150–151, 162, 164
Santa Barbara, University of California, 112, 164
Santayana, George, 143
Schaflander, Gerald M., 122
Schiller, Friedrich, 84
School of Journalism, University of Missouri, 98
school of night, 198
Schwartz, Caroline A., 39
Schwartz, Jack J., 2, 95
Schwartz, Jonathan F., 28
Schwartz, Judith M., 157
Schwartz, Katharine E., 39, 193

Sealts, Merton M., Jr., 182
Searle, John, 205
self-esteem myth, 120–121
Shaara, Michael, 82, 158
Shakespeare, William, 67, 76, 85, 92, 94, 114, 139, 176, 186, 190, 198, 218, 219, 240, 246
Shapiro, Barbara, 219
Shawcross, John T., 186
Shaw, George Bernard, 240
Sheedy, Charles, CSC, 32
Shelley, Percy Bysshe, 140
Sheridan, Richard Brinsley, 189
Sidney, Sir Philip, 139
Sinatra, Frank, 67
Singal, Daniel J., 122
sixties radicals, 115, 125, 138
Smith, Adam, 200
Smith, Peter, 29
Smollett, Tobias, 213
Snow, C. P., 205
Sober, Elliott, 204
Socrates, 216
Sokal, Alan, 205
Sophocles, 163, 205
Sousa, John Philip, 169
Southern California, University of, 11, 97
Sowell, Thomas, 116, 118, 159, 160, 165
Spenser, Edmund, 185
Sperling, John, 95
Spinoza, Baruch, 198
Sprat, Thomas, 198
Springsteen, Bruce, 138
Squire, James, 118
Stanford University, 3, 72, 77, 78, 159
Steenbock, Harry, 210
Steffens, Lincoln, 129
Steiger, Rod, 136
Steiner, George, 202, 205, 213, 214–219
Stewart, Potter, 95
Stites, Richard, 230
St. John's College, 68
St. Louis University, 19
Stoker, Bram, 240
Stossel, John, 22
Strauss, Leo, 63, 66
Studies in English Literature, 176
Summers, Clyde, 161
Sutton, Preston M., 73

Swift, Jonathan, 67, 177, 193–194
Synge, John Millington, 163
Syracuse University, 135

Tampopo, 179
teaching evaluations, student, 233–234
Tennessee, University of, 11
Texas A&M University, 54
Texas, University of, Austin, 11
Texas, University of, El Paso, 2
Thiel, Peter, 158, 167
Thompson, Kristin, 180
Thoreau, Henry David, 188
Thorne, Kip, 28
Thrale, Hester, 113
Thrones, Game of, 46
Tillstrom, Burr, 109
Tindall, William York, 195
Todorov, Tzvetan, 205
Traub, James, 94
Truman, Harry S., 136, 201
trustees, role of, 221
Tuchman, Gaye, 235
Tufnel, Nigel principle, 187
Tulane University, 3
Turing, Alan, 9, 93
Twain, Mark, 201
twigging, 177

UCLA, 160, 162, 164
Uncle Ben, 179
US News, 8
Ustinov, Peter, 34

Vanderbilt, Cornelius, 85
Vanderbilt University, 40
Vassar College, 54
Veblen, Thorstein, 45, 245
Vesalius, Andreas, 219
Vickers, Brian, 205
victimology, 119
Virgil, 219
Virginia, University of, 63, 69, 74, 224
vocational programming, 110
Vohs, Kathleen, 121
Voltaire (François-Marie Arouet), 114

Walzer, Michael, 225

WARF (Wisconsin Alumni Research Foundation), 28, 118, 175, 210
War Horse, 108
Washington State University, 10
Washington University in St. Louis, 54, 207
Watson, James, 231
Watt, Stephen, 189
Wayne State University, 136
Wedgwood, Josiah, 113
Weinberg, Jack, 127
Wellek, René, 205
Wertheimer, Mark, 170
West, Cornel, 159
West Point (United States Military Academy), ix, 33, 54, 58, 67, 87, 93, 110, 169, 195
Wharton School, 72, 98
Whitehead, Alfred North, 67, 198
Wilhelm, Ian, 28
Wilkins, John, Bishop, 219
Willetts, David, 108
William and Mary, College of, 54
Williams and Connelly, 6
Williams College, 159
Willingham, Daniel, 69–70, 133
Wisconsin, University of, Madison, ix, x, 6, 9, 16, 28, 54, 83, 93, 107, 118, 125, 135, 165, 173, 175, 182, 184, 186, 204, 205, 207, 210, 213, 234, 236
Wisconsin, University of, Oshkosh, 10
Wittgenstein, Ludwig, 246
Wittreich, Joseph A., Jr., 125, 186
Wollstonecraft, Mary, 42
Wood, Peter, 156–159
Woods, Tiger, 158
Wootton, David, 15
Wordsworth, William, 85, 121, 138, 139, 140–141
Wren, Christopher, 113, 198
Wrighton, Mark, 225

Yale University, 6, 40, 52, 54, 63, 72, 78, 80, 96, 112, 135, 161, 164, 223, 238, 244
Yeats, William Butler, 67

About the Author

Richard B. Schwartz is Dean of the College of Arts and Science and Professor of English, *emeritus* at the University of Missouri, Columbia. He previously taught at the United States Military Academy, the University of Wisconsin, Madison, and Georgetown University. He served in the capacity of associate graduate dean for the humanities, graduate dean, arts and science dean and interim provost for twenty-nine years. A Romnes Fellow at the University of Wisconsin, Madison, he has received awards from the Institute for Research in the Humanities, the American Council of Learned Societies and (twice) the National Endowment for the Humanities. He is an authority on Samuel Johnson, eighteenth-century intellectual and social history and contemporary American genre fiction. He is the author/coauthor/editor of twenty books and a top 500 reviewer, Vine voice and top contributor in Philosophy for Amazon.com. His wife, Judith A. Schwartz, recently retired as Executive Director of the Lifelong Learning Institute at Washington University in St. Louis; their son Jonathan is Executive Director of Campaign Management at Tufts University. Visit the author at www.richardbschwartz.com.

Also by Richard B. Schwartz

CRITICISM

Samuel Johnson and the New Science

Samuel Johnson and the Problem of Evil

Boswell's Johnson: A Preface to the Life

Daily Life in Johnson's London

After the Death of Literature

Nice and Noir: Contemporary American Crime Fiction

The Wounds that Heal: Heroism and Human Development
(with Judith A. Schwartz)

ed. *The Plays of Arthur Murphy, 4 vols.*

ed. *Theory and Tradition in Eighteenth-Century Studies*

MEMOIRS

The Biggest City in America: A Fifties Boyhood in Ohio

Accidental Soldier: A Reserve Officer at West Point in the Vietnam Era

Also by Richard B. Schwartz

FICTION

Frozen Stare
The Last Voice You Hear
Proof of Purchase
Into the Dark

EBOOK

Is a College Education Still Worth the Price? A Dean's Sobering Perspective

www.ingramcontent.com/pod-product-compliance
Lightning Source LLC
Chambersburg PA
CBHW030131240426
43672CB00005B/103